COLLECTION EDITOR: **JENNIFER GRÜNWALD**
ASSISTANT EDITOR: **SARAH BRUNSTAD**
ASSOCIATE MANAGING EDITOR: **ALEX STARBUCK**
EDITOR, SPECIAL PROJECTS: **MARK D. BEAZLEY**
SENIOR EDITOR, SPECIAL PROJECTS: **JEFF YOUNGQUIST**
SVP PRINT, SALES & MARKETING: **DAVID GABRIEL**

EDITOR IN CHIEF: **AXEL ALONSO**
CHIEF CREATIVE OFFICER: **JOE QUESADA**
PUBLISHER: **DAN BUCKLEY**
EXECUTIVE PRODUCER: **ALAN FINE**

AVENGERS: TIME RUNS OUT VOL. 4. Contains material originally published in magazine form as AVENGERS #43-44 and NEW AVENGERS #31-33. First printing 2015. ISBN# 978-0-7851-9224-4. Published by MARVEL WORLDWIDE, INC., a subsidiary of MARVEL ENTERTAINMENT, LLC. OFFICE OF PUBLICATION: 135 West 50th Street, New York, NY 10020. Copyright © 2015 MARVEL No similarity between any of the names, characters, persons, and/or institutions in this magazine with those of any living or dead person or institution is intended, and any such similarity which may exist is purely coincidental. **Printed in the U.S.A.** ALAN FINE, President, Marvel Entertainment; DAN BUCKLEY, President, TV, Publishing and Brand Management; JOE QUESADA, Chief Creative Officer; TOM BREVOORT, SVP of Publishing; DAVID BOGART, SVP of Operations & Procurement, Publishing; C.B. CEBULSKI, VP of International Development & Brand Management; DAVID GABRIEL, SVP Print, Sales & Marketing; JIM O'KEEFE, VP of Operations & Logistics; DAN CARR, Executive Director of Publishing Technology; SUSAN CRESPI, Editorial Operations Manager; ALEX MORALES, Publishing Operations Manager; STAN LEE, Chairman Emeritus. For information regarding advertising in Marvel Comics or on Marvel.com, please contact Jonathan Rheingold, VP of Custom Solutions & Ad Sales, at jrheingold@marvel.com. For Marvel subscription inquiries, please call 800-217-9158. **Manufactured between 4/17/2015 and 6/1/2015** by R.R. DONNELLEY, INC., SALEM, VA, USA.

10 9 8 7 6 5 4 3 2 1

AVENGERS

WRITER: **JONATHAN HICKMAN**

NEW AVENGERS #31
ARTIST: **KEV WALKER**
COLOR ARTIST: **FRANK MARTIN**
LETTERER: **VC'S JOE CARAMAGNA**
COVER ART: **IN-HYUK LEE**

NEW AVENGERS #32
ARTIST: **MIKE DEODATO**
COLOR ARTIST: **FRANK MARTIN**
LETTERER: **VC'S JOE CARAMAGNA**
COVER ART: **ADAM KUBERT & FRANK MARTIN**

NEW AVENGERS #33
ARTIST: **MIKE DEODATO**
COLOR ARTIST: **FRANK MARTIN**
LETTERER: **VC'S JOE CARAMAGNA**
COVER ART: **GABRIELE DELL'OTTO**

AVENGERS #43
ARTIST: **KEV WALKER**
COLOR ARTIST: **FRANK MARTIN**
LETTERER: **VC'S CORY PETIT**
COVER ART: **STEFANO CASELLI & SUNDER RAJ**

AVENGERS #44
ARTISTS: **STEFANO CASELLI & KEV WALKER**
COLOR ARTIST: **FRANK MARTIN**
LETTERER: **VC'S CORY PETIT**
COVER ART: **DUSTIN WEAVER & JUSTIN PONSOR**

ASSOCIATE EDITOR: **JAKE THOMAS**
EDITORS: **TOM BREVOORT** WITH **WIL MOSS**
AVENGERS CREATED BY STAN LEE & JACK KIRBY

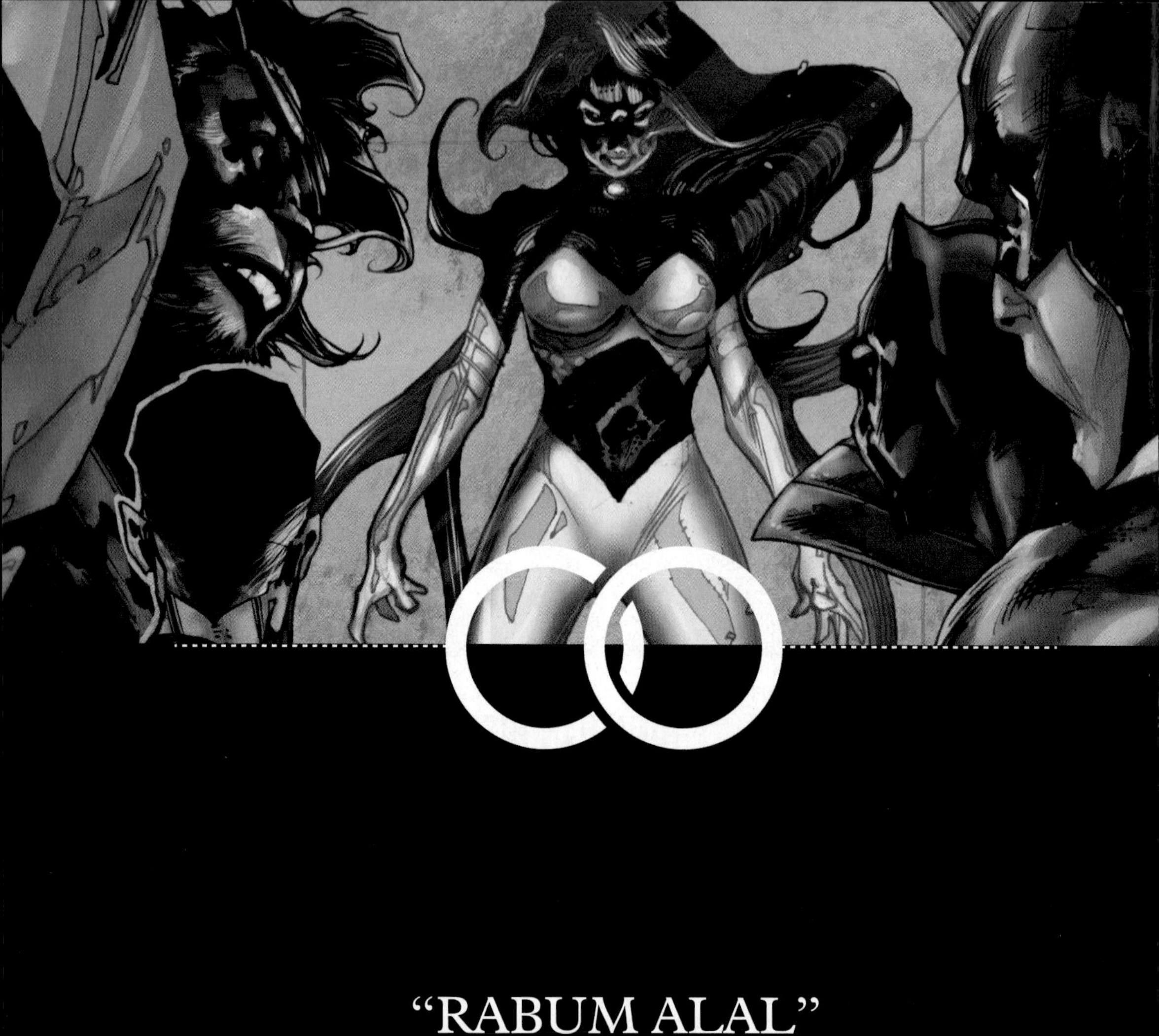

“RABUM ALAL”

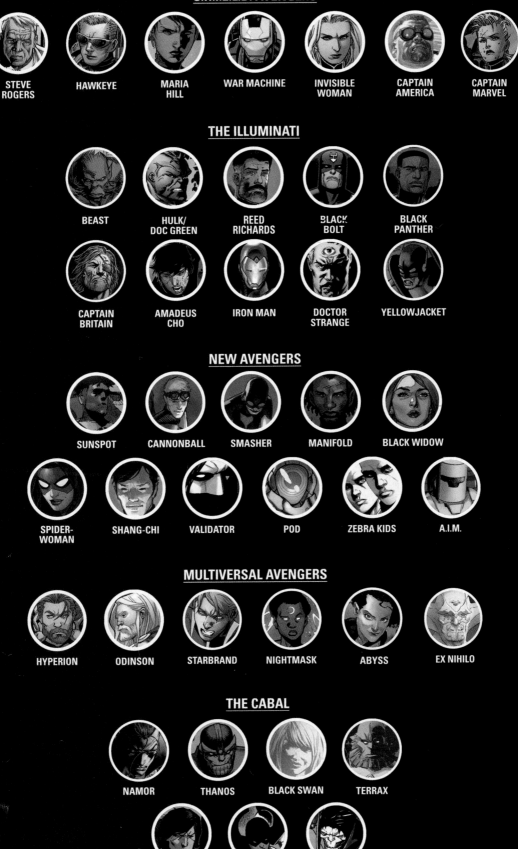

S.H.I.E.L.D. AVENGERS

STEVE ROGERS • HAWKEYE • MARIA HILL • WAR MACHINE • INVISIBLE WOMAN • CAPTAIN AMERICA • CAPTAIN MARVEL

THE ILLUMINATI

BEAST • HULK/DOC GREEN • REED RICHARDS • BLACK BOLT • BLACK PANTHER

CAPTAIN BRITAIN • AMADEUS CHO • IRON MAN • DOCTOR STRANGE • YELLOWJACKET

NEW AVENGERS

SUNSPOT • CANNONBALL • SMASHER • MANIFOLD • BLACK WIDOW

SPIDER-WOMAN • SHANG-CHI • VALIDATOR • POD • ZEBRA KIDS • A.I.M.

MULTIVERSAL AVENGERS

HYPERION • ODINSON • STARBRAND • NIGHTMASK • ABYSS • EX NIHILO

THE CABAL

NAMOR • THANOS • BLACK SWAN • TERRAX

MAXIMUS • PROXIMA MIDNIGHT • CORVUS GLAIVE

PREVIOUSLY IN NEW AVENGERS

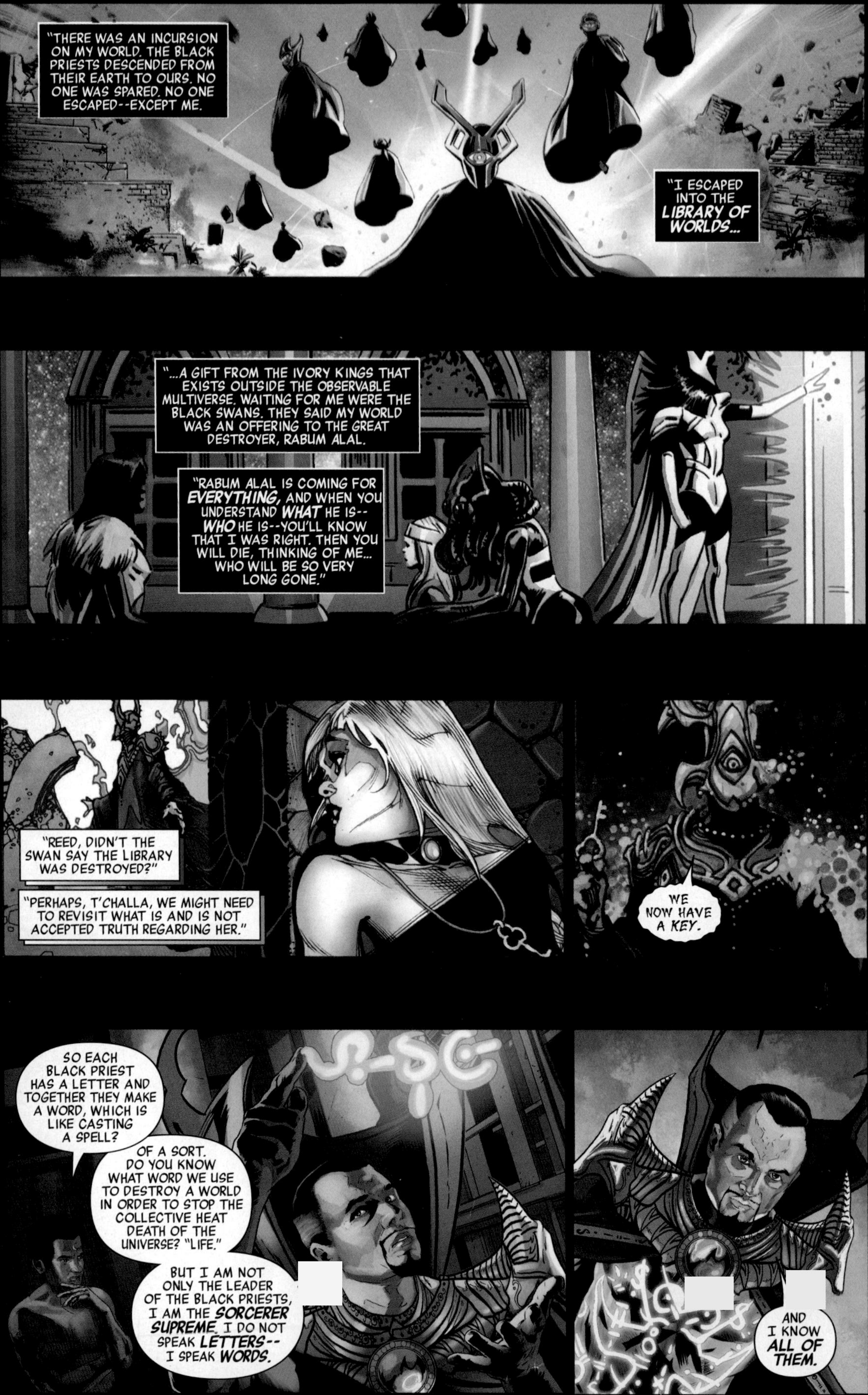
"THERE WAS AN INCURSION ON MY WORLD. THE BLACK PRIESTS DESCENDED FROM THEIR EARTH TO OURS. NO ONE WAS SPARED. NO ONE ESCAPED--EXCEPT ME.
"I ESCAPED INTO THE LIBRARY OF WORLDS...
"...A GIFT FROM THE IVORY KINGS THAT EXISTS OUTSIDE THE OBSERVABLE MULTIVERSE. WAITING FOR ME WERE THE BLACK SWANS. THEY SAID MY WORLD WAS AN OFFERING TO THE GREAT DESTROYER, RABUM ALAL.
"RABUM ALAL IS COMING FOR EVERYTHING, AND WHEN YOU UNDERSTAND WHAT HE IS--WHO HE IS--YOU'LL KNOW THAT I WAS RIGHT. THEN YOU WILL DIE, THINKING OF ME... WHO WILL BE SO VERY LONG GONE."
"REED, DIDN'T THE SWAN SAY THE LIBRARY WAS DESTROYED?"
"PERHAPS, T'CHALLA, WE MIGHT NEED TO REVISIT WHAT IS AND IS NOT ACCEPTED TRUTH REGARDING HER."
WE NOW HAVE A KEY.
SO EACH BLACK PRIEST HAS A LETTER AND TOGETHER THEY MAKE A WORD, WHICH IS LIKE CASTING A SPELL?
OF A SORT. DO YOU KNOW WHAT WORD WE USE TO DESTROY A WORLD IN ORDER TO STOP THE COLLECTIVE HEAT DEATH OF THE UNIVERSE? "LIFE."
BUT I AM NOT ONLY THE LEADER OF THE BLACK PRIESTS, I AM THE SORCERER SUPREME. I DO NOT SPEAK LETTERS--I SPEAK WORDS.
AND I KNOW ALL OF THEM.

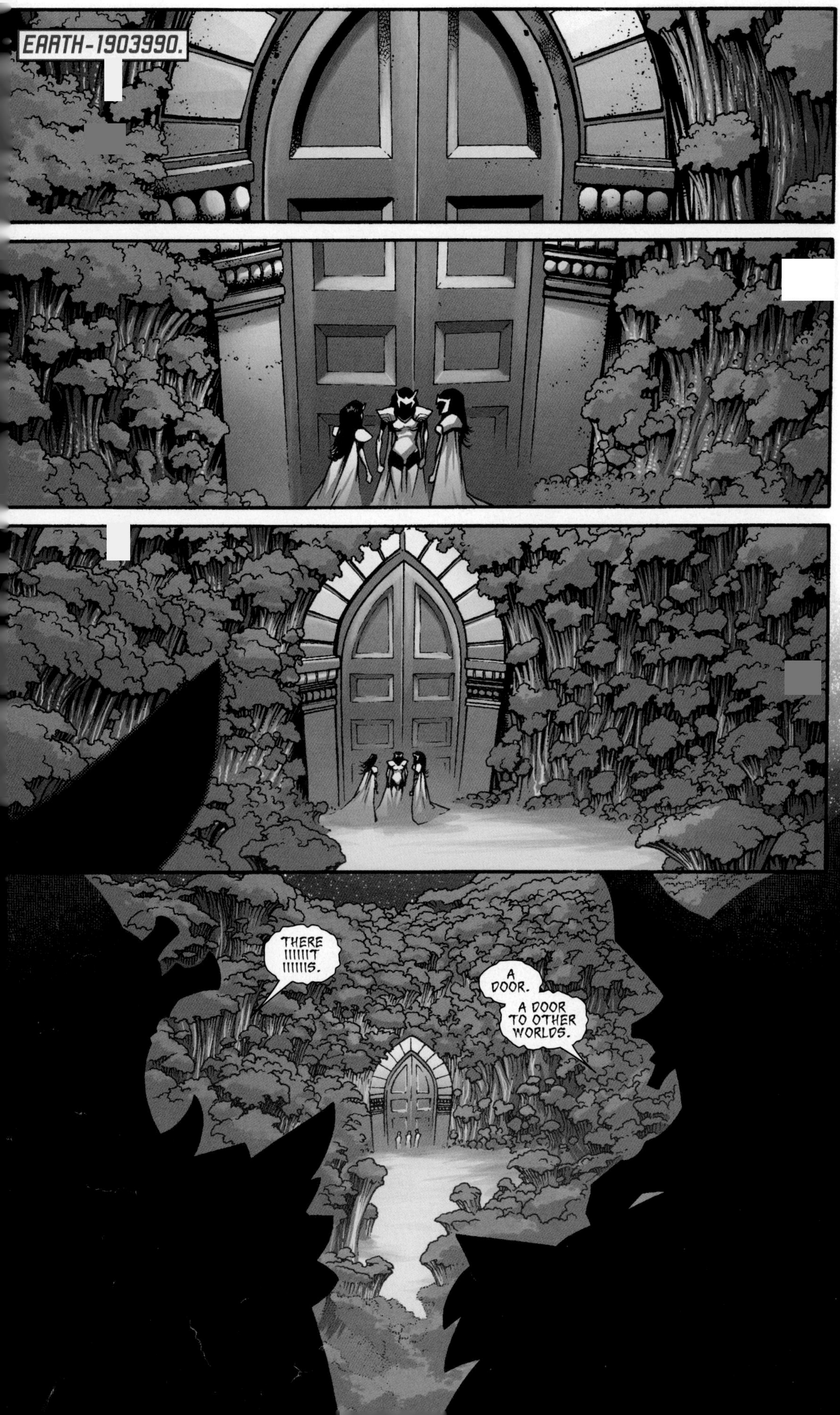
EARTH-1903990.
THERE IIIIIIT IIIIIIS.
A DOOR.
A DOOR TO OTHER WORLDS.

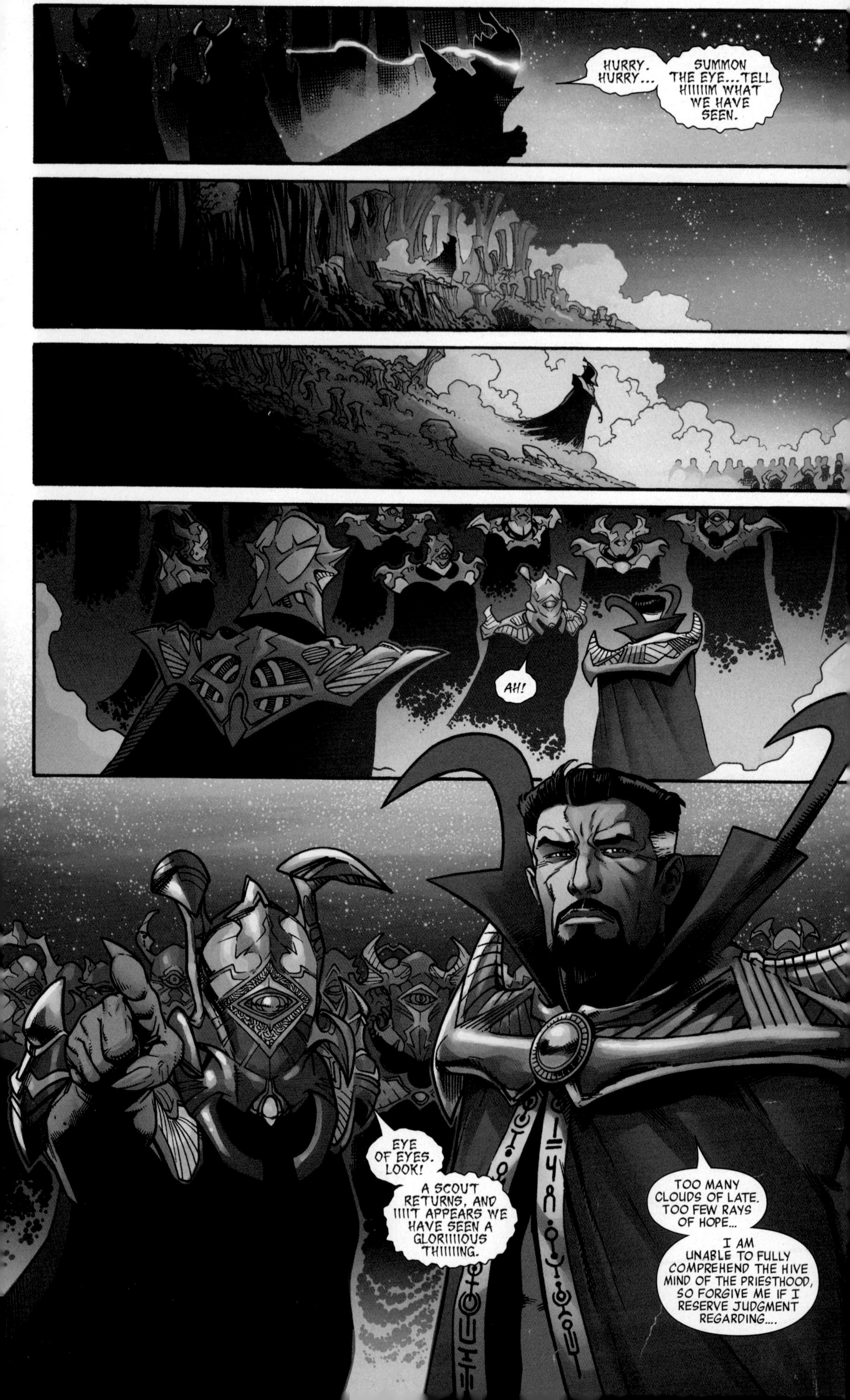
HURRY. HURRY...
SUMMON THE EYE...TELL HIIIIIM WHAT WE HAVE SEEN.
AH!
EYE OF EYES. LOOK!
A SCOUT RETURNS, AND IIIIT APPEARS WE HAVE SEEN A GLORIIIIOUS THIIIIING.
TOO MANY CLOUDS OF LATE. TOO FEW RAYS OF HOPE...
I AM UNABLE TO FULLY COMPREHEND THE HIVE MIND OF THE PRIESTHOOD, SO FORGIVE ME IF I RESERVE JUDGMENT REGARDING....

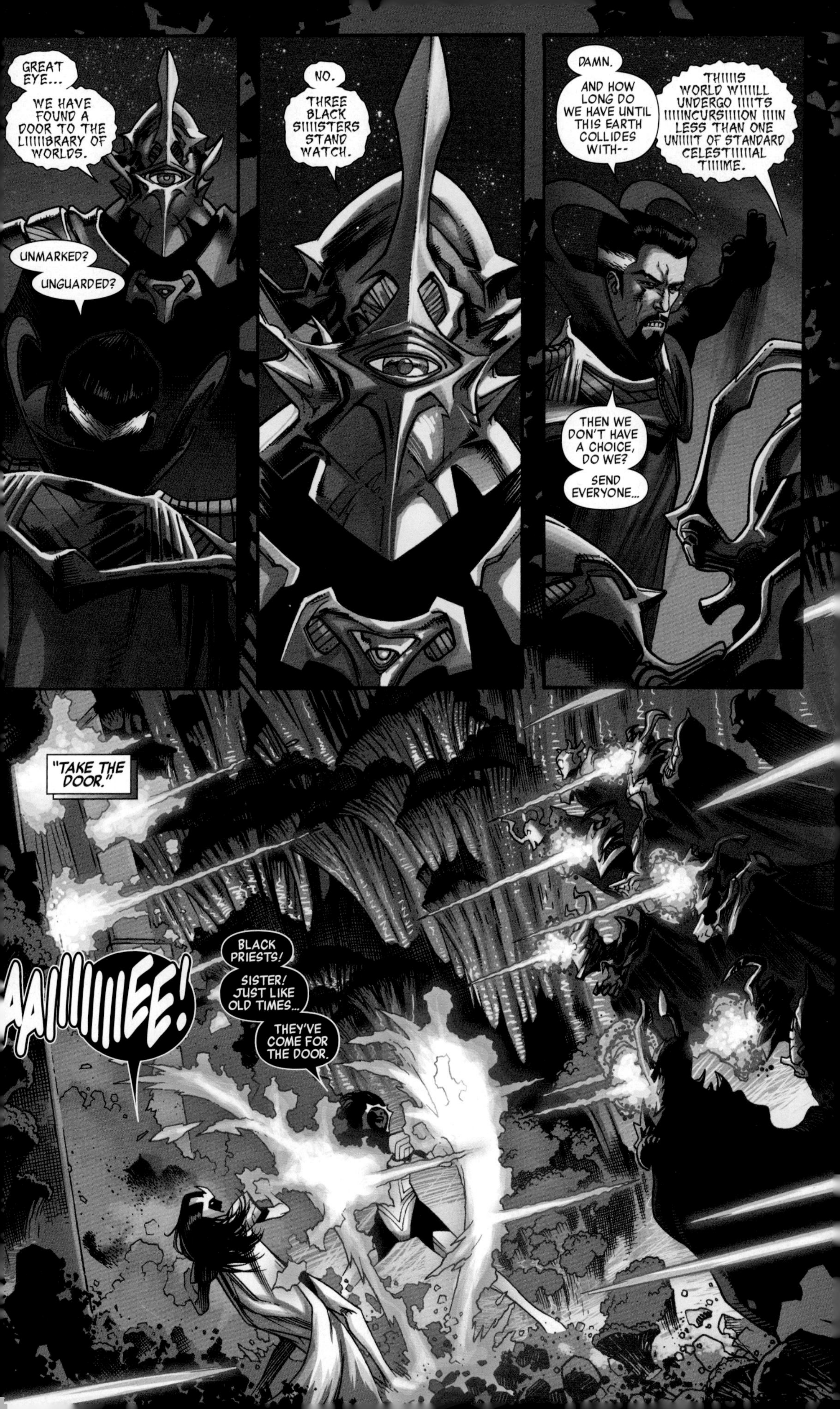
GREAT EYE...
WE HAVE FOUND A DOOR TO THE LIIIIIBRARY OF WORLDS.
UNMARKED?
UNGUARDED?
NO.
THREE BLACK SIIIISTERS STAND WATCH.
DAMN.
AND HOW LONG DO WE HAVE UNTIL THIS EARTH COLLIDES WITH--
THIIIIS WORLD WIIIIILL UNDERGO IIIITS IIIIIINCURSIIIION IIIIN LESS THAN ONE UNIIIIT OF STANDARD CELESTIIIIIAL TIIIIME.
THEN WE DON'T HAVE A CHOICE, DO WE?
SEND EVERYONE...
"TAKE THE DOOR."
AAIIIIIIIEE!
BLACK PRIESTS!
SISTER! JUST LIKE OLD TIMES...
THEY'VE COME FOR THE DOOR.

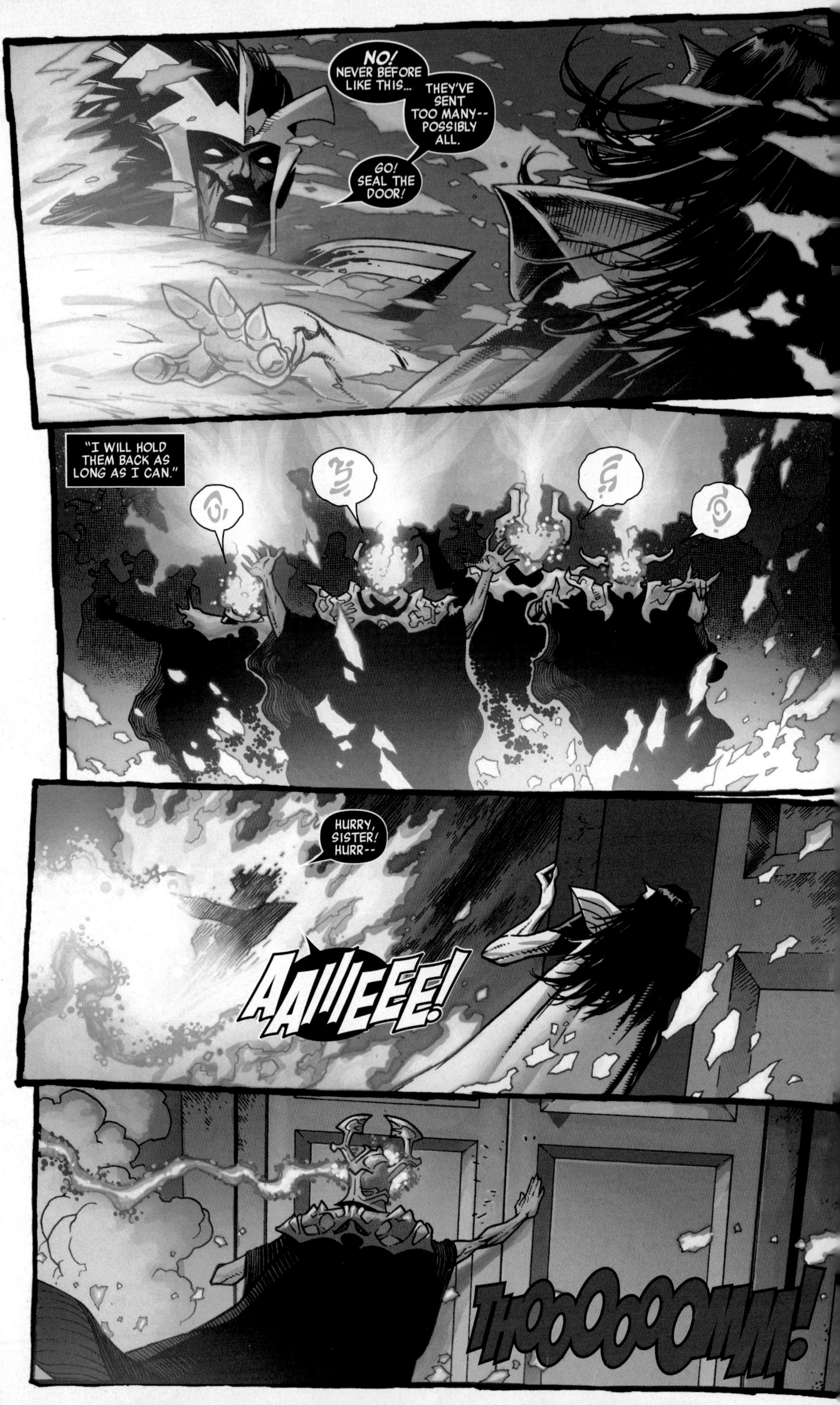
NO! NEVER BEFORE LIKE THIS...
THEY'VE SENT TOO MANY-- POSSIBLY ALL.
GO! SEAL THE DOOR!
"I WILL HOLD THEM BACK AS LONG AS I CAN."
HURRY, SISTER! HURR--
AAIIIEEE!
THOOOOOOMM!

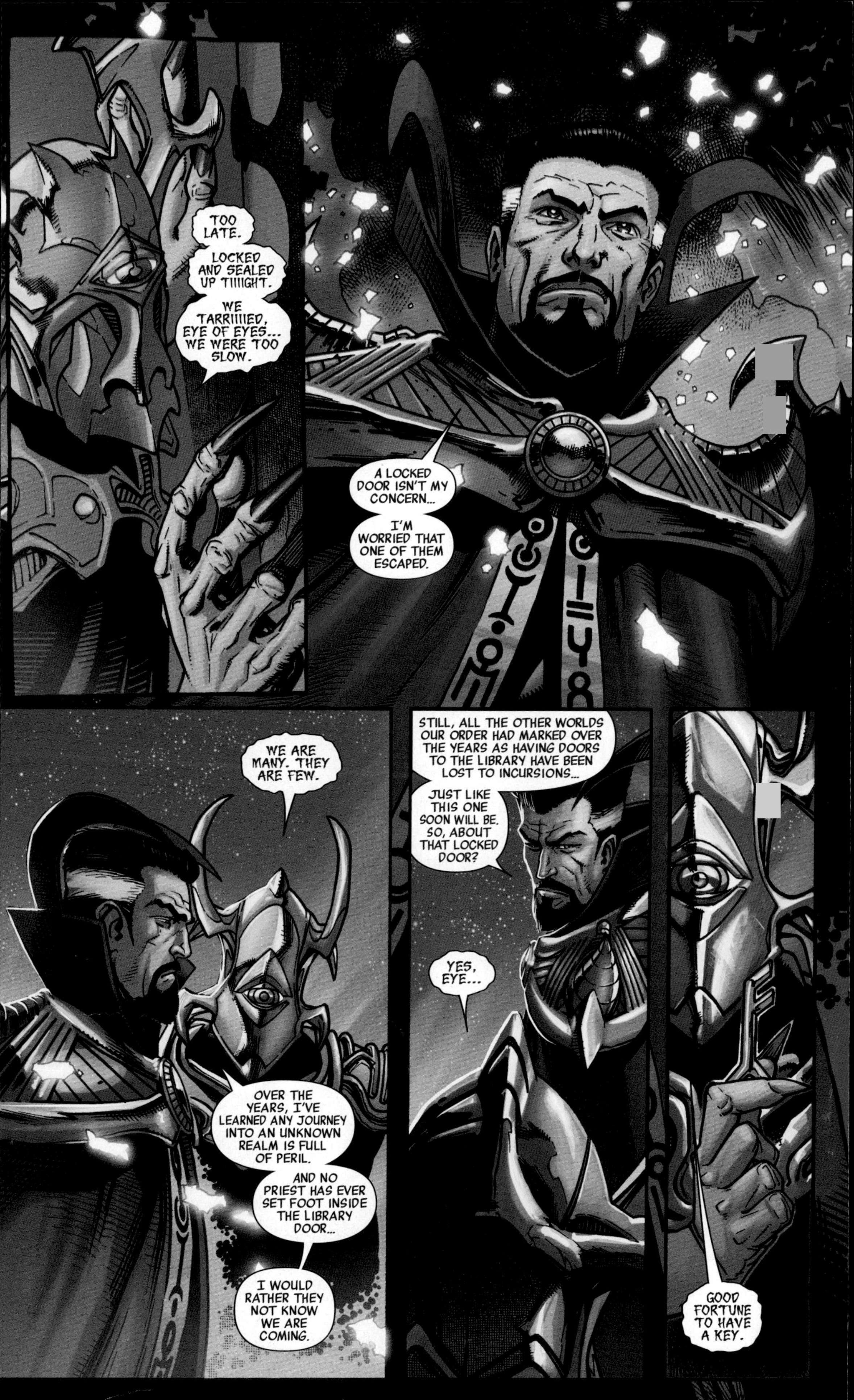
TOO LATE.
LOCKED AND SEALED UP TIIIIGHT.
WE TARRIIIIED, EYE OF EYES... WE WERE TOO SLOW.
A LOCKED DOOR ISN'T MY CONCERN...
I'M WORRIED THAT ONE OF THEM ESCAPED.
WE ARE MANY. THEY ARE FEW.
OVER THE YEARS, I'VE LEARNED ANY JOURNEY INTO AN UNKNOWN REALM IS FULL OF PERIL.
AND NO PRIEST HAS EVER SET FOOT INSIDE THE LIBRARY DOOR...
I WOULD RATHER THEY NOT KNOW WE ARE COMING.
STILL, ALL THE OTHER WORLDS OUR ORDER HAD MARKED OVER THE YEARS AS HAVING DOORS TO THE LIBRARY HAVE BEEN LOST TO INCURSIONS...
JUST LIKE THIS ONE SOON WILL BE. SO, ABOUT THAT LOCKED DOOR?
YES, EYE...
GOOD FORTUNE TO HAVE A KEY.

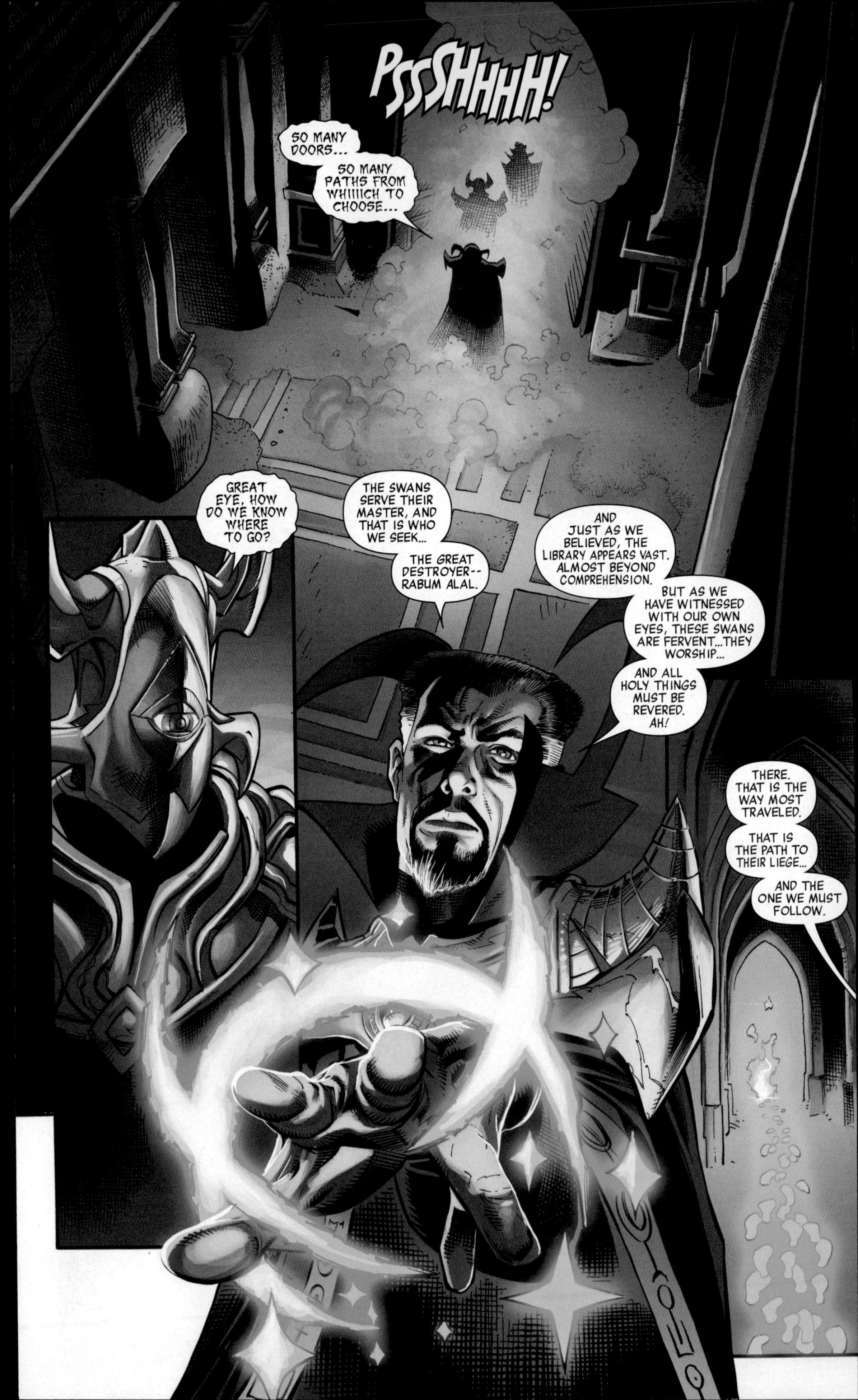
PSSSHHHH!
SO MANY DOORS...
SO MANY PATHS FROM WHIIIICH TO CHOOSE...
GREAT EYE, HOW DO WE KNOW WHERE TO GO?
THE SWANS SERVE THEIR MASTER, AND THAT IS WHO WE SEEK...
THE GREAT DESTROYER-- RABUM ALAL.
AND JUST AS WE BELIEVED, THE LIBRARY APPEARS VAST. ALMOST BEYOND COMPREHENSION.
BUT AS WE HAVE WITNESSED WITH OUR OWN EYES, THESE SWANS ARE FERVENT...THEY WORSHIP...
AND ALL HOLY THINGS MUST BE REVERED. AH!
THERE. THAT IS THE WAY MOST TRAVELED.
THAT IS THE PATH TO THEIR LIEGE...
AND THE ONE WE MUST FOLLOW.

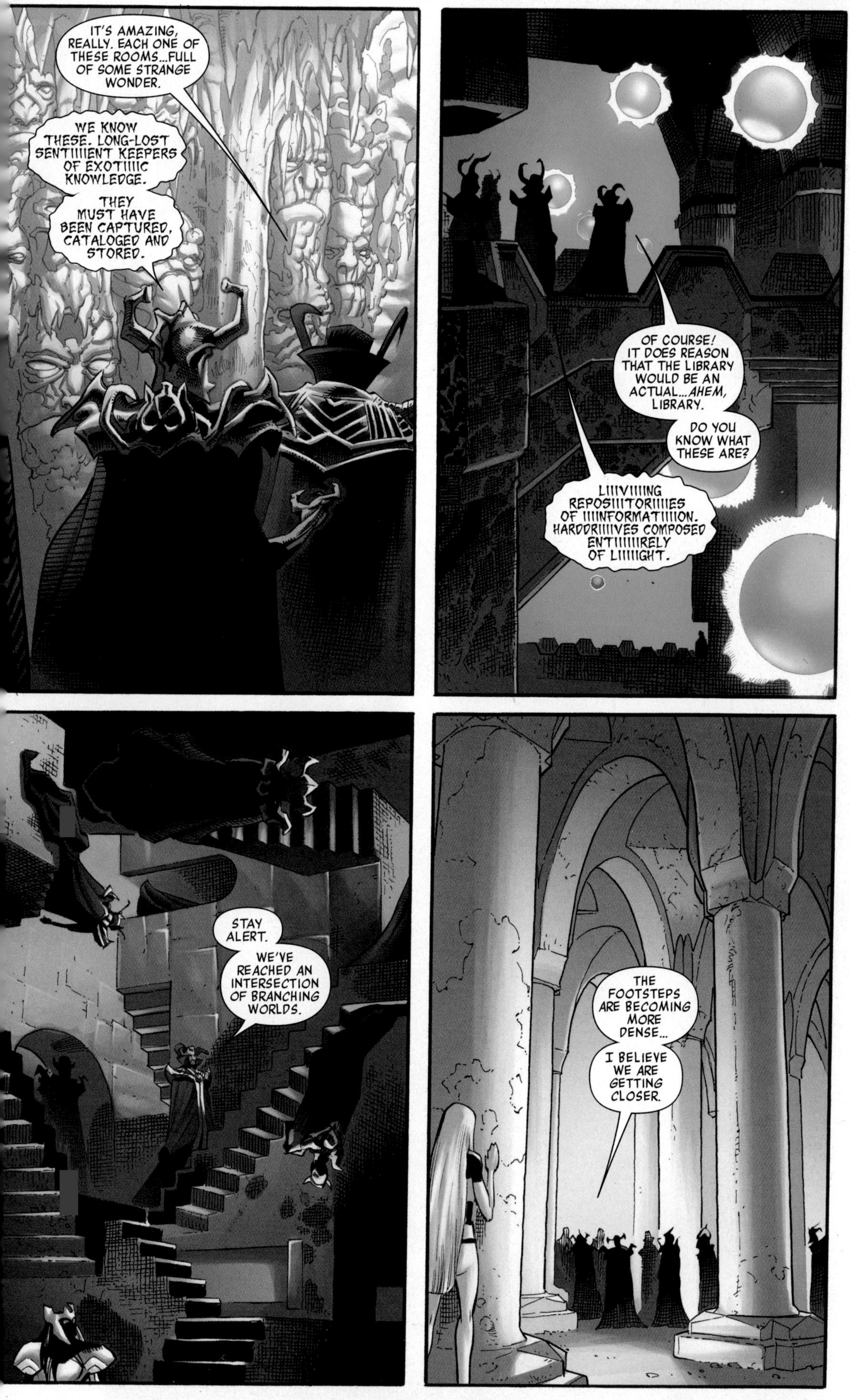
IT'S AMAZING, REALLY. EACH ONE OF THESE ROOMS...FULL OF SOME STRANGE WONDER.
WE KNOW THESE. LONG-LOST SENTIIIIENT KEEPERS OF EXOTIIIIC KNOWLEDGE.
THEY MUST HAVE BEEN CAPTURED, CATALOGED AND STORED.
OF COURSE! IT DOES REASON THAT THE LIBRARY WOULD BE AN ACTUAL...*AHEM*, LIBRARY.
DO YOU KNOW WHAT THESE ARE?
LIIIVIIIING REPOSIIIITORIIIIES OF IIIINFORMATIIIION. HARDDRIIIIVES COMPOSED ENTIIIIIIRELY OF LIIIIGHT.
STAY ALERT.
WE'VE REACHED AN INTERSECTION OF BRANCHING WORLDS.
THE FOOTSTEPS ARE BECOMING MORE DENSE...
I BELIEVE WE ARE GETTING CLOSER.

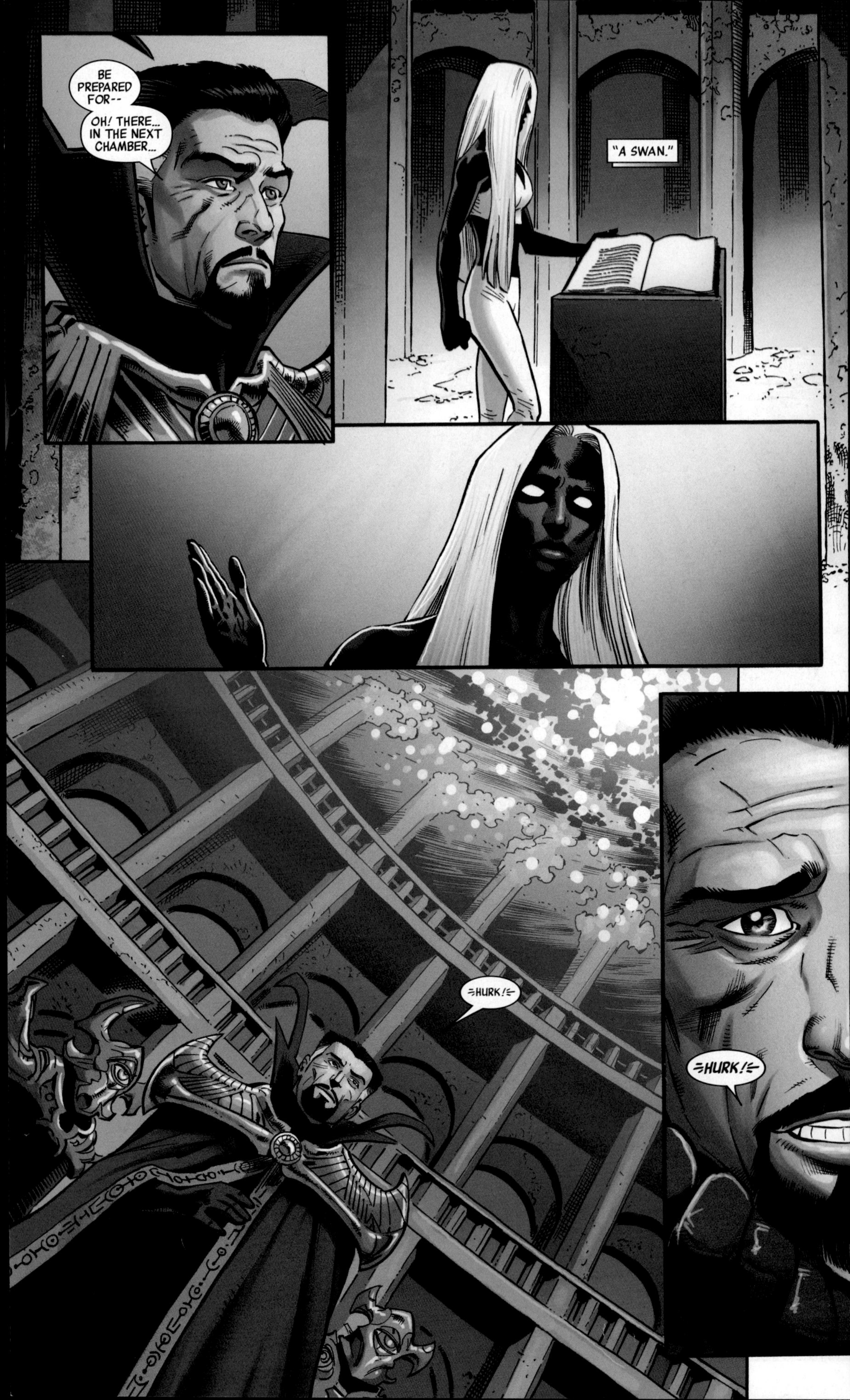
BE PREPARED FOR--
OH! THERE... IN THE NEXT CHAMBER...
"A SWAN."
HURK!
HURK!

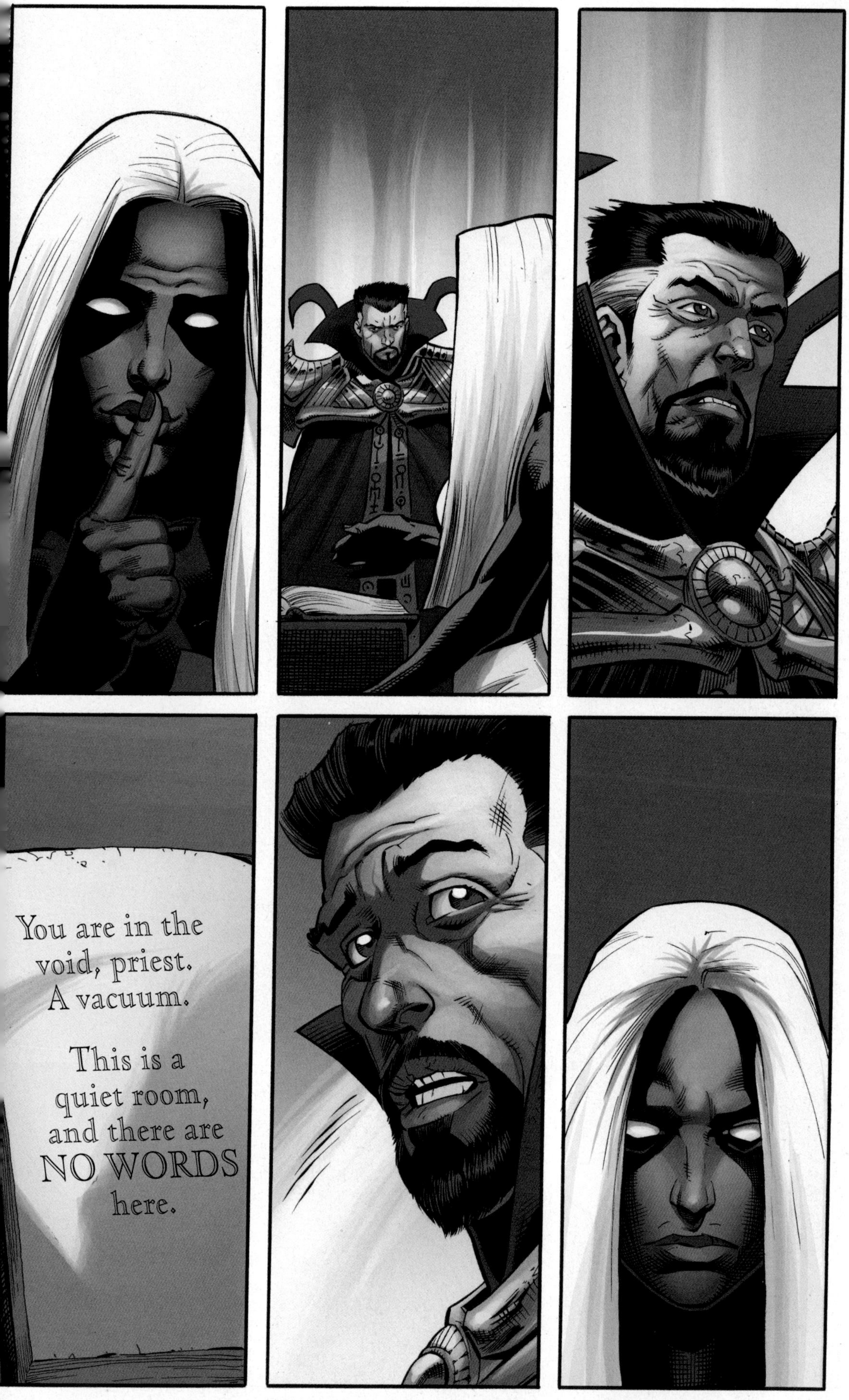
You are in the void, priest. A vacuum.
This is a quiet room, and there are NO WORDS here.

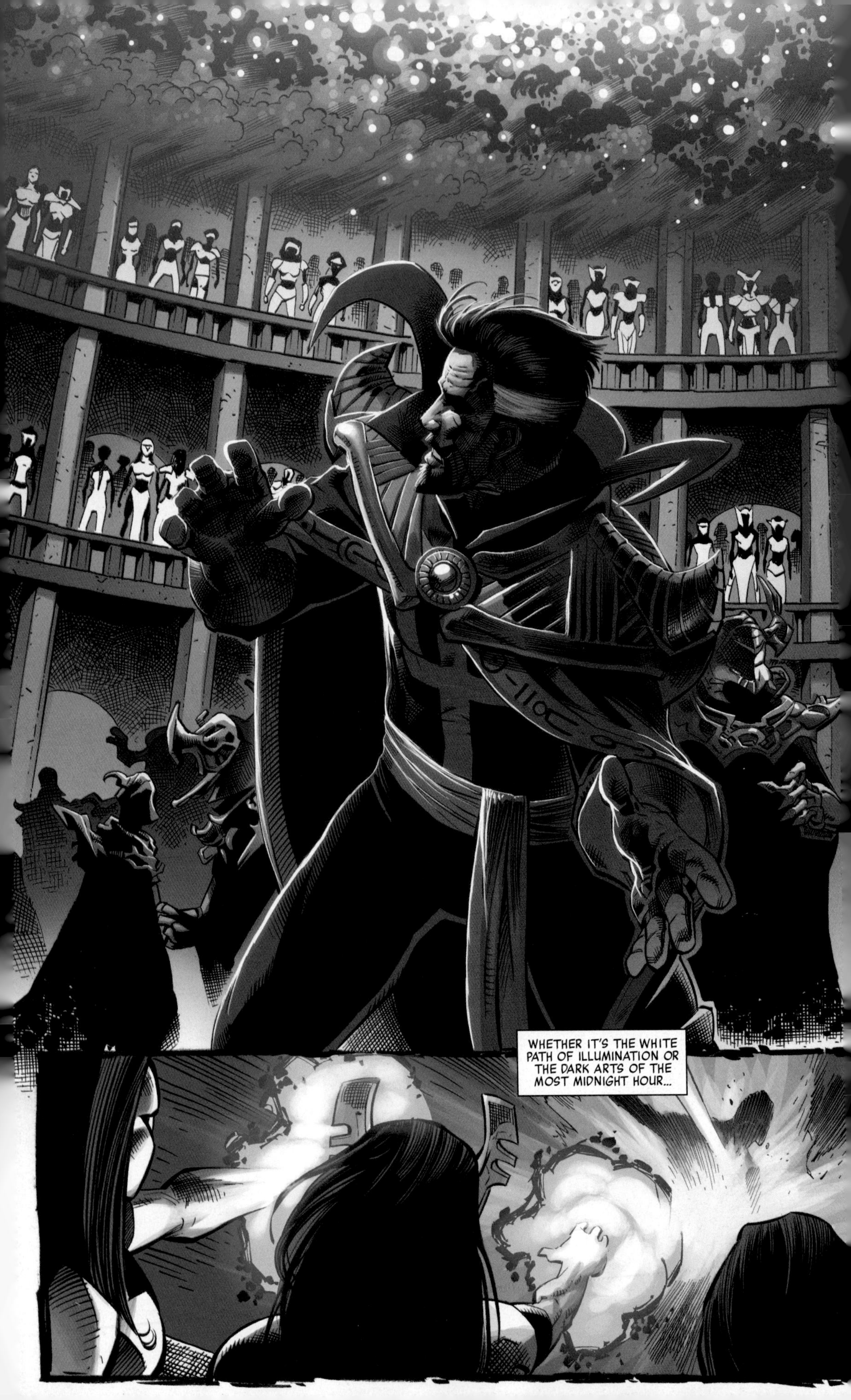
WHETHER IT'S THE WHITE PATH OF ILLUMINATION OR THE DARK ARTS OF THE MOST MIDNIGHT HOUR...

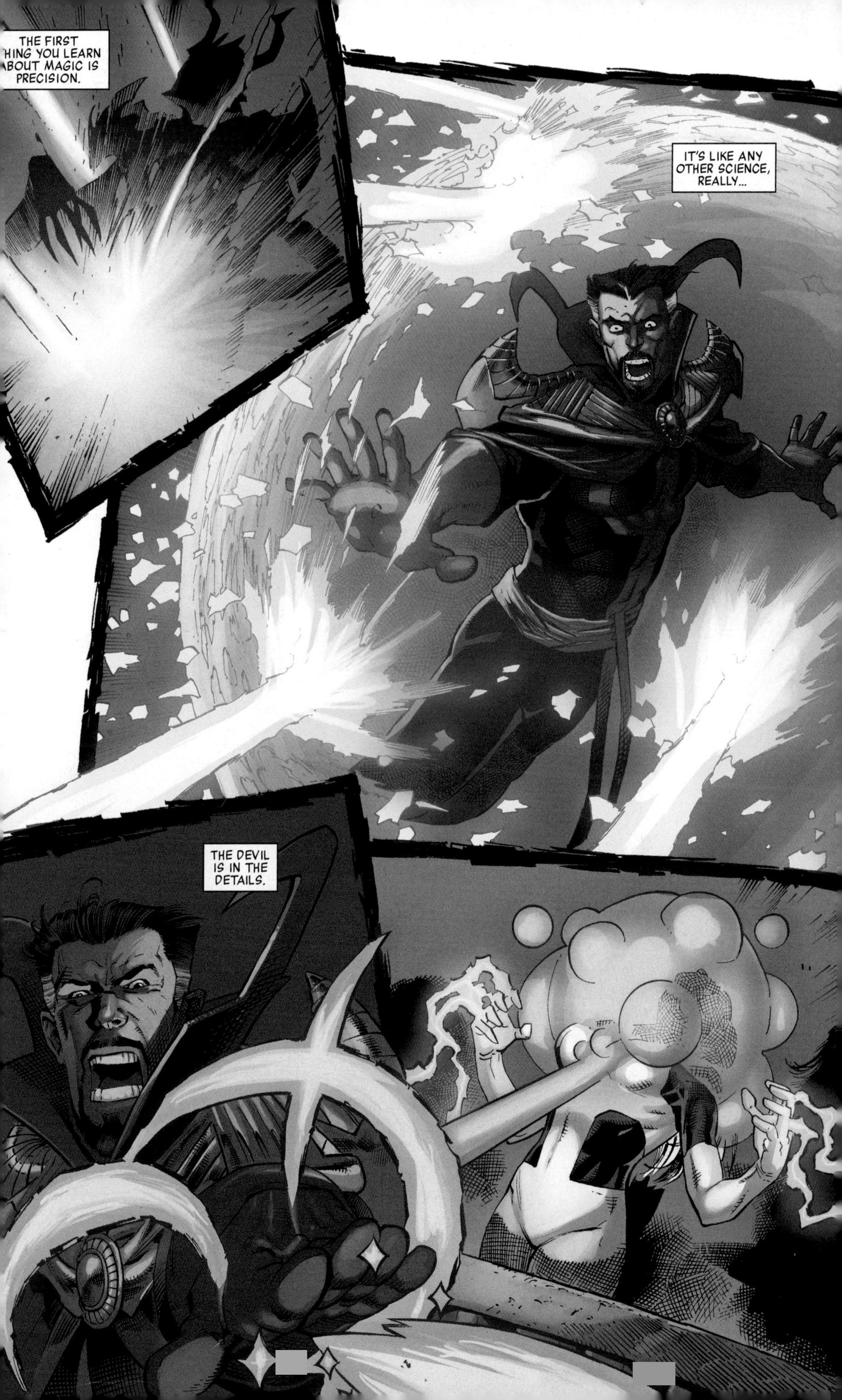
THE FIRST THING YOU LEARN ABOUT MAGIC IS PRECISION.
IT'S LIKE ANY OTHER SCIENCE, REALLY...
THE DEVIL IS IN THE DETAILS.

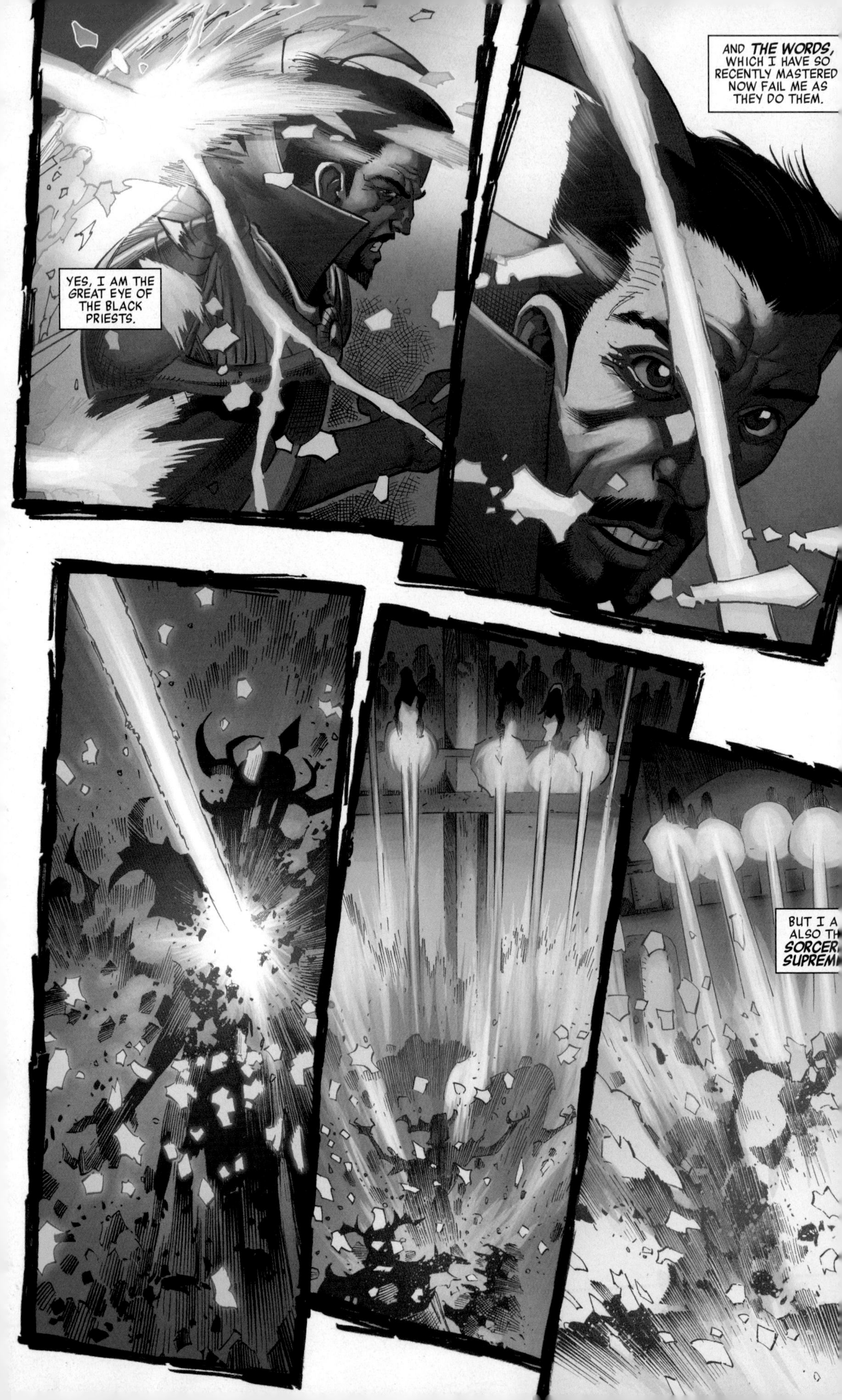
YES, I AM THE GREAT EYE OF THE BLACK PRIESTS.
AND THE WORDS, WHICH I HAVE SO RECENTLY MASTERED NOW FAIL ME AS THEY DO THEM.
BUT I A ALSO TH SORCER SUPREM

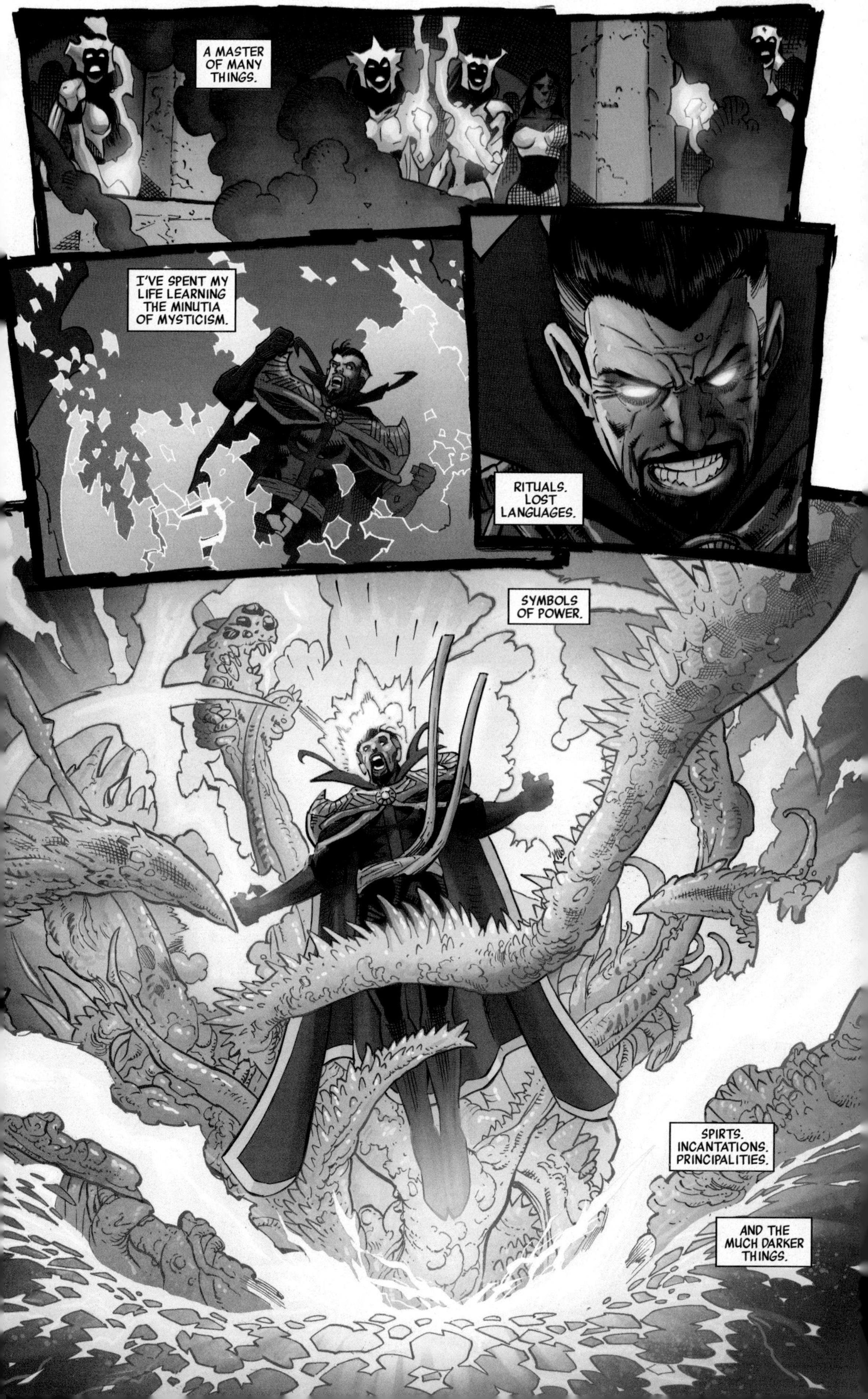
A MASTER OF MANY THINGS.
I'VE SPENT MY LIFE LEARNING THE MINUTIA OF MYSTICISM.
RITUALS. LOST LANGUAGES.
SYMBOLS OF POWER.
SPIRTS. INCANTATIONS. PRINCIPALITIES.
AND THE MUCH DARKER THINGS.

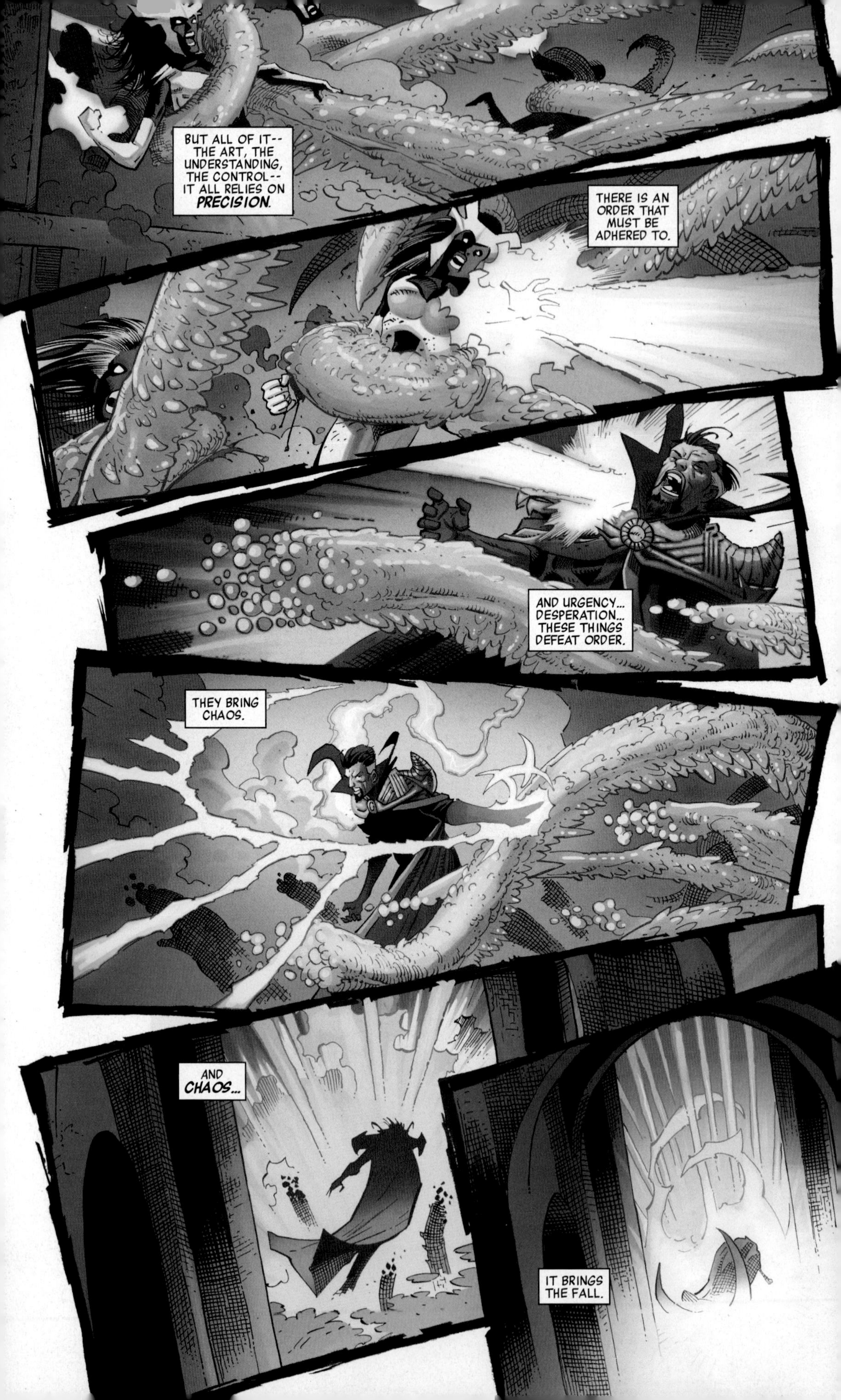
BUT ALL OF IT-- THE ART, THE UNDERSTANDING, THE CONTROL-- IT ALL RELIES ON **PRECISION**.
THERE IS AN ORDER THAT MUST BE ADHERED TO.
AND URGENCY... DESPERATION... THESE THINGS DEFEAT ORDER.
THEY BRING CHAOS.
AND **CHAOS**...
IT BRINGS THE FALL.

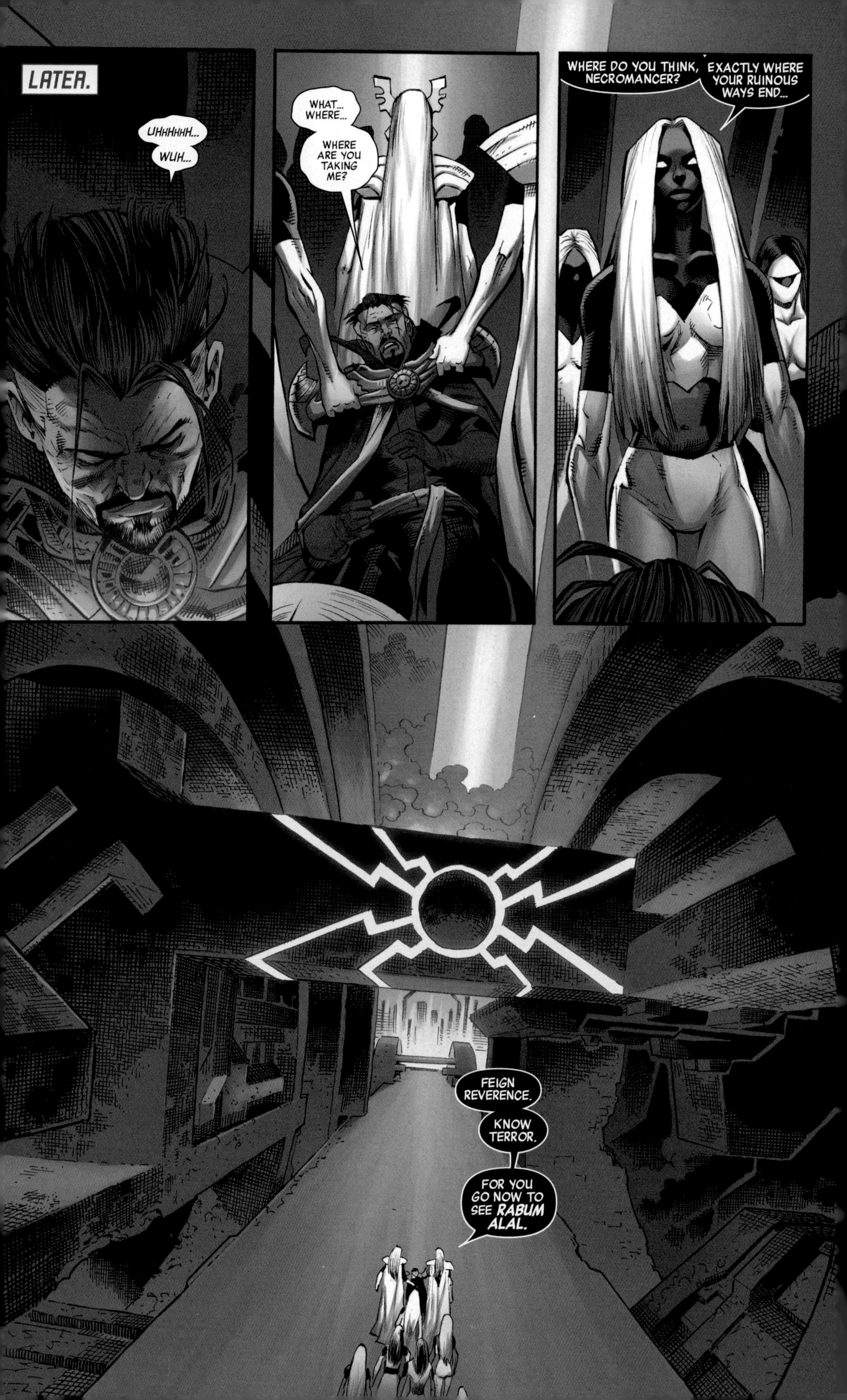
LATER.
UHHHHHH... WUH...
WHAT... WHERE...
WHERE ARE YOU TAKING ME?
WHERE DO YOU THINK, NECROMANCER?
EXACTLY WHERE YOUR RUINOUS WAYS END...
FEIGN REVERENCE.
KNOW TERROR.
FOR YOU GO NOW TO SEE RABUM ALAL.

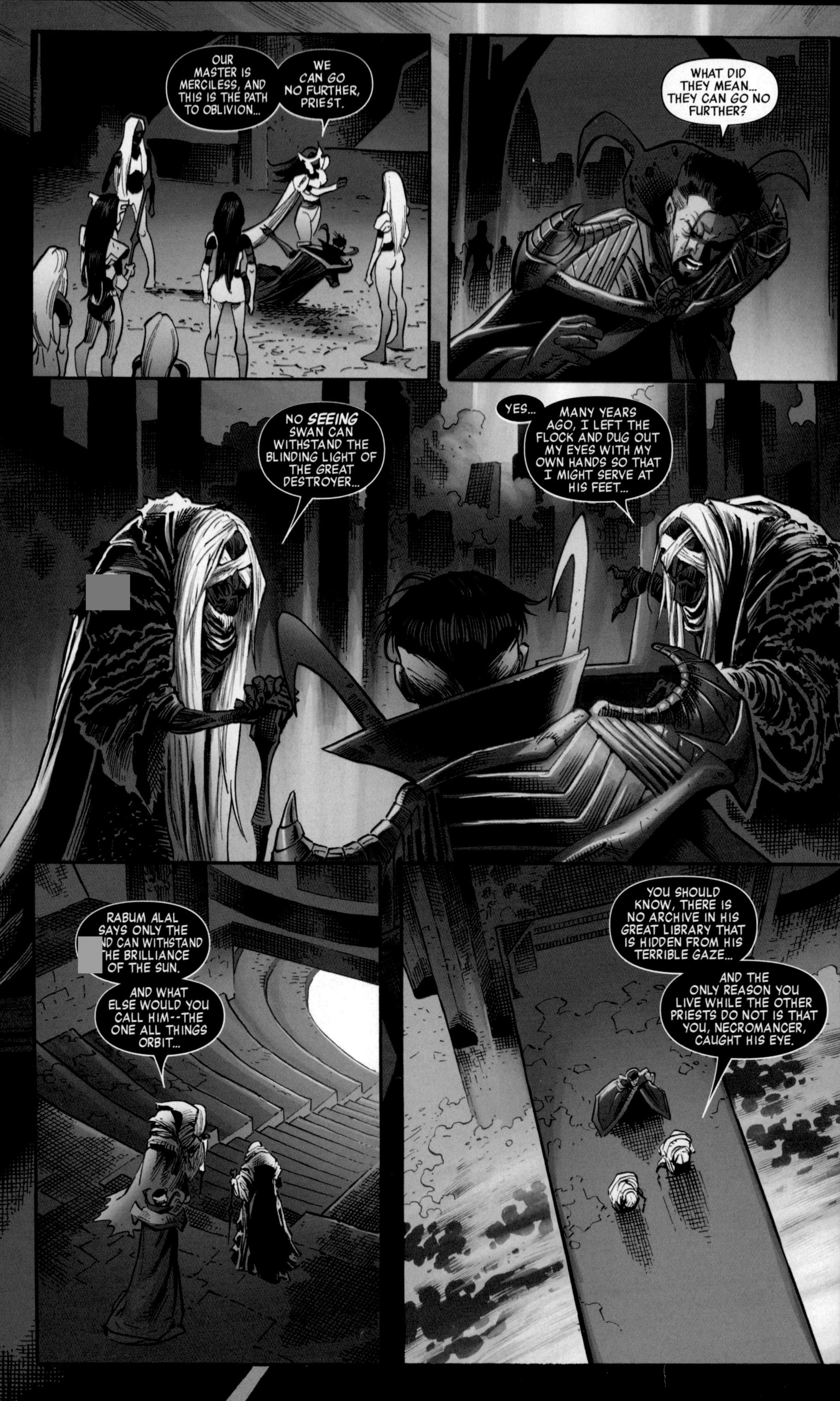
OUR MASTER IS MERCILESS, AND THIS IS THE PATH TO OBLIVION...
WE CAN GO NO FURTHER, PRIEST.
WHAT DID THEY MEAN... THEY CAN GO NO FURTHER?
NO SEEING SWAN CAN WITHSTAND THE BLINDING LIGHT OF THE GREAT DESTROYER...
YES...
MANY YEARS AGO, I LEFT THE FLOCK AND DUG OUT MY EYES WITH MY OWN HANDS SO THAT I MIGHT SERVE AT HIS FEET...
RABUM ALAL SAYS ONLY THE
ND CAN WITHSTAND THE BRILLIANCE OF THE SUN.
AND WHAT ELSE WOULD YOU CALL HIM--THE ONE ALL THINGS ORBIT...
YOU SHOULD KNOW, THERE IS NO ARCHIVE IN HIS GREAT LIBRARY THAT IS HIDDEN FROM HIS TERRIBLE GAZE...
AND THE ONLY REASON YOU LIVE WHILE THE OTHER PRIESTS DO NOT IS THAT YOU, NECROMANCER, CAUGHT HIS EYE.

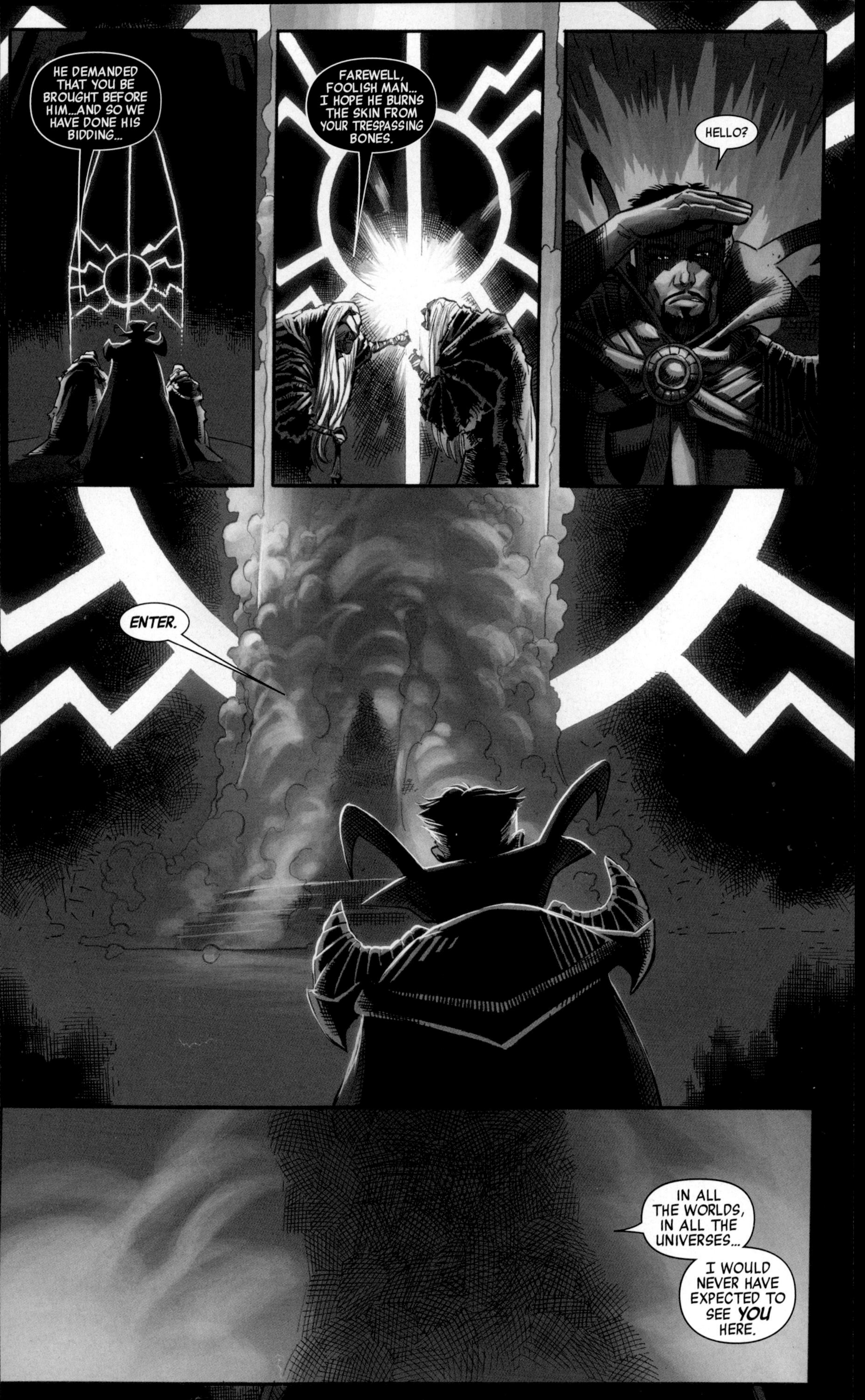
HE DEMANDED THAT YOU BE BROUGHT BEFORE HIM...AND SO WE HAVE DONE HIS BIDDING...
FAREWELL, FOOLISH MAN... I HOPE HE BURNS THE SKIN FROM YOUR TRESPASSING BONES.
HELLO?
ENTER.
IN ALL THE WORLDS, IN ALL THE UNIVERSES...
I WOULD NEVER HAVE EXPECTED TO SEE YOU HERE.

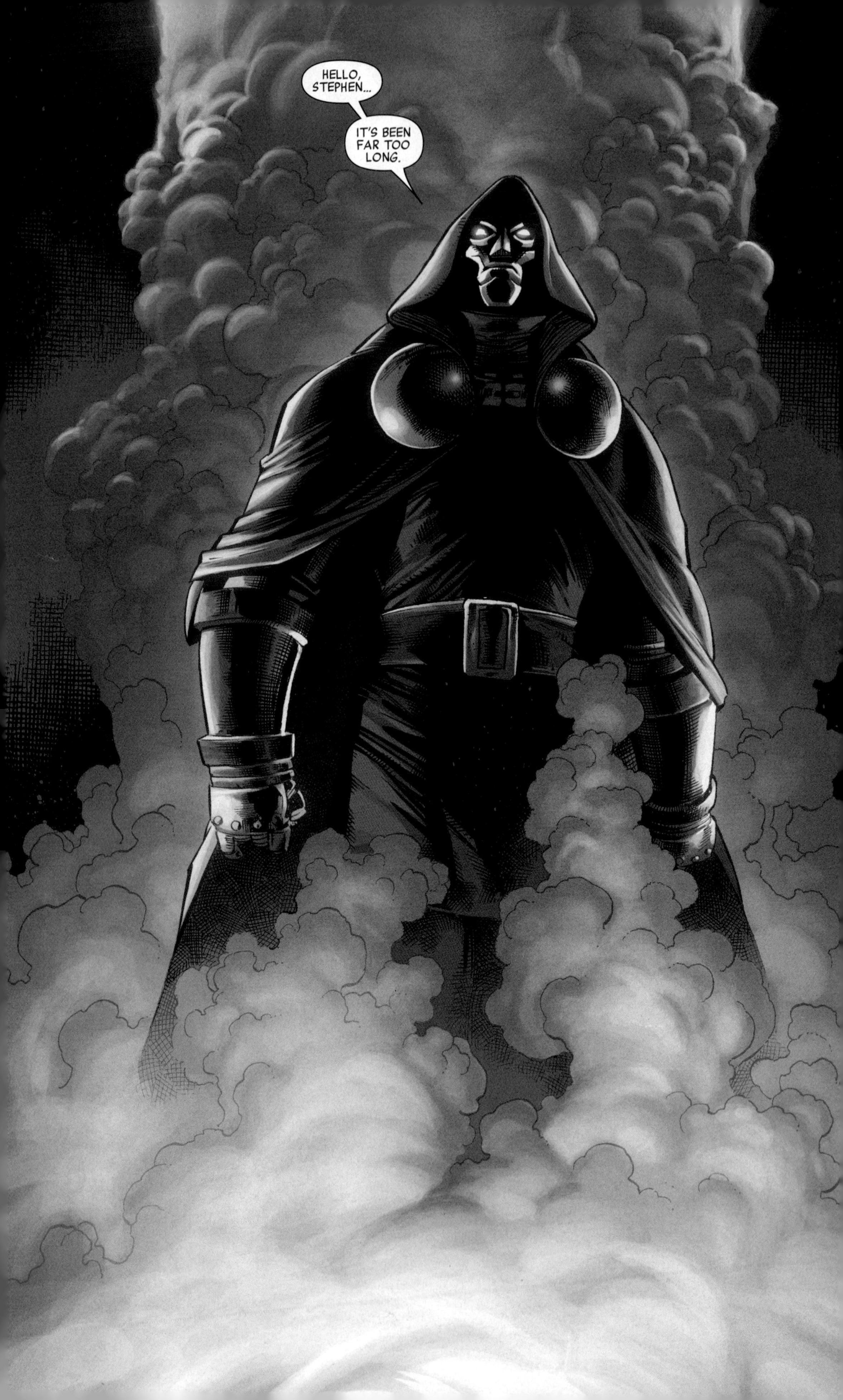
HELLO, STEPHEN...
IT'S BEEN FAR TOO LONG.

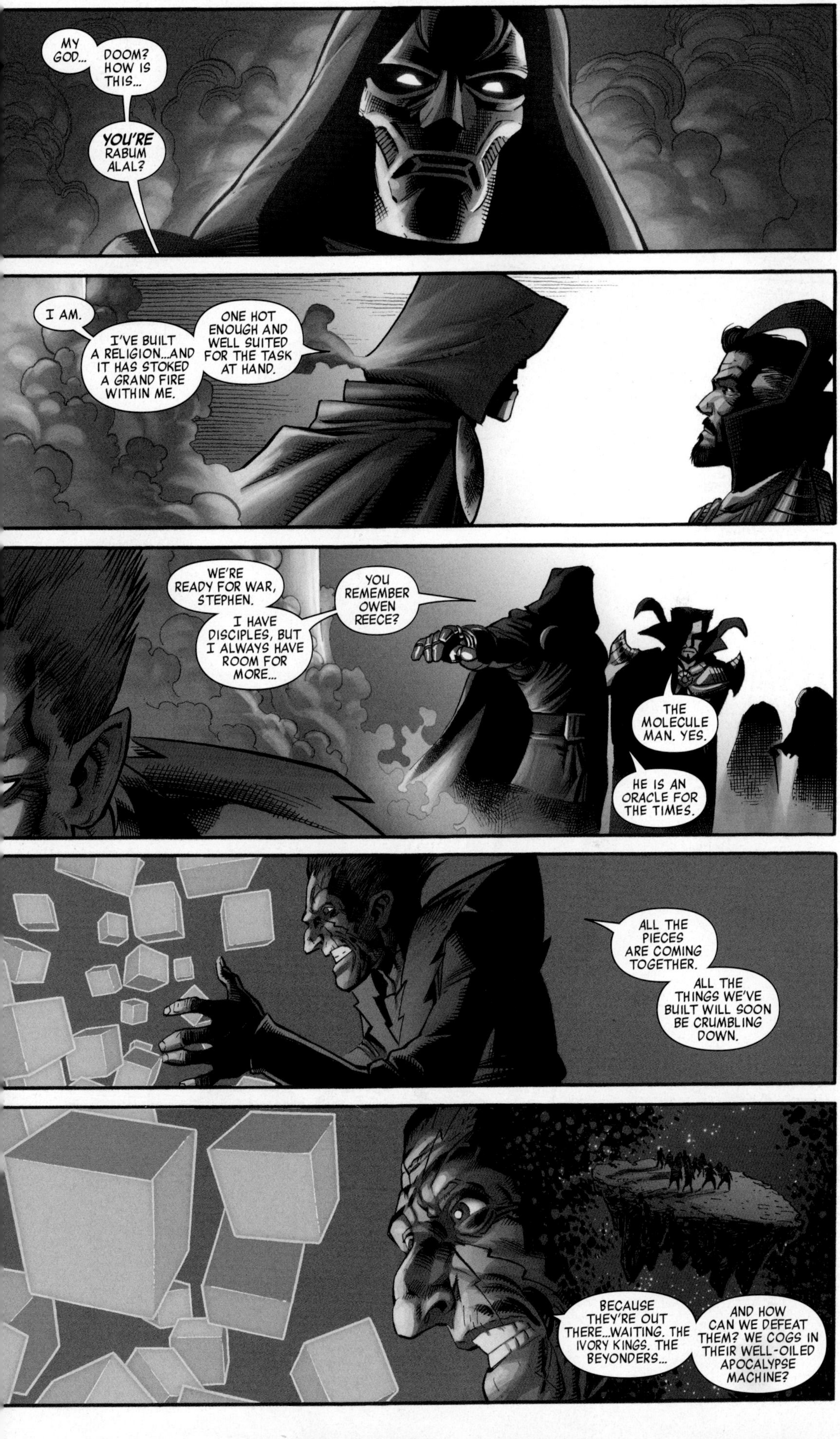
MY GOD...
DOOM? HOW IS THIS...
YOU'RE RABUM ALAL?
I AM.
I'VE BUILT A RELIGION...AND IT HAS STOKED A GRAND FIRE WITHIN ME.
ONE HOT ENOUGH AND WELL SUITED FOR THE TASK AT HAND.
WE'RE READY FOR WAR, STEPHEN.
I HAVE DISCIPLES, BUT I ALWAYS HAVE ROOM FOR MORE...
YOU REMEMBER OWEN REECE?
THE MOLECULE MAN. YES.
HE IS AN ORACLE FOR THE TIMES.
ALL THE PIECES ARE COMING TOGETHER.
ALL THE THINGS WE'VE BUILT WILL SOON BE CRUMBLING DOWN.
BECAUSE THEY'RE OUT THERE...WAITING. THE IVORY KINGS. THE BEYONDERS...
AND HOW CAN WE DEFEAT THEM? WE COGS IN THEIR WELL-OILED APOCALYPSE MACHINE?

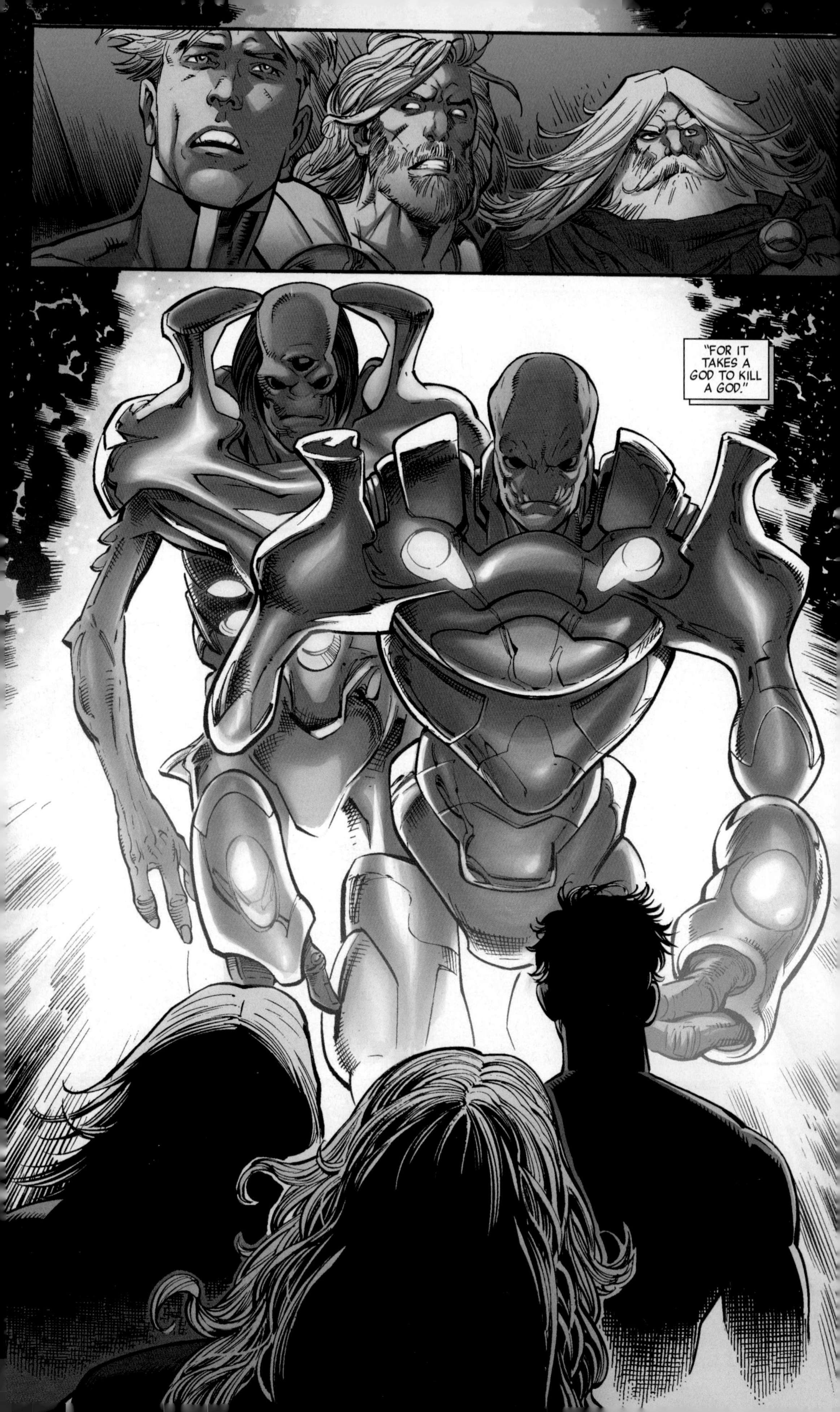
"FOR IT TAKES A GOD TO KILL A GOD."

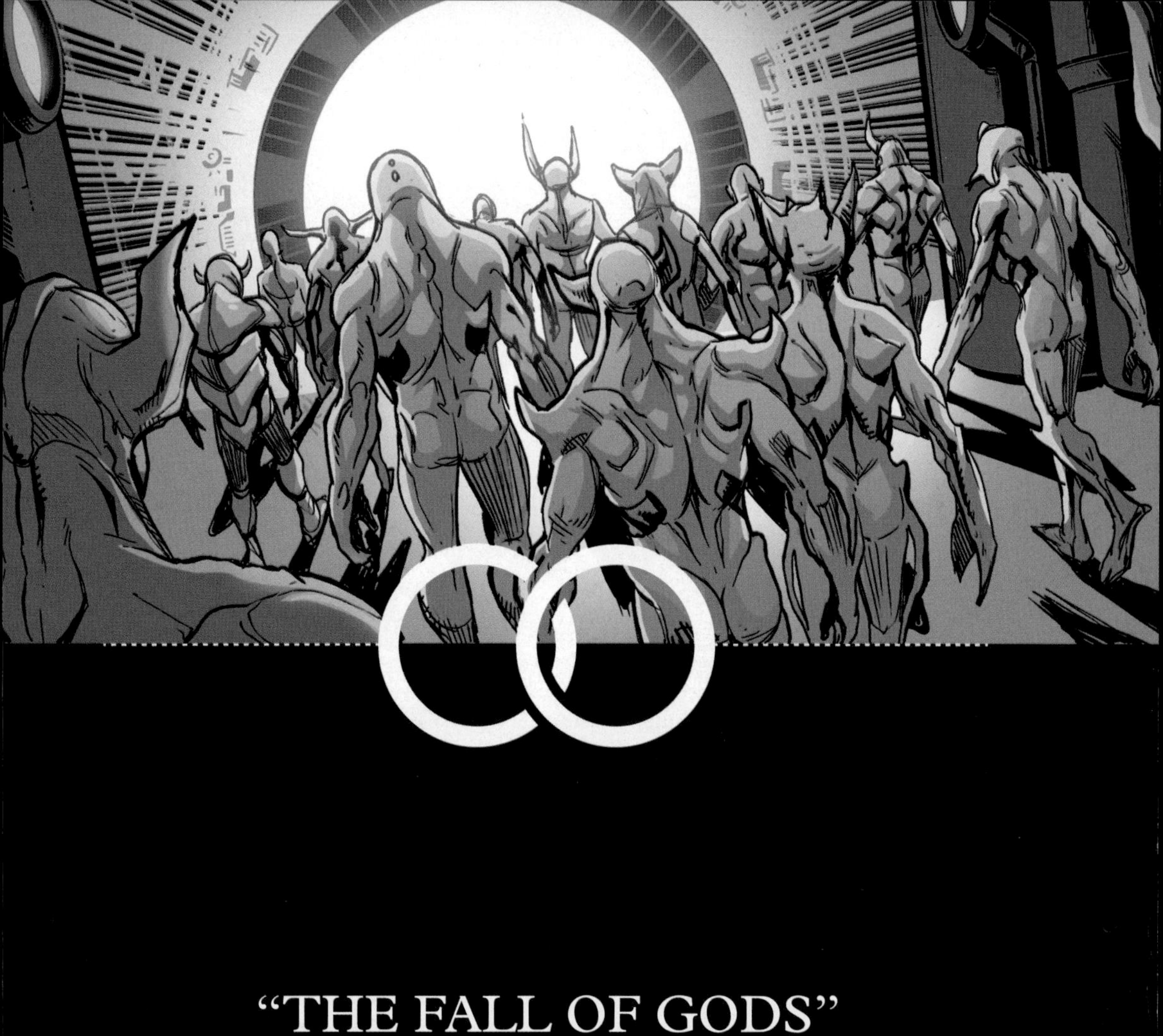

"THE FALL OF GODS"

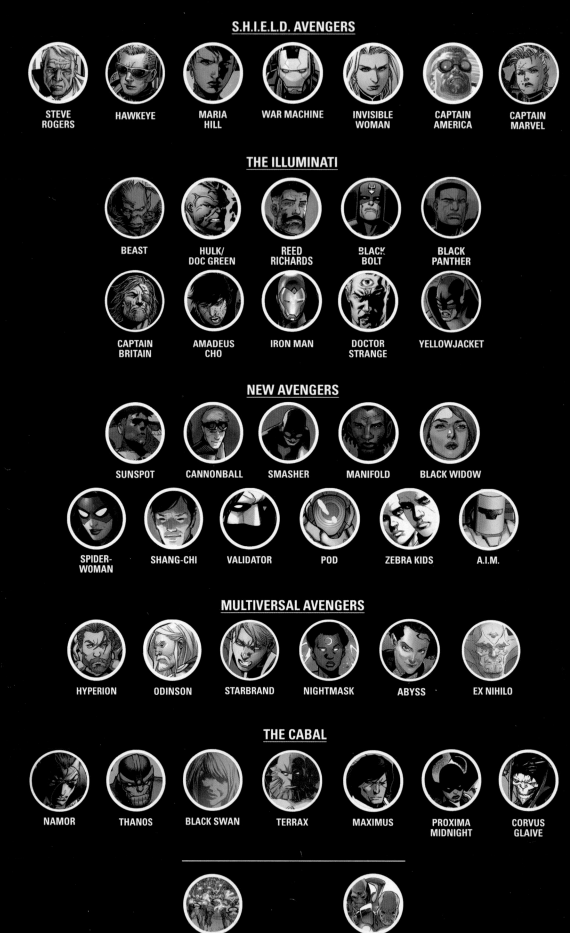

S.H.I.E.L.D. AVENGERS

STEVE ROGERS • HAWKEYE • MARIA HILL • WAR MACHINE • INVISIBLE WOMAN • CAPTAIN AMERICA • CAPTAIN MARVEL

THE ILLUMINATI

BEAST • HULK/DOC GREEN • REED RICHARDS • BLACK BOLT • BLACK PANTHER

CAPTAIN BRITAIN • AMADEUS CHO • IRON MAN • DOCTOR STRANGE • YELLOWJACKET

NEW AVENGERS

SUNSPOT • CANNONBALL • SMASHER • MANIFOLD • BLACK WIDOW

SPIDER-WOMAN • SHANG-CHI • VALIDATOR • POD • ZEBRA KIDS • A.I.M.

MULTIVERSAL AVENGERS

HYPERION • ODINSON • STARBRAND • NIGHTMASK • ABYSS • EX NIHILO

THE CABAL

NAMOR • THANOS • BLACK SWAN • TERRAX • MAXIMUS • PROXIMA MIDNIGHT • CORVUS GLAIVE

EX NIHILII • BEYONDERS

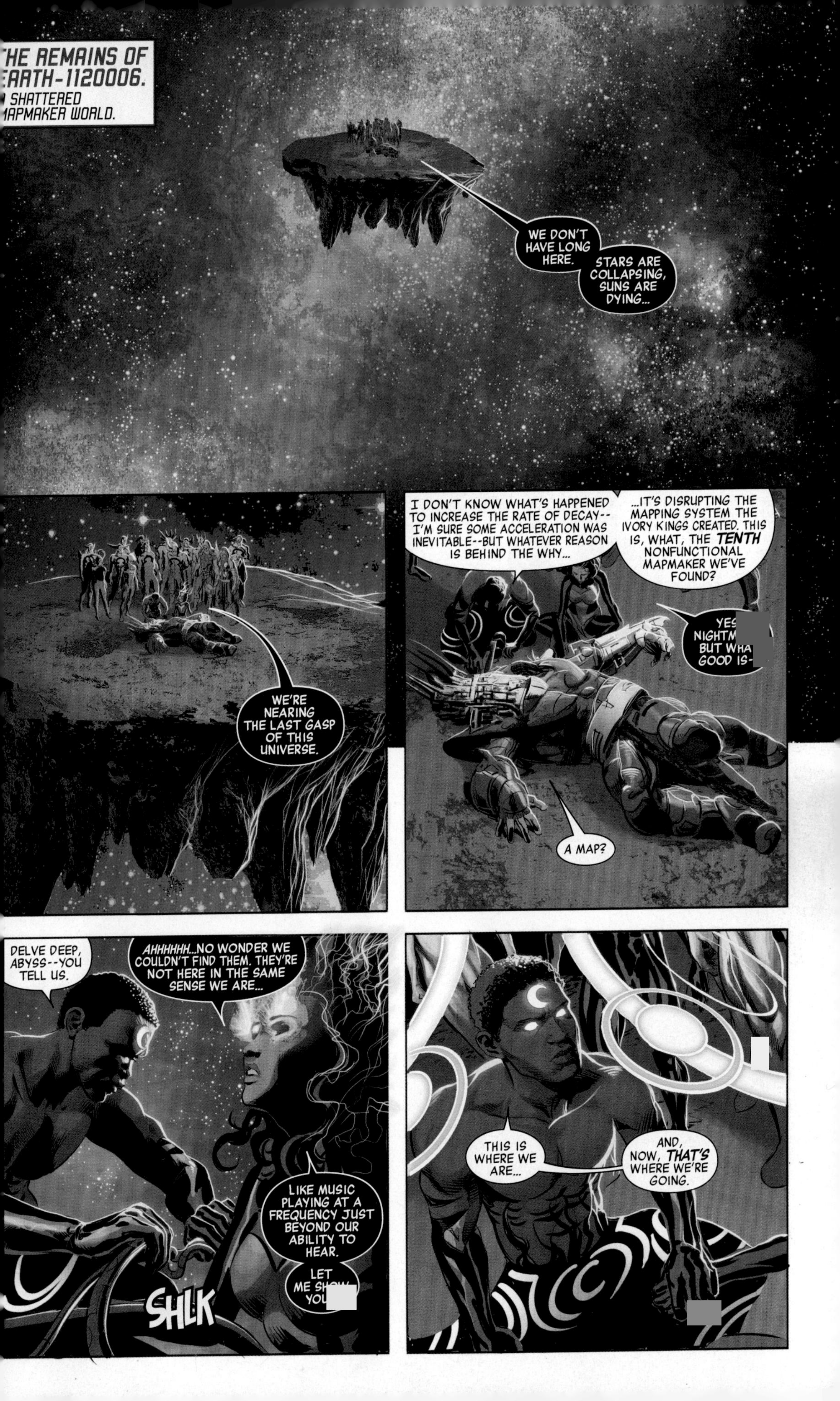

HE REMAINS OF EARTH-1120006.
SHATTERED APMAKER WORLD.
WE DON'T HAVE LONG HERE.
STARS ARE COLLAPSING, SUNS ARE DYING...
WE'RE NEARING THE LAST GASP OF THIS UNIVERSE.
I DON'T KNOW WHAT'S HAPPENED TO INCREASE THE RATE OF DECAY--I'M SURE SOME ACCELERATION WAS INEVITABLE--BUT WHATEVER REASON IS BEHIND THE WHY...
...IT'S DISRUPTING THE MAPPING SYSTEM THE IVORY KINGS CREATED. THIS IS, WHAT, THE TENTH NONFUNCTIONAL MAPMAKER WE'VE FOUND?
YES NIGHTM BUT WHA GOOD IS-
A MAP?
DELVE DEEP, ABYSS--YOU TELL US.
AHHHHHH...NO WONDER WE COULDN'T FIND THEM. THEY'RE NOT HERE IN THE SAME SENSE WE ARE...
LIKE MUSIC PLAYING AT A FREQUENCY JUST BEYOND OUR ABILITY TO HEAR.
LET ME SHOW YOU
SHLK
THIS IS WHERE WE ARE...
AND, NOW, THAT'S WHERE WE'RE GOING.

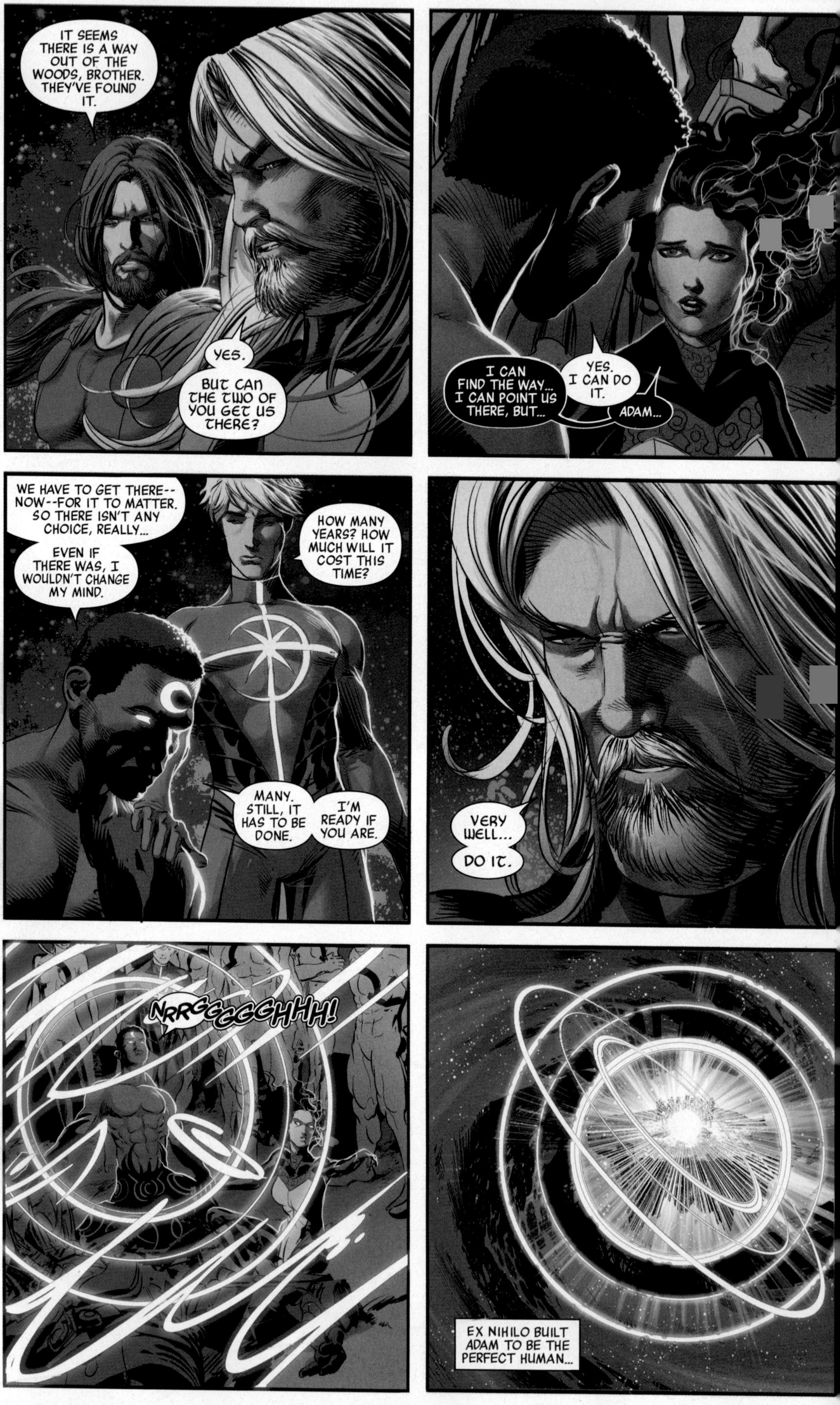
IT SEEMS THERE IS A WAY OUT OF THE WOODS, BROTHER. THEY'VE FOUND IT.
YES.
BUT CAN THE TWO OF YOU GET US THERE?
I CAN FIND THE WAY... I CAN POINT US THERE, BUT...
YES. I CAN DO IT.
ADAM...
WE HAVE TO GET THERE--NOW--FOR IT TO MATTER. SO THERE ISN'T ANY CHOICE, REALLY...
EVEN IF THERE WAS, I WOULDN'T CHANGE MY MIND.
HOW MANY YEARS? HOW MUCH WILL IT COST THIS TIME?
MANY. STILL, IT HAS TO BE DONE.
I'M READY IF YOU ARE.
VERY WELL...
DO IT.
NRRGGGGGHHH!
EX NIHILO BUILT ADAM TO BE THE PERFECT HUMAN...

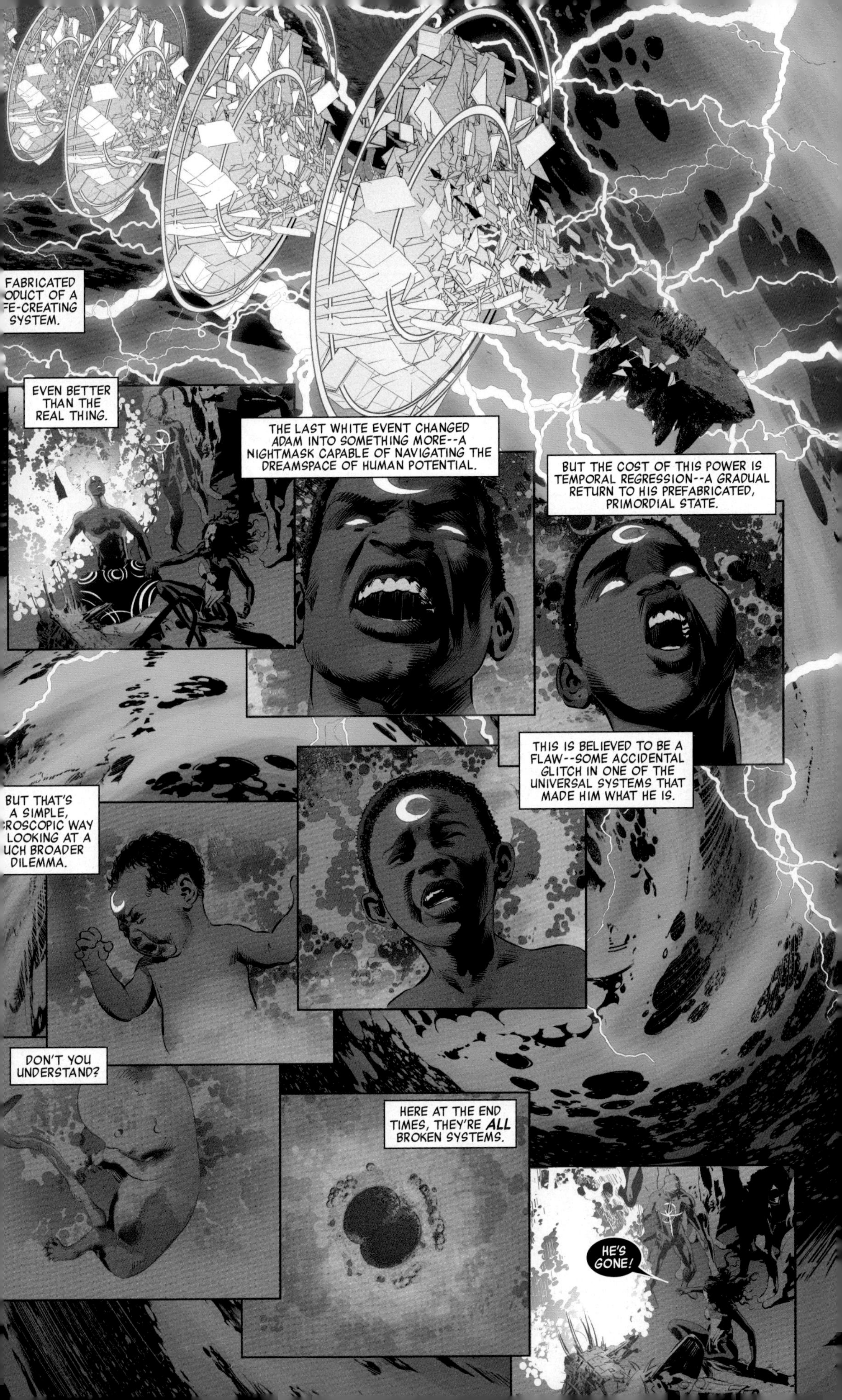
FABRICATED
ODUCT OF A
FE-CREATING
SYSTEM.
EVEN BETTER THAN THE REAL THING.
THE LAST WHITE EVENT CHANGED ADAM INTO SOMETHING MORE--A NIGHTMASK CAPABLE OF NAVIGATING THE DREAMSPACE OF HUMAN POTENTIAL.
BUT THE COST OF THIS POWER IS TEMPORAL REGRESSION--A GRADUAL RETURN TO HIS PREFABRICATED, PRIMORDIAL STATE.
THIS IS BELIEVED TO BE A FLAW--SOME ACCIDENTAL GLITCH IN ONE OF THE UNIVERSAL SYSTEMS THAT MADE HIM WHAT HE IS.
BUT THAT'S
A SIMPLE,
CROSCOPIC WAY
LOOKING AT A
UCH BROADER
DILEMMA.
DON'T YOU UNDERSTAND?
HERE AT THE END TIMES, THEY'RE ALL BROKEN SYSTEMS.
HE'S GONE!

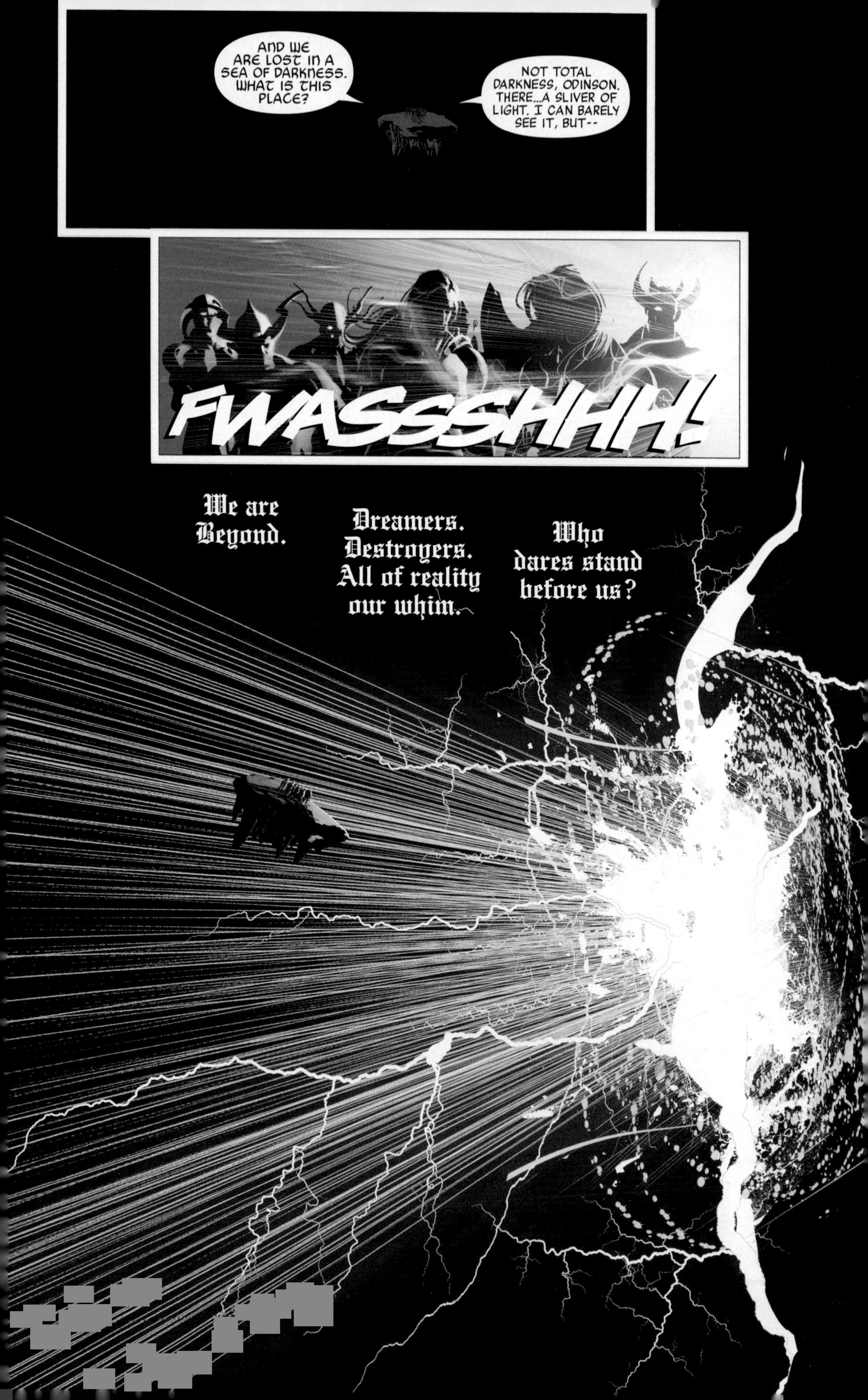
AND WE ARE LOST IN A SEA OF DARKNESS. WHAT IS THIS PLACE?
NOT TOTAL DARKNESS, ODINSON. THERE...A SLIVER OF LIGHT. I CAN BARELY SEE IT, BUT--
FWASSSHHH!
We are Beyond.
Dreamers. Destroyers. All of reality our whim.
Who dares stand before us?

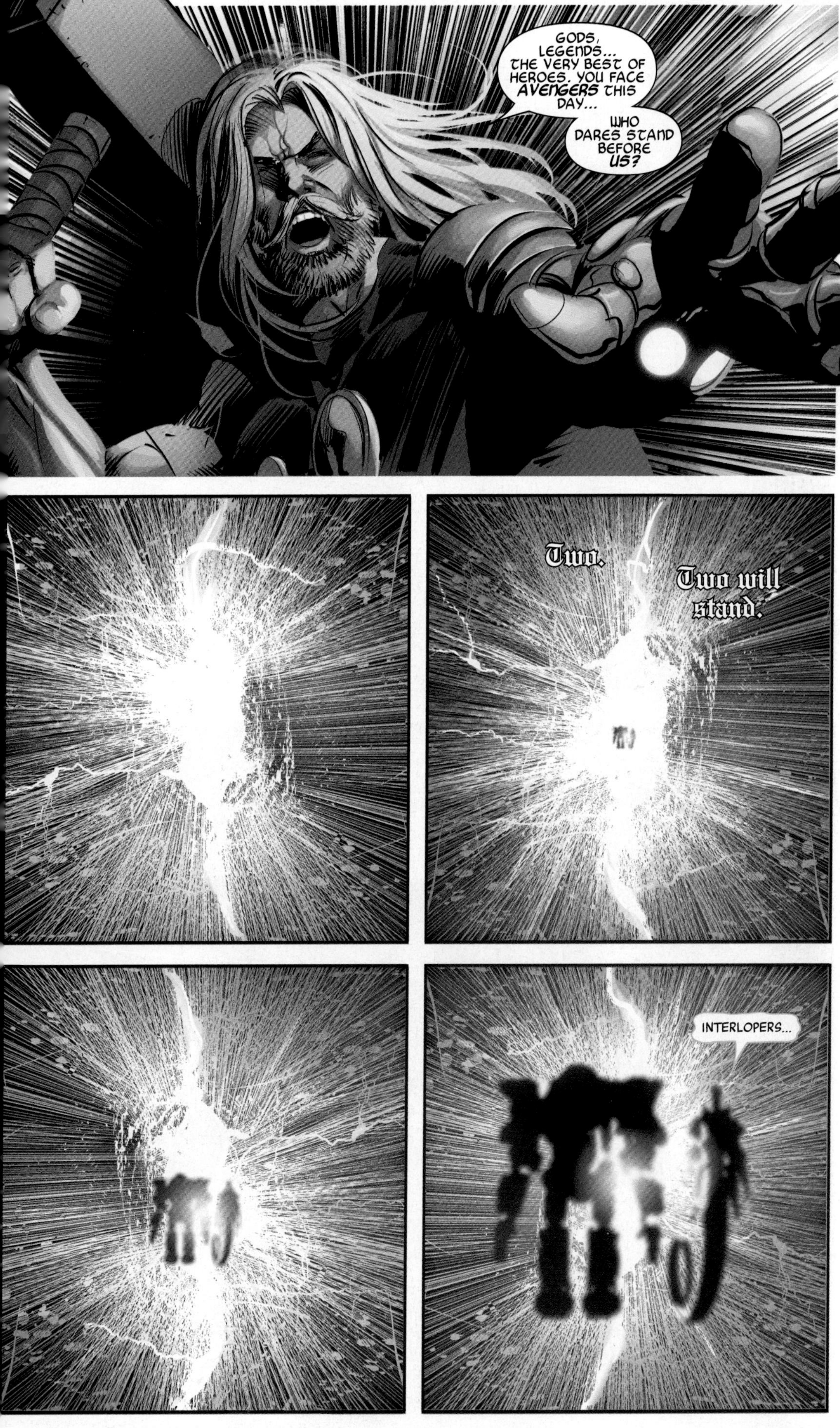
GODS, LEGENDS... THE VERY BEST OF HEROES. YOU FACE AVENGERS THIS DAY...
WHO DARES STAND BEFORE US?
Two.
Two will stand.
INTERLOPERS...

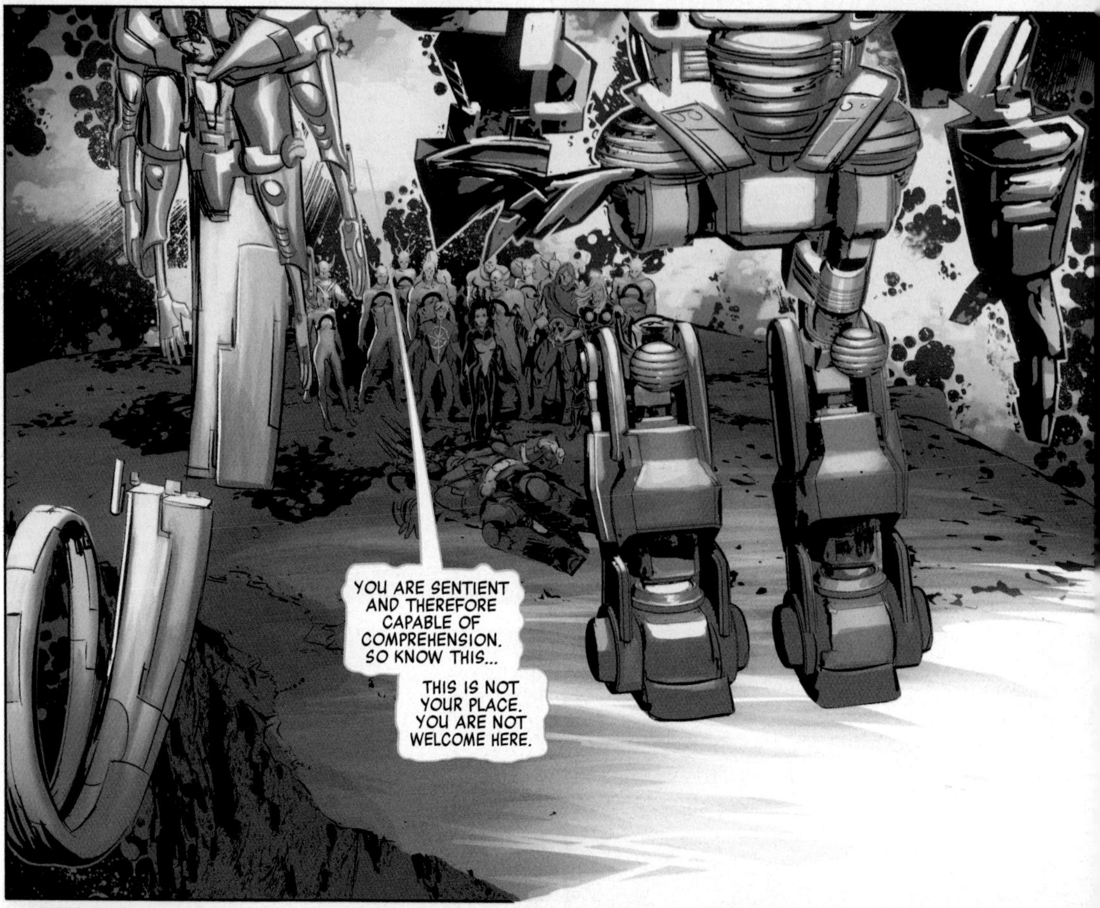
YOU ARE SENTIENT AND THEREFORE CAPABLE OF COMPREHENSION. SO KNOW THIS...
THIS IS NOT YOUR PLACE. YOU ARE NOT WELCOME HERE.

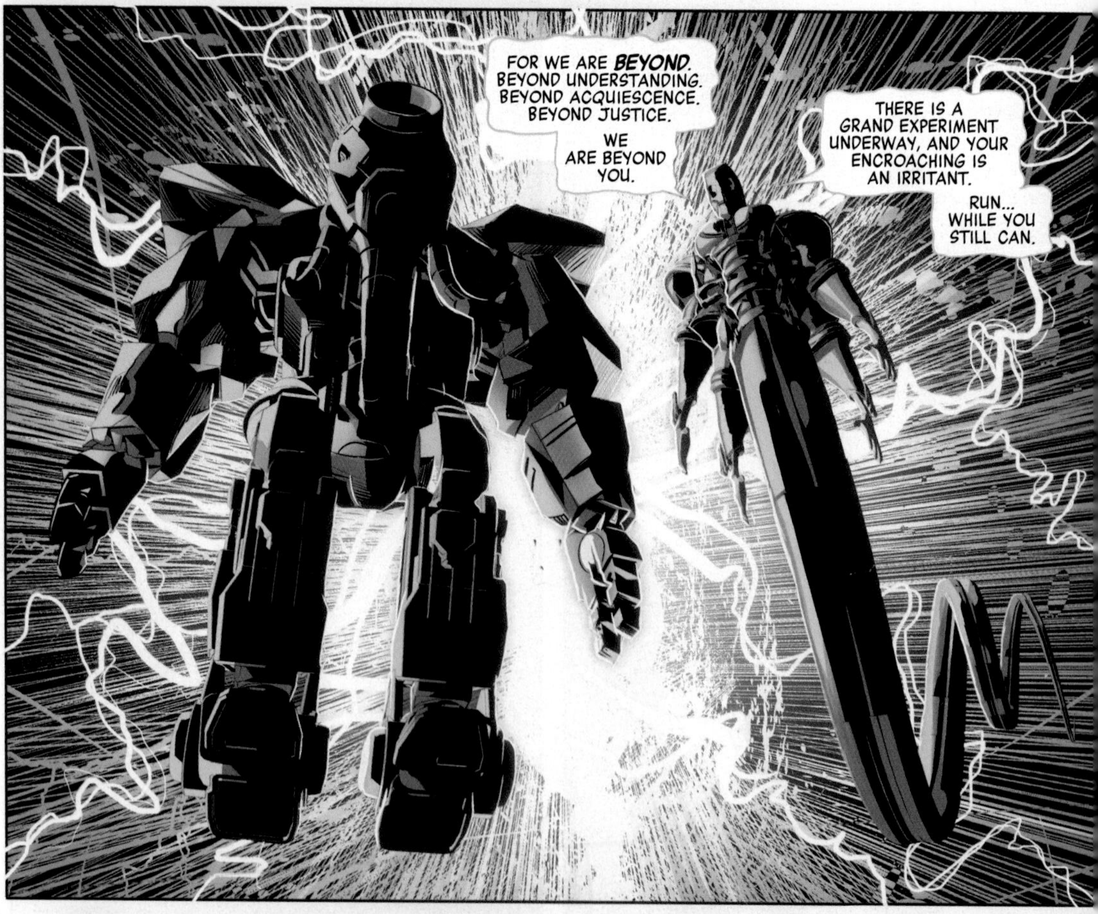
FOR WE ARE BEYOND. BEYOND UNDERSTANDING. BEYOND ACQUIESCENCE. BEYOND JUSTICE.
WE ARE BEYOND YOU.
THERE IS A GRAND EXPERIMENT UNDERWAY, AND YOUR ENCROACHING IS AN IRRITANT.
RUN... WHILE YOU STILL CAN.

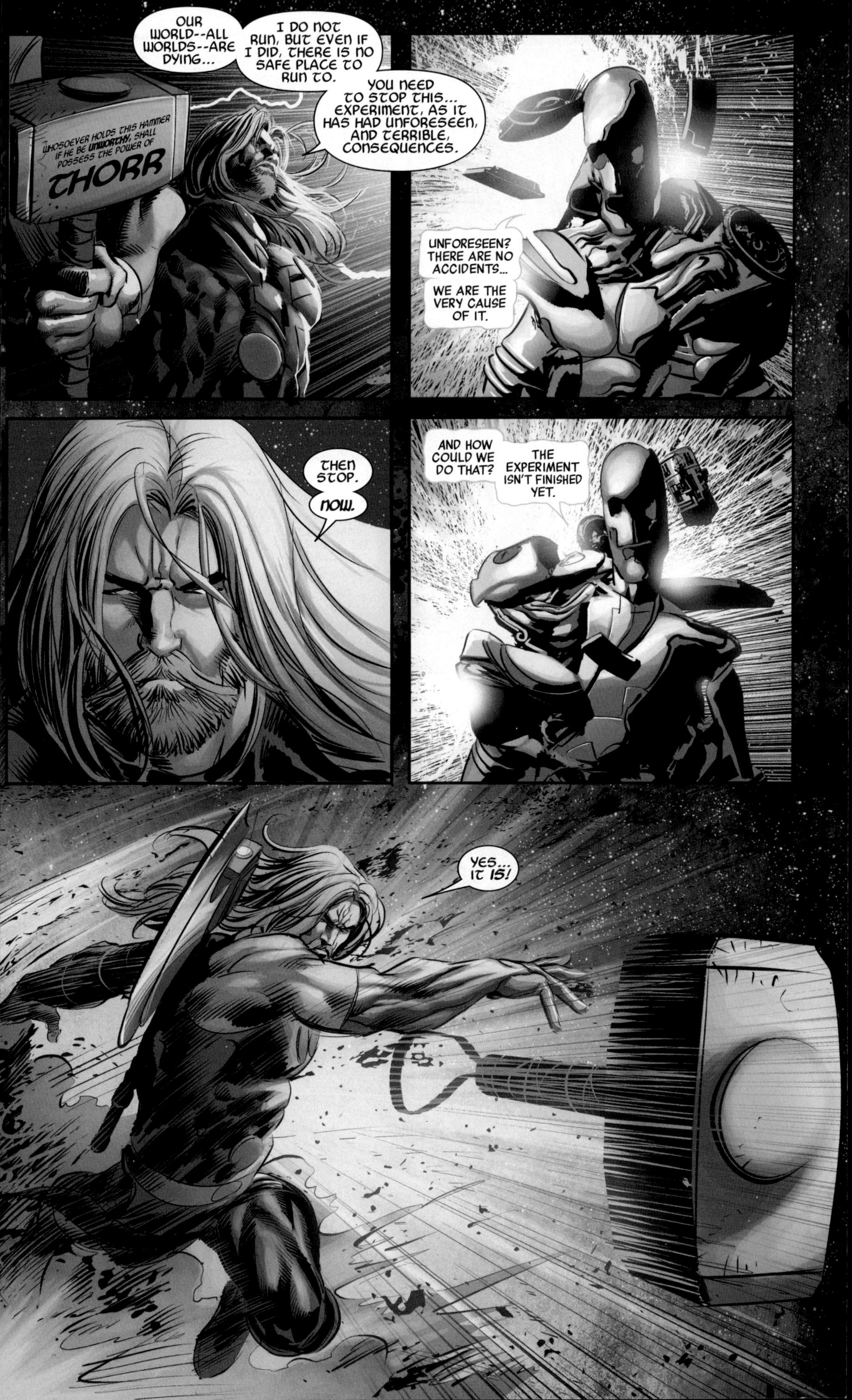
OUR WORLD--ALL WORLDS--ARE DYING...
I DO NOT RUN, BUT EVEN IF I DID, THERE IS NO SAFE PLACE TO RUN TO.
YOU NEED TO STOP THIS... EXPERIMENT, AS IT HAS HAD UNFORESEEN, AND TERRIBLE, CONSEQUENCES.
WHOSOEVER HOLDS THIS HAMMER IF HE BE UNWORTHY, SHALL POSSESS THE POWER OF
THORR
UNFORESEEN? THERE ARE NO ACCIDENTS...
WE ARE THE VERY CAUSE OF IT.
THEN STOP.
NOW.
AND HOW COULD WE DO THAT?
THE EXPERIMENT ISN'T FINISHED YET.
YES... IT IS!

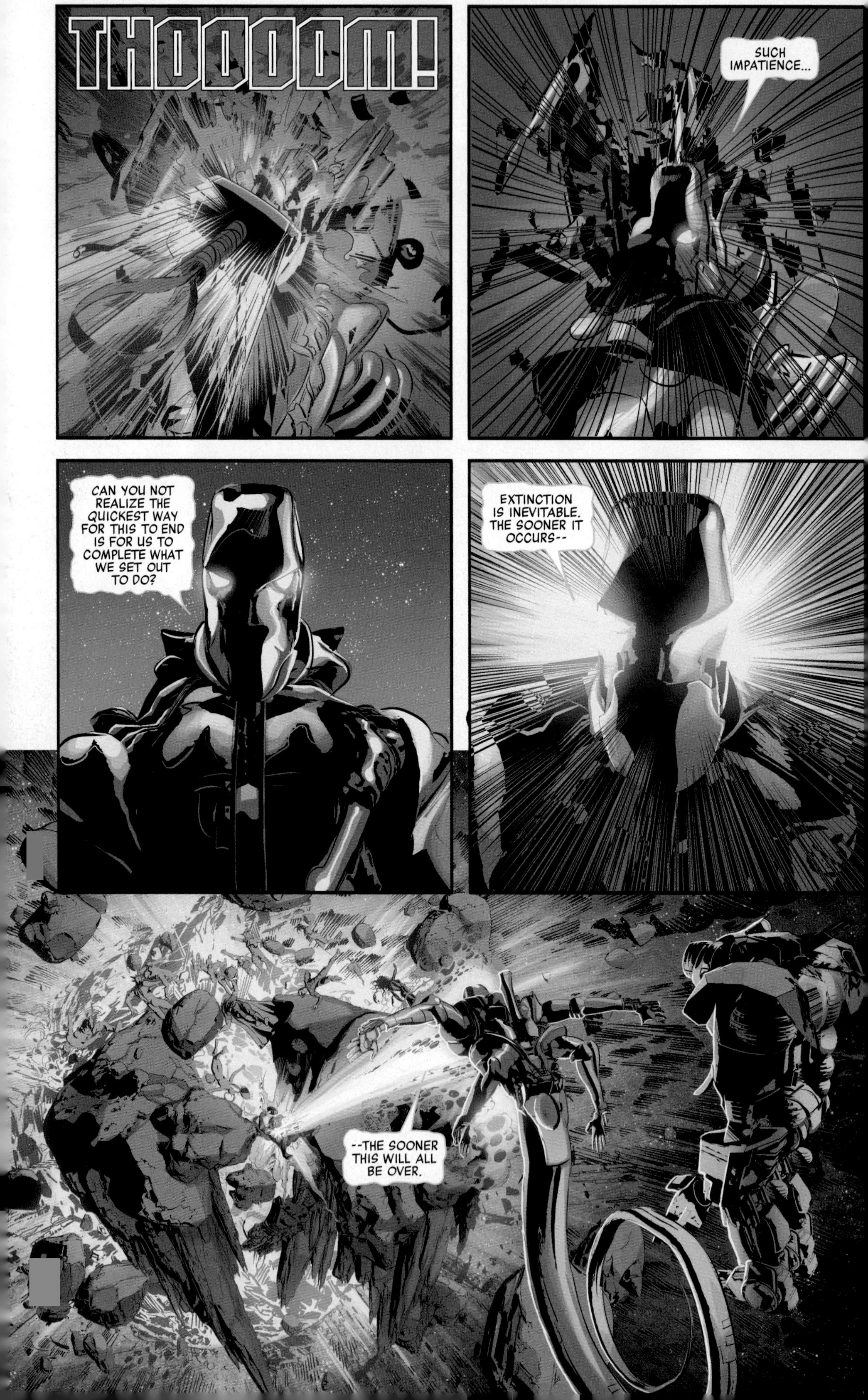
THOOOOM!
SUCH IMPATIENCE...
CAN YOU NOT REALIZE THE QUICKEST WAY FOR THIS TO END IS FOR US TO COMPLETE WHAT WE SET OUT TO DO?
EXTINCTION IS INEVITABLE. THE SOONER IT OCCURS--
--THE SOONER THIS WILL ALL BE OVER.

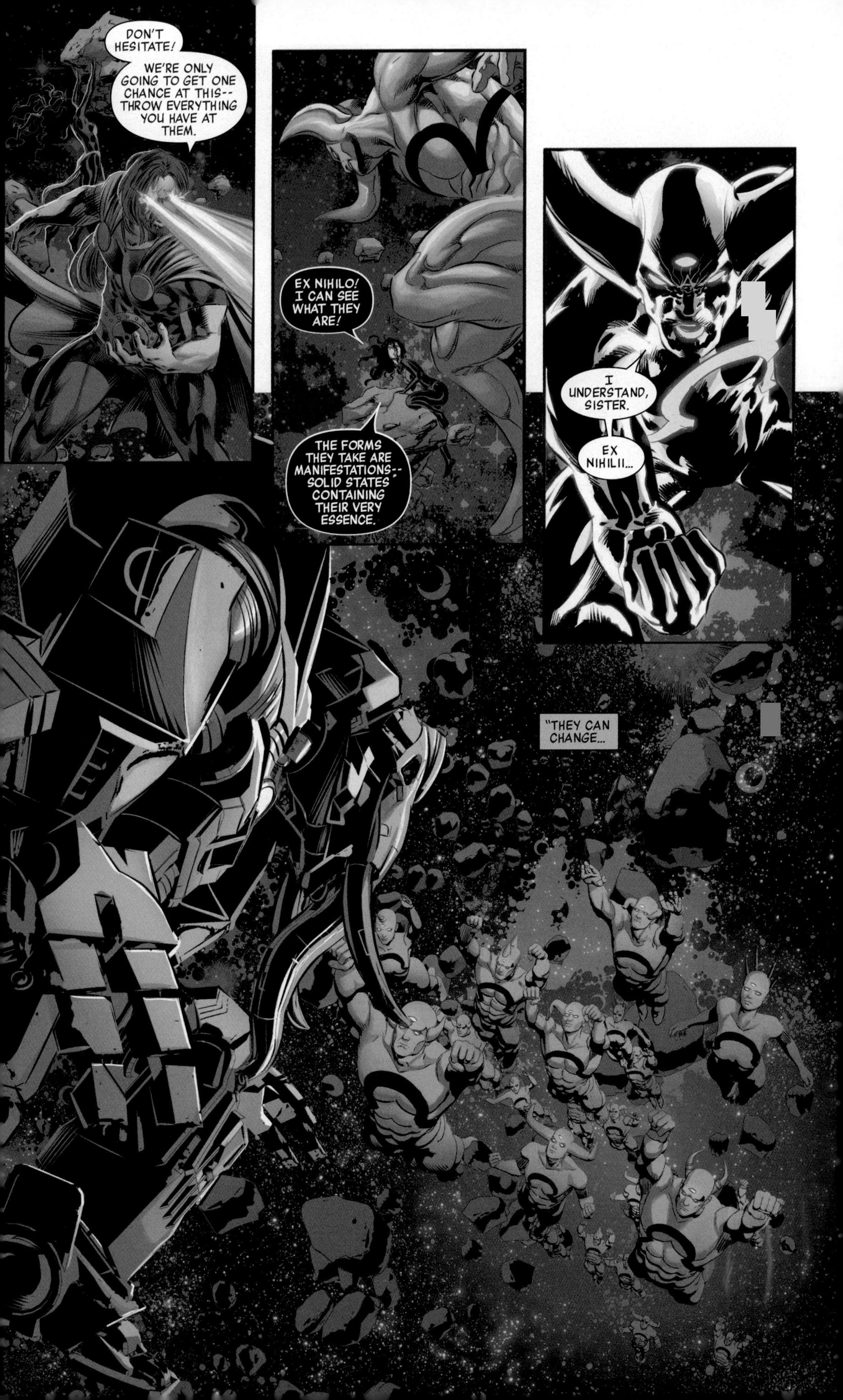
DON'T HESITATE!
WE'RE ONLY GOING TO GET ONE CHANCE AT THIS--THROW EVERYTHING YOU HAVE AT THEM.
EX NIHILO! I CAN SEE WHAT THEY ARE!
THE FORMS THEY TAKE ARE MANIFESTATIONS--SOLID STATES CONTAINING THEIR VERY ESSENCE.
I UNDERSTAND, SISTER.
EX NIHILII...
"THEY CAN CHANGE...

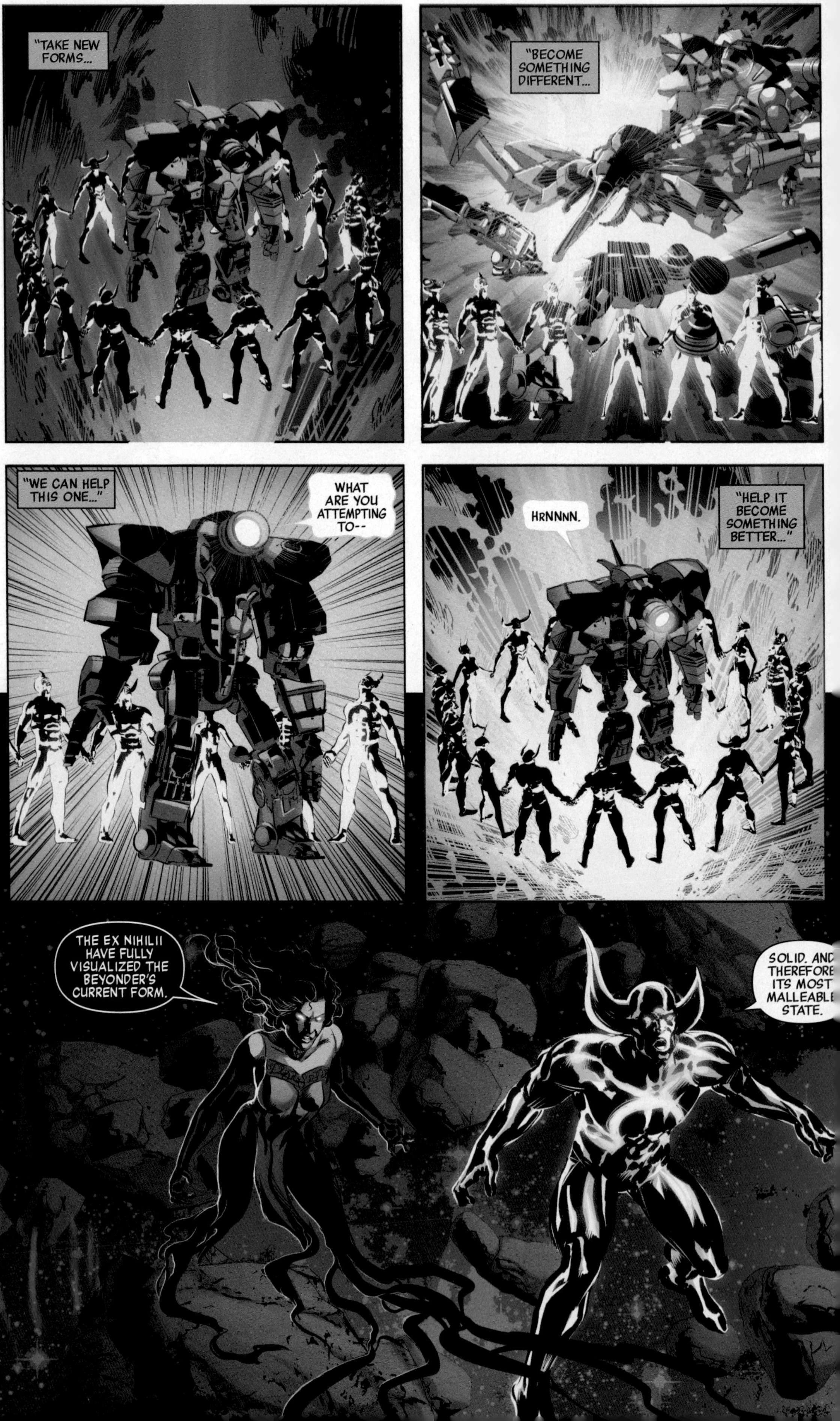
"TAKE NEW FORMS...
"BECOME SOMETHING DIFFERENT...
"WE CAN HELP THIS ONE..."
WHAT ARE YOU ATTEMPTING TO--
HRNNNN.
"HELP IT BECOME SOMETHING BETTER..."
THE EX NIHILII HAVE FULLY VISUALIZED THE BEYONDER'S CURRENT FORM.
SOLID. AND THEREFORE ITS MOST MALLEABLE STATE.

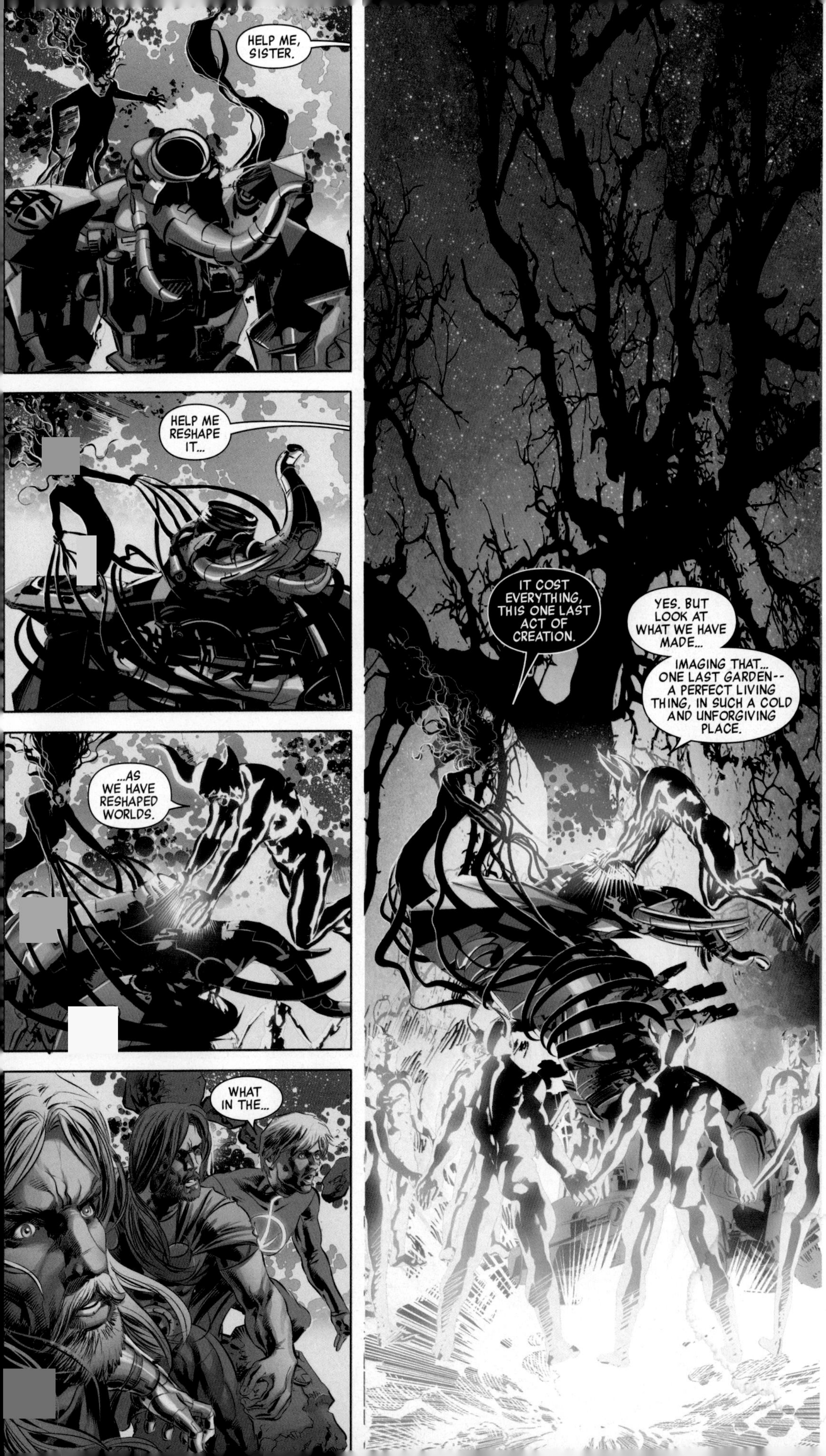
HELP ME, SISTER.
HELP ME RESHAPE IT...
...AS WE HAVE RESHAPED WORLDS.
WHAT IN THE...
IT COST EVERYTHING, THIS ONE LAST ACT OF CREATION.
YES. BUT LOOK AT WHAT WE HAVE MADE...
IMAGING THAT... ONE LAST GARDEN-- A PERFECT LIVING THING, IN SUCH A COLD AND UNFORGIVING PLACE.

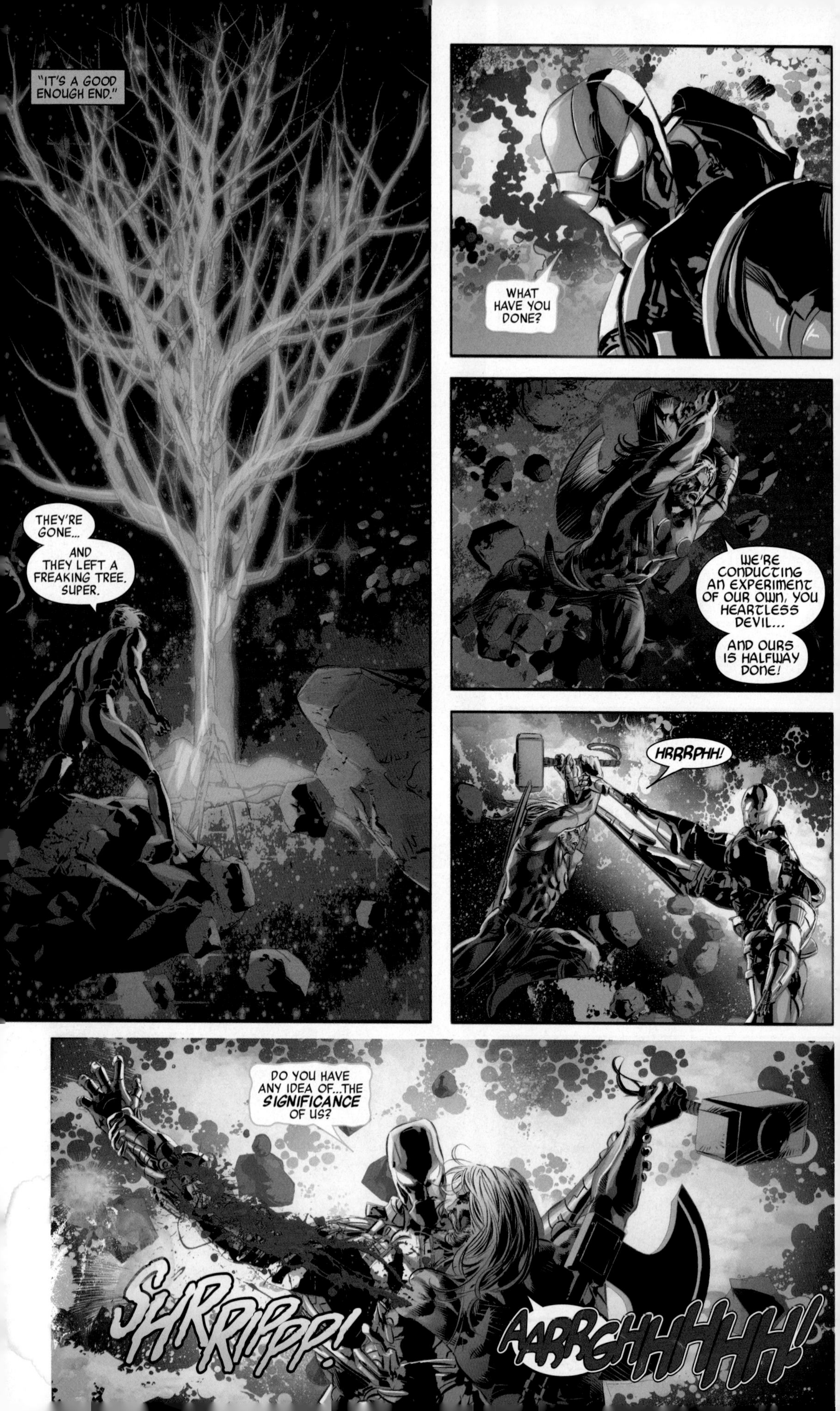
"IT'S A GOOD ENOUGH END."
THEY'RE GONE...
AND THEY LEFT A FREAKING TREE. SUPER.
WHAT HAVE YOU DONE?
WE'RE CONDUCTING AN EXPERIMENT OF OUR OWN, YOU HEARTLESS DEVIL...
AND OURS IS HALFWAY DONE!
HRRRPHH!
DO YOU HAVE ANY IDEA OF...THE SIGNIFICANCE OF US?
SHRRIPPP!
AARRGHHHHHH!

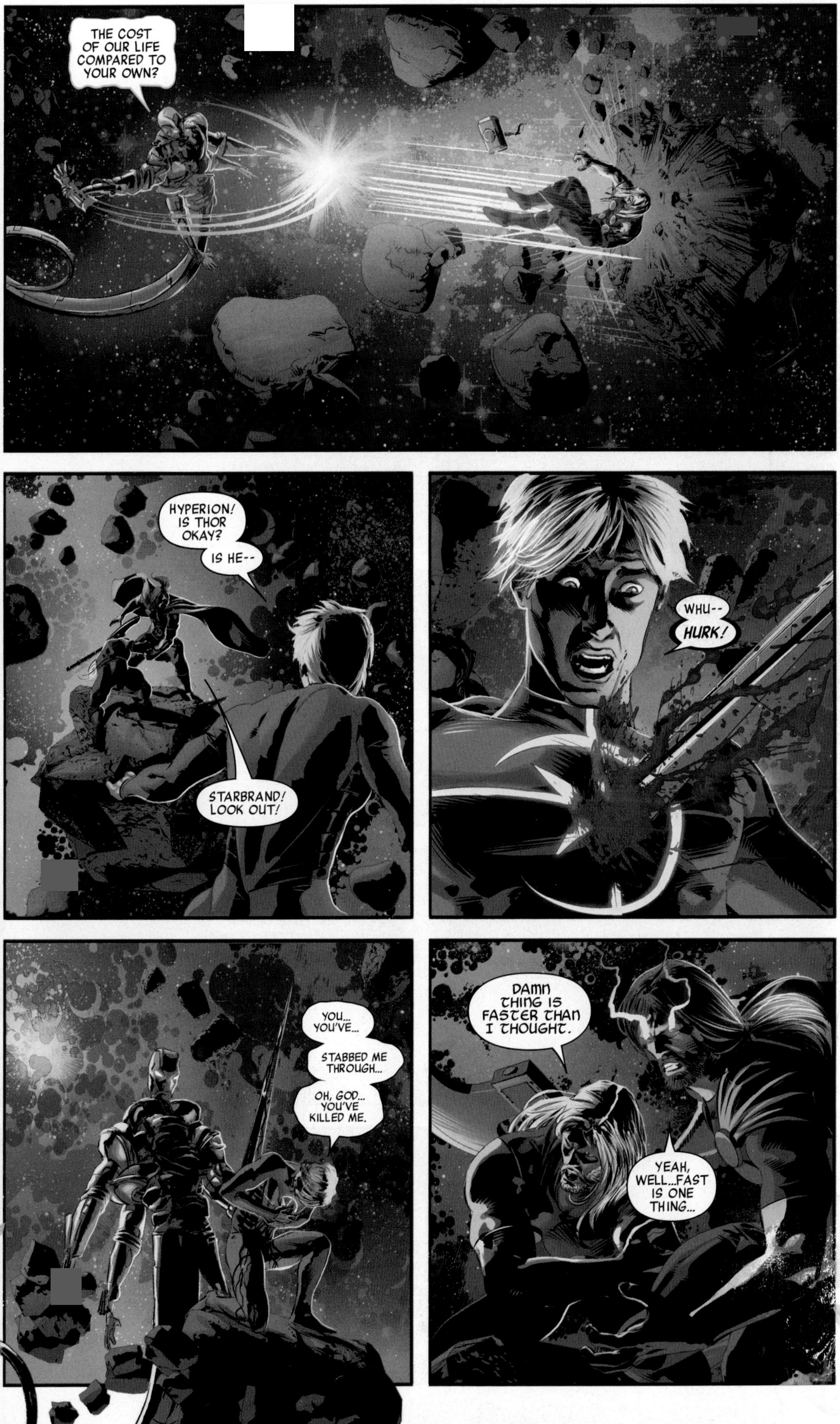
THE COST OF OUR LIFE COMPARED TO YOUR OWN?
HYPERION! IS THOR OKAY?
IS HE--
STARBRAND! LOOK OUT!
WHU--
HURK!
YOU... YOU'VE...
STABBED ME THROUGH...
OH, GOD... YOU'VE KILLED ME.
DAMN THING IS FASTER THAN I THOUGHT.
YEAH, WELL...FAST IS ONE THING...

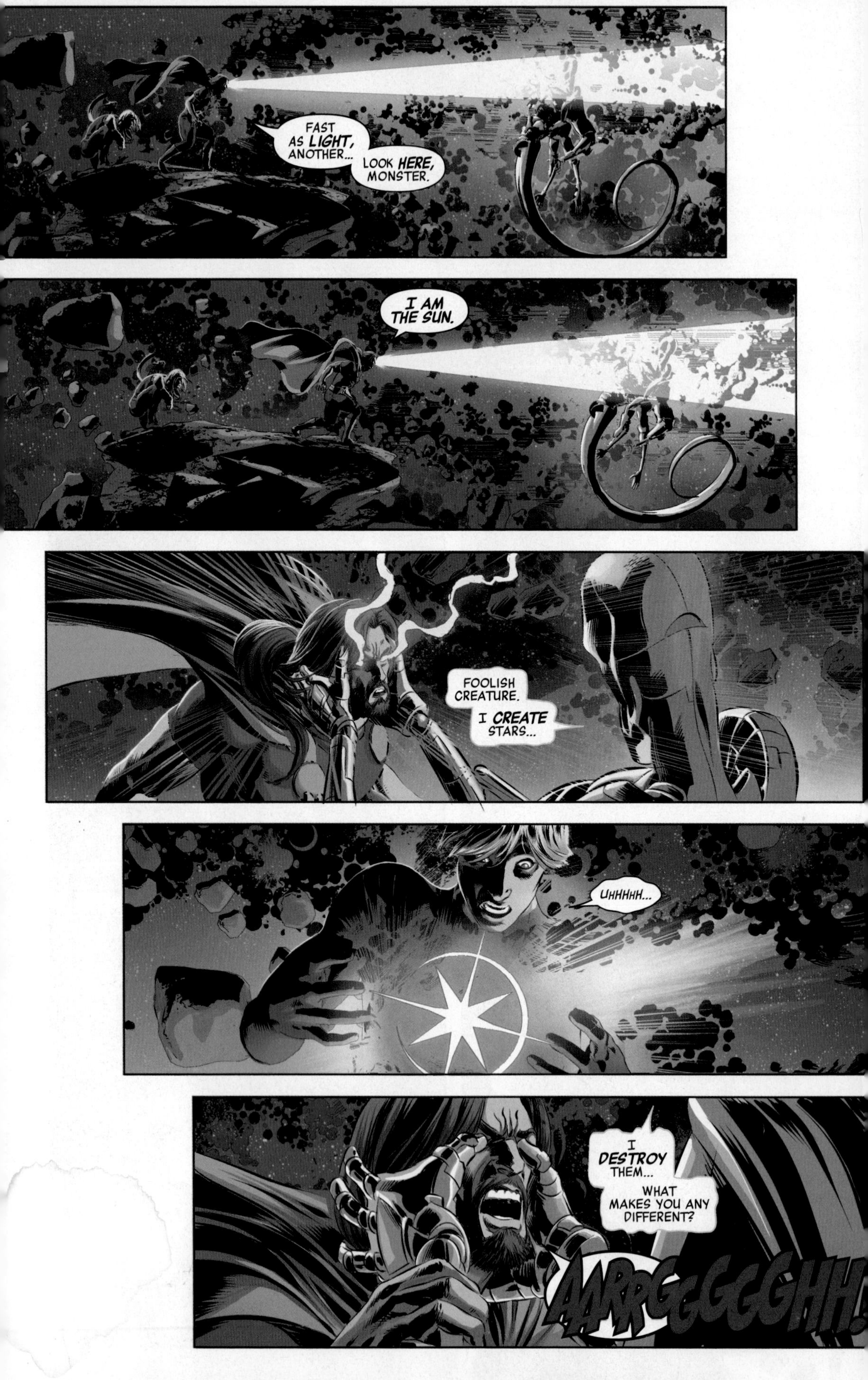
FAST AS LIGHT, ANOTHER...
LOOK HERE, MONSTER.
I AM THE SUN.
FOOLISH CREATURE.
I CREATE STARS...
UHHHHH...
I DESTROY THEM...
WHAT MAKES YOU ANY DIFFERENT?
AARRGGGGGHH!

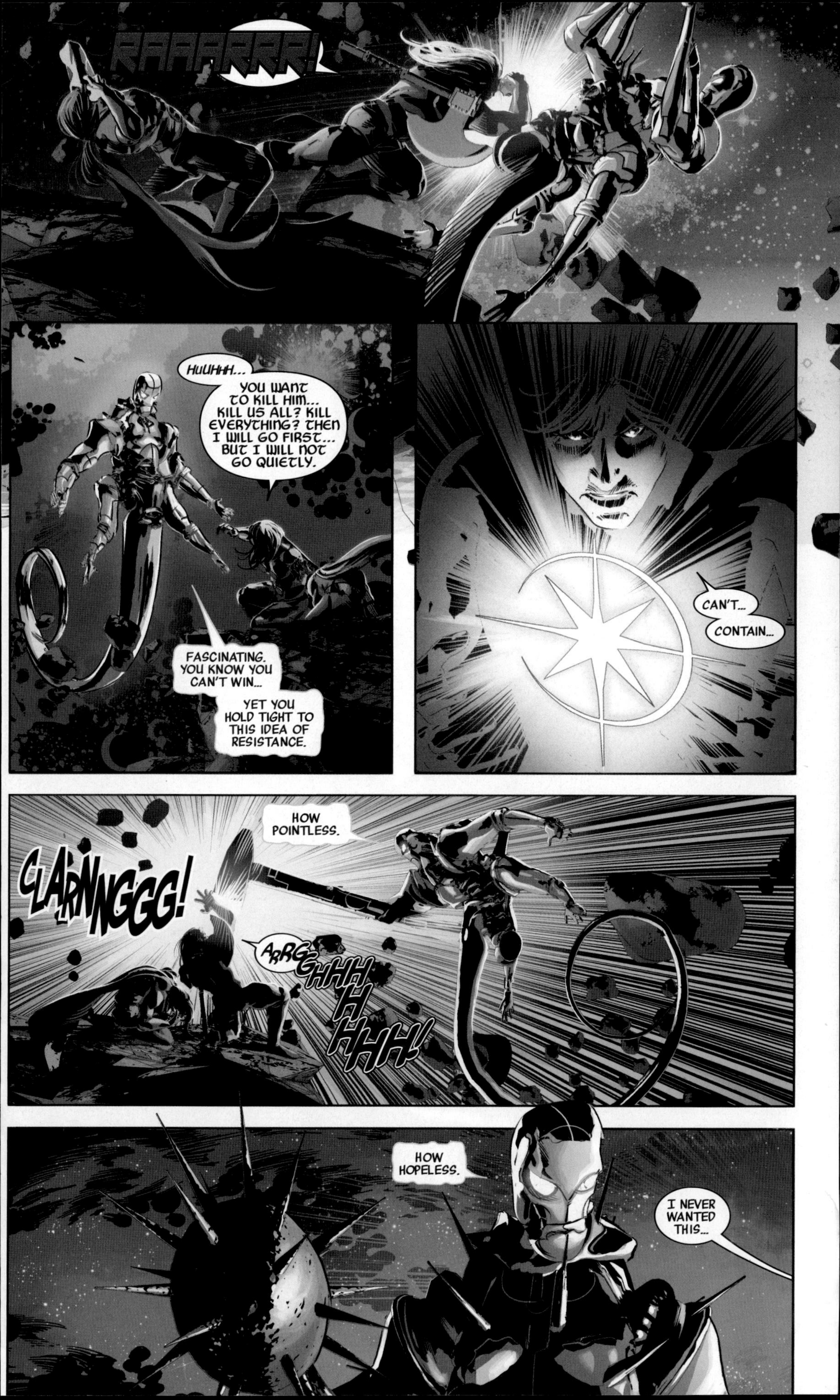

RAAARRR!
HUUHHH...
YOU WANT TO KILL HIM... KILL US ALL? KILL EVERYTHING? THEN I WILL GO FIRST... BUT I WILL NOT GO QUIETLY.
FASCINATING. YOU KNOW YOU CAN'T WIN...
YET YOU HOLD TIGHT TO THIS IDEA OF RESISTANCE.
CAN'T...
CONTAIN...
HOW POINTLESS.
CLARNNGGG!
ARRGGHHHHHHH!
HOW HOPELESS.
I NEVER WANTED THIS...

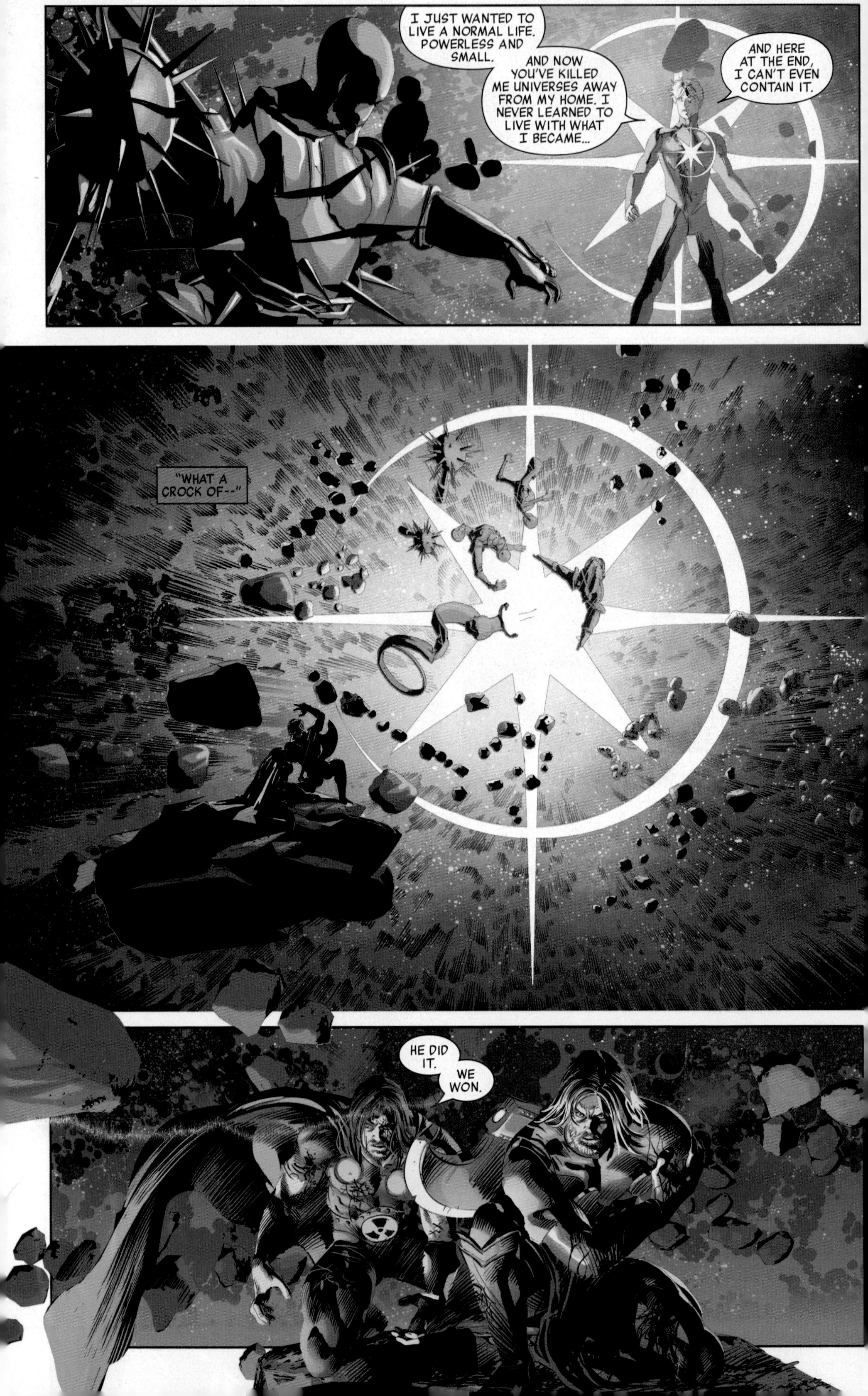
I JUST WANTED TO LIVE A NORMAL LIFE. POWERLESS AND SMALL.
AND NOW YOU'VE KILLED ME UNIVERSES AWAY FROM MY HOME. I NEVER LEARNED TO LIVE WITH WHAT I BECAME...
AND HERE AT THE END, I CAN'T EVEN CONTAIN IT.
"WHAT A CROCK OF--"
HE DID IT.
WE WON.

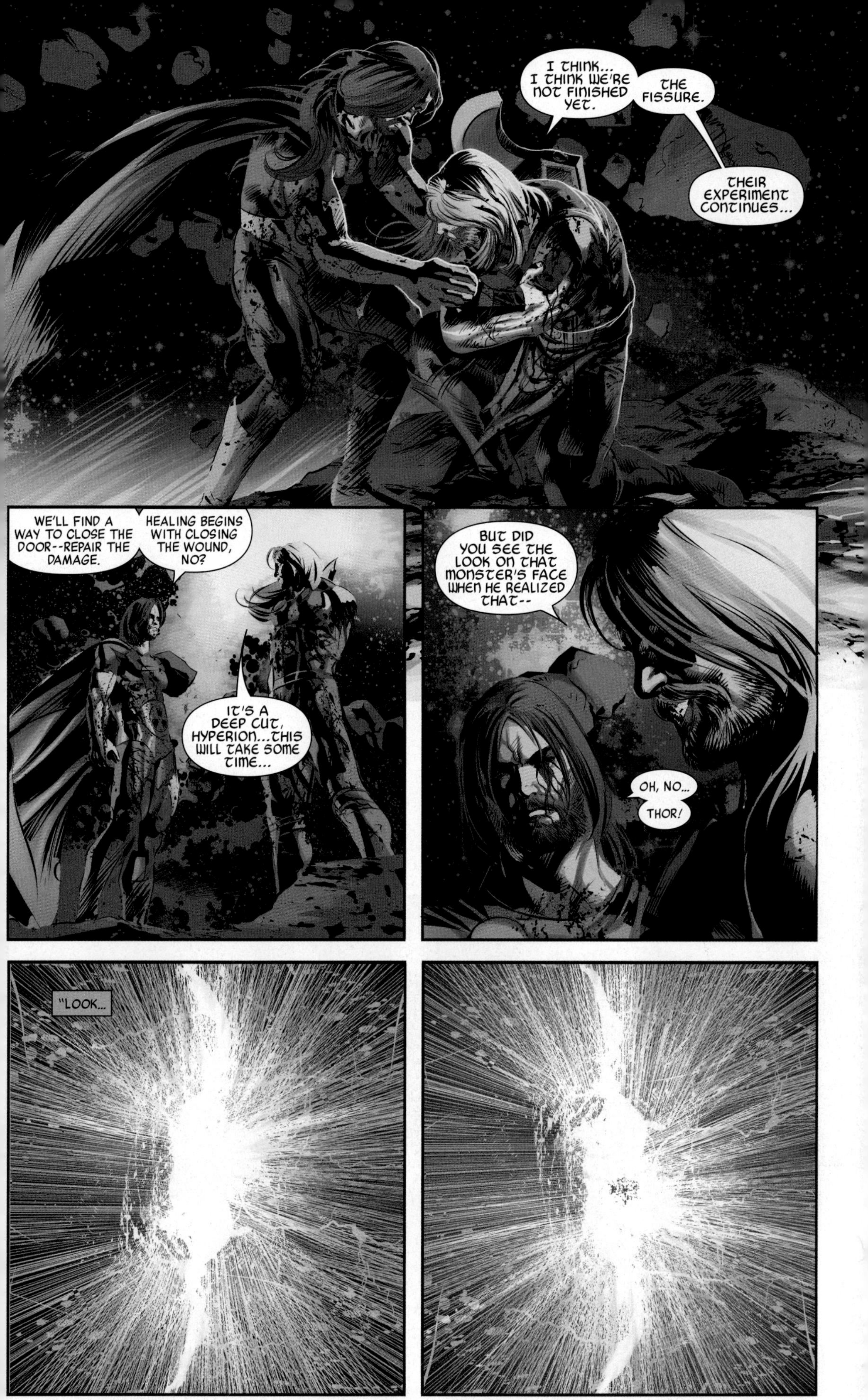

I THINK... I THINK WE'RE NOT FINISHED YET.
THE FISSURE.
THEIR EXPERIMENT CONTINUES...
WE'LL FIND A WAY TO CLOSE THE DOOR--REPAIR THE DAMAGE.
HEALING BEGINS WITH CLOSING THE WOUND, NO?
IT'S A DEEP CUT, HYPERION...THIS WILL TAKE SOME TIME...
BUT DID YOU SEE THE LOOK ON THAT MONSTER'S FACE WHEN HE REALIZED THAT--
OH, NO...
THOR!
"LOOK...

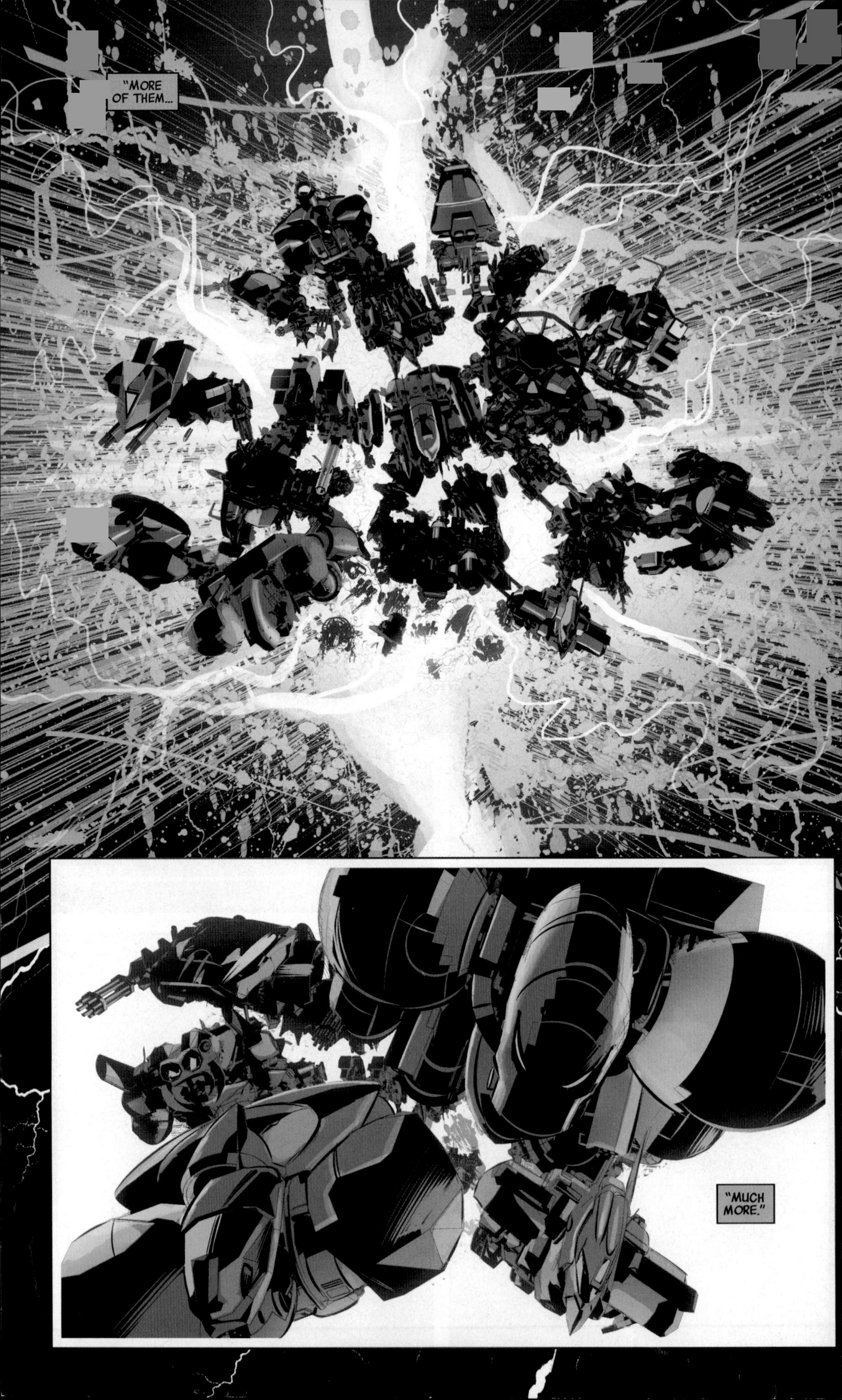
"MORE OF THEM...
"MUCH MORE."

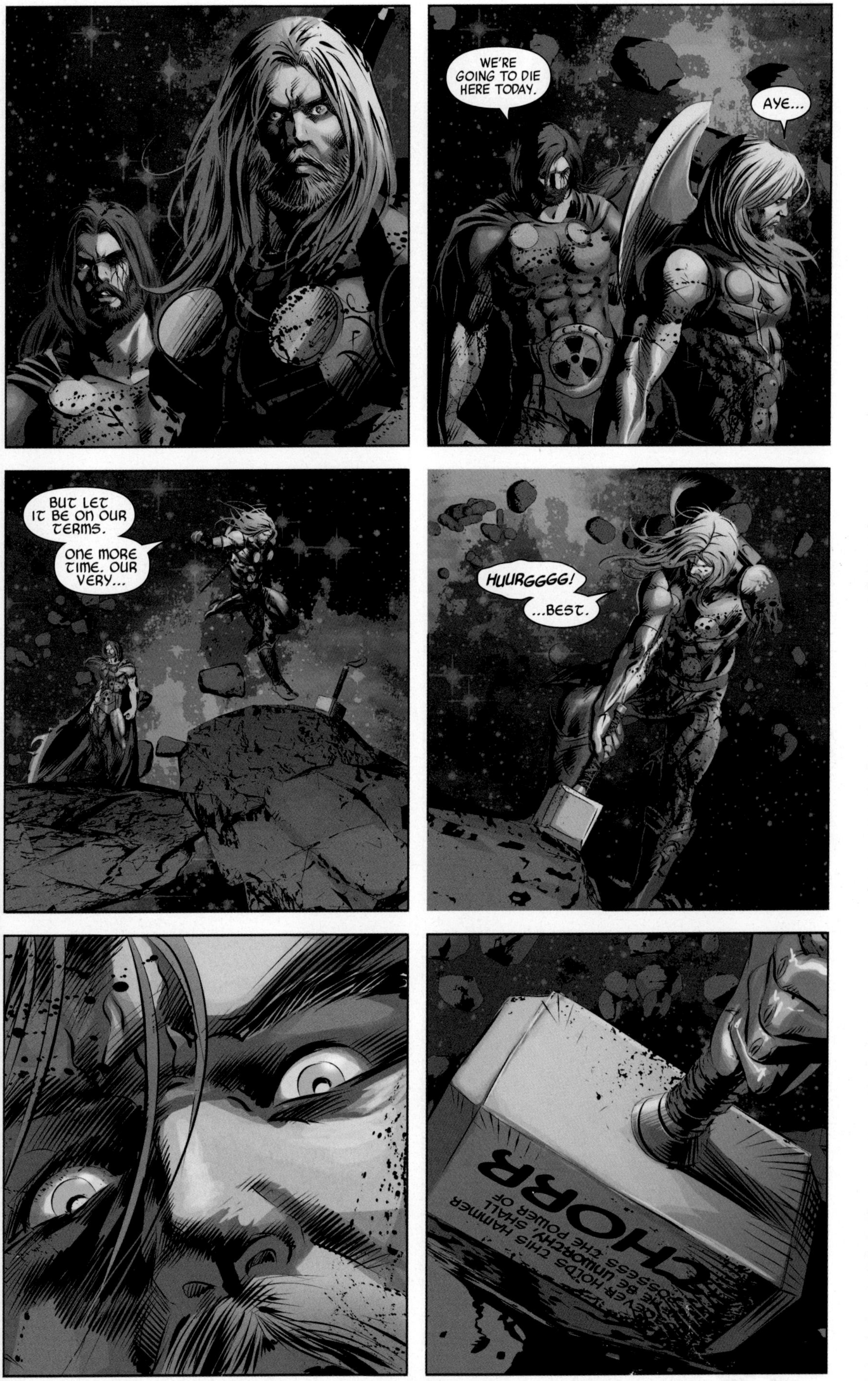
WE'RE GOING TO DIE HERE TODAY.
AYE...
BUT LET IT BE ON OUR TERMS.
ONE MORE TIME. OUR VERY...
HUURGGGG!
...BEST.

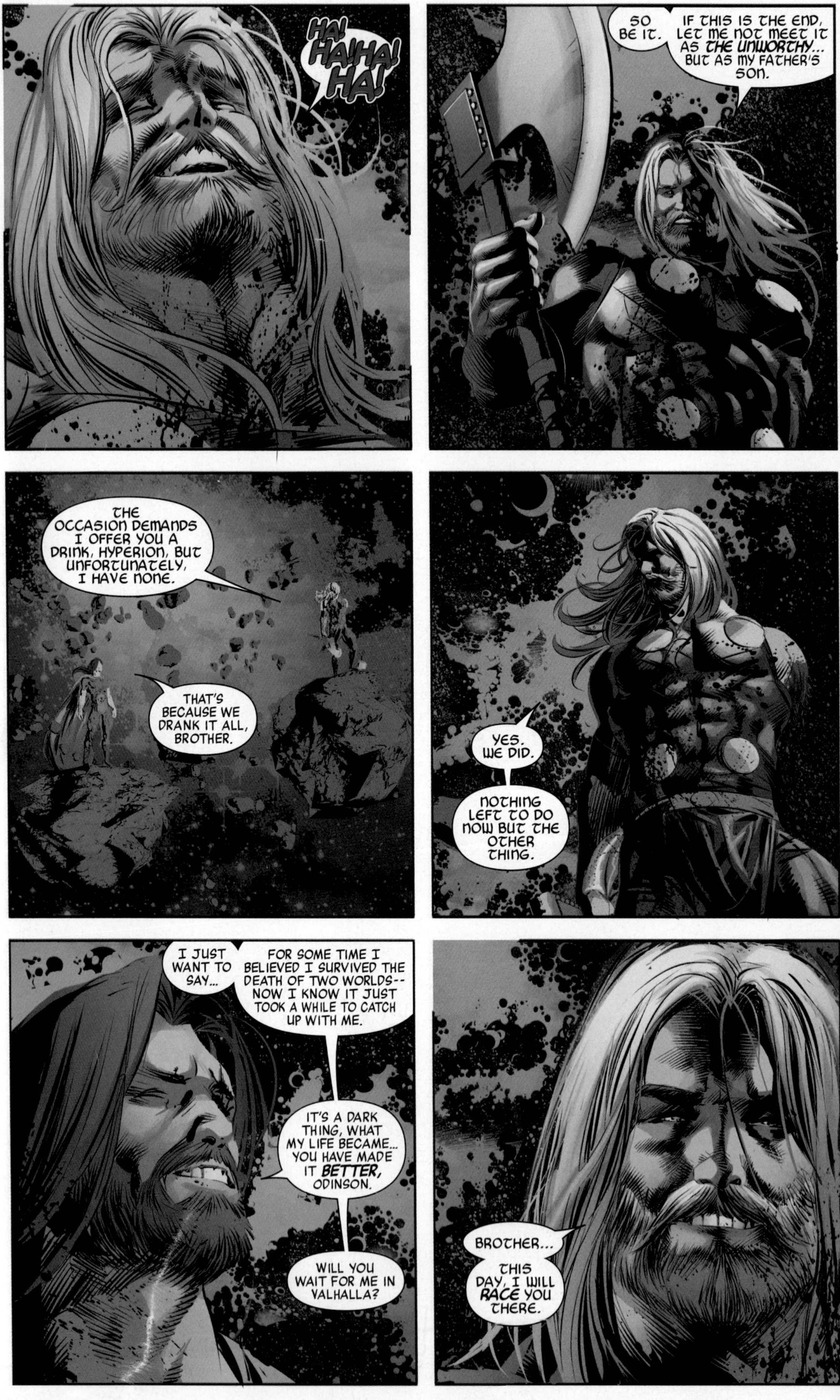
HA! HA!HA! HA!
SO BE IT.
IF THIS IS THE END, LET ME NOT MEET IT AS THE UNWORTHY... BUT AS MY FATHER'S SON.
THE OCCASION DEMANDS I OFFER YOU A DRINK, HYPERION, BUT UNFORTUNATELY, I HAVE NONE.
THAT'S BECAUSE WE DRANK IT ALL, BROTHER.
YES. WE DID.
NOTHING LEFT TO DO NOW BUT THE OTHER THING.
I JUST WANT TO SAY...
FOR SOME TIME I BELIEVED I SURVIVED THE DEATH OF TWO WORLDS-- NOW I KNOW IT JUST TOOK A WHILE TO CATCH UP WITH ME.
IT'S A DARK THING, WHAT MY LIFE BECAME... YOU HAVE MADE IT BETTER, ODINSON.
WILL YOU WAIT FOR ME IN VALHALLA?
BROTHER...
THIS DAY, I WILL RACE YOU THERE.

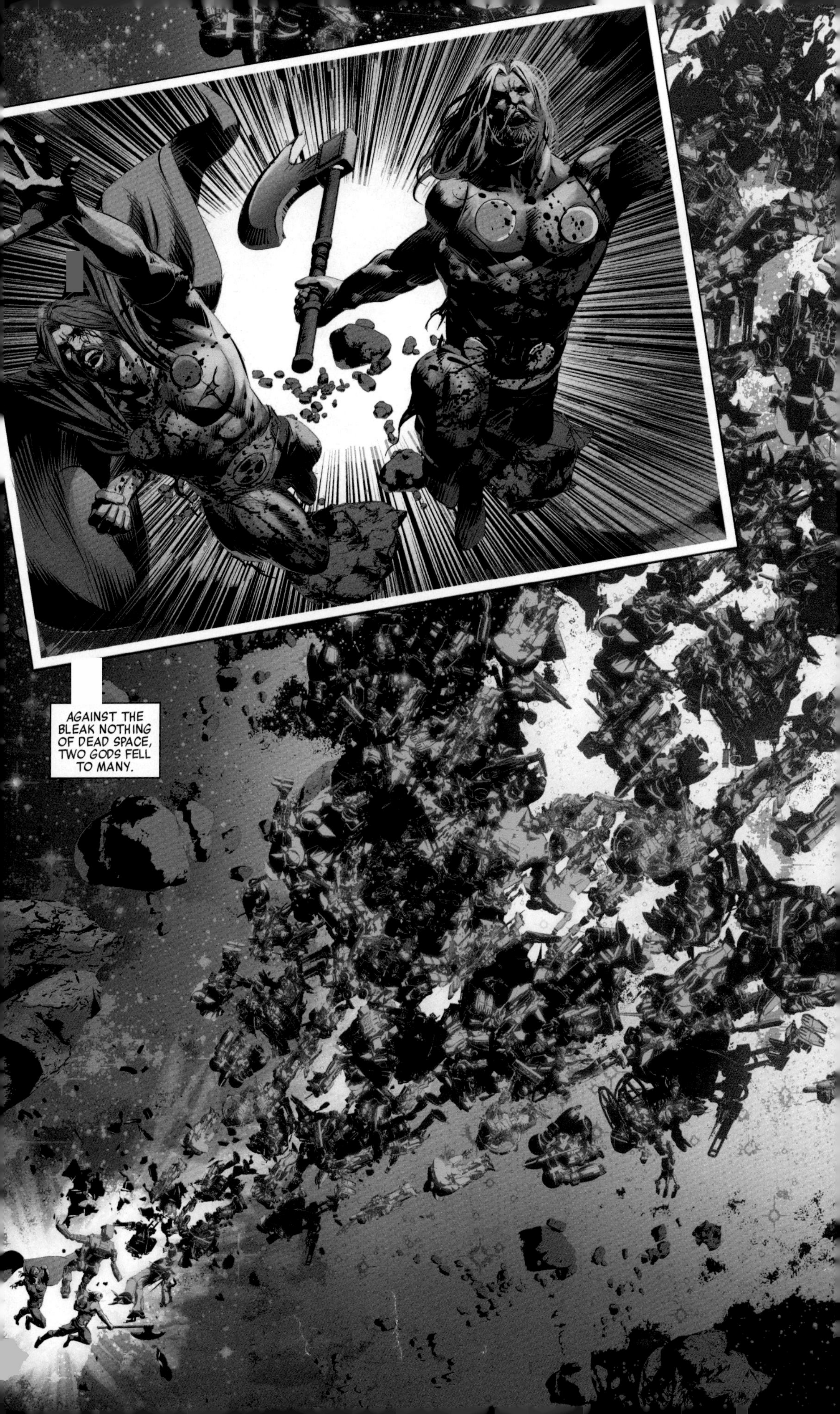
AGAINST THE BLEAK NOTHING OF DEAD SPACE, TWO GODS FELL TO MANY.

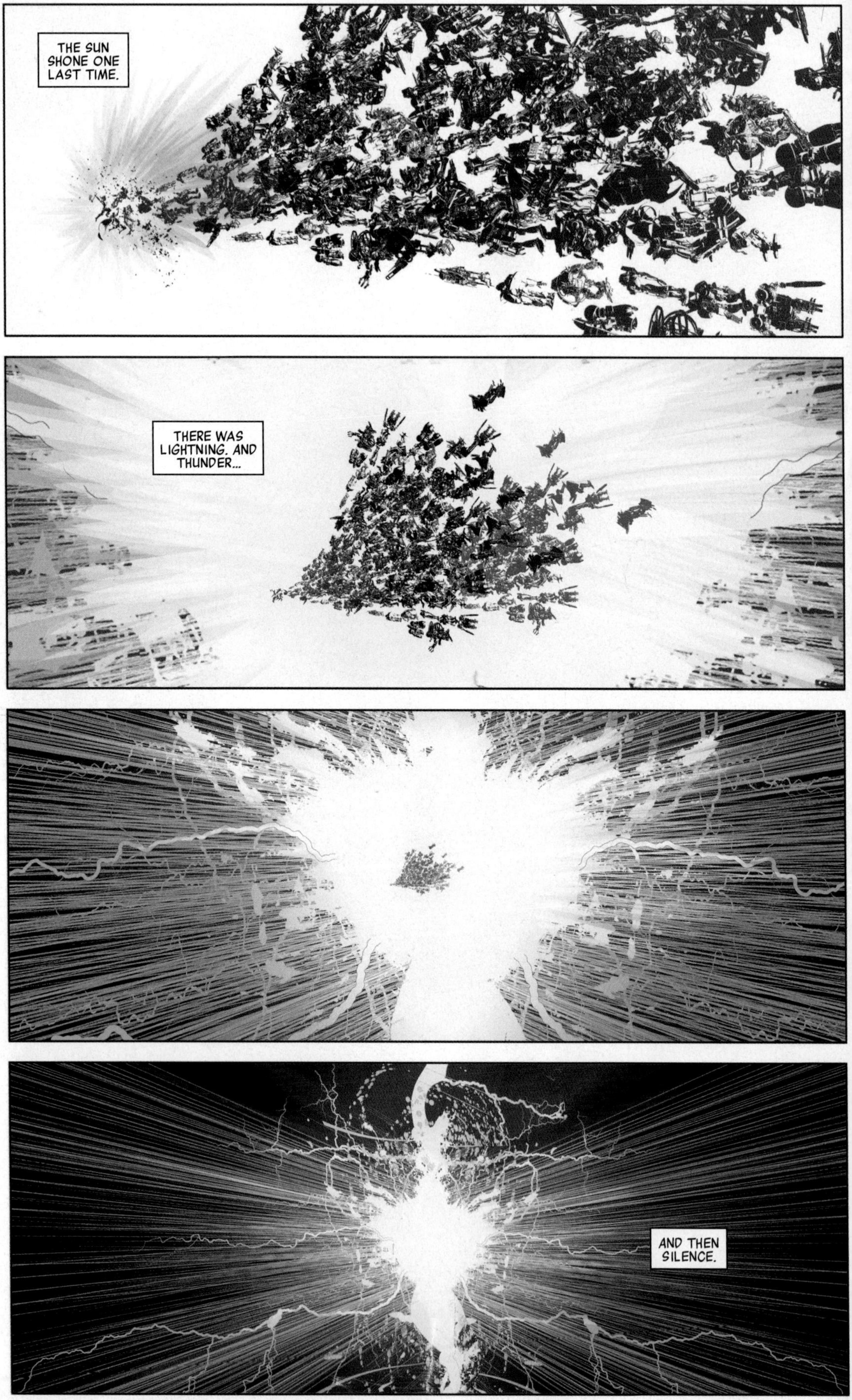
THE SUN SHONE ONE LAST TIME.
THERE WAS LIGHTNING. AND THUNDER...
AND THEN SILENCE.

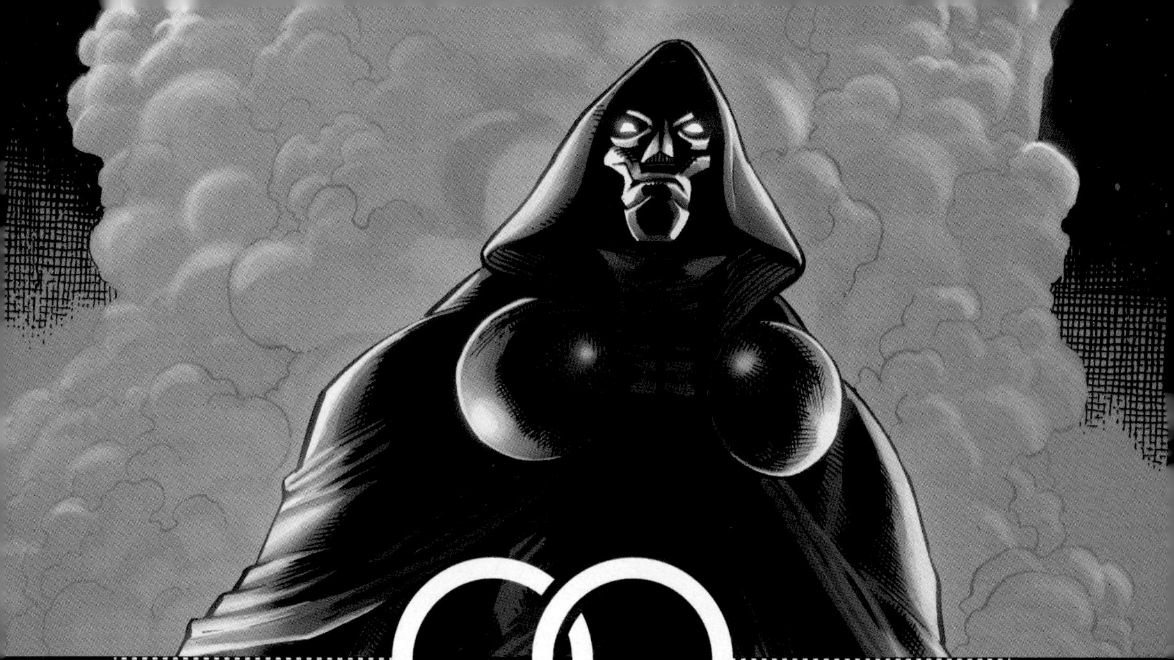

"IN LATVERIA, THE FLOWERS DIE IN SUMMER"

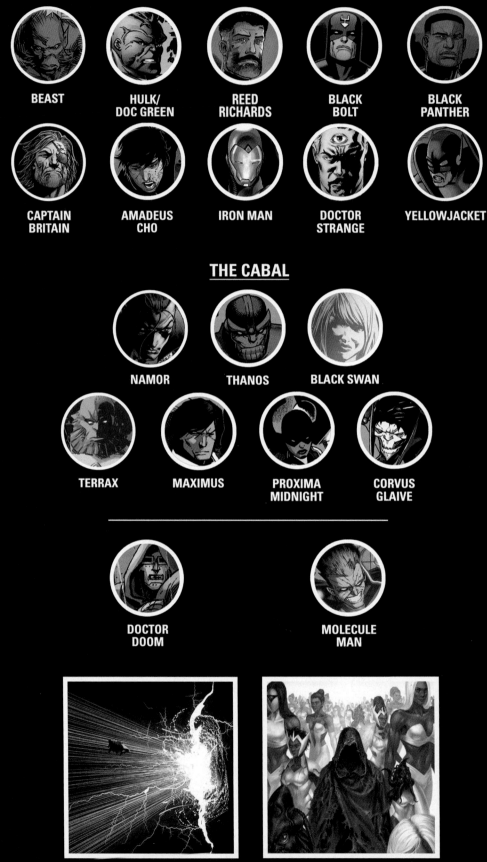

THE ILLUMINATI

BEAST

HULK/
DOC GREEN

REED
RICHARDS

BLACK
BOLT

BLACK
PANTHER

CAPTAIN
BRITAIN

AMADEUS
CHO

IRON MAN

DOCTOR
STRANGE

YELLOWJACKET

THE CABAL

NAMOR

THANOS

BLACK SWAN

TERRAX

MAXIMUS

PROXIMA
MIDNIGHT

CORVUS
GLAIVE

DOCTOR
DOOM

MOLECULE
MAN

BEYONDERS

BLACK SWANS

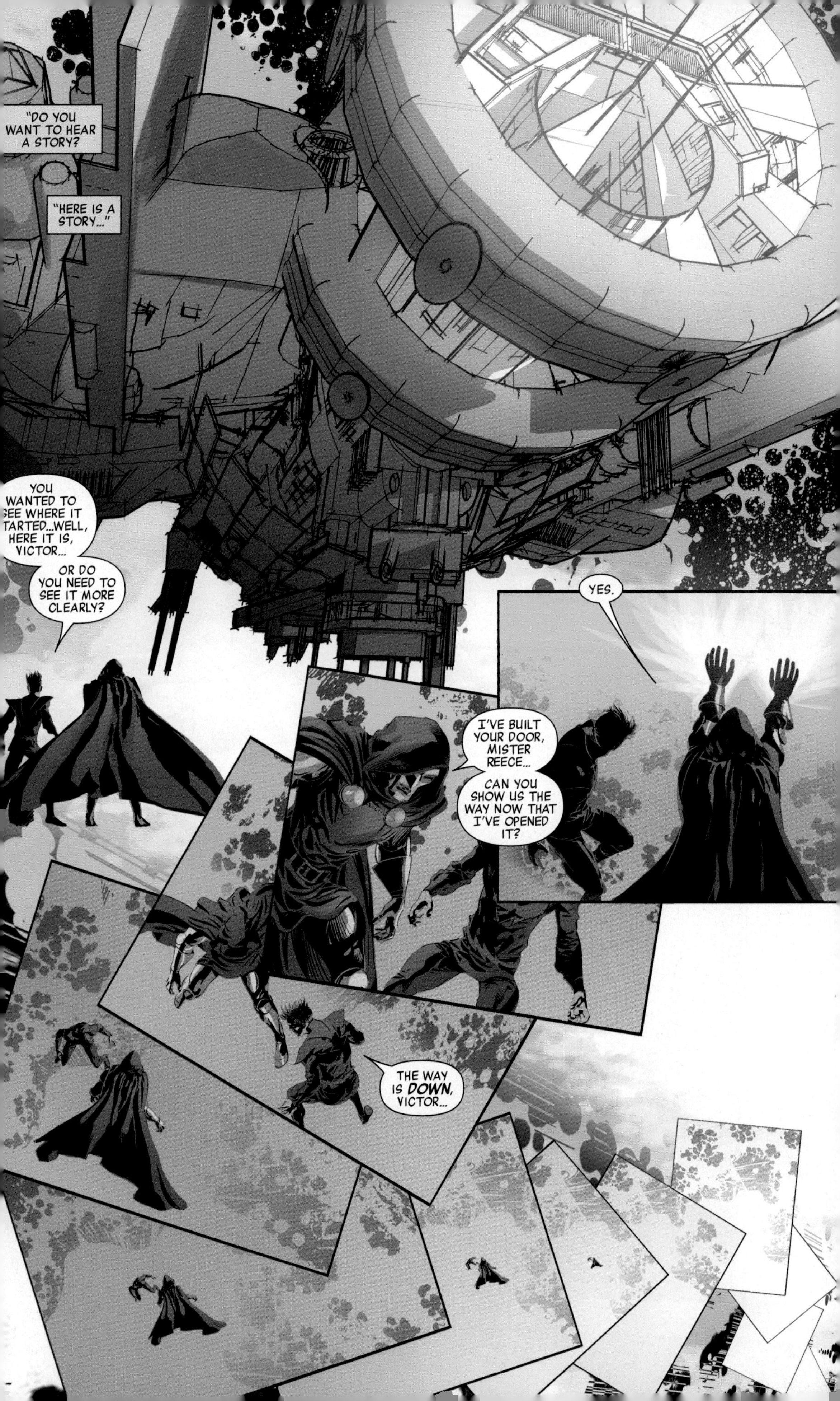
"DO YOU WANT TO HEAR A STORY?
"HERE IS A STORY..."
YOU WANTED TO SEE WHERE IT STARTED...WELL, HERE IT IS, VICTOR...
OR DO YOU NEED TO SEE IT MORE CLEARLY?
YES.
I'VE BUILT YOUR DOOR, MISTER REECE...
CAN YOU SHOW US THE WAY NOW THAT I'VE OPENED IT?
THE WAY IS *DOWN*, VICTOR...

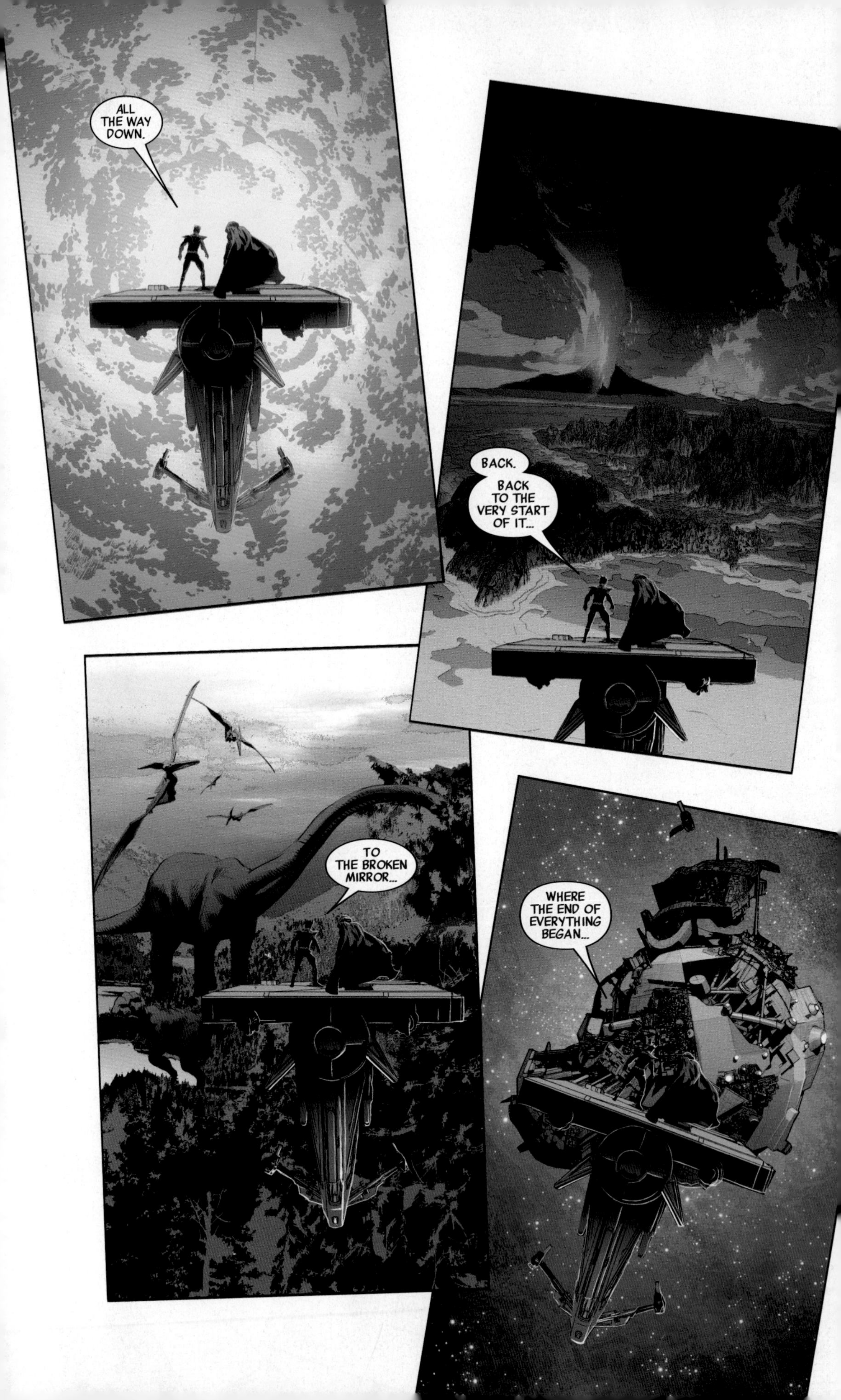
ALL THE WAY DOWN.
BACK.
BACK TO THE VERY START OF IT...
TO THE BROKEN MIRROR...
WHERE THE END OF EVERYTHING BEGAN...

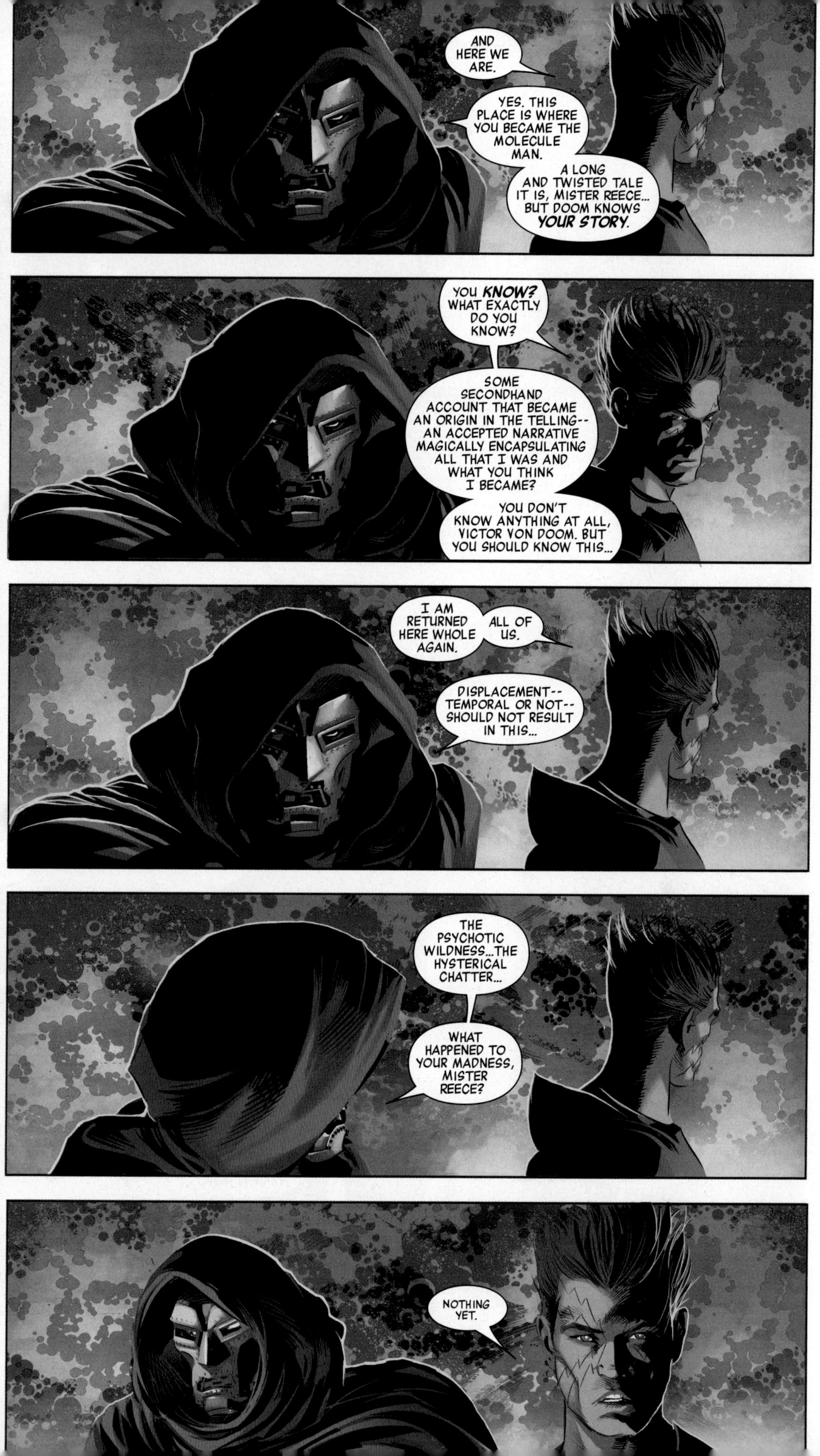

AND HERE WE ARE.
YES. THIS PLACE IS WHERE YOU BECAME THE MOLECULE MAN.
A LONG AND TWISTED TALE IT IS, MISTER REECE... BUT DOOM KNOWS *YOUR STORY*.
YOU *KNOW?* WHAT EXACTLY DO YOU KNOW?
SOME SECONDHAND ACCOUNT THAT BECAME AN ORIGIN IN THE TELLING-- AN ACCEPTED NARRATIVE MAGICALLY ENCAPSULATING ALL THAT I WAS AND WHAT YOU THINK I BECAME?
YOU DON'T KNOW ANYTHING AT ALL, VICTOR VON DOOM. BUT YOU SHOULD KNOW THIS...
I AM RETURNED HERE WHOLE AGAIN.
ALL OF US.
DISPLACEMENT-- TEMPORAL OR NOT-- SHOULD NOT RESULT IN THIS...
THE PSYCHOTIC WILDNESS...THE HYSTERICAL CHATTER...
WHAT HAPPENED TO YOUR MADNESS, MISTER REECE?
NOTHING YET.

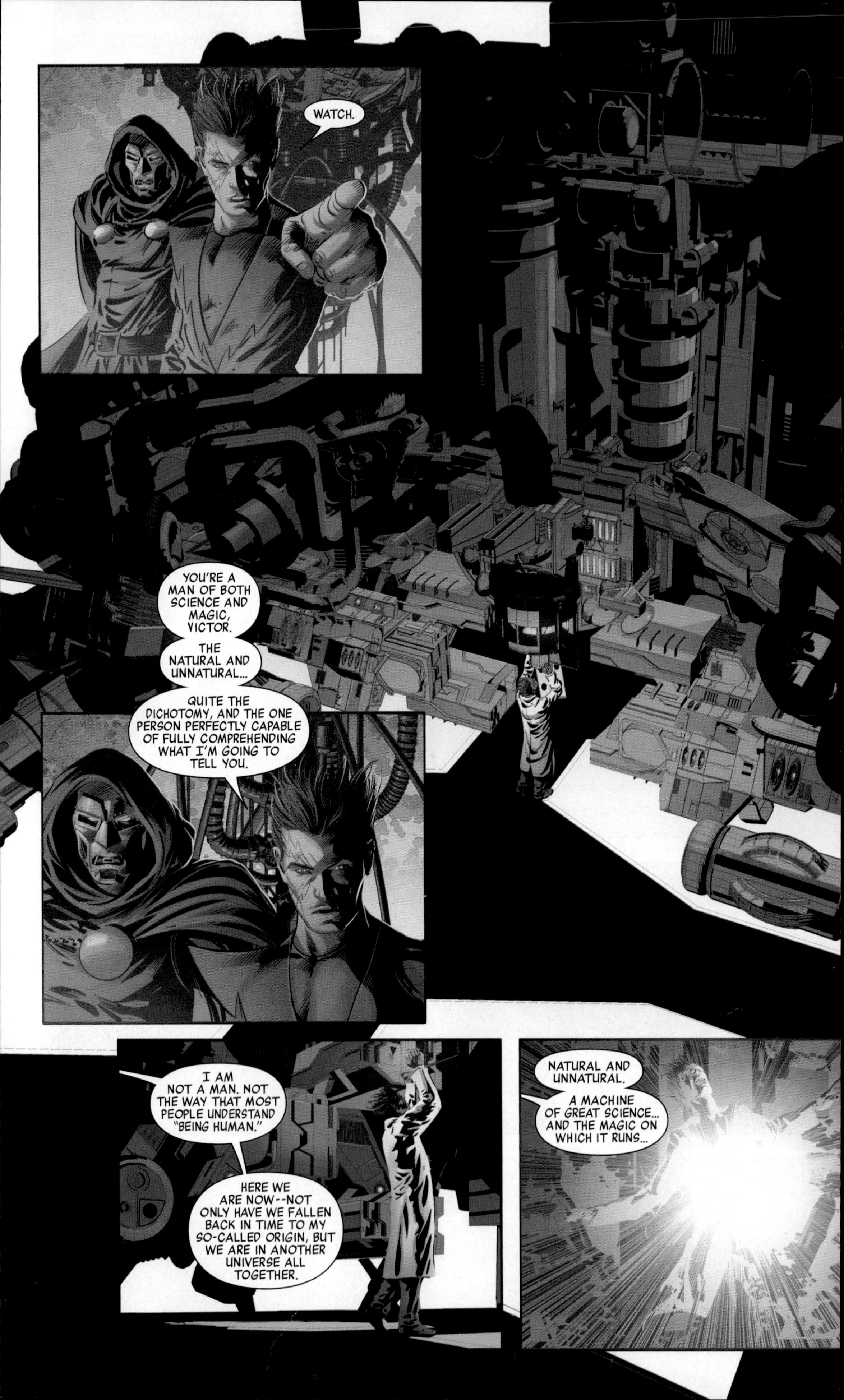
WATCH.
YOU'RE A MAN OF BOTH SCIENCE AND MAGIC, VICTOR.
THE NATURAL AND UNNATURAL...
QUITE THE DICHOTOMY, AND THE ONE PERSON PERFECTLY CAPABLE OF FULLY COMPREHENDING WHAT I'M GOING TO TELL YOU.
I AM NOT A MAN. NOT THE WAY THAT MOST PEOPLE UNDERSTAND "BEING HUMAN."
HERE WE ARE NOW--NOT ONLY HAVE WE FALLEN BACK IN TIME TO MY SO-CALLED ORIGIN, BUT WE ARE IN ANOTHER UNIVERSE ALL TOGETHER.
NATURAL AND UNNATURAL.
A MACHINE OF GREAT SCIENCE... AND THE MAGIC ON WHICH IT RUNS...

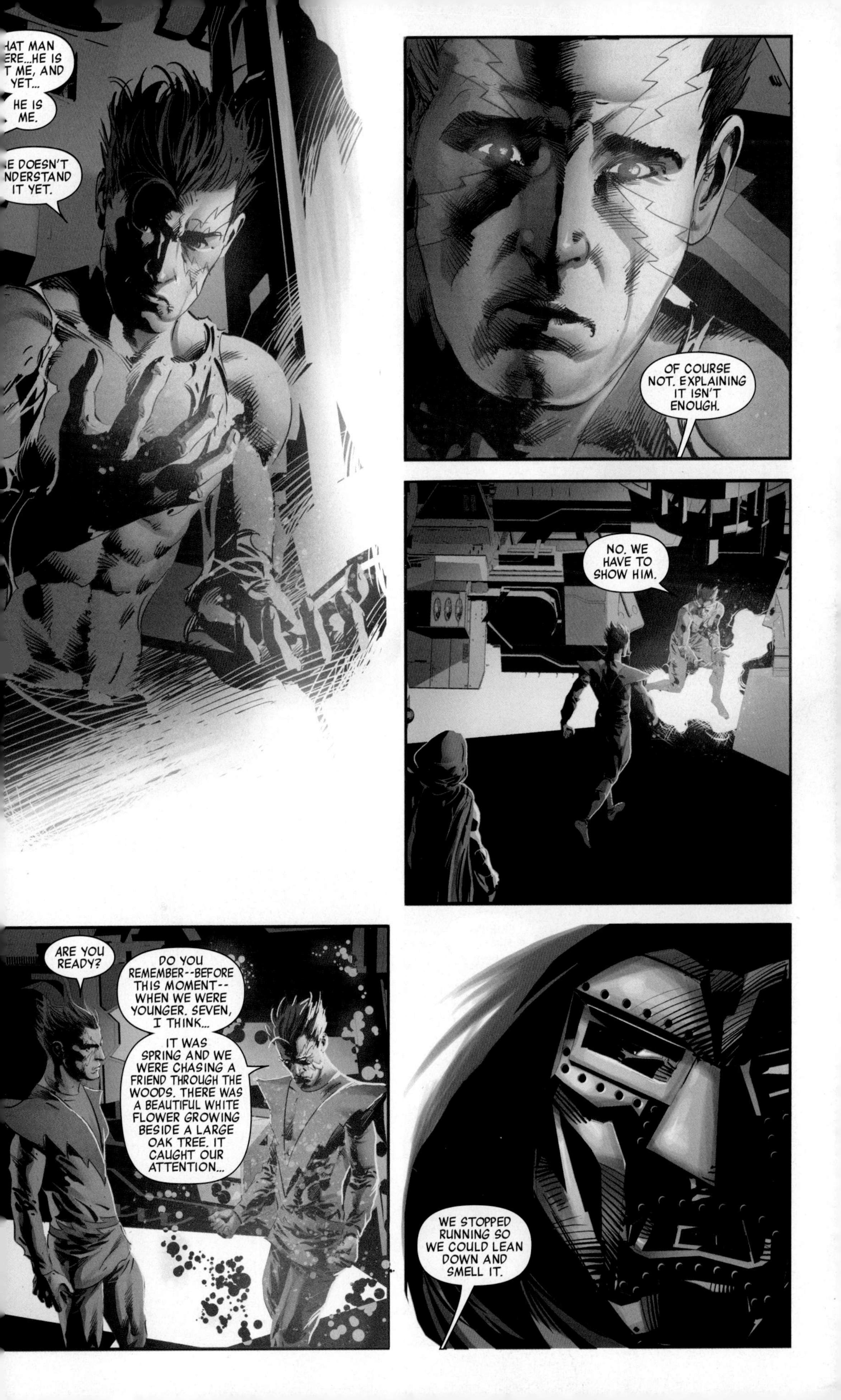
HAT MAN
ERE...HE IS
T ME, AND
YET...
HE IS
ME.
E DOESN'T
NDERSTAND
IT YET.
OF COURSE NOT. EXPLAINING IT ISN'T ENOUGH.
NO. WE HAVE TO SHOW HIM.
ARE YOU READY?
DO YOU REMEMBER--BEFORE THIS MOMENT--WHEN WE WERE YOUNGER. SEVEN, I THINK...
IT WAS SPRING AND WE WERE CHASING A FRIEND THROUGH THE WOODS. THERE WAS A BEAUTIFUL WHITE FLOWER GROWING BESIDE A LARGE OAK TREE. IT CAUGHT OUR ATTENTION...
WE STOPPED RUNNING SO WE COULD LEAN DOWN AND SMELL IT.

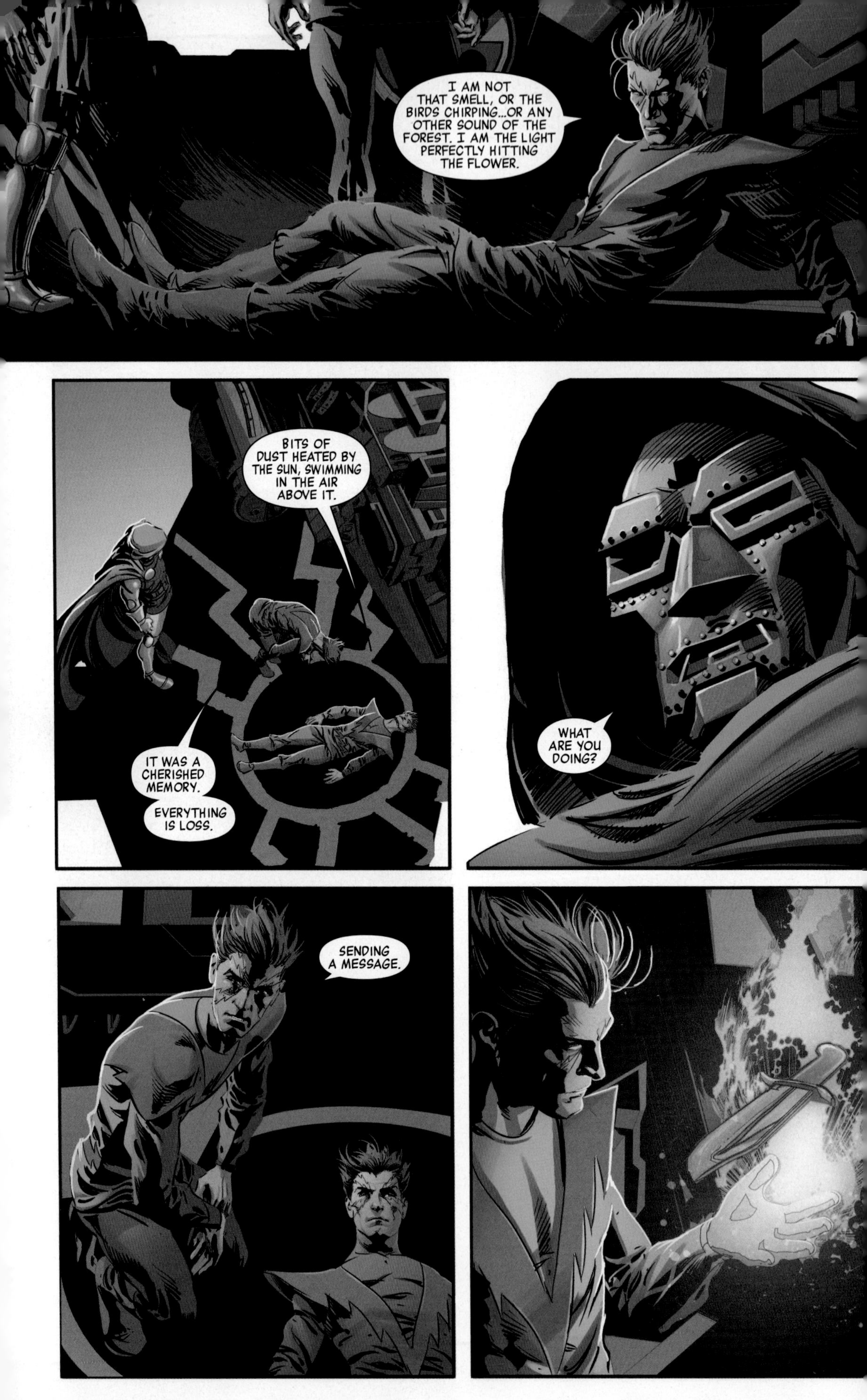
I AM NOT THAT SMELL, OR THE BIRDS CHIRPING...OR ANY OTHER SOUND OF THE FOREST. I AM THE LIGHT PERFECTLY HITTING THE FLOWER.
BITS OF DUST HEATED BY THE SUN, SWIMMING IN THE AIR ABOVE IT.
IT WAS A CHERISHED MEMORY.
EVERYTHING IS LOSS.
WHAT ARE YOU DOING?
SENDING A MESSAGE.

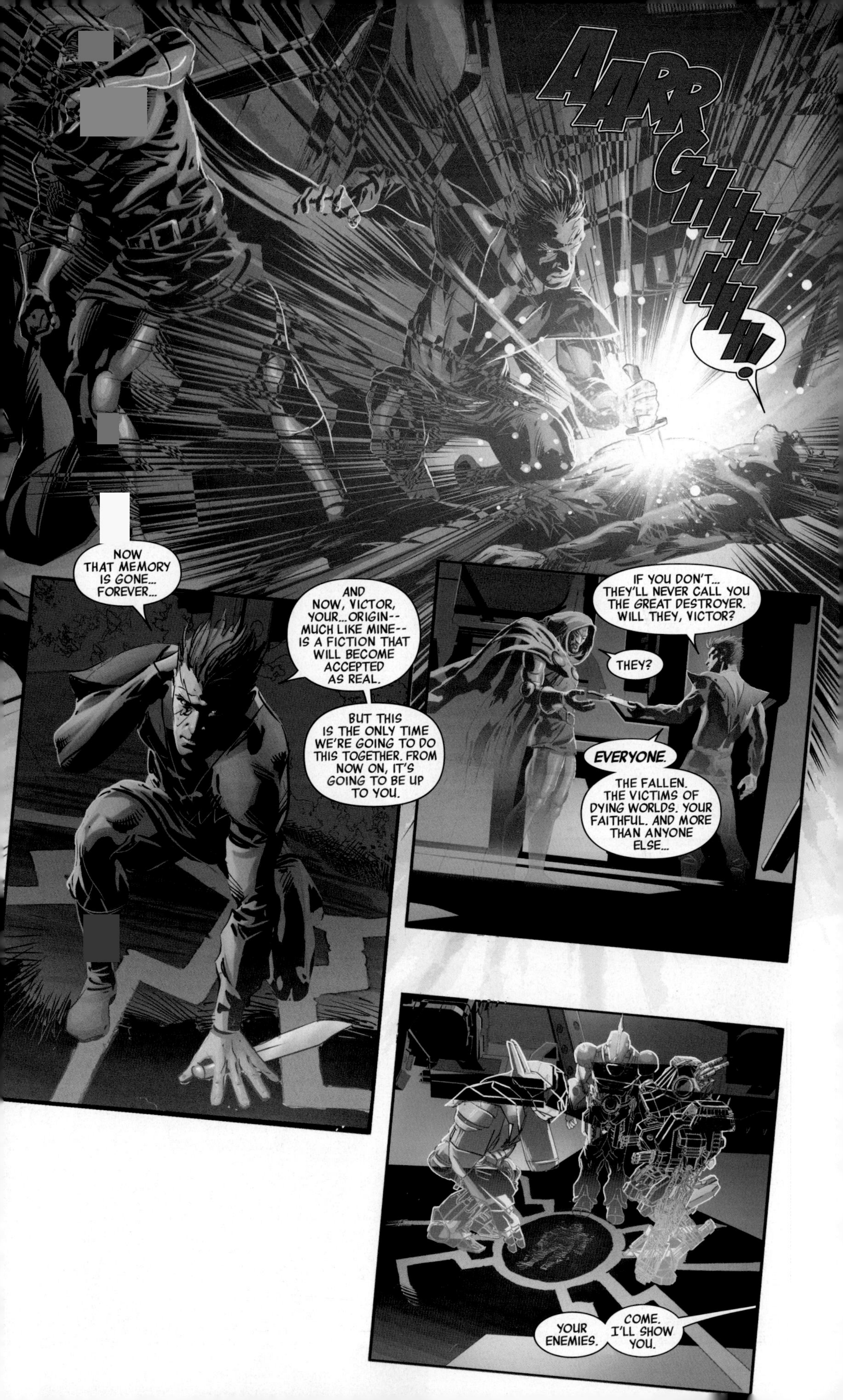
AARRGHHHHHH!
NOW THAT MEMORY IS GONE... FOREVER...
AND NOW, VICTOR, YOUR...ORIGIN-- MUCH LIKE MINE-- IS A FICTION THAT WILL BECOME ACCEPTED AS REAL.
BUT THIS IS THE ONLY TIME WE'RE GOING TO DO THIS TOGETHER. FROM NOW ON, IT'S GOING TO BE UP TO YOU.
IF YOU DON'T... THEY'LL NEVER CALL YOU THE GREAT DESTROYER. WILL THEY, VICTOR?
THEY?
EVERYONE.
THE FALLEN. THE VICTIMS OF DYING WORLDS. YOUR FAITHFUL. AND MORE THAN ANYONE ELSE...
YOUR ENEMIES.
COME. I'LL SHOW YOU.

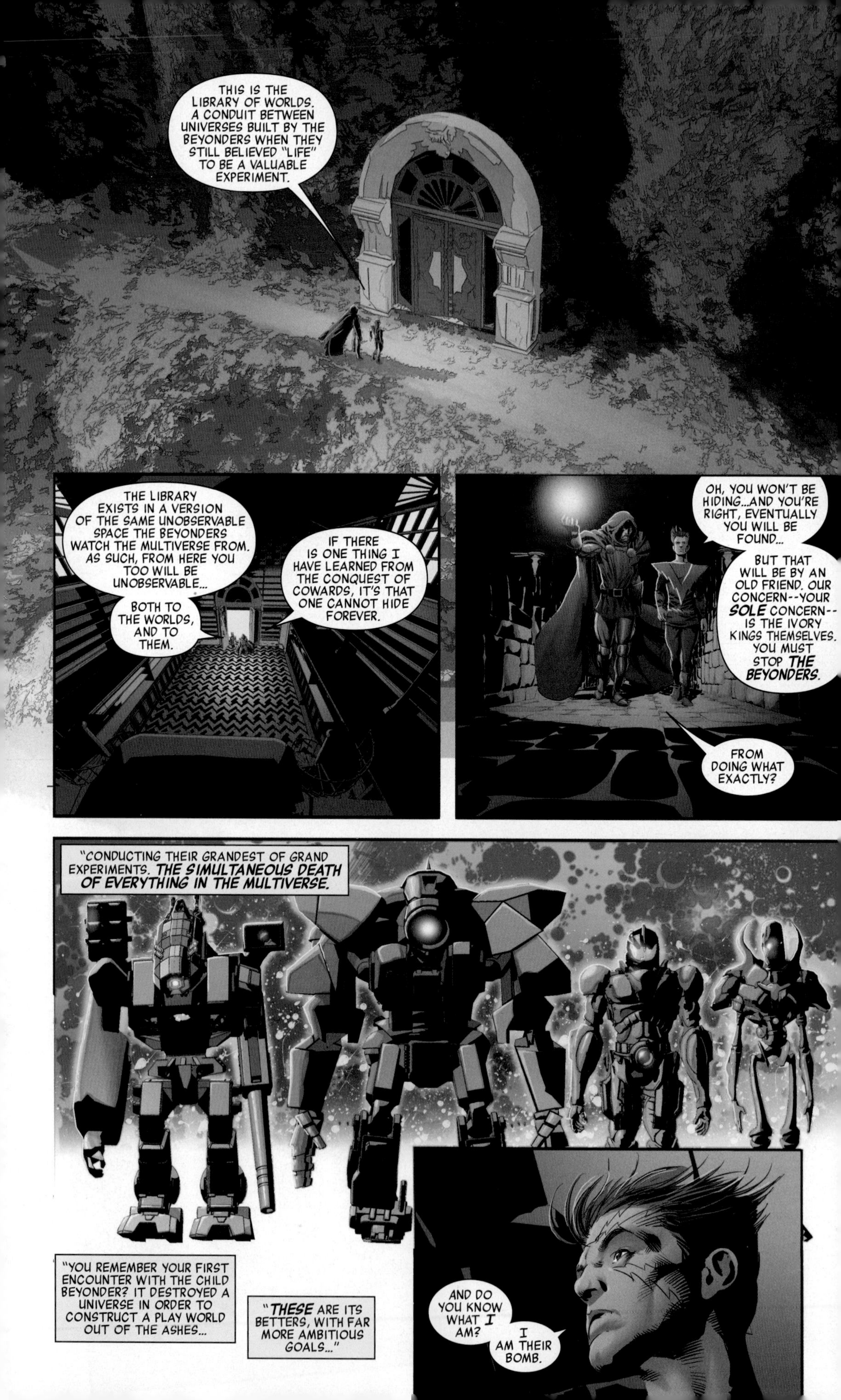
THIS IS THE LIBRARY OF WORLDS. A CONDUIT BETWEEN UNIVERSES BUILT BY THE BEYONDERS WHEN THEY STILL BELIEVED "LIFE" TO BE A VALUABLE EXPERIMENT.
THE LIBRARY EXISTS IN A VERSION OF THE SAME UNOBSERVABLE SPACE THE BEYONDERS WATCH THE MULTIVERSE FROM. AS SUCH, FROM HERE YOU TOO WILL BE UNOBSERVABLE...
BOTH TO THE WORLDS, AND TO THEM.
IF THERE IS ONE THING I HAVE LEARNED FROM THE CONQUEST OF COWARDS, IT'S THAT ONE CANNOT HIDE FOREVER.
OH, YOU WON'T BE HIDING...AND YOU'RE RIGHT, EVENTUALLY YOU WILL BE FOUND...
BUT THAT WILL BE BY AN OLD FRIEND. OUR CONCERN--YOUR SOLE CONCERN--IS THE IVORY KINGS THEMSELVES. YOU MUST STOP THE BEYONDERS.
FROM DOING WHAT EXACTLY?
"CONDUCTING THEIR GRANDEST OF GRAND EXPERIMENTS. THE SIMULTANEOUS DEATH OF EVERYTHING IN THE MULTIVERSE.
"YOU REMEMBER YOUR FIRST ENCOUNTER WITH THE CHILD BEYONDER? IT DESTROYED A UNIVERSE IN ORDER TO CONSTRUCT A PLAY WORLD OUT OF THE ASHES...
"THESE ARE ITS BETTERS, WITH FAR MORE AMBITIOUS GOALS..."
AND DO YOU KNOW WHAT I AM?
I AM THEIR BOMB.

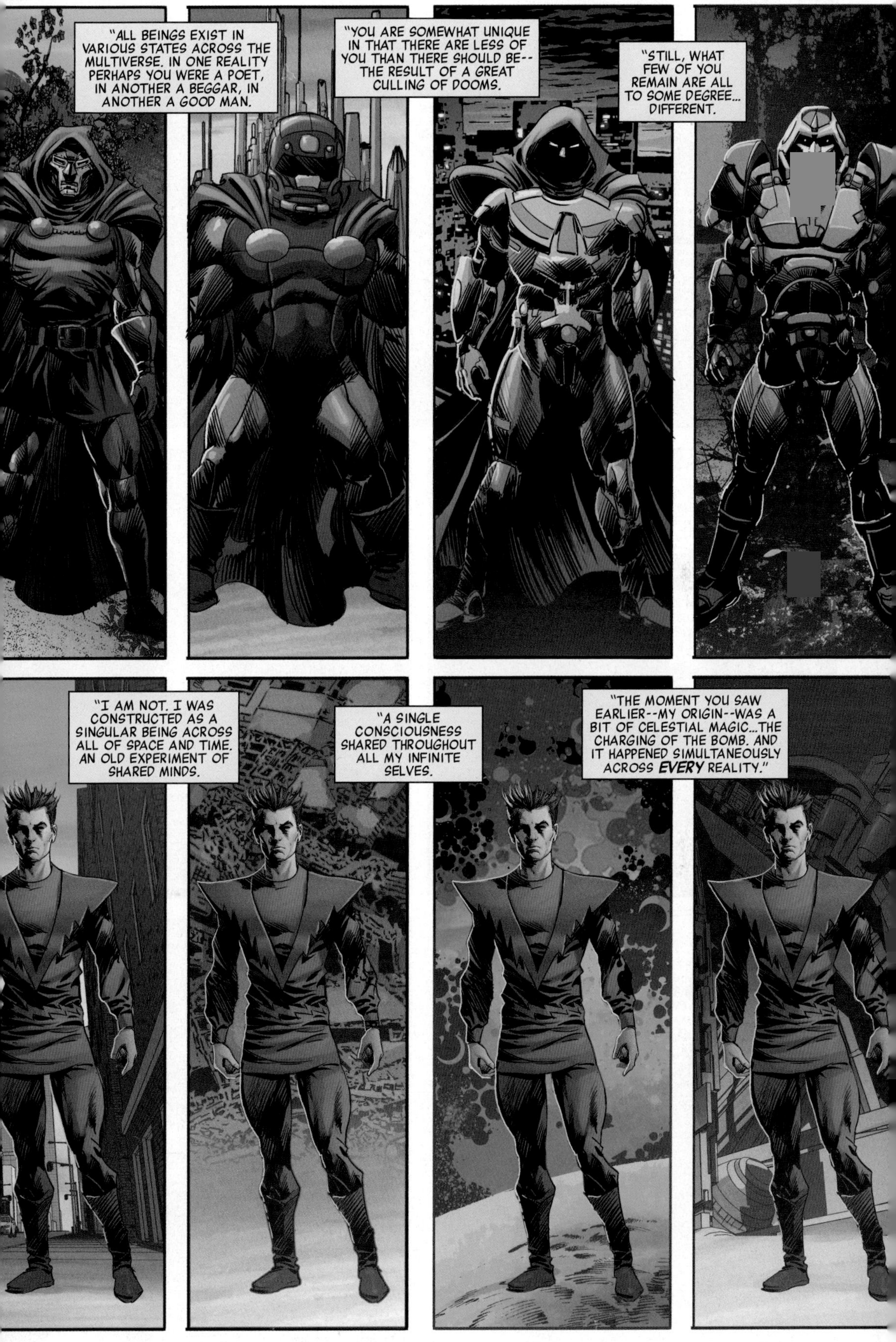
"ALL BEINGS EXIST IN VARIOUS STATES ACROSS THE MULTIVERSE. IN ONE REALITY PERHAPS YOU WERE A POET, IN ANOTHER A BEGGAR, IN ANOTHER A GOOD MAN.
"YOU ARE SOMEWHAT UNIQUE IN THAT THERE ARE LESS OF YOU THAN THERE SHOULD BE-- THE RESULT OF A GREAT CULLING OF DOOMS.
"STILL, WHAT FEW OF YOU REMAIN ARE ALL TO SOME DEGREE... DIFFERENT.
"I AM NOT. I WAS CONSTRUCTED AS A SINGULAR BEING ACROSS ALL OF SPACE AND TIME. AN OLD EXPERIMENT OF SHARED MINDS.
"A SINGLE CONSCIOUSNESS SHARED THROUGHOUT ALL MY INFINITE SELVES.
"THE MOMENT YOU SAW EARLIER--MY ORIGIN--WAS A BIT OF CELESTIAL MAGIC...THE CHARGING OF THE BOMB. AND IT HAPPENED SIMULTANEOUSLY ACROSS EVERY REALITY."

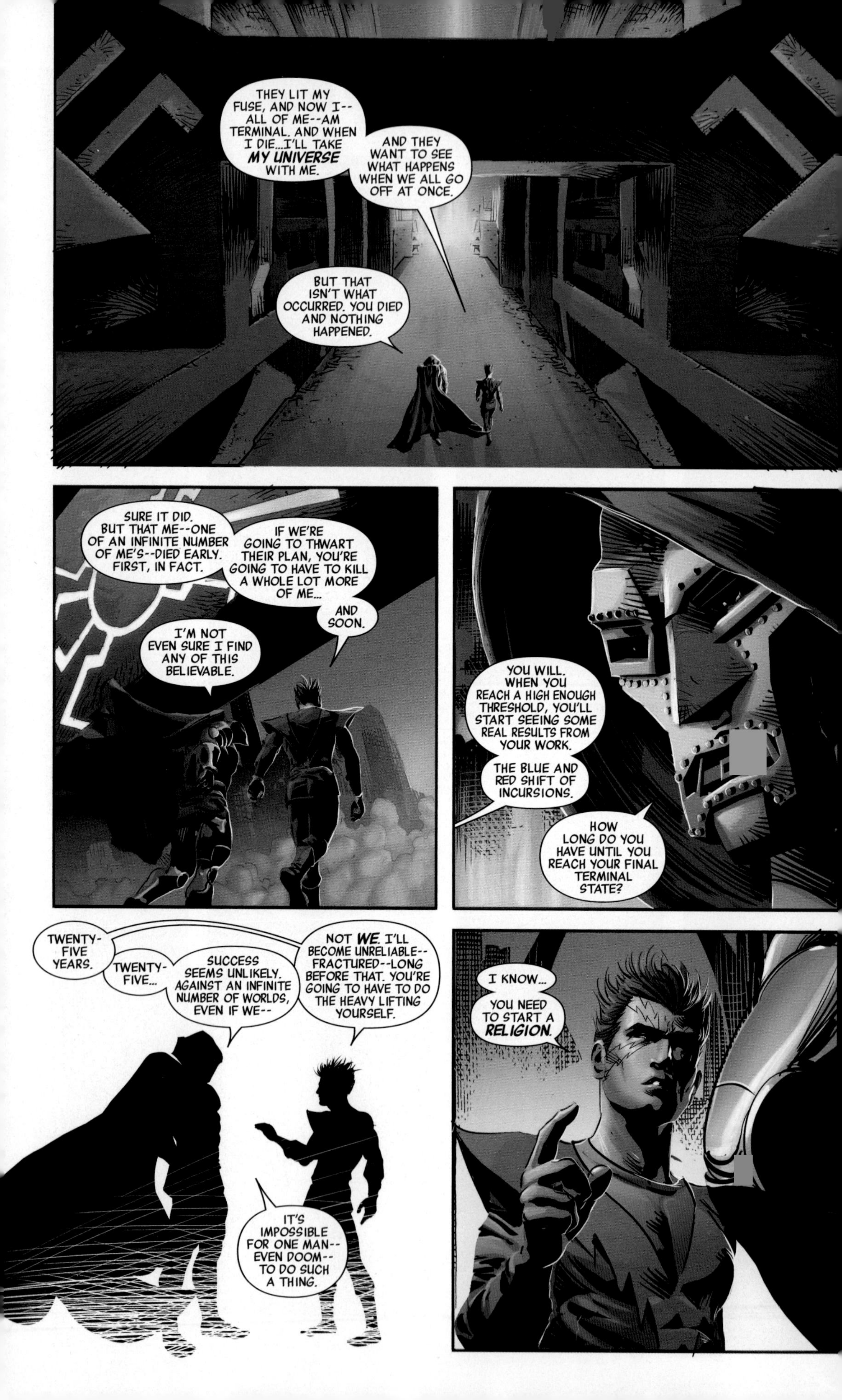

THEY LIT MY FUSE, AND NOW I-- ALL OF ME--AM TERMINAL. AND WHEN I DIE...I'LL TAKE **MY UNIVERSE** WITH ME.
AND THEY WANT TO SEE WHAT HAPPENS WHEN WE ALL GO OFF AT ONCE.
BUT THAT ISN'T WHAT OCCURRED. YOU DIED AND NOTHING HAPPENED.
SURE IT DID. BUT THAT ME--ONE OF AN INFINITE NUMBER OF ME'S--DIED EARLY. FIRST, IN FACT.
IF WE'RE GOING TO THWART THEIR PLAN, YOU'RE GOING TO HAVE TO KILL A WHOLE LOT MORE OF ME...
AND SOON.
I'M NOT EVEN SURE I FIND ANY OF THIS BELIEVABLE.
YOU WILL. WHEN YOU REACH A HIGH ENOUGH THRESHOLD, YOU'LL START SEEING SOME REAL RESULTS FROM YOUR WORK.
THE BLUE AND RED SHIFT OF INCURSIONS.
HOW LONG DO YOU HAVE UNTIL YOU REACH YOUR FINAL TERMINAL STATE?
TWENTY-FIVE YEARS.
TWENTY-FIVE...
SUCCESS SEEMS UNLIKELY. AGAINST AN INFINITE NUMBER OF WORLDS, EVEN IF WE--
NOT **WE**. I'LL BECOME UNRELIABLE--FRACTURED--LONG BEFORE THAT. YOU'RE GOING TO HAVE TO DO THE HEAVY LIFTING YOURSELF.
IT'S IMPOSSIBLE FOR ONE MAN--EVEN DOOM--TO DO SUCH A THING.
I KNOW...
YOU NEED TO START A **RELIGION**.

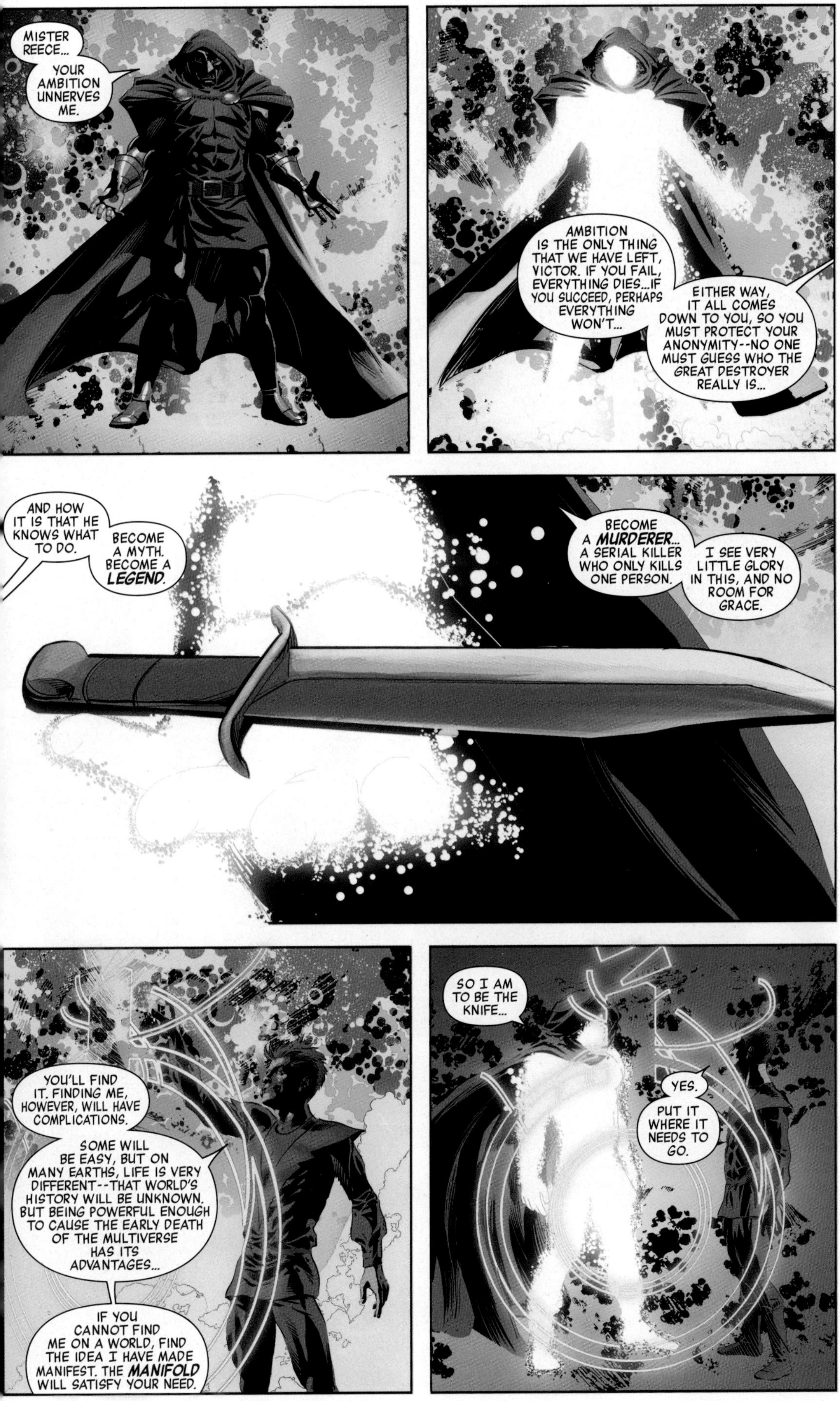
MISTER REECE...
YOUR AMBITION UNNERVES ME.
AMBITION IS THE ONLY THING THAT WE HAVE LEFT, VICTOR. IF YOU FAIL, EVERYTHING DIES...IF YOU SUCCEED, PERHAPS EVERYTHING WON'T...
EITHER WAY, IT ALL COMES DOWN TO YOU, SO YOU MUST PROTECT YOUR ANONYMITY--NO ONE MUST GUESS WHO THE GREAT DESTROYER REALLY IS...
AND HOW IT IS THAT HE KNOWS WHAT TO DO.
BECOME A MYTH. BECOME A *LEGEND*.
BECOME A ***MURDERER***... A SERIAL KILLER WHO ONLY KILLS ONE PERSON.
I SEE VERY LITTLE GLORY IN THIS, AND NO ROOM FOR GRACE.
YOU'LL FIND IT. FINDING ME, HOWEVER, WILL HAVE COMPLICATIONS.
SOME WILL BE EASY, BUT ON MANY EARTHS, LIFE IS VERY DIFFERENT--THAT WORLD'S HISTORY WILL BE UNKNOWN. BUT BEING POWERFUL ENOUGH TO CAUSE THE EARLY DEATH OF THE MULTIVERSE HAS ITS ADVANTAGES...
IF YOU CANNOT FIND ME ON A WORLD, FIND THE IDEA I HAVE MADE MANIFEST. THE ***MANIFOLD*** WILL SATISFY YOUR NEED.
SO I AM TO BE THE KNIFE...
YES.
PUT IT WHERE IT NEEDS TO GO.

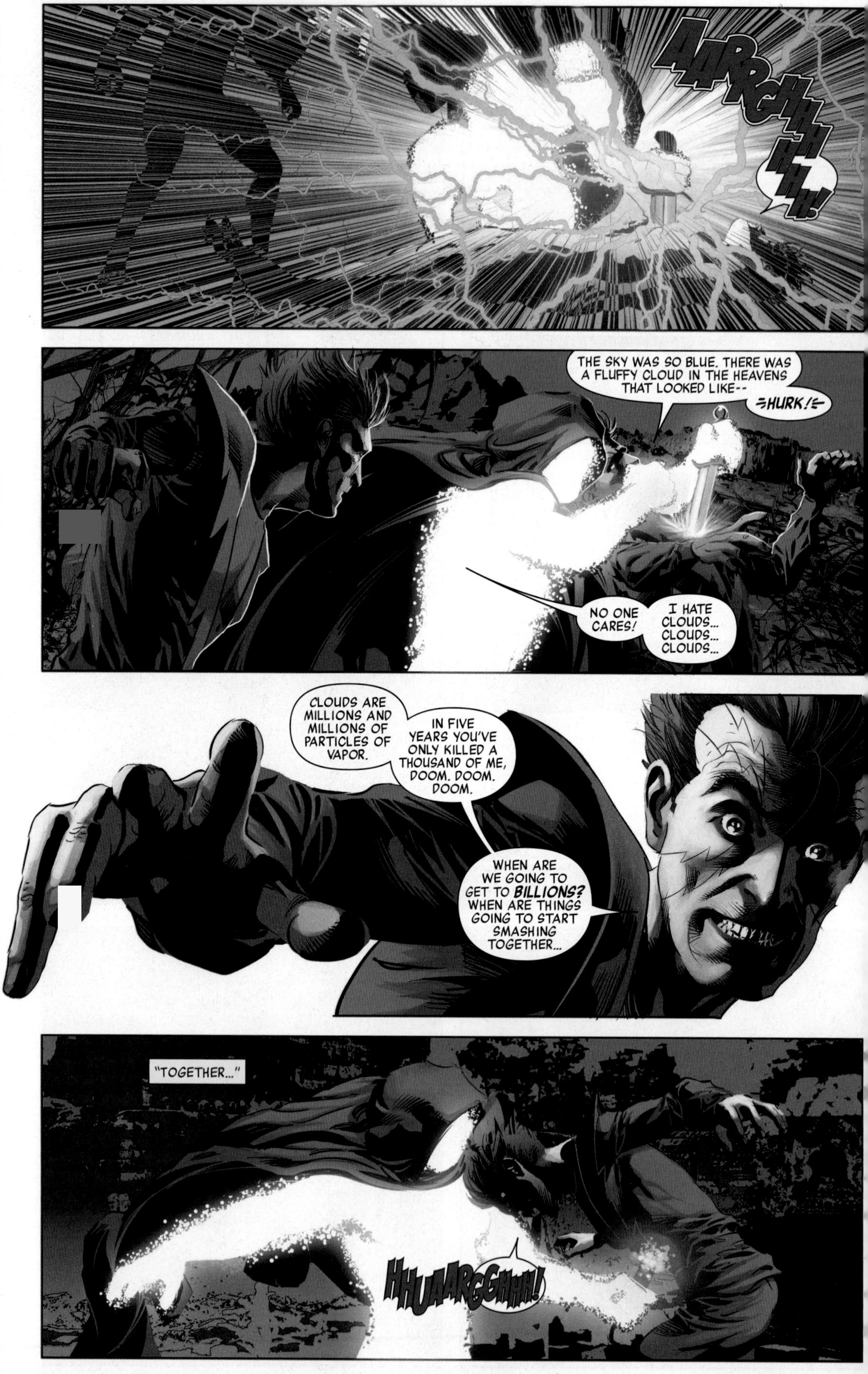
AARRGHHHHHH!
THE SKY WAS SO BLUE. THERE WAS A FLUFFY CLOUD IN THE HEAVENS THAT LOOKED LIKE--
HURK!
NO ONE CARES!
I HATE CLOUDS... CLOUDS... CLOUDS...
CLOUDS ARE MILLIONS AND MILLIONS OF PARTICLES OF VAPOR.
IN FIVE YEARS YOU'VE ONLY KILLED A THOUSAND OF ME, DOOM. DOOM. DOOM.
WHEN ARE WE GOING TO GET TO BILLIONS? WHEN ARE THINGS GOING TO START SMASHING TOGETHER...
"TOGETHER..."
HHUAARGGHHH!

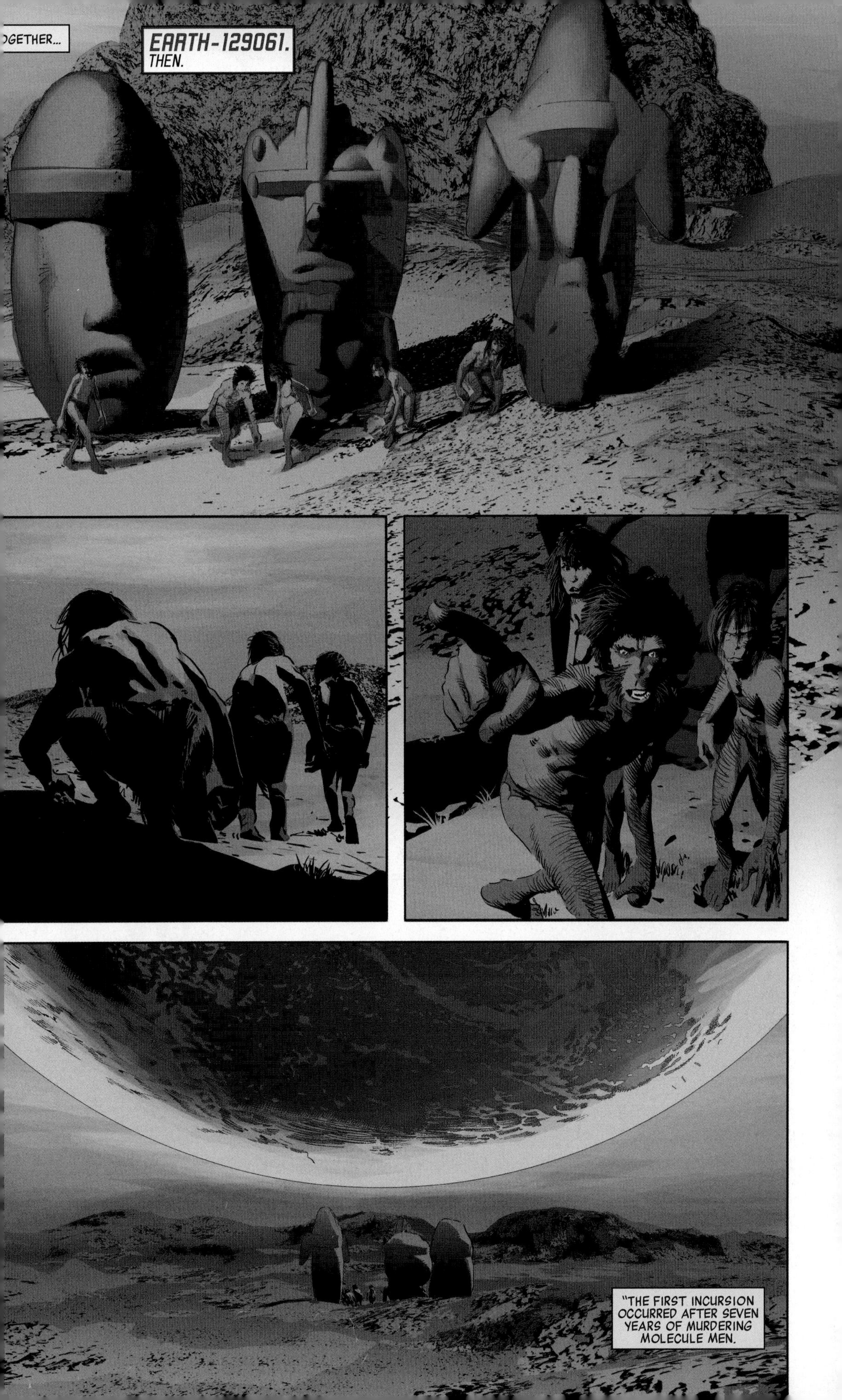

...OGETHER...
EARTH-129061.
THEN.
"THE FIRST INCURSION OCCURRED AFTER SEVEN YEARS OF MURDERING MOLECULE MEN.

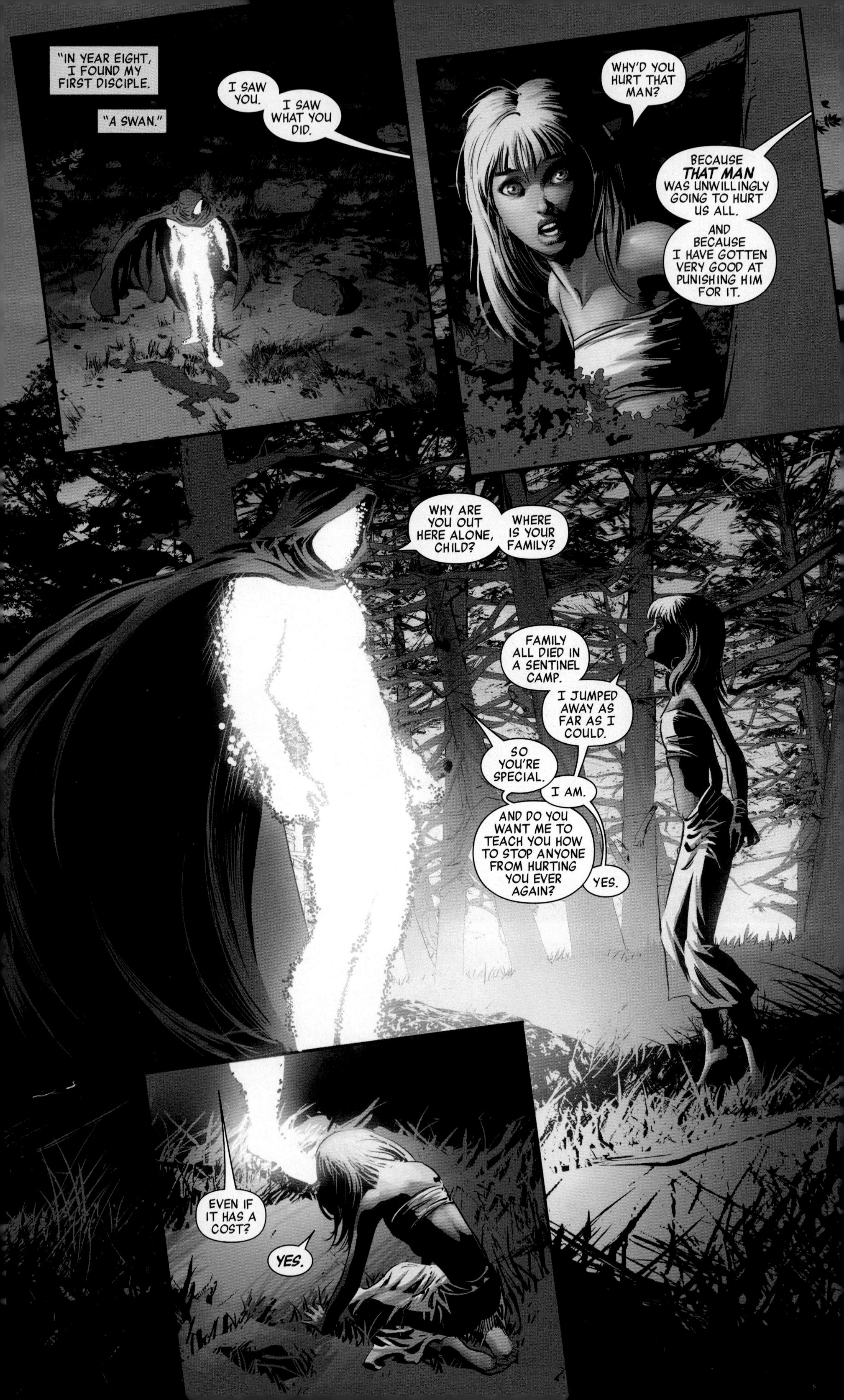
"IN YEAR EIGHT, I FOUND MY FIRST DISCIPLE.
"A SWAN."
I SAW YOU.
I SAW WHAT YOU DID.
WHY'D YOU HURT THAT MAN?
BECAUSE THAT MAN WAS UNWILLINGLY GOING TO HURT US ALL.
AND BECAUSE I HAVE GOTTEN VERY GOOD AT PUNISHING HIM FOR IT.
WHY ARE YOU OUT HERE ALONE, CHILD?
WHERE IS YOUR FAMILY?
FAMILY ALL DIED IN A SENTINEL CAMP.
I JUMPED AWAY AS FAR AS I COULD.
SO YOU'RE SPECIAL.
I AM.
AND DO YOU WANT ME TO TEACH YOU HOW TO STOP ANYONE FROM HURTING YOU EVER AGAIN?
YES.
EVEN IF IT HAS A COST?
YES.

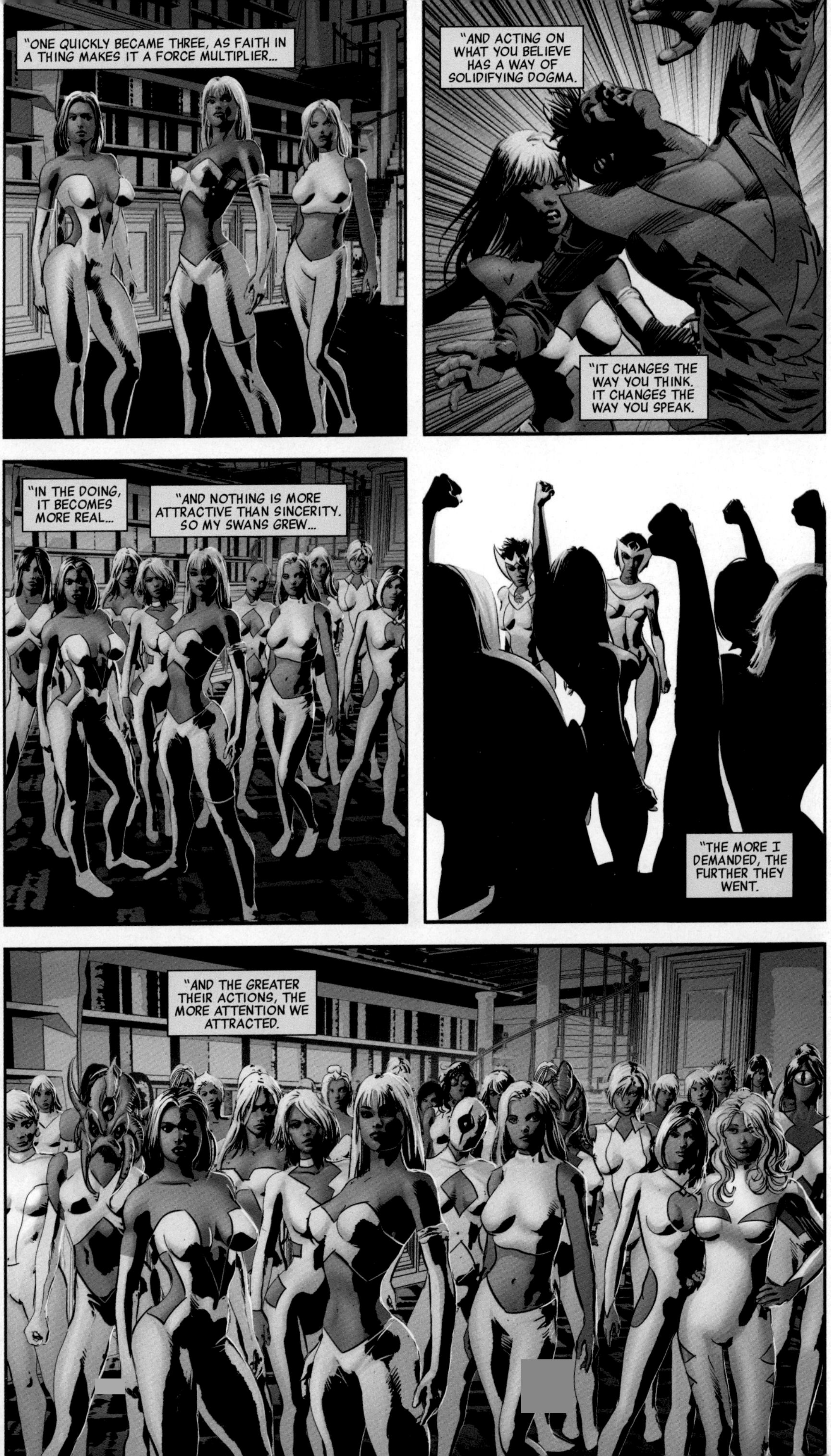
"ONE QUICKLY BECAME THREE, AS FAITH IN A THING MAKES IT A FORCE MULTIPLIER...
"AND ACTING ON WHAT YOU BELIEVE HAS A WAY OF SOLIDIFYING DOGMA.
"IT CHANGES THE WAY YOU THINK. IT CHANGES THE WAY YOU SPEAK.
"IN THE DOING, IT BECOMES MORE REAL...
"AND NOTHING IS MORE ATTRACTIVE THAN SINCERITY. SO MY SWANS GREW...
"THE MORE I DEMANDED, THE FURTHER THEY WENT.
"AND THE GREATER THEIR ACTIONS, THE MORE ATTENTION WE ATTRACTED.

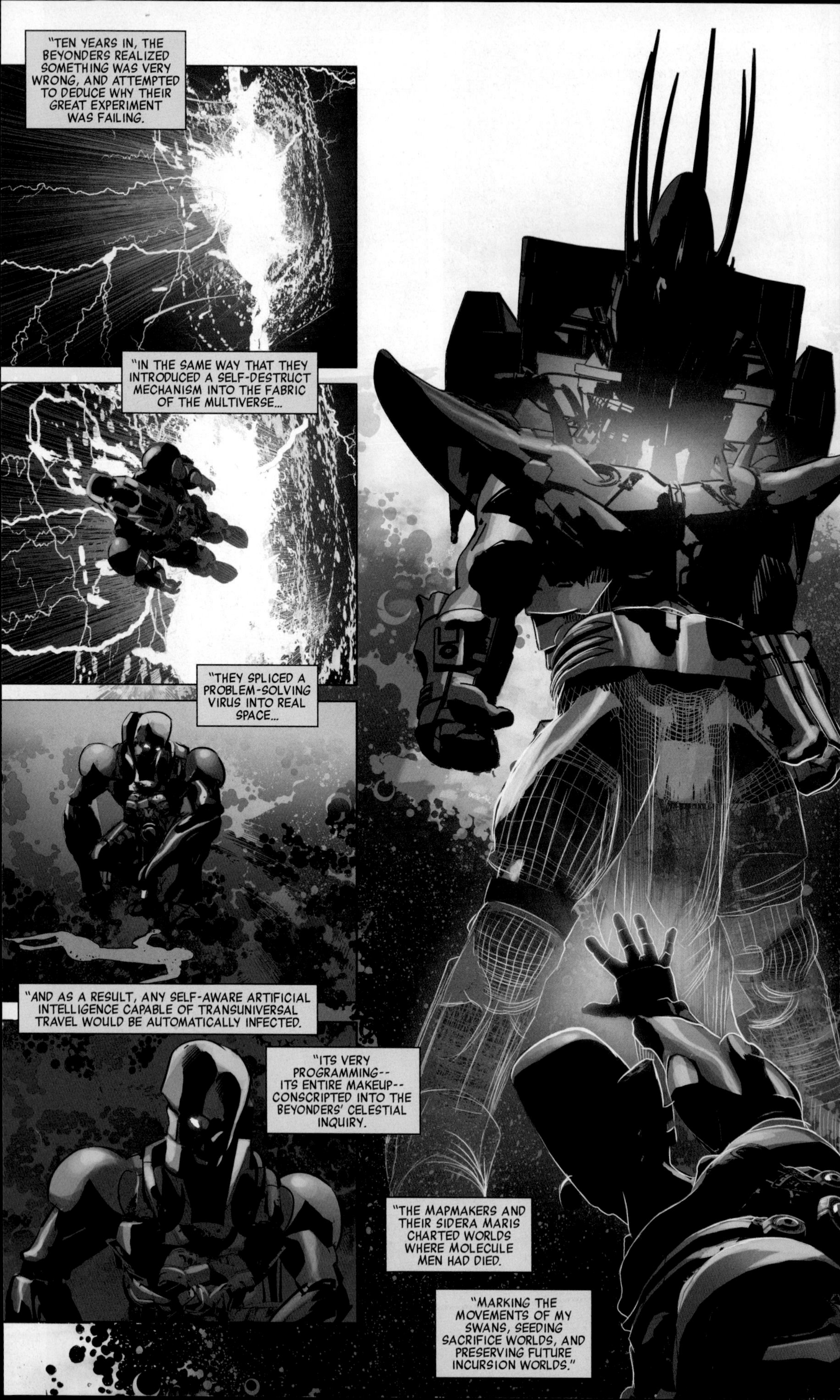
"TEN YEARS IN, THE BEYONDERS REALIZED SOMETHING WAS VERY WRONG, AND ATTEMPTED TO DEDUCE WHY THEIR GREAT EXPERIMENT WAS FAILING.
"IN THE SAME WAY THAT THEY INTRODUCED A SELF-DESTRUCT MECHANISM INTO THE FABRIC OF THE MULTIVERSE...
"THEY SPLICED A PROBLEM-SOLVING VIRUS INTO REAL SPACE...
"AND AS A RESULT, ANY SELF-AWARE ARTIFICIAL INTELLIGENCE CAPABLE OF TRANSUNIVERSAL TRAVEL WOULD BE AUTOMATICALLY INFECTED.
"ITS VERY PROGRAMMING-- ITS ENTIRE MAKEUP-- CONSCRIPTED INTO THE BEYONDERS' CELESTIAL INQUIRY.
"THE MAPMAKERS AND THEIR SIDERA MARIS CHARTED WORLDS WHERE MOLECULE MEN HAD DIED.
"MARKING THE MOVEMENTS OF MY SWANS, SEEDING SACRIFICE WORLDS, AND PRESERVING FUTURE INCURSION WORLDS."

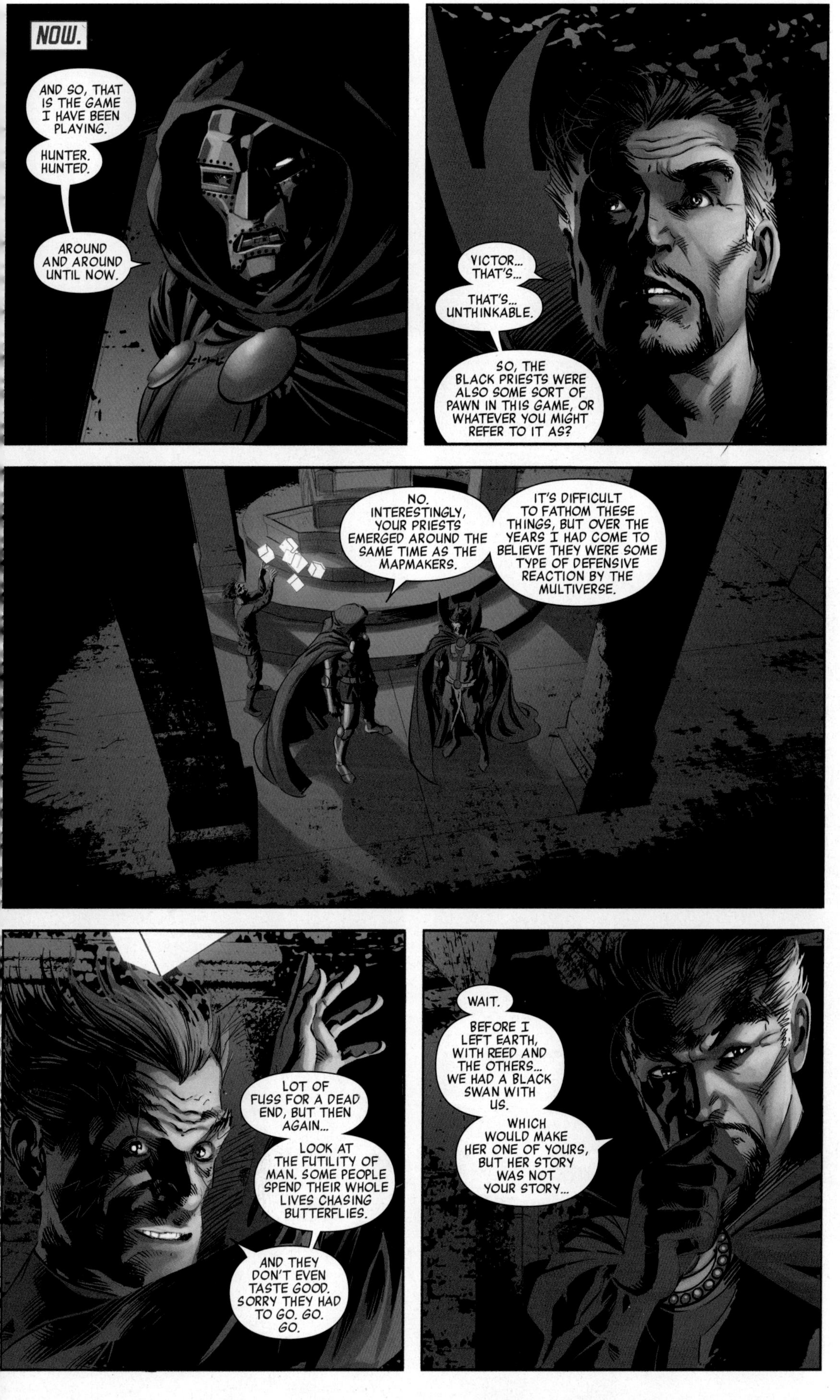
NOW.
AND SO, THAT IS THE GAME I HAVE BEEN PLAYING.
HUNTER. HUNTED.
AROUND AND AROUND UNTIL NOW.
VICTOR... THAT'S...
THAT'S... UNTHINKABLE.
SO, THE BLACK PRIESTS WERE ALSO SOME SORT OF PAWN IN THIS GAME, OR WHATEVER YOU MIGHT REFER TO IT AS?
NO. INTERESTINGLY, YOUR PRIESTS EMERGED AROUND THE SAME TIME AS THE MAPMAKERS.
IT'S DIFFICULT TO FATHOM THESE THINGS, BUT OVER THE YEARS I HAD COME TO BELIEVE THEY WERE SOME TYPE OF DEFENSIVE REACTION BY THE MULTIVERSE.
LOT OF FUSS FOR A DEAD END, BUT THEN AGAIN...
LOOK AT THE FUTILITY OF MAN. SOME PEOPLE SPEND THEIR WHOLE LIVES CHASING BUTTERFLIES.
AND THEY DON'T EVEN TASTE GOOD. SORRY THEY HAD TO GO. GO. GO.
WAIT.
BEFORE I LEFT EARTH, WITH REED AND THE OTHERS... WE HAD A BLACK SWAN WITH US.
WHICH WOULD MAKE HER ONE OF YOURS, BUT HER STORY WAS NOT YOUR STORY...

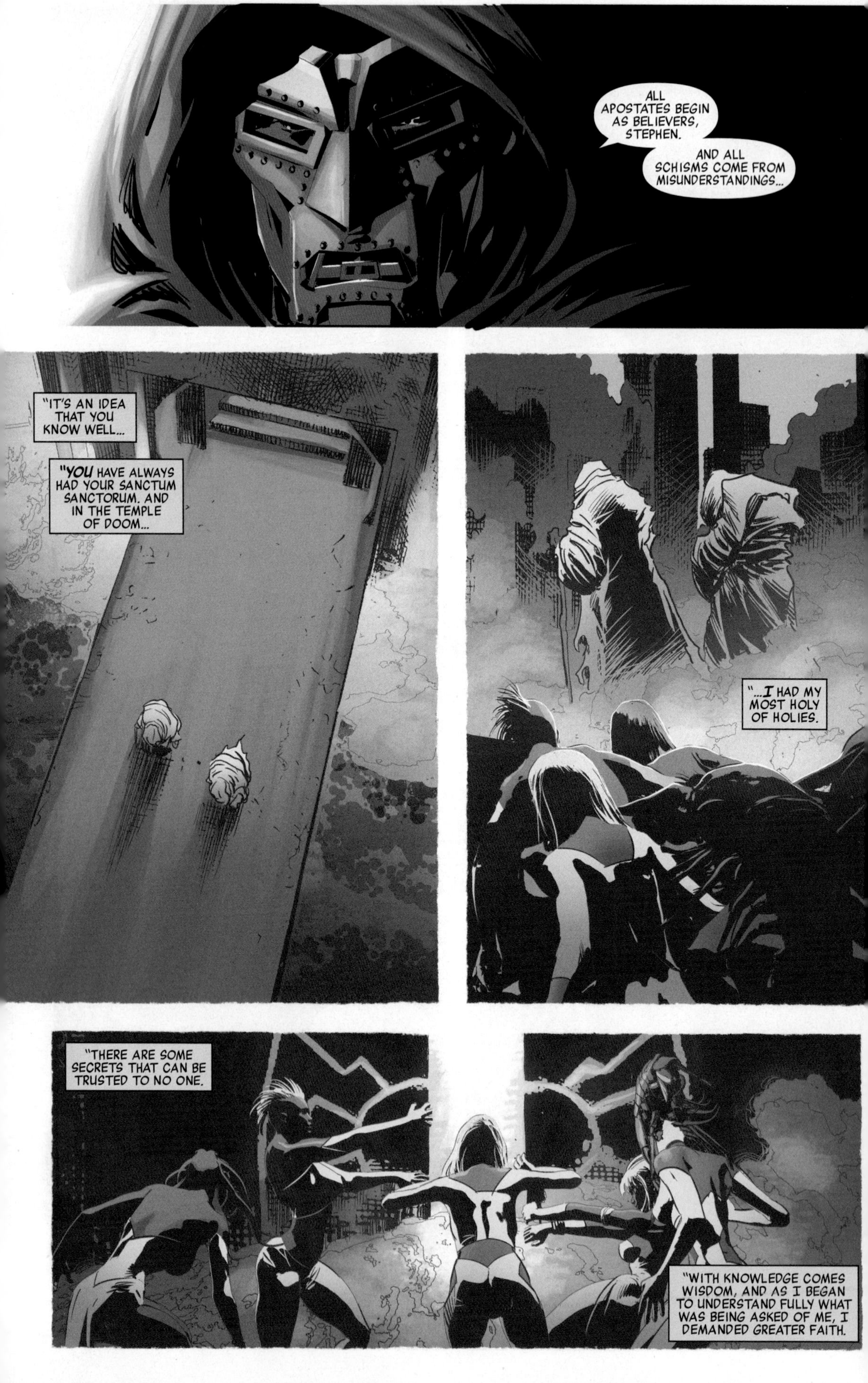

ALL APOSTATES BEGIN AS BELIEVERS, STEPHEN.
AND ALL SCHISMS COME FROM MISUNDERSTANDINGS...
"IT'S AN IDEA THAT YOU KNOW WELL...
"YOU HAVE ALWAYS HAD YOUR SANCTUM SANCTORUM. AND IN THE TEMPLE OF DOOM...
"...I HAD MY MOST HOLY OF HOLIES.
"THERE ARE SOME SECRETS THAT CAN BE TRUSTED TO NO ONE.
"WITH KNOWLEDGE COMES WISDOM, AND AS I BEGAN TO UNDERSTAND FULLY WHAT WAS BEING ASKED OF ME, I DEMANDED GREATER FAITH.

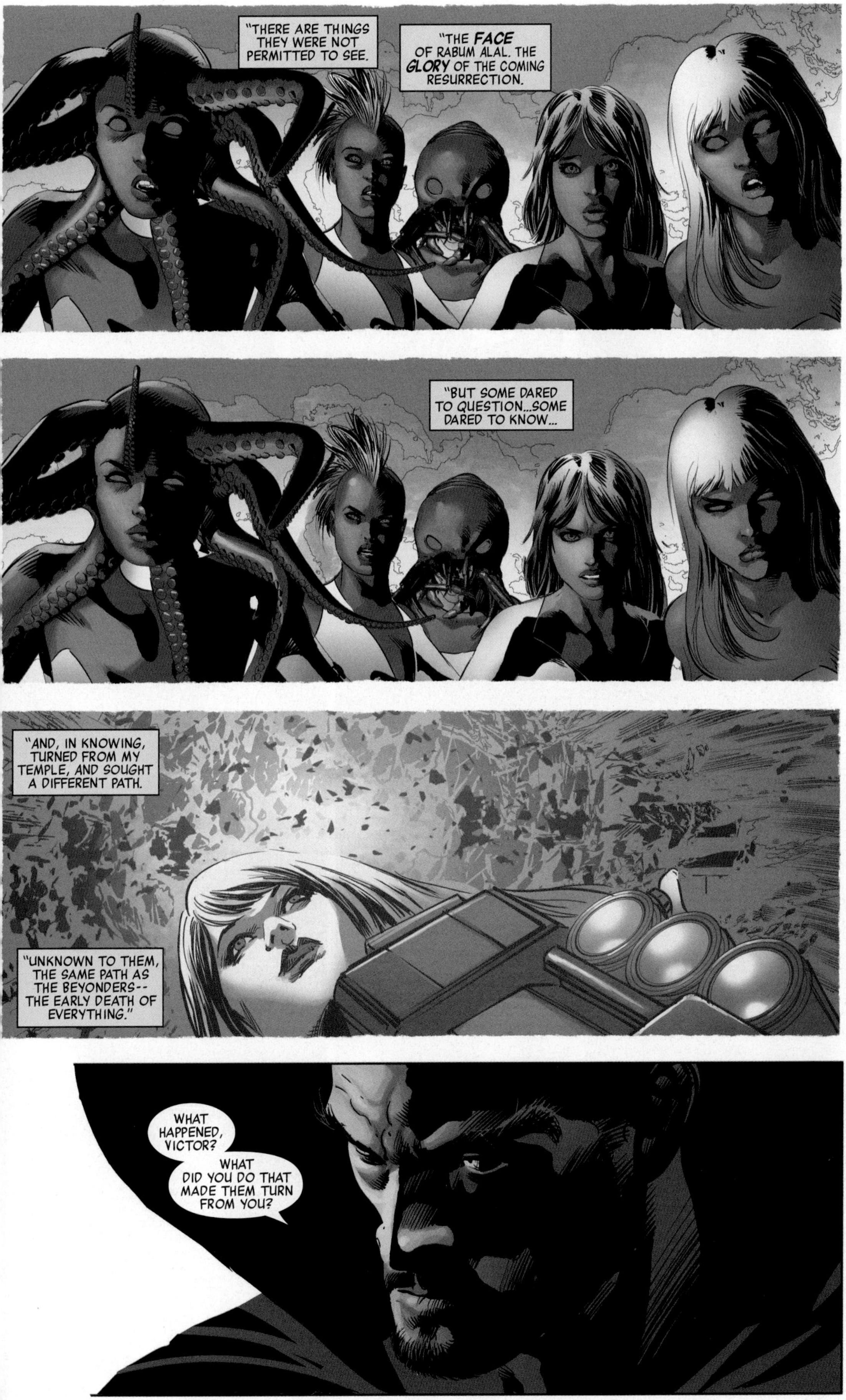

"THERE ARE THINGS THEY WERE NOT PERMITTED TO SEE.
"THE FACE OF RABUM ALAL. THE GLORY OF THE COMING RESURRECTION.
"BUT SOME DARED TO QUESTION...SOME DARED TO KNOW...
"AND, IN KNOWING, TURNED FROM MY TEMPLE, AND SOUGHT A DIFFERENT PATH.
"UNKNOWN TO THEM, THE SAME PATH AS THE BEYONDERS-- THE EARLY DEATH OF EVERYTHING."
WHAT HAPPENED, VICTOR?
WHAT DID YOU DO THAT MADE THEM TURN FROM YOU?

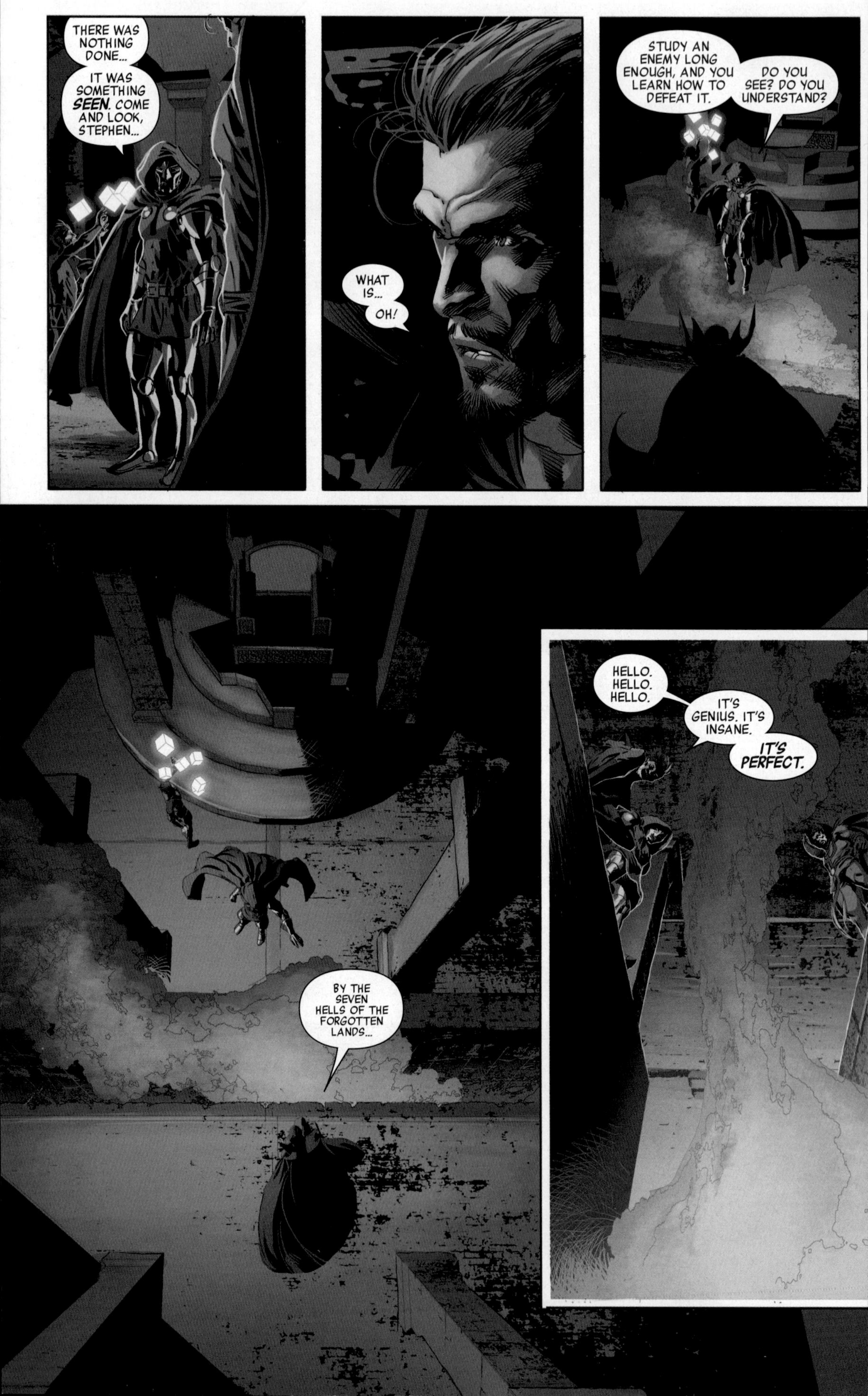

THERE WAS NOTHING DONE...
IT WAS SOMETHING **SEEN**. COME AND LOOK, STEPHEN...
WHAT IS...
OH!
STUDY AN ENEMY LONG ENOUGH, AND YOU LEARN HOW TO DEFEAT IT.
DO YOU SEE? DO YOU UNDERSTAND?
BY THE SEVEN HELLS OF THE FORGOTTEN LANDS...
HELLO. HELLO. HELLO.
IT'S GENIUS. IT'S INSANE.
IT'S PERFECT.

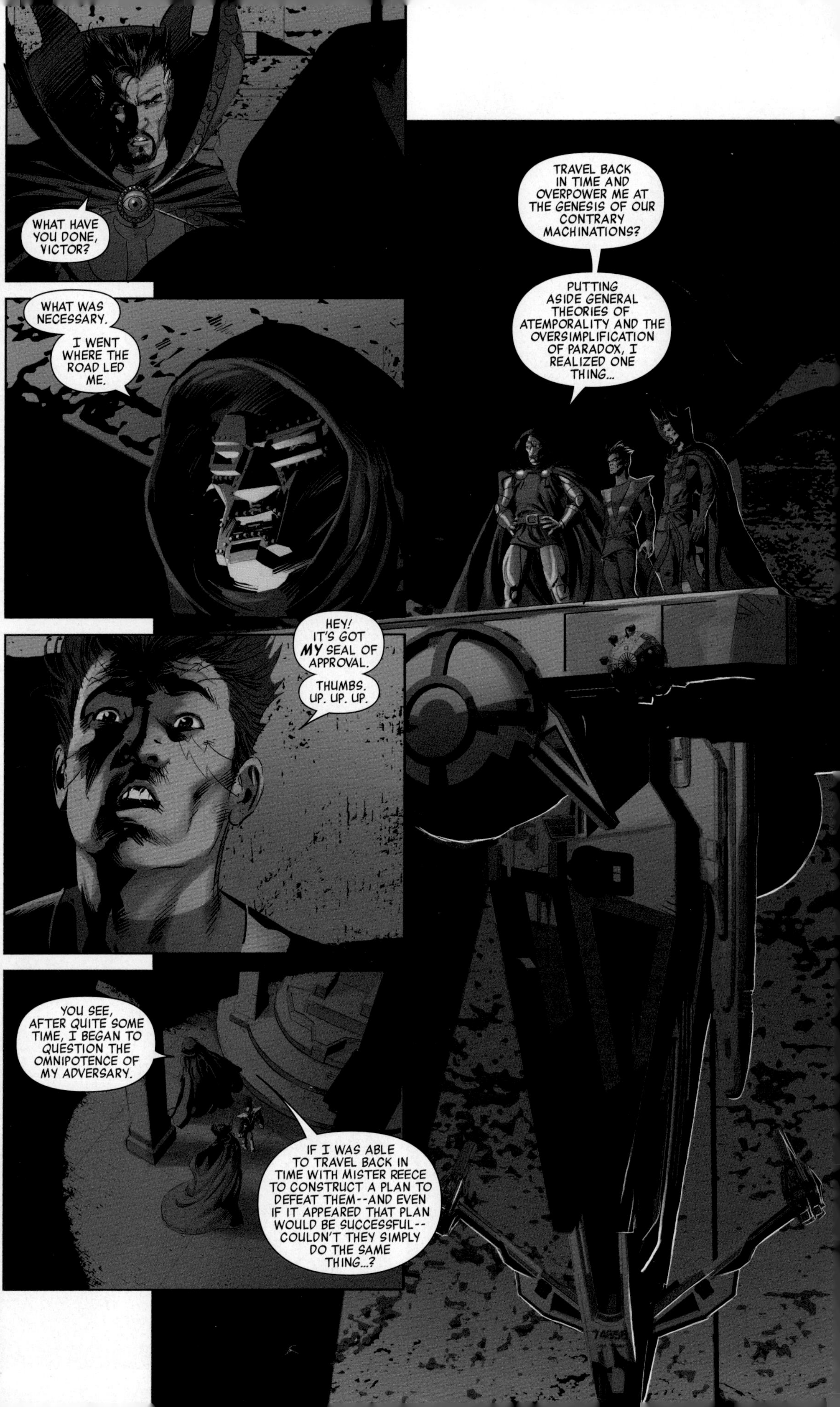
WHAT HAVE YOU DONE, VICTOR?
WHAT WAS NECESSARY.
I WENT WHERE THE ROAD LED ME.
TRAVEL BACK IN TIME AND OVERPOWER ME AT THE GENESIS OF OUR CONTRARY MACHINATIONS?
PUTTING ASIDE GENERAL THEORIES OF ATEMPORALITY AND THE OVERSIMPLIFICATION OF PARADOX, I REALIZED ONE THING...
HEY! IT'S GOT **MY** SEAL OF APPROVAL.
THUMBS. UP. UP. UP.
YOU SEE, AFTER QUITE SOME TIME, I BEGAN TO QUESTION THE OMNIPOTENCE OF MY ADVERSARY.
IF I WAS ABLE TO TRAVEL BACK IN TIME WITH MISTER REECE TO CONSTRUCT A PLAN TO DEFEAT THEM--AND EVEN IF IT APPEARED THAT PLAN WOULD BE SUCCESSFUL--COULDN'T THEY SIMPLY DO THE SAME THING...?

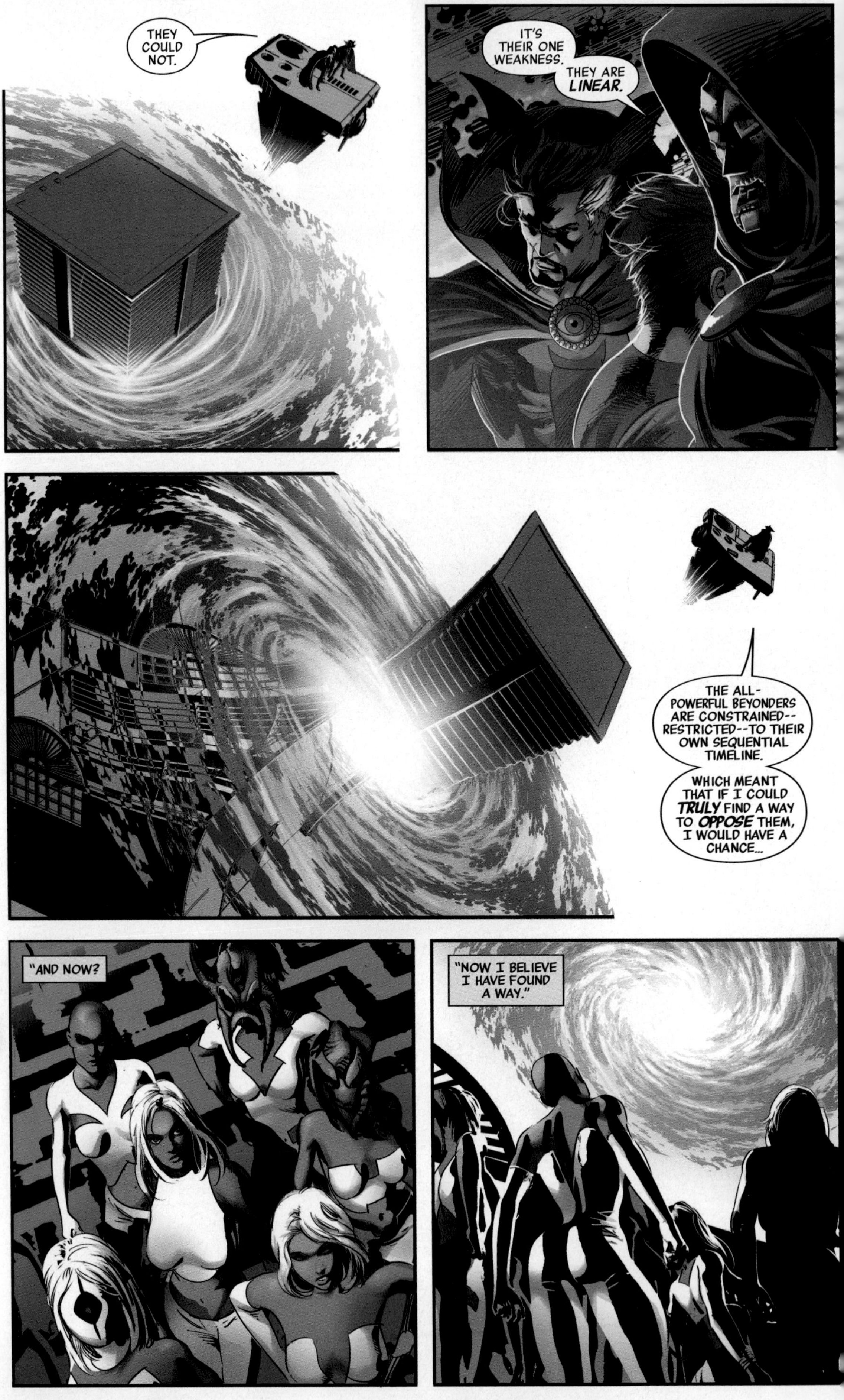
THEY COULD NOT.
IT'S THEIR ONE WEAKNESS.
THEY ARE LINEAR.
THE ALL-POWERFUL BEYONDERS ARE CONSTRAINED--RESTRICTED--TO THEIR OWN SEQUENTIAL TIMELINE.
WHICH MEANT THAT IF I COULD TRULY FIND A WAY TO OPPOSE THEM, I WOULD HAVE A CHANCE...
"AND NOW?
"NOW I BELIEVE I HAVE FOUND A WAY."

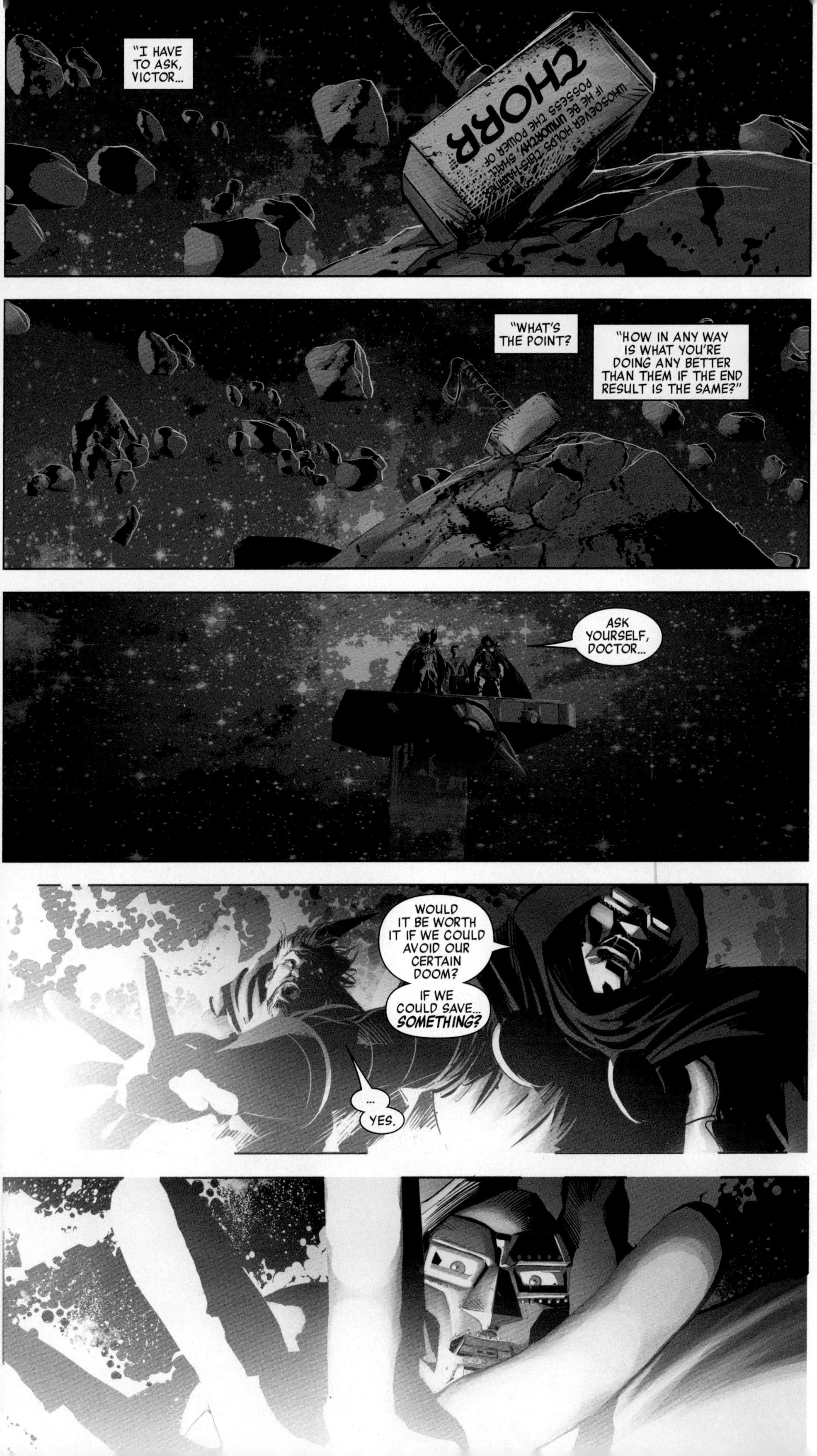
"I HAVE TO ASK, VICTOR...
WHOSOEVER HOLDS THIS HAMMER, IF HE BE UNWORTHY, SHALL POSSESS THE POWER OF
THOR
"WHAT'S THE POINT?
"HOW IN ANY WAY IS WHAT YOU'RE DOING ANY BETTER THAN THEM IF THE END RESULT IS THE SAME?"
ASK YOURSELF, DOCTOR...
WOULD IT BE WORTH IT IF WE COULD AVOID OUR CERTAIN DOOM?
IF WE COULD SAVE... ***SOMETHING?***
... YES.

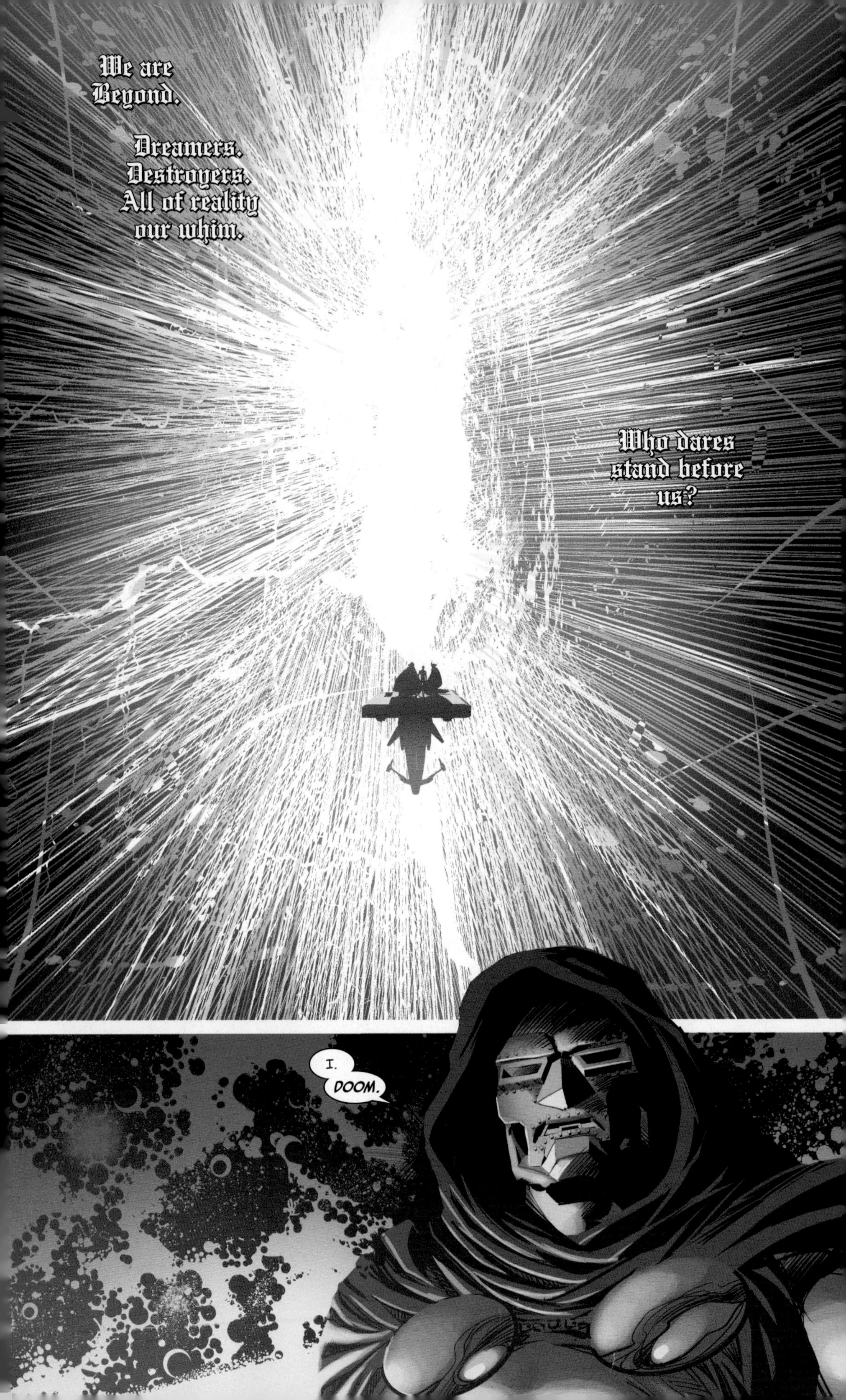
We are Beyond.
Dreamers. Destroyers. All of reality our whim.
Who dares stand before us?
I.
DOOM.

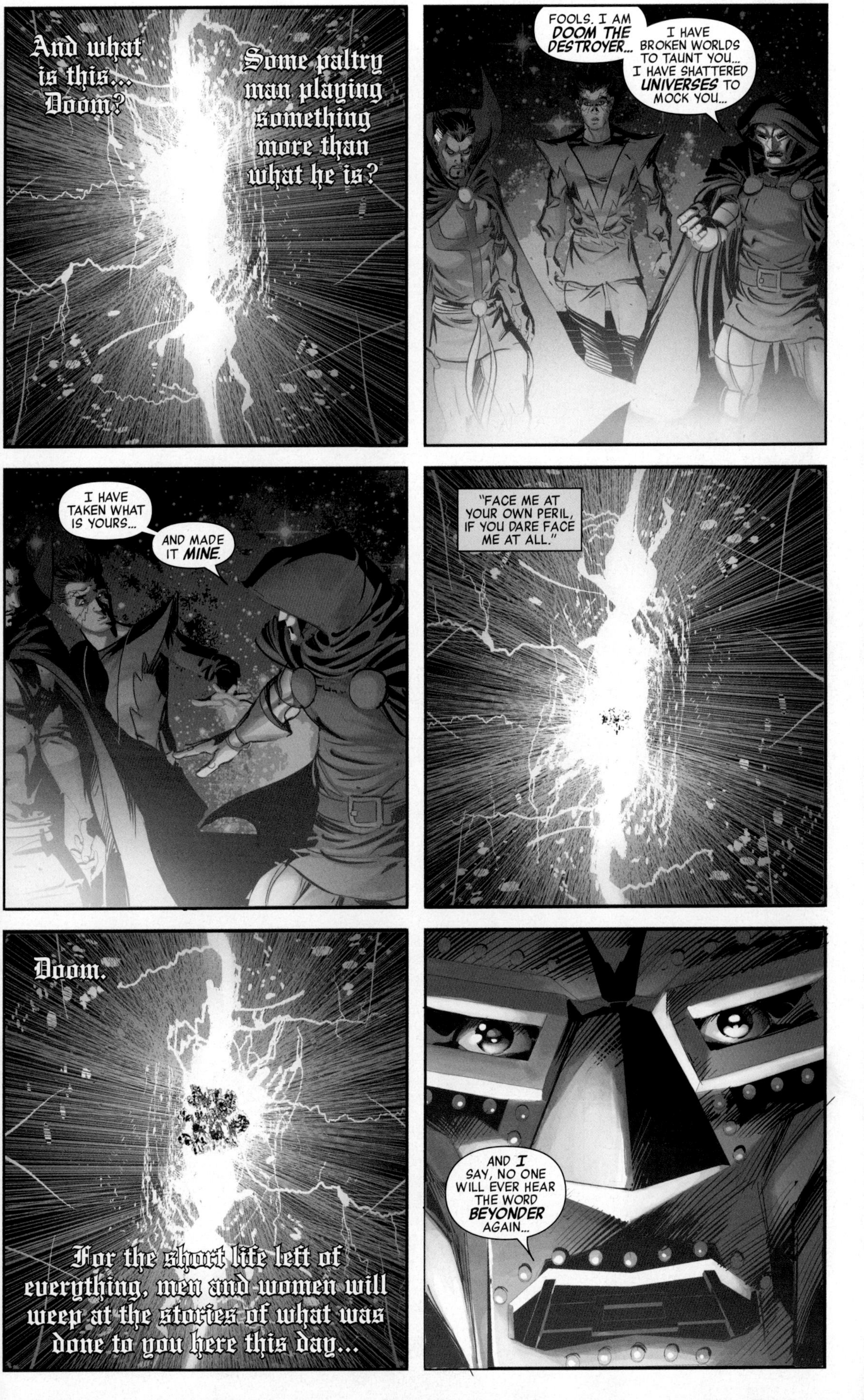
And what is this... Doom?
Some paltry man playing something more than what he is?
FOOLS. I AM DOOM THE DESTROYER...
I HAVE BROKEN WORLDS TO TAUNT YOU... I HAVE SHATTERED UNIVERSES TO MOCK YOU...
I HAVE TAKEN WHAT IS YOURS...
AND MADE IT MINE.
"FACE ME AT YOUR OWN PERIL, IF YOU DARE FACE ME AT ALL."
Doom.
For the short life left of everything, men and women will weep at the stories of what was done to you here this day...
AND I SAY, NO ONE WILL EVER HEAR THE WORD BEYONDER AGAIN...

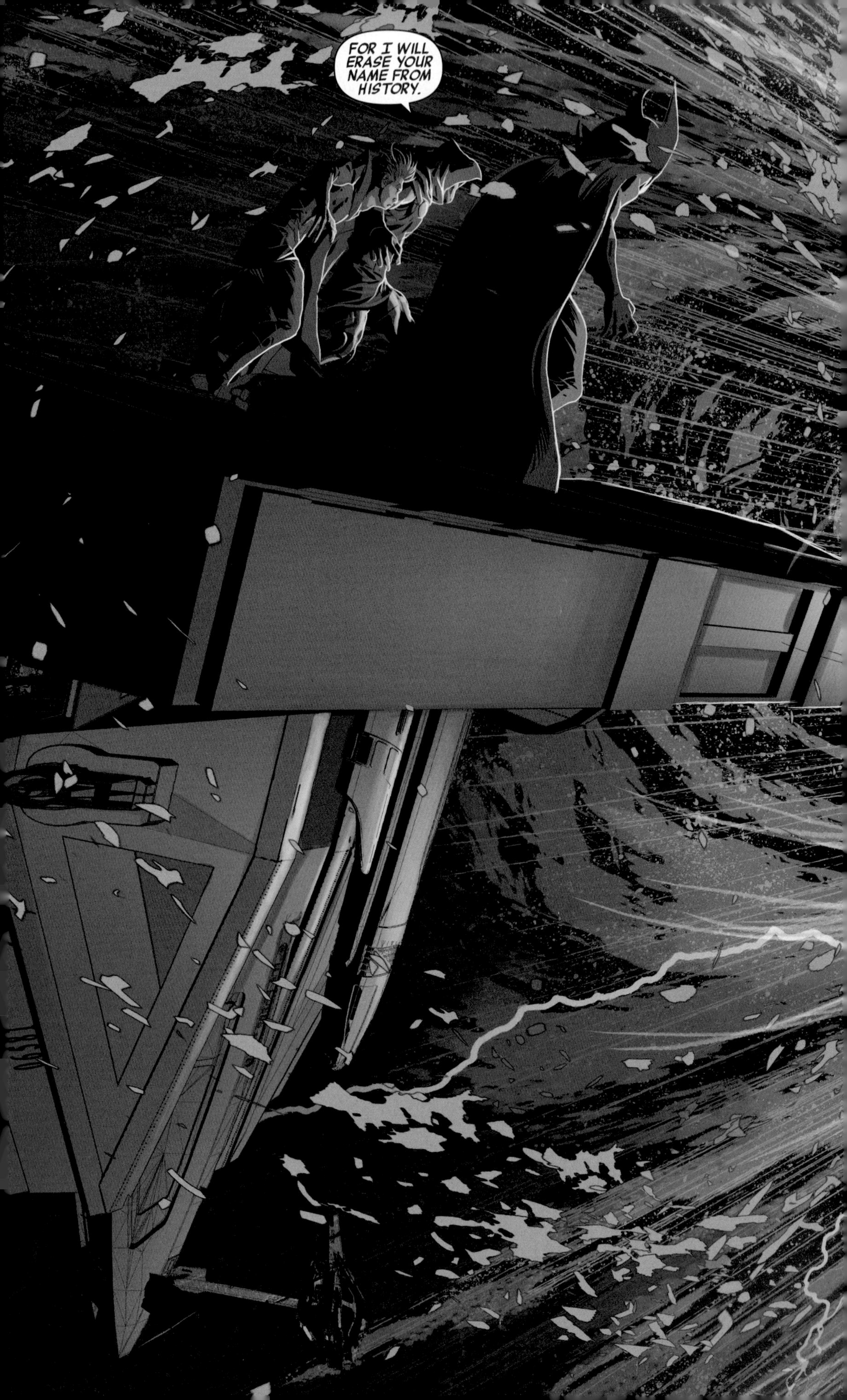
FOR I WILL ERASE YOUR NAME FROM HISTORY.

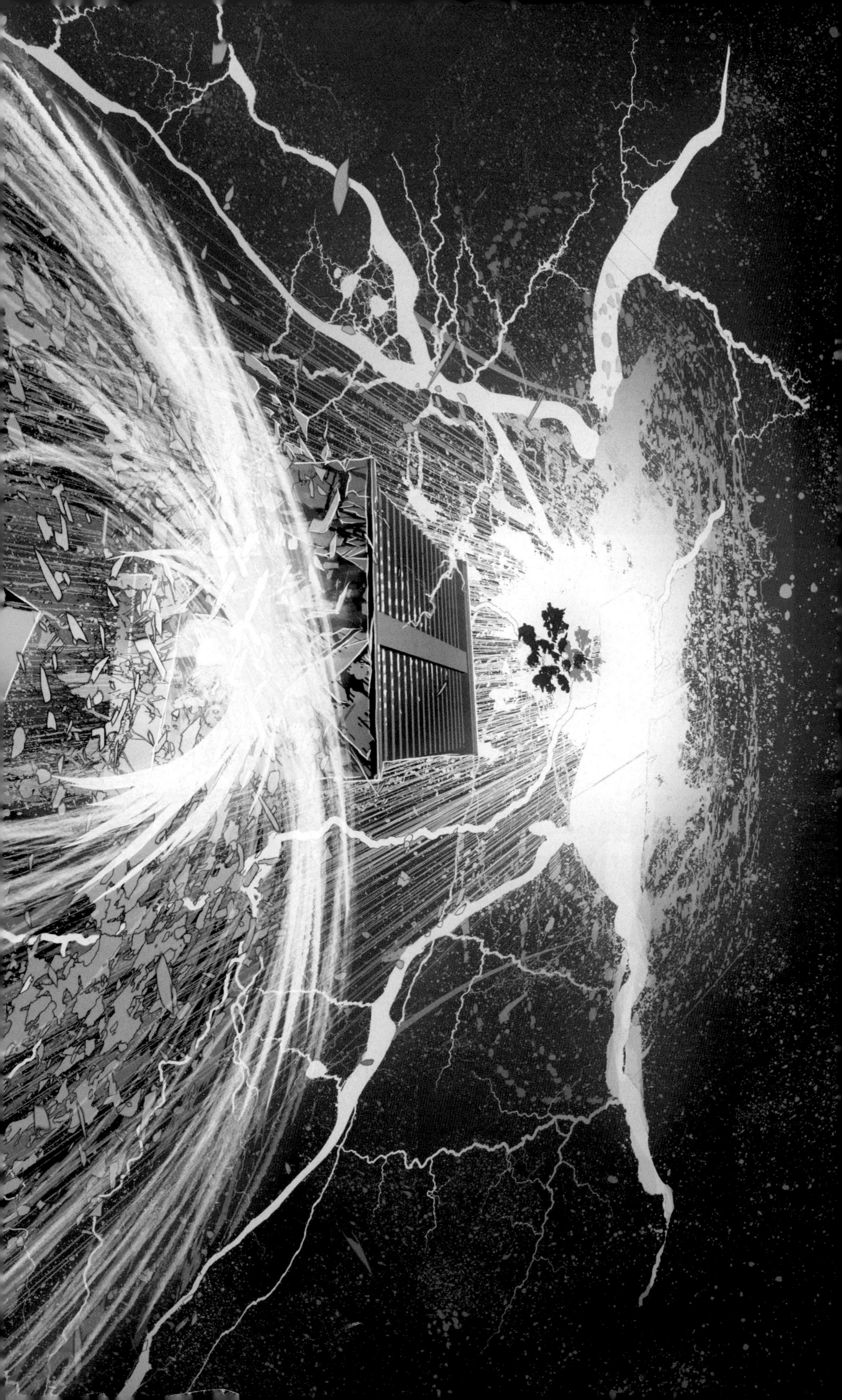

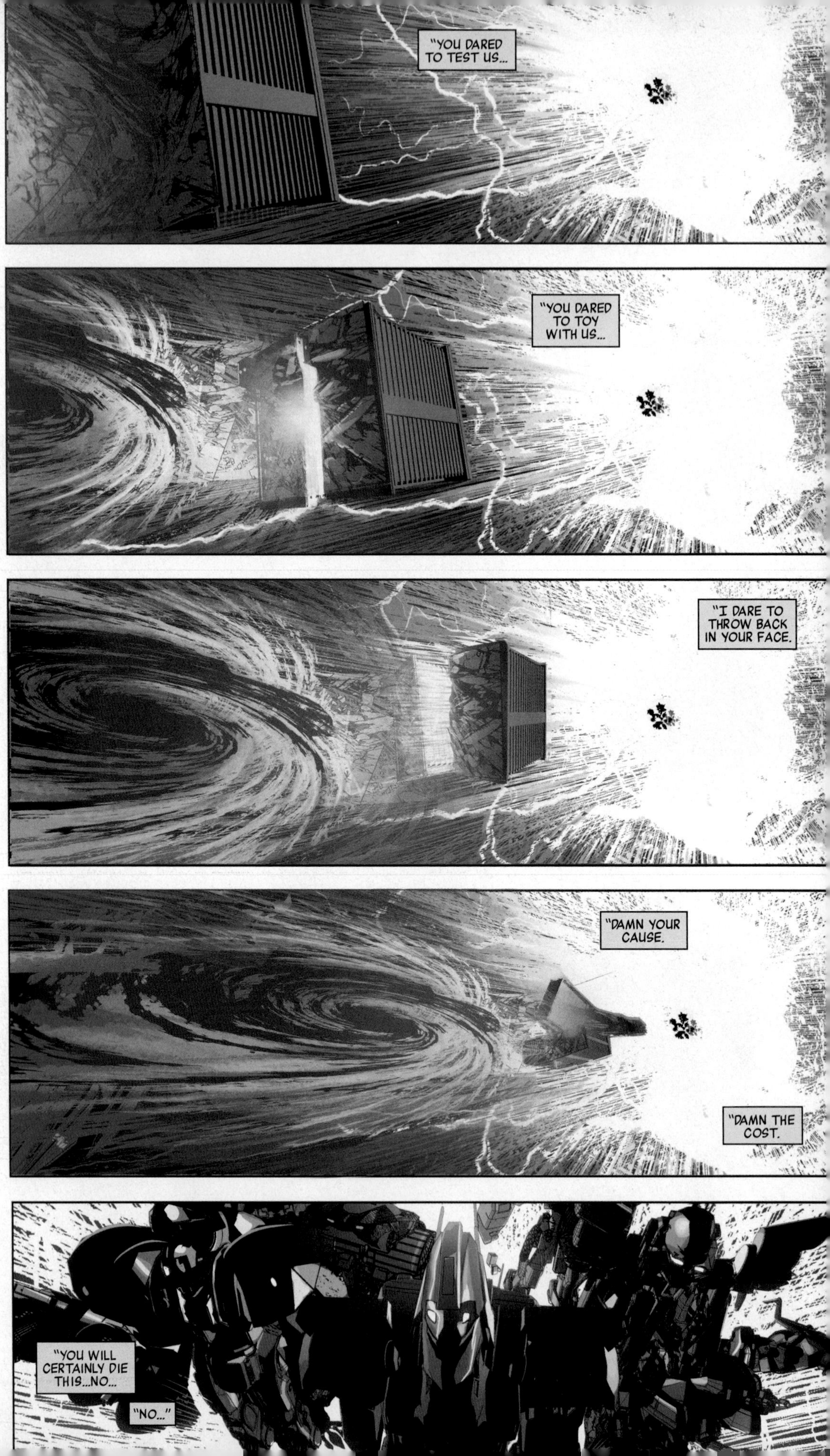
"YOU DARED TO TEST US...
"YOU DARED TO TOY WITH US...
"I DARE TO THROW BACK IN YOUR FACE.
"DAMN YOUR CAUSE.
"DAMN THE COST.
"YOU WILL CERTAINLY DIE THIS...NO...
"NO..."

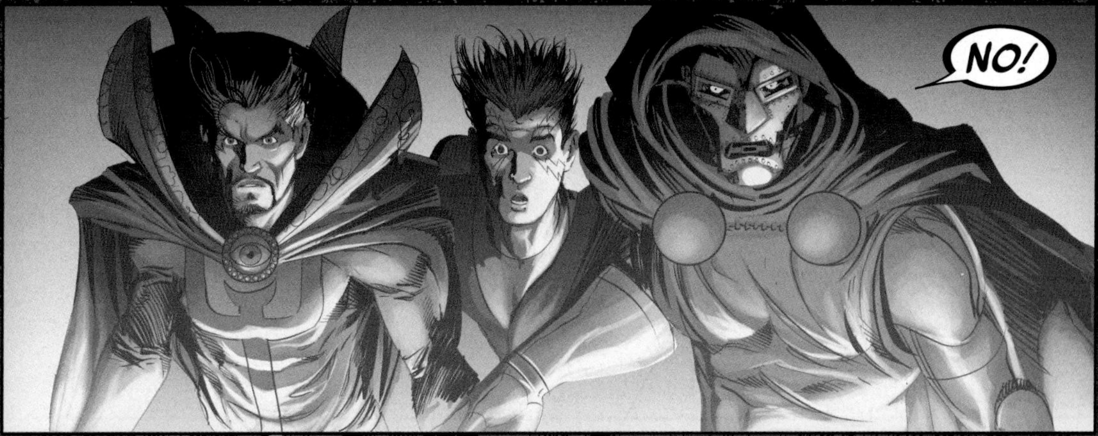
NO!

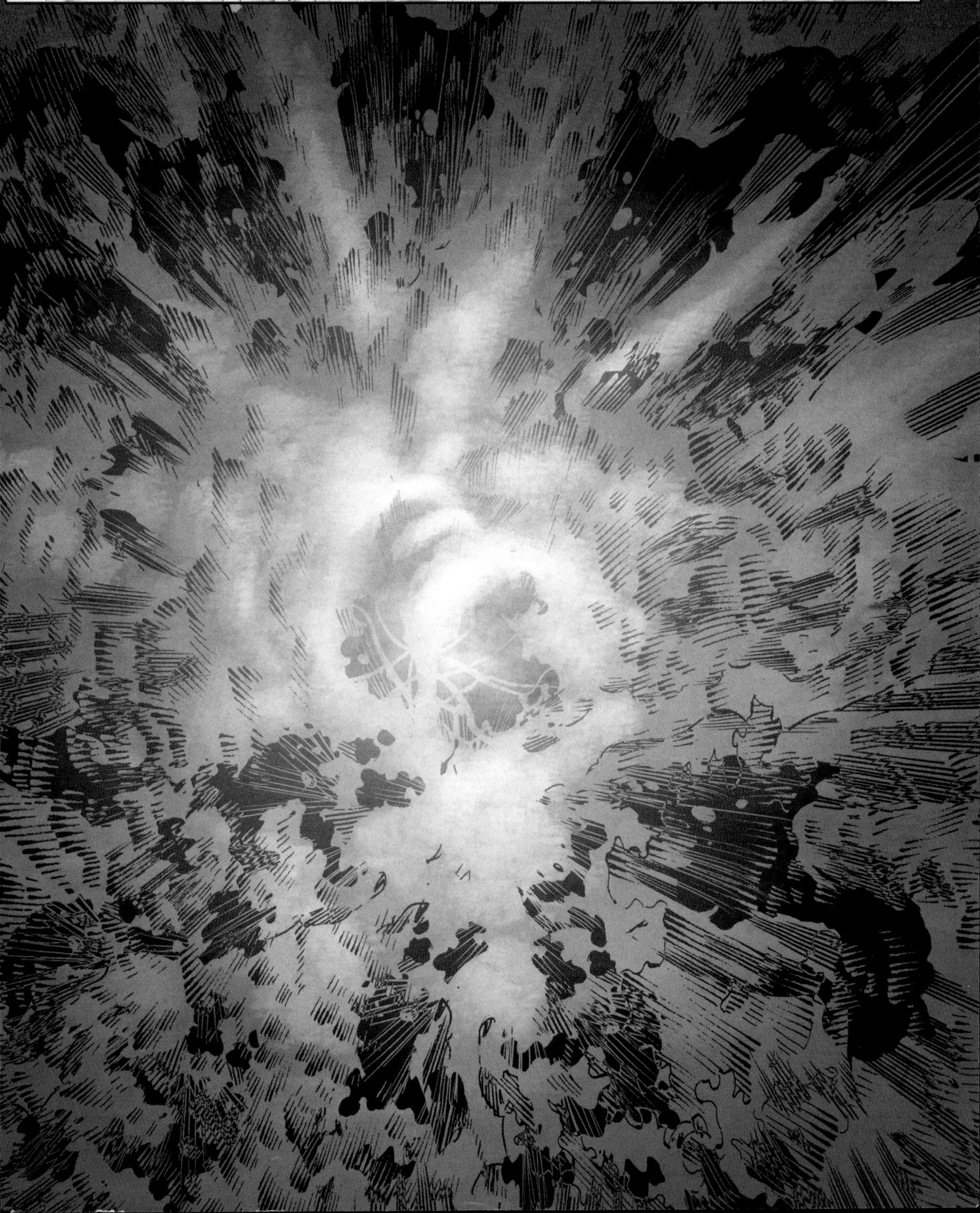

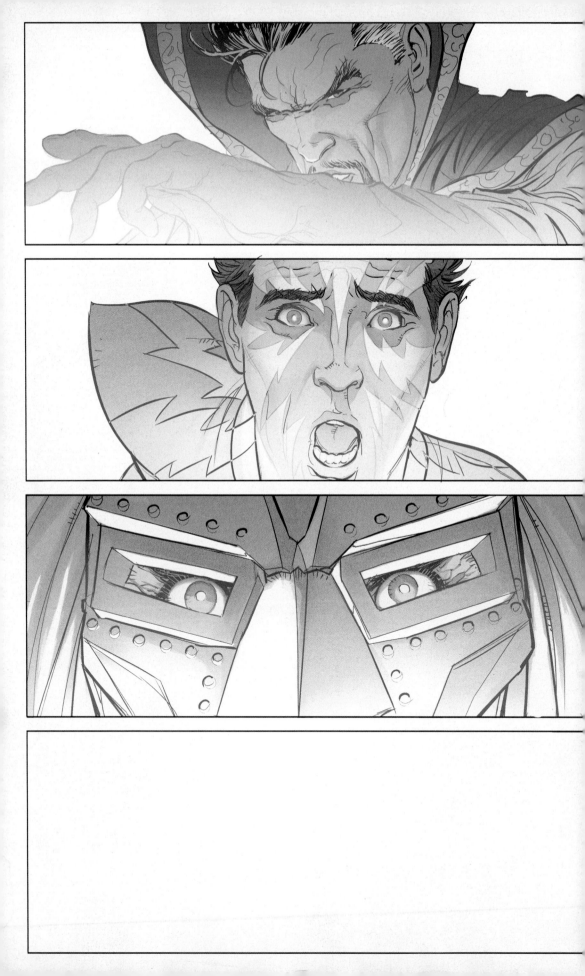

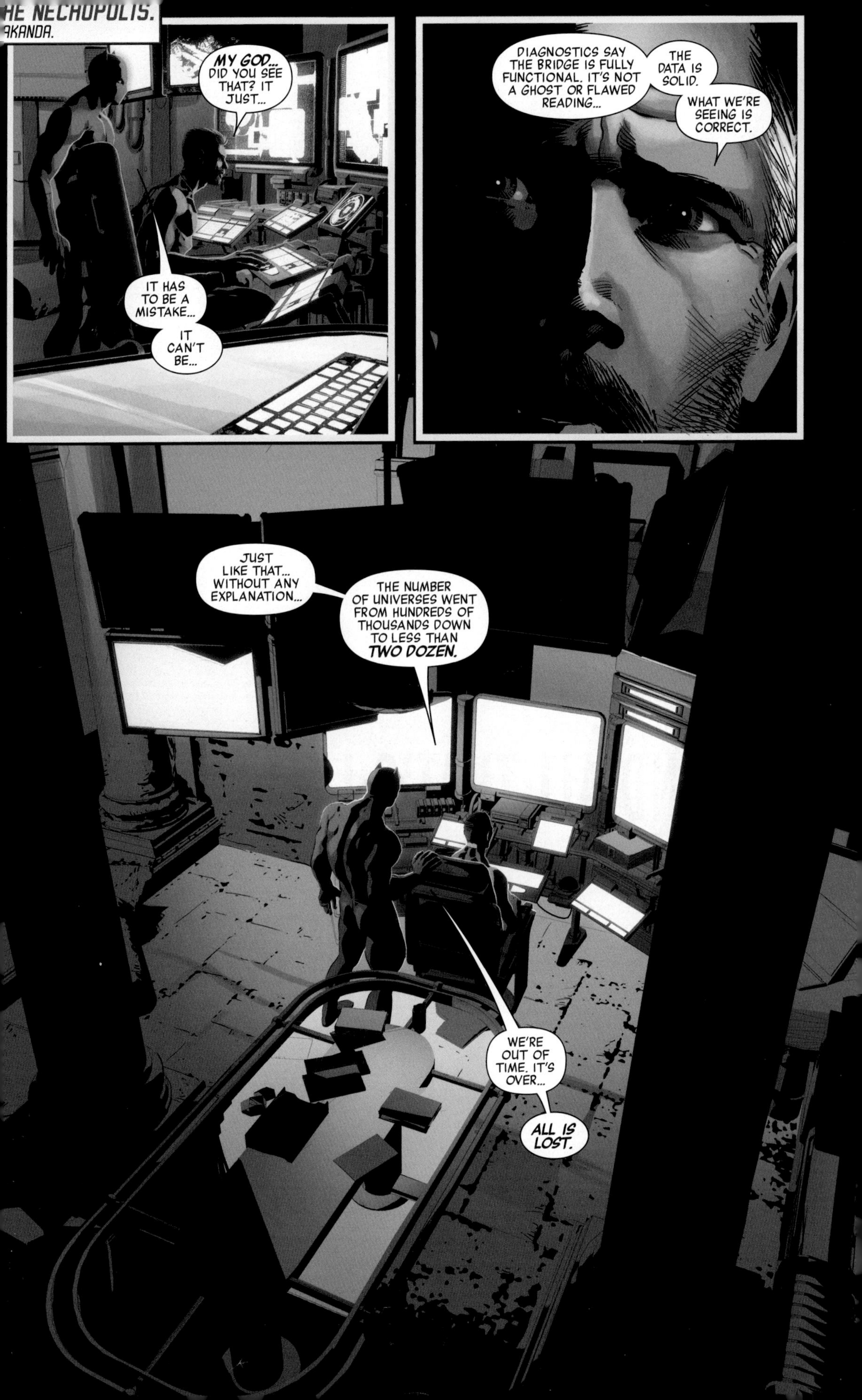
HE NECROPOLIS.
AKANDA.
MY GOD... DID YOU SEE THAT? IT JUST...
IT HAS TO BE A MISTAKE...
IT CAN'T BE...
DIAGNOSTICS SAY THE BRIDGE IS FULLY FUNCTIONAL. IT'S NOT A GHOST OR FLAWED READING...
THE DATA IS SOLID.
WHAT WE'RE SEEING IS CORRECT.
JUST LIKE THAT... WITHOUT ANY EXPLANATION...
THE NUMBER OF UNIVERSES WENT FROM HUNDREDS OF THOUSANDS DOWN TO LESS THAN TWO DOZEN.
WE'RE OUT OF TIME. IT'S OVER...
ALL IS LOST.

"...AND ALL THAT'S LEFT IS ASHES"

THE ILLUMINATI

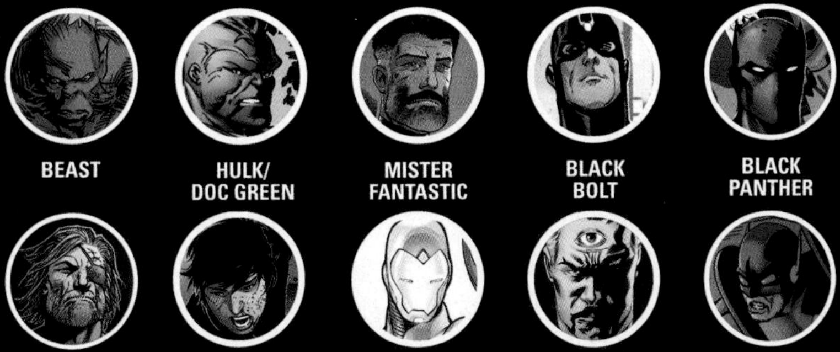

BEAST · HULK/DOC GREEN · MISTER FANTASTIC · BLACK BOLT · BLACK PANTHER
CAPTAIN BRITAIN · AMADEUS CHO · IRON MAN · DOCTOR STRANGE · YELLOWJACKET

S.H.I.E.L.D. AVENGERS

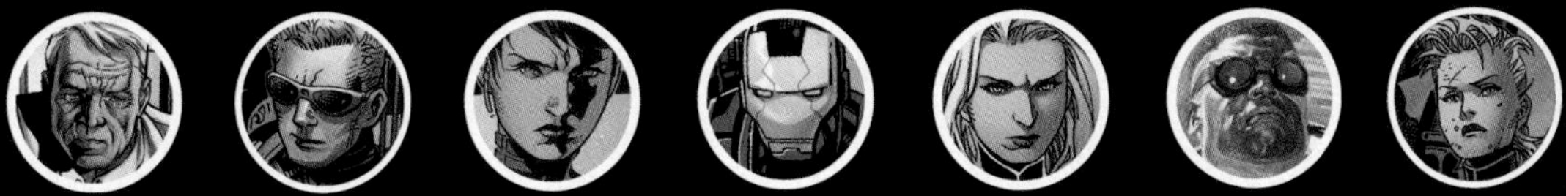

STEVE ROGERS · HAWKEYE · MARIA HILL · WAR MACHINE · INVISIBLE WOMAN · CAPTAIN AMERICA · CAPTAIN MARVEL

NEW AVENGERS

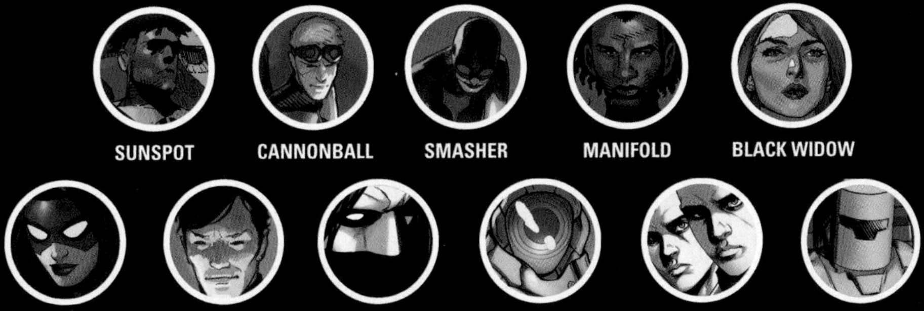

SUNSPOT · CANNONBALL · SMASHER · MANIFOLD · BLACK WIDOW
SPIDER-WOMAN · SHANG-CHI · VALIDATOR · POD · ZEBRA KIDS · A.I.M.

THE CABAL

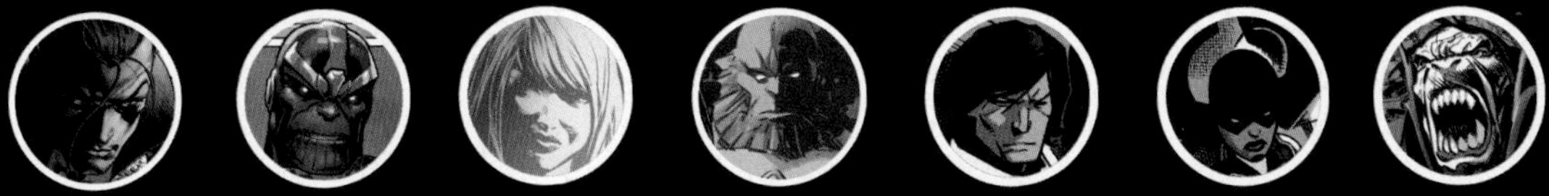

NAMOR · THANOS · BLACK SWAN · TERRAX · MAXIMUS · PROXIMA MIDNIGHT · CORVUS GLAIVE

THE GUARDIANS OF THE GALAXY

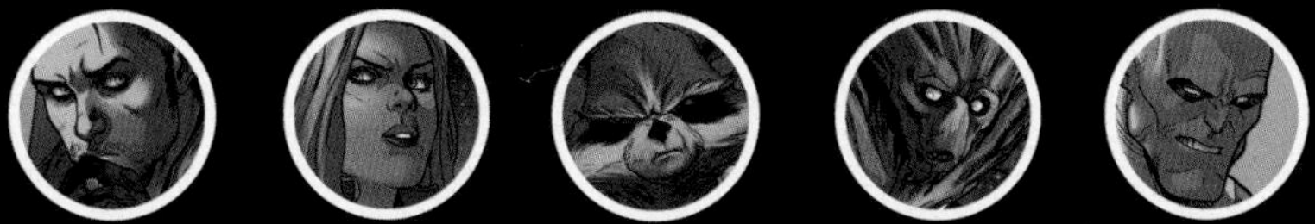

STAR-LORD · GAMORA · ROCKET RACCOON · GROOT · DRAX

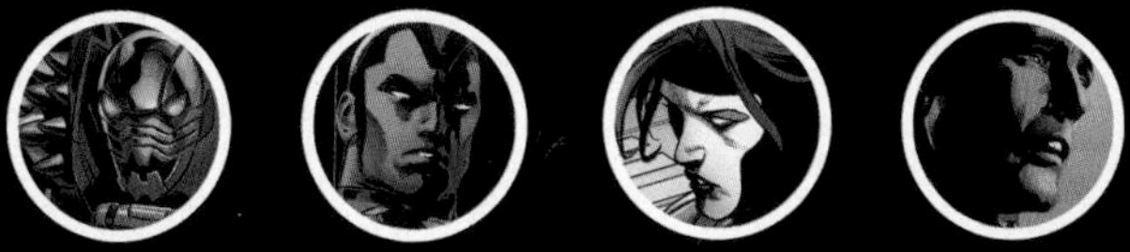

ANNIHILUS · GLADIATOR · ORACLE · MENTOR

PREVIOUSLY IN AVENGERS

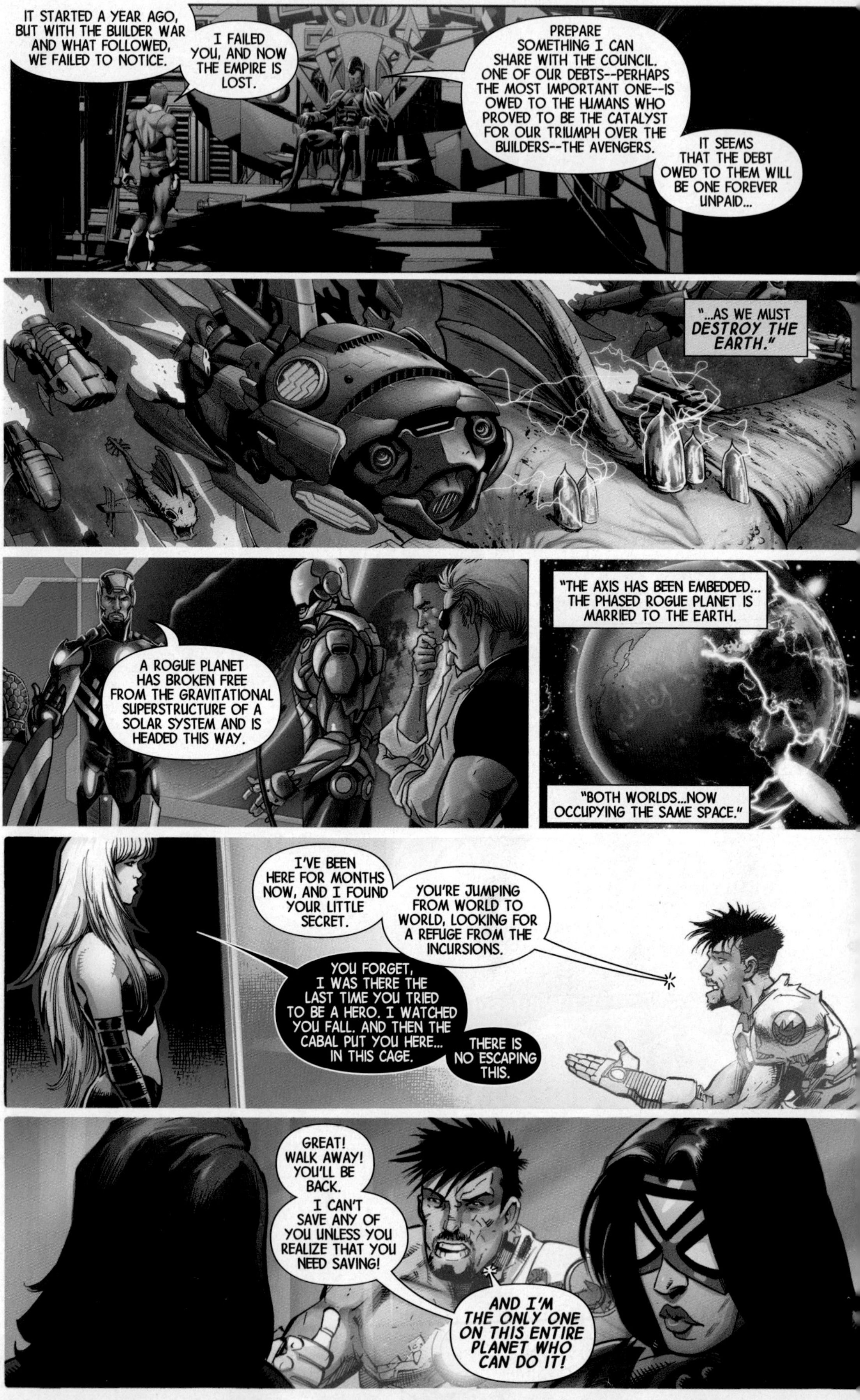
IT STARTED A YEAR AGO, BUT WITH THE BUILDER WAR AND WHAT FOLLOWED, WE FAILED TO NOTICE.
I FAILED YOU, AND NOW THE EMPIRE IS LOST.
PREPARE SOMETHING I CAN SHARE WITH THE COUNCIL. ONE OF OUR DEBTS--PERHAPS THE MOST IMPORTANT ONE--IS OWED TO THE HUMANS WHO PROVED TO BE THE CATALYST FOR OUR TRIUMPH OVER THE BUILDERS--THE AVENGERS.
IT SEEMS THAT THE DEBT OWED TO THEM WILL BE ONE FOREVER UNPAID...
"...AS WE MUST *DESTROY THE EARTH.*"
A ROGUE PLANET HAS BROKEN FREE FROM THE GRAVITATIONAL SUPERSTRUCTURE OF A SOLAR SYSTEM AND IS HEADED THIS WAY.
"THE AXIS HAS BEEN EMBEDDED... THE PHASED ROGUE PLANET IS MARRIED TO THE EARTH.
"BOTH WORLDS...NOW OCCUPYING THE SAME SPACE."
I'VE BEEN HERE FOR MONTHS NOW, AND I FOUND YOUR LITTLE SECRET.
YOU'RE JUMPING FROM WORLD TO WORLD, LOOKING FOR A REFUGE FROM THE INCURSIONS.
YOU FORGET, I WAS THERE THE LAST TIME YOU TRIED TO BE A HERO. I WATCHED YOU FALL. AND THEN THE CABAL PUT YOU HERE... IN THIS CAGE.
THERE IS NO ESCAPING THIS.
GREAT! WALK AWAY! YOU'LL BE BACK.
I CAN'T SAVE ANY OF YOU UNLESS YOU REALIZE THAT YOU NEED SAVING!
AND I'M THE ONLY ONE ON THIS ENTIRE PLANET WHO CAN DO IT!

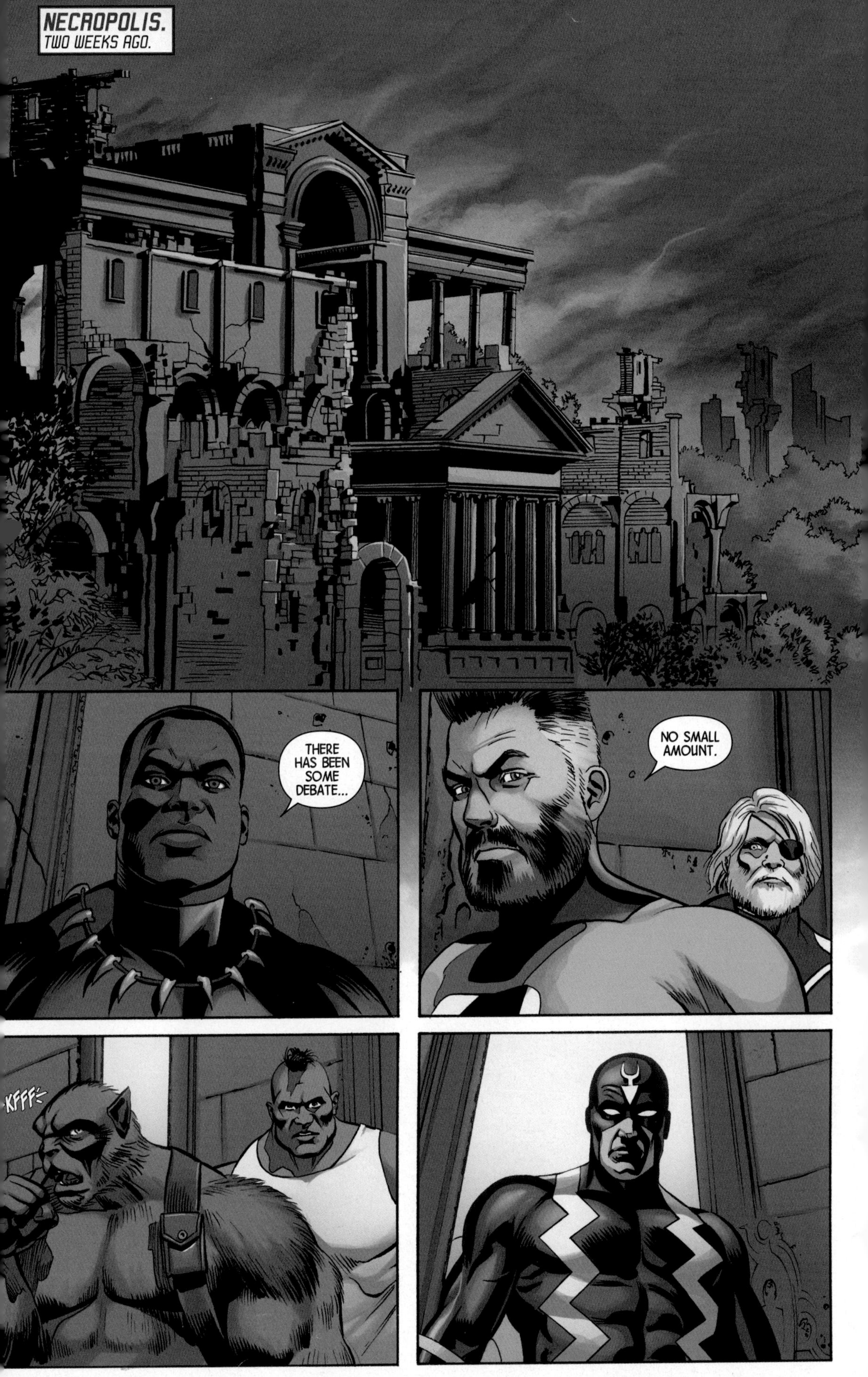
NECROPOLIS.
TWO WEEKS AGO.
THERE HAS BEEN SOME DEBATE...
NO SMALL AMOUNT.
KFFF

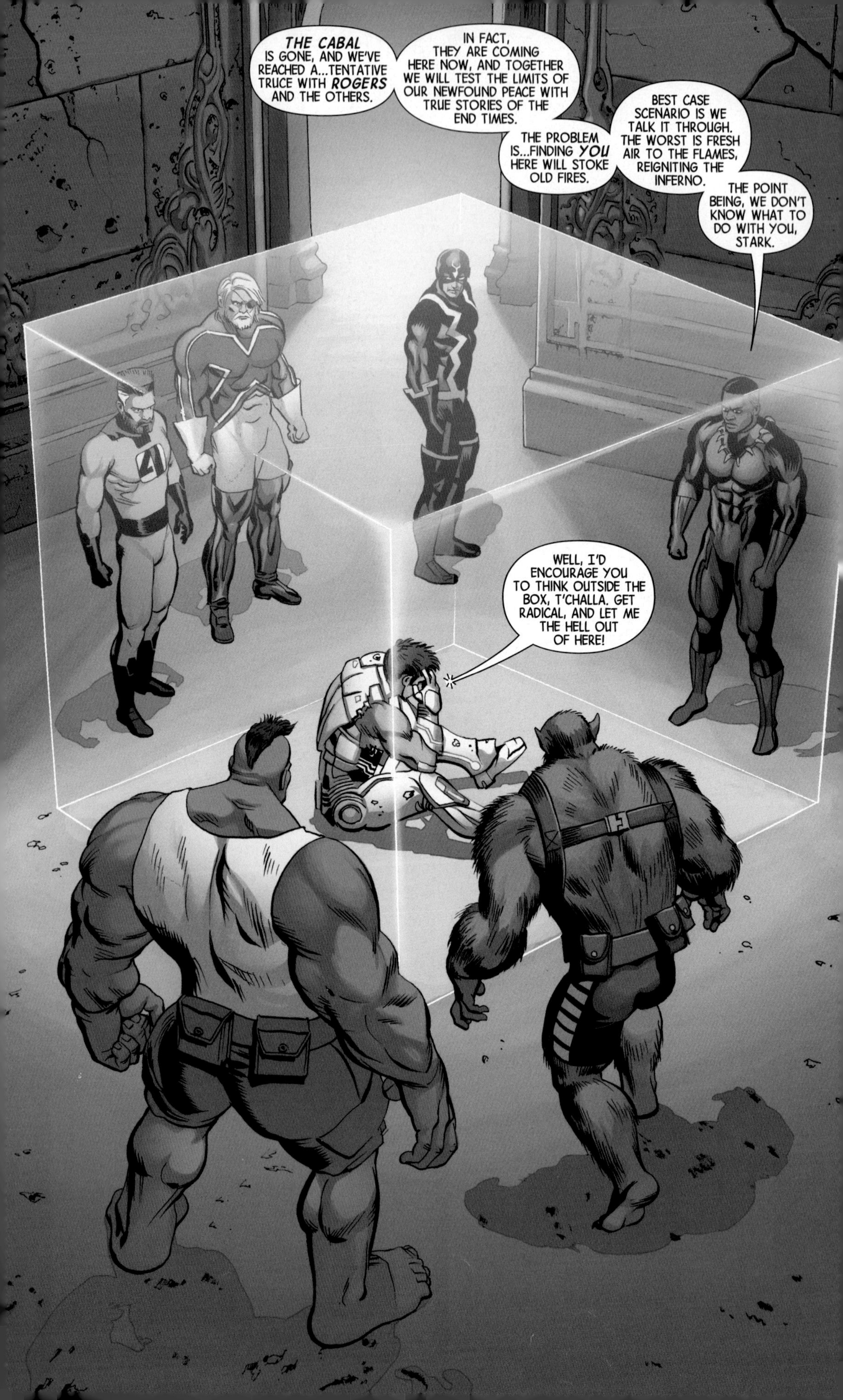
THE CABAL IS GONE, AND WE'VE REACHED A...TENTATIVE TRUCE WITH ROGERS AND THE OTHERS.
IN FACT, THEY ARE COMING HERE NOW, AND TOGETHER WE WILL TEST THE LIMITS OF OUR NEWFOUND PEACE WITH TRUE STORIES OF THE END TIMES.
THE PROBLEM IS...FINDING YOU HERE WILL STOKE OLD FIRES.
BEST CASE SCENARIO IS WE TALK IT THROUGH. THE WORST IS FRESH AIR TO THE FLAMES, REIGNITING THE INFERNO.
THE POINT BEING, WE DON'T KNOW WHAT TO DO WITH YOU, STARK.
WELL, I'D ENCOURAGE YOU TO THINK OUTSIDE THE BOX, T'CHALLA. GET RADICAL, AND LET ME THE HELL OUT OF HERE!

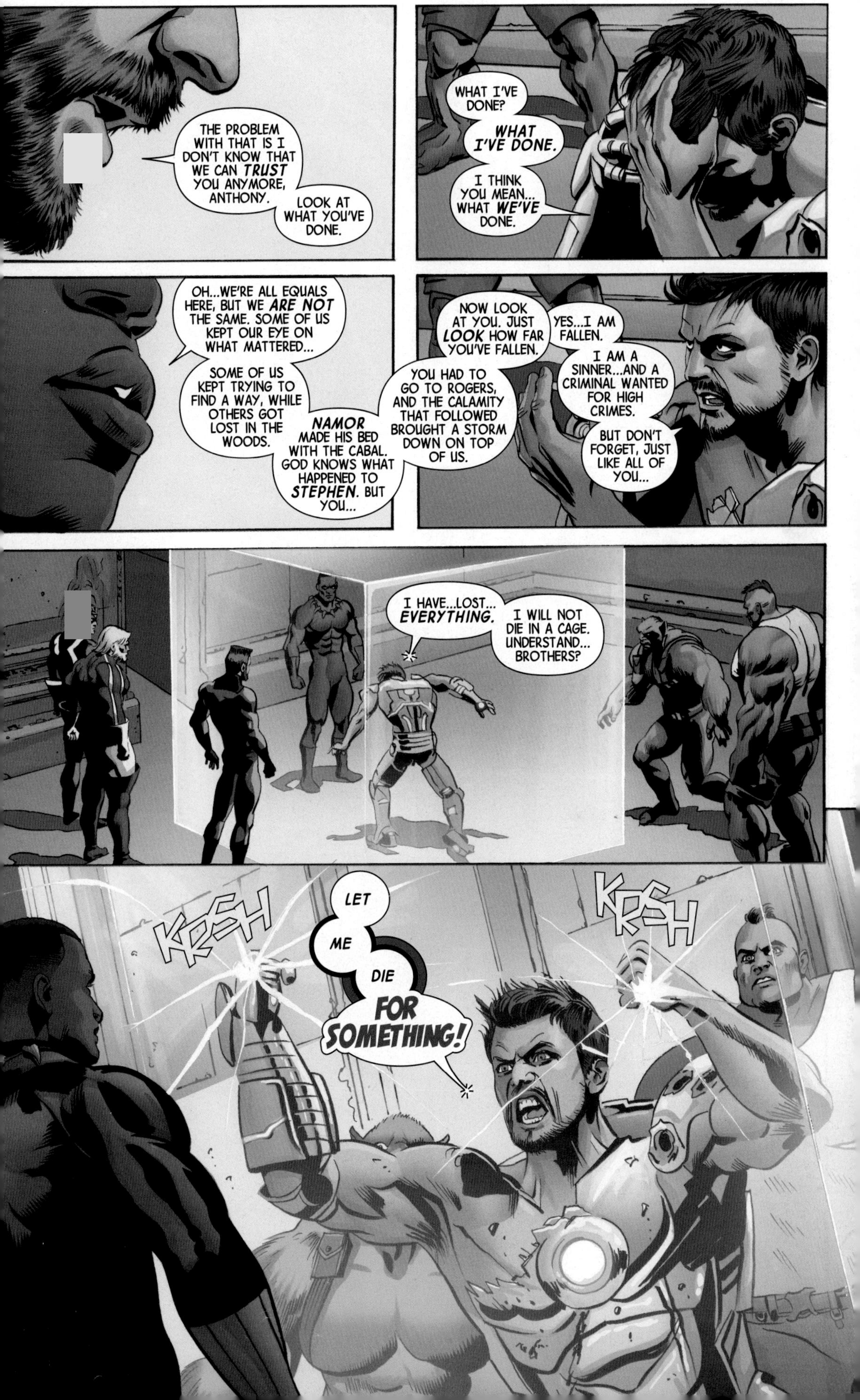
THE PROBLEM WITH THAT IS I DON'T KNOW THAT WE CAN TRUST YOU ANYMORE, ANTHONY.
LOOK AT WHAT YOU'VE DONE.
WHAT I'VE DONE?
WHAT I'VE DONE.
I THINK YOU MEAN... WHAT WE'VE DONE.
OH...WE'RE ALL EQUALS HERE, BUT WE ARE NOT THE SAME. SOME OF US KEPT OUR EYE ON WHAT MATTERED...
SOME OF US KEPT TRYING TO FIND A WAY, WHILE OTHERS GOT LOST IN THE WOODS.
NAMOR MADE HIS BED WITH THE CABAL. GOD KNOWS WHAT HAPPENED TO STEPHEN. BUT YOU...
YOU HAD TO GO TO ROGERS, AND THE CALAMITY THAT FOLLOWED BROUGHT A STORM DOWN ON TOP OF US.
NOW LOOK AT YOU. JUST LOOK HOW FAR YOU'VE FALLEN.
YES...I AM FALLEN.
I AM A SINNER...AND A CRIMINAL WANTED FOR HIGH CRIMES.
BUT DON'T FORGET, JUST LIKE ALL OF YOU...
I HAVE...LOST... EVERYTHING.
I WILL NOT DIE IN A CAGE. UNDERSTAND... BROTHERS?
KRSH
LET ME DIE FOR SOMETHING!
KRSH

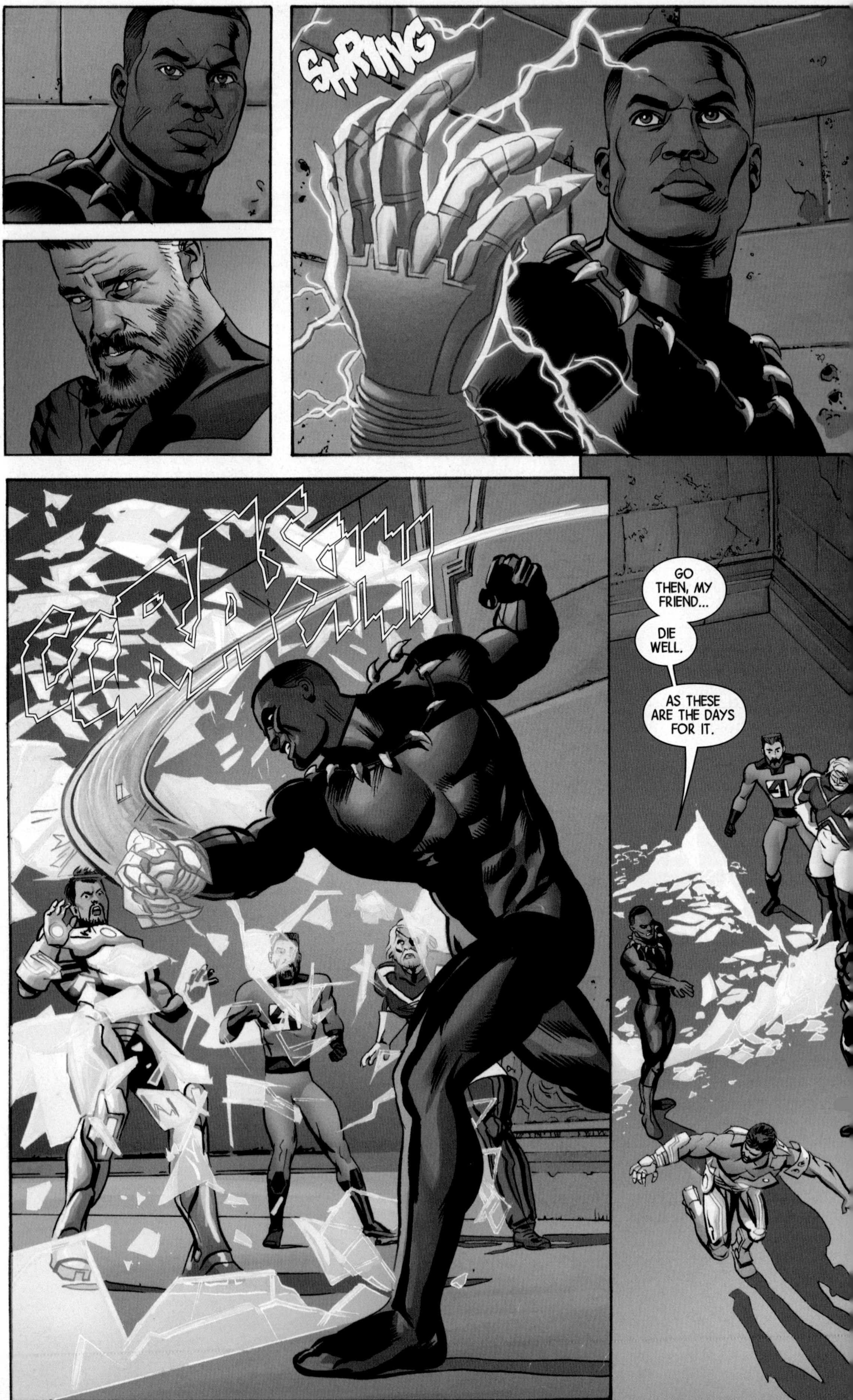
SHING
GO THEN, MY FRIEND...
DIE WELL.
AS THESE ARE THE DAYS FOR IT.

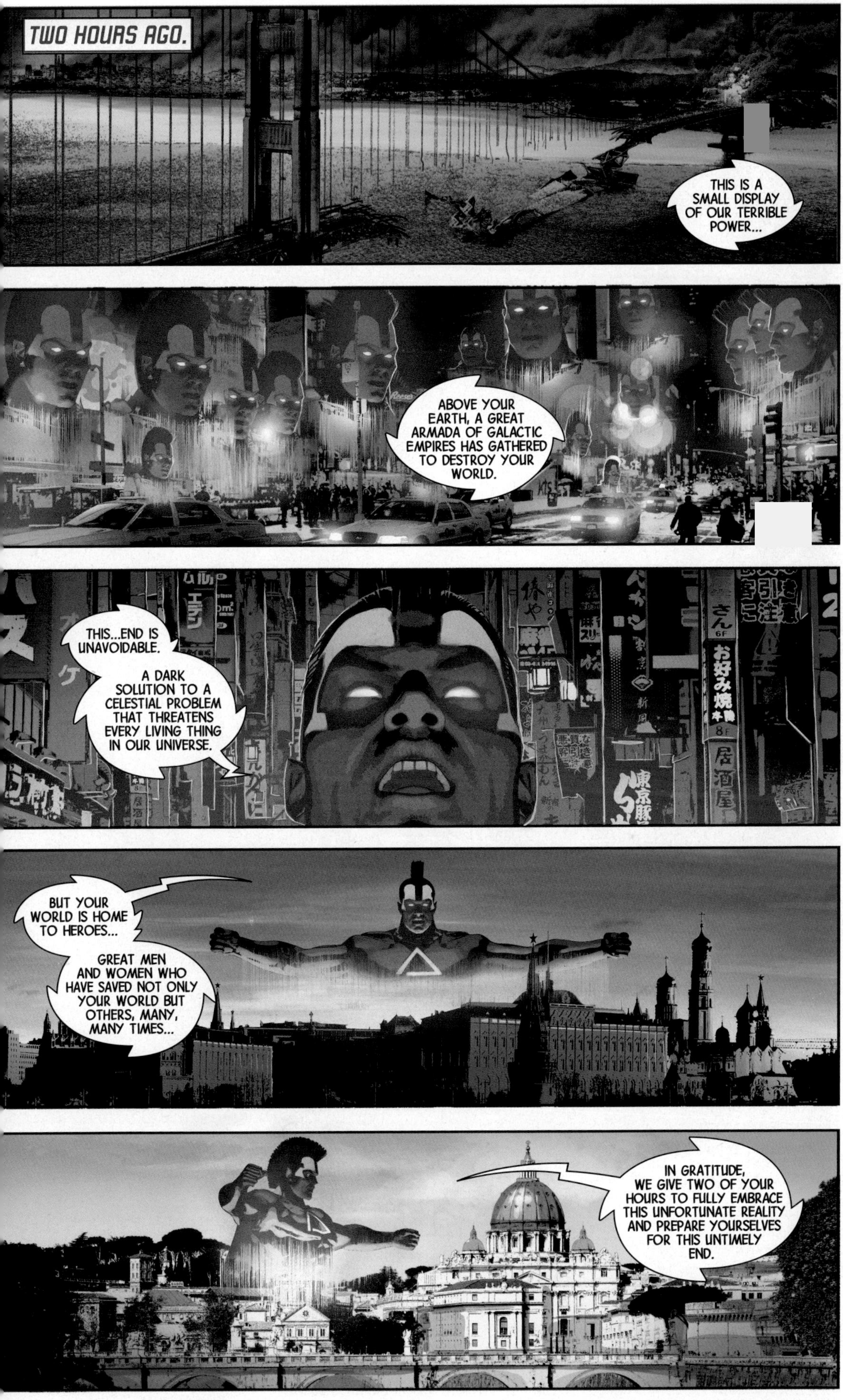
TWO HOURS AGO.
THIS IS A SMALL DISPLAY OF OUR TERRIBLE POWER...
ABOVE YOUR EARTH, A GREAT ARMADA OF GALACTIC EMPIRES HAS GATHERED TO DESTROY YOUR WORLD.
THIS...END IS UNAVOIDABLE.
A DARK SOLUTION TO A CELESTIAL PROBLEM THAT THREATENS EVERY LIVING THING IN OUR UNIVERSE.
BUT YOUR WORLD IS HOME TO HEROES...
GREAT MEN AND WOMEN WHO HAVE SAVED NOT ONLY YOUR WORLD BUT OTHERS, MANY, MANY TIMES...
IN GRATITUDE, WE GIVE TWO OF YOUR HOURS TO FULLY EMBRACE THIS UNFORTUNATE REALITY AND PREPARE YOURSELVES FOR THIS UNTIMELY END.

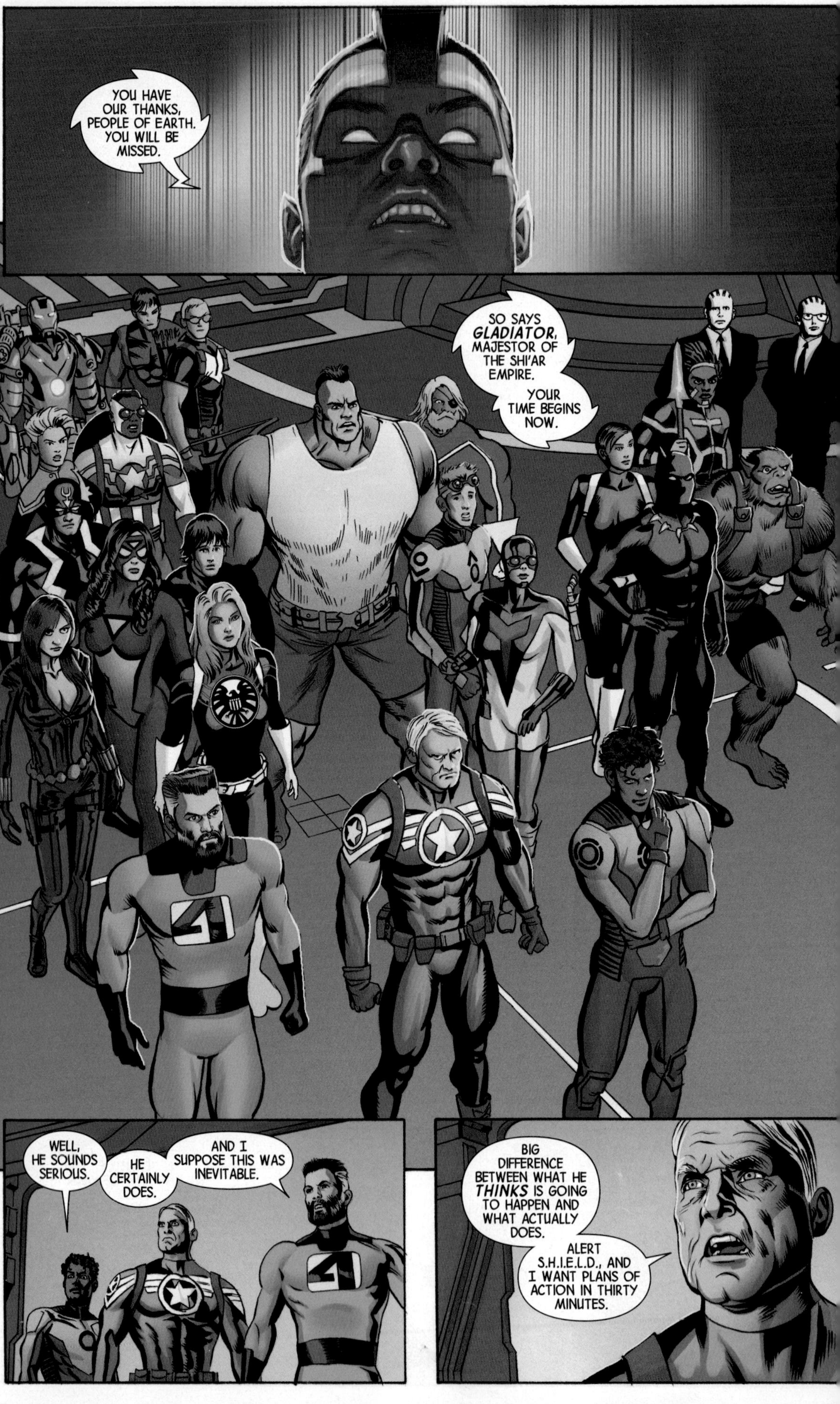
YOU HAVE OUR THANKS, PEOPLE OF EARTH. YOU WILL BE MISSED.
SO SAYS GLADIATOR, MAJESTOR OF THE SHI'AR EMPIRE.
YOUR TIME BEGINS NOW.
WELL, HE SOUNDS SERIOUS.
HE CERTAINLY DOES.
AND I SUPPOSE THIS WAS INEVITABLE.
BIG DIFFERENCE BETWEEN WHAT HE THINKS IS GOING TO HAPPEN AND WHAT ACTUALLY DOES.
ALERT S.H.I.E.L.D., AND I WANT PLANS OF ACTION IN THIRTY MINUTES.

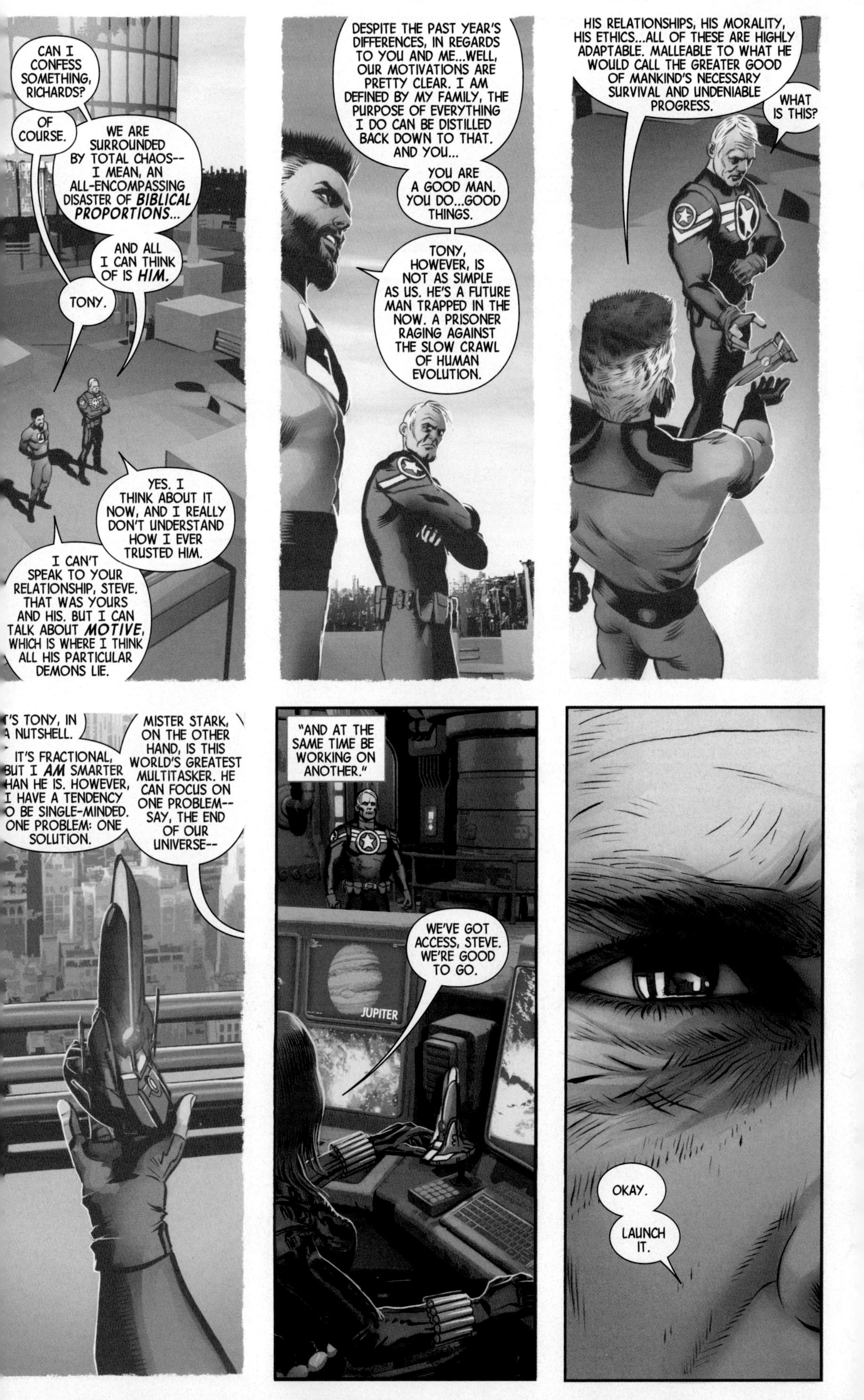

CAN I CONFESS SOMETHING, RICHARDS?
OF COURSE.
WE ARE SURROUNDED BY TOTAL CHAOS-- I MEAN, AN ALL-ENCOMPASSING DISASTER OF BIBLICAL PROPORTIONS...
AND ALL I CAN THINK OF IS HIM.
TONY.
YES. I THINK ABOUT IT NOW, AND I REALLY DON'T UNDERSTAND HOW I EVER TRUSTED HIM.
I CAN'T SPEAK TO YOUR RELATIONSHIP, STEVE. THAT WAS YOURS AND HIS. BUT I CAN TALK ABOUT MOTIVE, WHICH IS WHERE I THINK ALL HIS PARTICULAR DEMONS LIE.
DESPITE THE PAST YEAR'S DIFFERENCES, IN REGARDS TO YOU AND ME...WELL, OUR MOTIVATIONS ARE PRETTY CLEAR. I AM DEFINED BY MY FAMILY, THE PURPOSE OF EVERYTHING I DO CAN BE DISTILLED BACK DOWN TO THAT. AND YOU...
YOU ARE A GOOD MAN. YOU DO...GOOD THINGS.
TONY, HOWEVER, IS NOT AS SIMPLE AS US. HE'S A FUTURE MAN TRAPPED IN THE NOW. A PRISONER RAGING AGAINST THE SLOW CRAWL OF HUMAN EVOLUTION.
HIS RELATIONSHIPS, HIS MORALITY, HIS ETHICS...ALL OF THESE ARE HIGHLY ADAPTABLE. MALLEABLE TO WHAT HE WOULD CALL THE GREATER GOOD OF MANKIND'S NECESSARY SURVIVAL AND UNDENIABLE PROGRESS.
WHAT IS THIS?
'S TONY, IN NUTSHELL.
IT'S FRACTIONAL, BUT I AM SMARTER HAN HE IS. HOWEVER, I HAVE A TENDENCY O BE SINGLE-MINDED. ONE PROBLEM: ONE SOLUTION.
MISTER STARK, ON THE OTHER HAND, IS THIS WORLD'S GREATEST MULTITASKER. HE CAN FOCUS ON ONE PROBLEM-- SAY, THE END OF OUR UNIVERSE--
"AND AT THE SAME TIME BE WORKING ON ANOTHER."
JUPITER
WE'VE GOT ACCESS, STEVE. WE'RE GOOD TO GO.
OKAY.
LAUNCH IT.

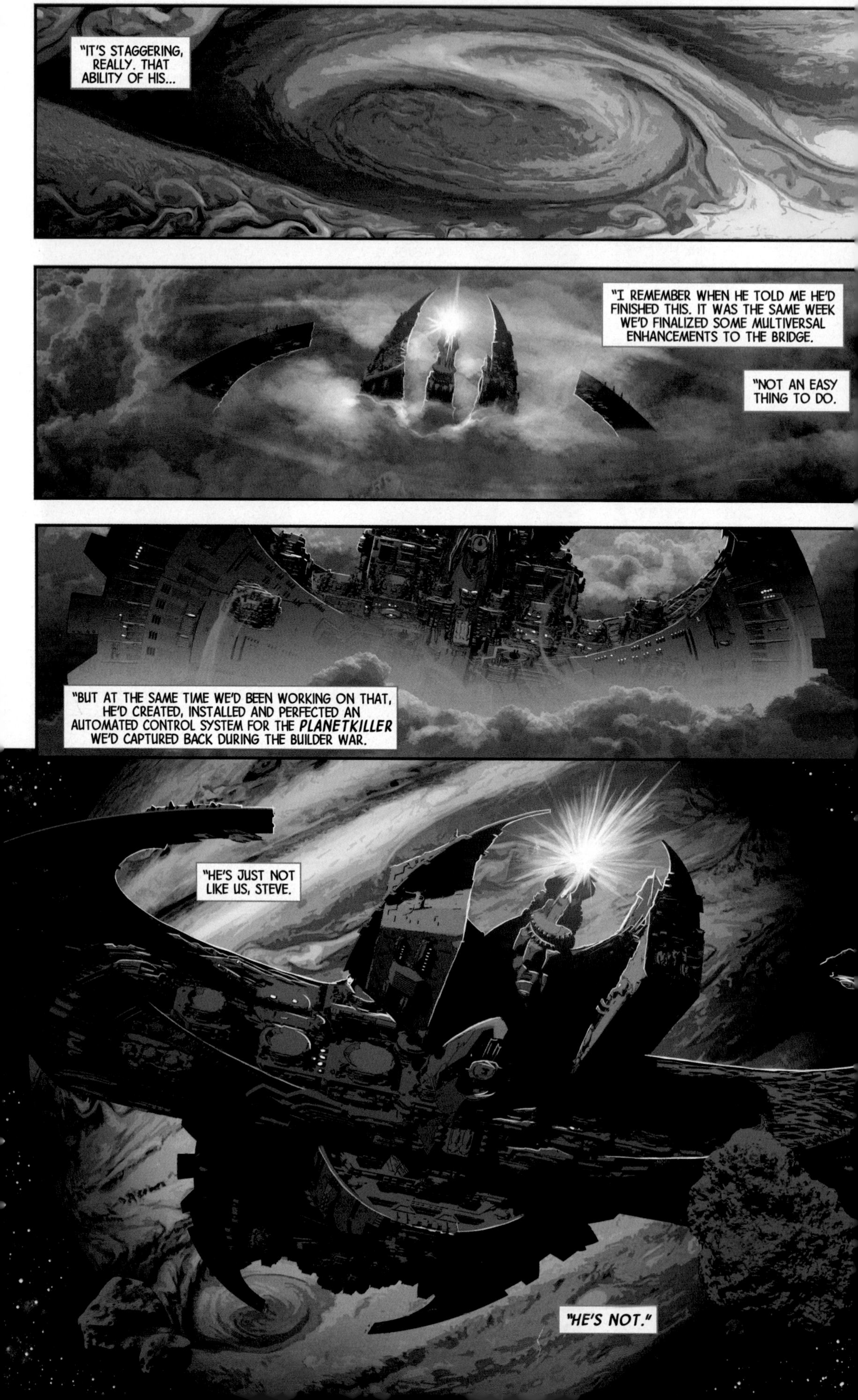
"IT'S STAGGERING, REALLY. THAT ABILITY OF HIS...
"I REMEMBER WHEN HE TOLD ME HE'D FINISHED THIS. IT WAS THE SAME WEEK WE'D FINALIZED SOME MULTIVERSAL ENHANCEMENTS TO THE BRIDGE.
"NOT AN EASY THING TO DO.
"BUT AT THE SAME TIME WE'D BEEN WORKING ON THAT, HE'D CREATED, INSTALLED AND PERFECTED AN AUTOMATED CONTROL SYSTEM FOR THE PLANETKILLER WE'D CAPTURED BACK DURING THE BUILDER WAR.
"HE'S JUST NOT LIKE US, STEVE.
"HE'S NOT."

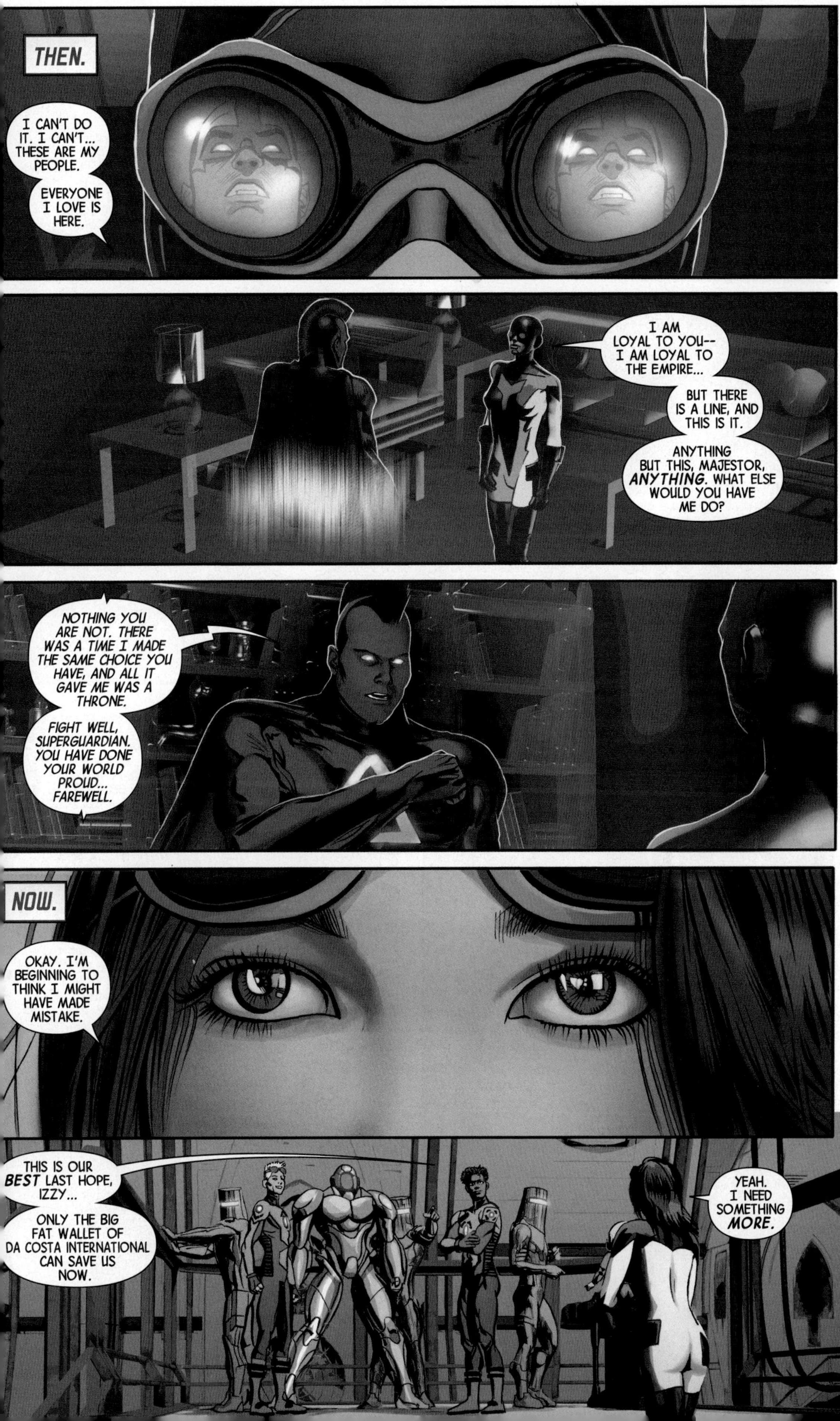
THEN.
I CAN'T DO IT. I CAN'T... THESE ARE MY PEOPLE.
EVERYONE I LOVE IS HERE.
I AM LOYAL TO YOU-- I AM LOYAL TO THE EMPIRE...
BUT THERE IS A LINE, AND THIS IS IT.
ANYTHING BUT THIS, MAJESTOR, ANYTHING. WHAT ELSE WOULD YOU HAVE ME DO?
NOTHING YOU ARE NOT. THERE WAS A TIME I MADE THE SAME CHOICE YOU HAVE, AND ALL IT GAVE ME WAS A THRONE.
FIGHT WELL, SUPERGUARDIAN. YOU HAVE DONE YOUR WORLD PROUD... FAREWELL.
NOW.
OKAY. I'M BEGINNING TO THINK I MIGHT HAVE MADE MISTAKE.
THIS IS OUR BEST LAST HOPE, IZZY...
ONLY THE BIG FAT WALLET OF DA COSTA INTERNATIONAL CAN SAVE US NOW.
YEAH. I NEED SOMETHING MORE.

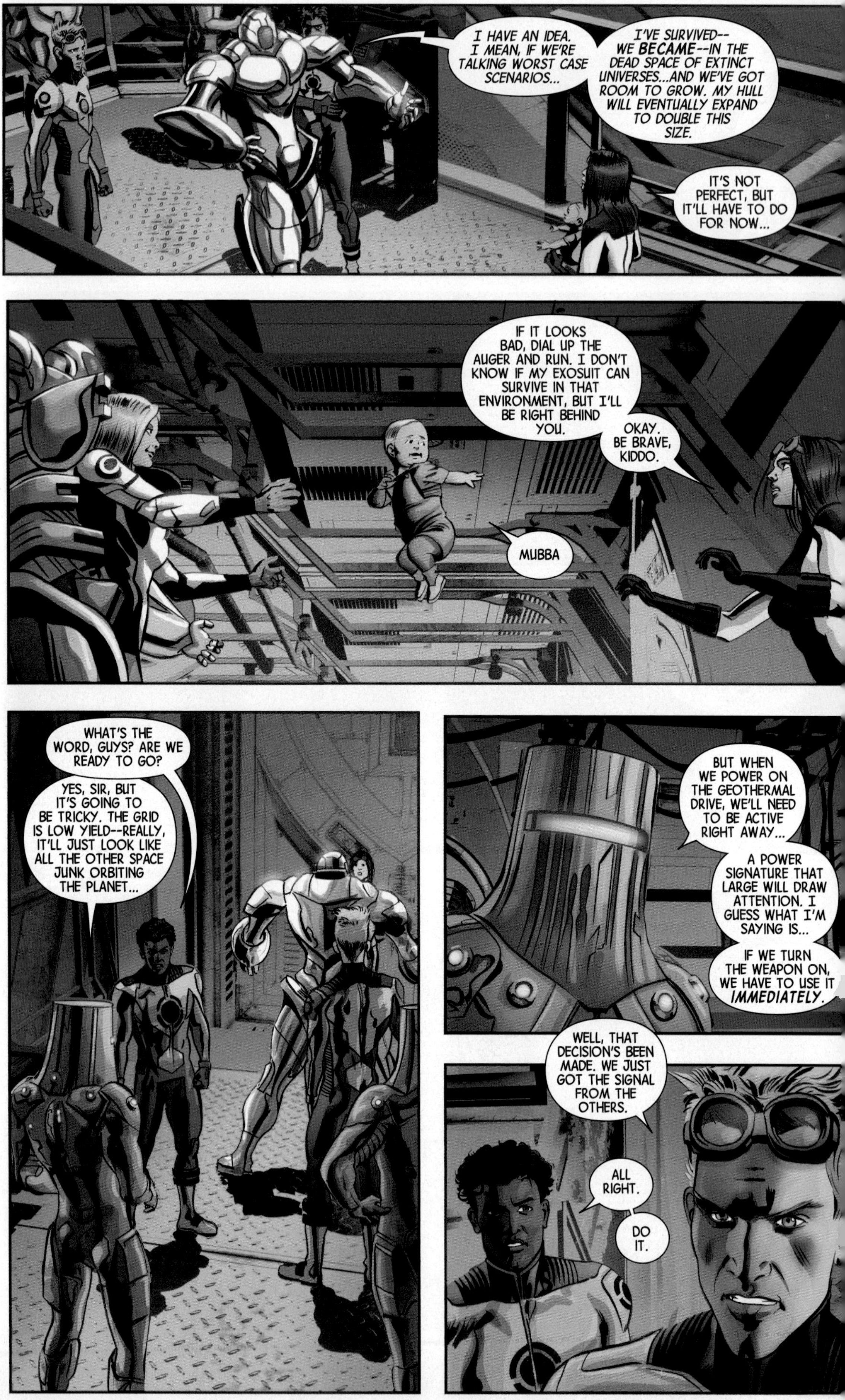
I HAVE AN IDEA. I MEAN, IF WE'RE TALKING WORST CASE SCENARIOS...
I'VE SURVIVED--WE BECAME--IN THE DEAD SPACE OF EXTINCT UNIVERSES...AND WE'VE GOT ROOM TO GROW. MY HULL WILL EVENTUALLY EXPAND TO DOUBLE THIS SIZE.
IT'S NOT PERFECT, BUT IT'LL HAVE TO DO FOR NOW...
IF IT LOOKS BAD, DIAL UP THE AUGER AND RUN. I DON'T KNOW IF MY EXOSUIT CAN SURVIVE IN THAT ENVIRONMENT, BUT I'LL BE RIGHT BEHIND YOU.
OKAY. BE BRAVE, KIDDO.
MUBBA
WHAT'S THE WORD, GUYS? ARE WE READY TO GO?
YES, SIR, BUT IT'S GOING TO BE TRICKY. THE GRID IS LOW YIELD--REALLY, IT'LL JUST LOOK LIKE ALL THE OTHER SPACE JUNK ORBITING THE PLANET...
BUT WHEN WE POWER ON THE GEOTHERMAL DRIVE, WE'LL NEED TO BE ACTIVE RIGHT AWAY...
A POWER SIGNATURE THAT LARGE WILL DRAW ATTENTION. I GUESS WHAT I'M SAYING IS...
IF WE TURN THE WEAPON ON, WE HAVE TO USE IT IMMEDIATELY.
WELL, THAT DECISION'S BEEN MADE. WE JUST GOT THE SIGNAL FROM THE OTHERS.
ALL RIGHT.
DO IT.

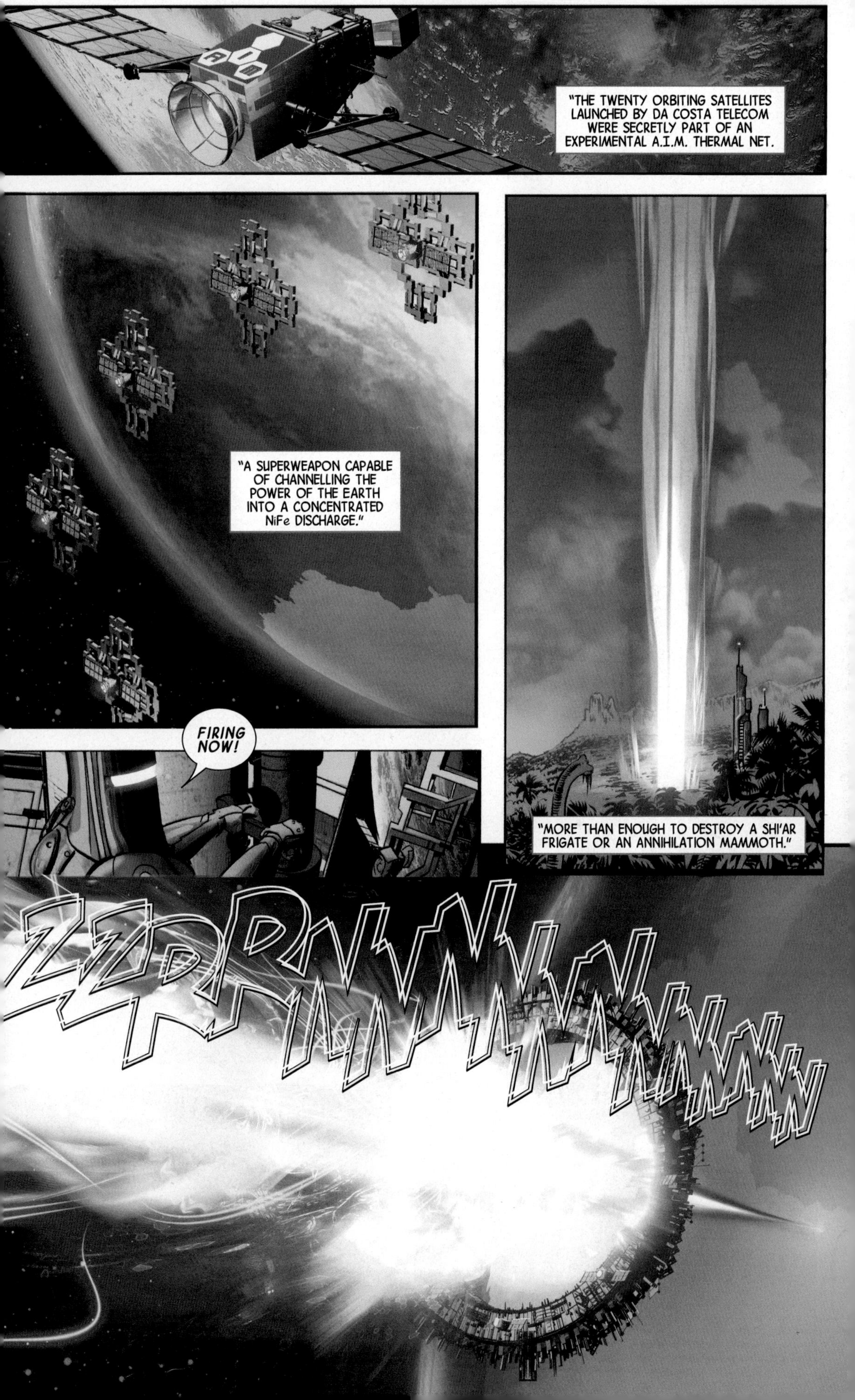
"THE TWENTY ORBITING SATELLITES LAUNCHED BY DA COSTA TELECOM WERE SECRETLY PART OF AN EXPERIMENTAL A.I.M. THERMAL NET.
"A SUPERWEAPON CAPABLE OF CHANNELLING THE POWER OF THE EARTH INTO A CONCENTRATED NiFe DISCHARGE."
"MORE THAN ENOUGH TO DESTROY A SHI'AR FRIGATE OR AN ANNIHILATION MAMMOTH."
FIRING NOW!
ZZRAKKOWWWWWWWWW

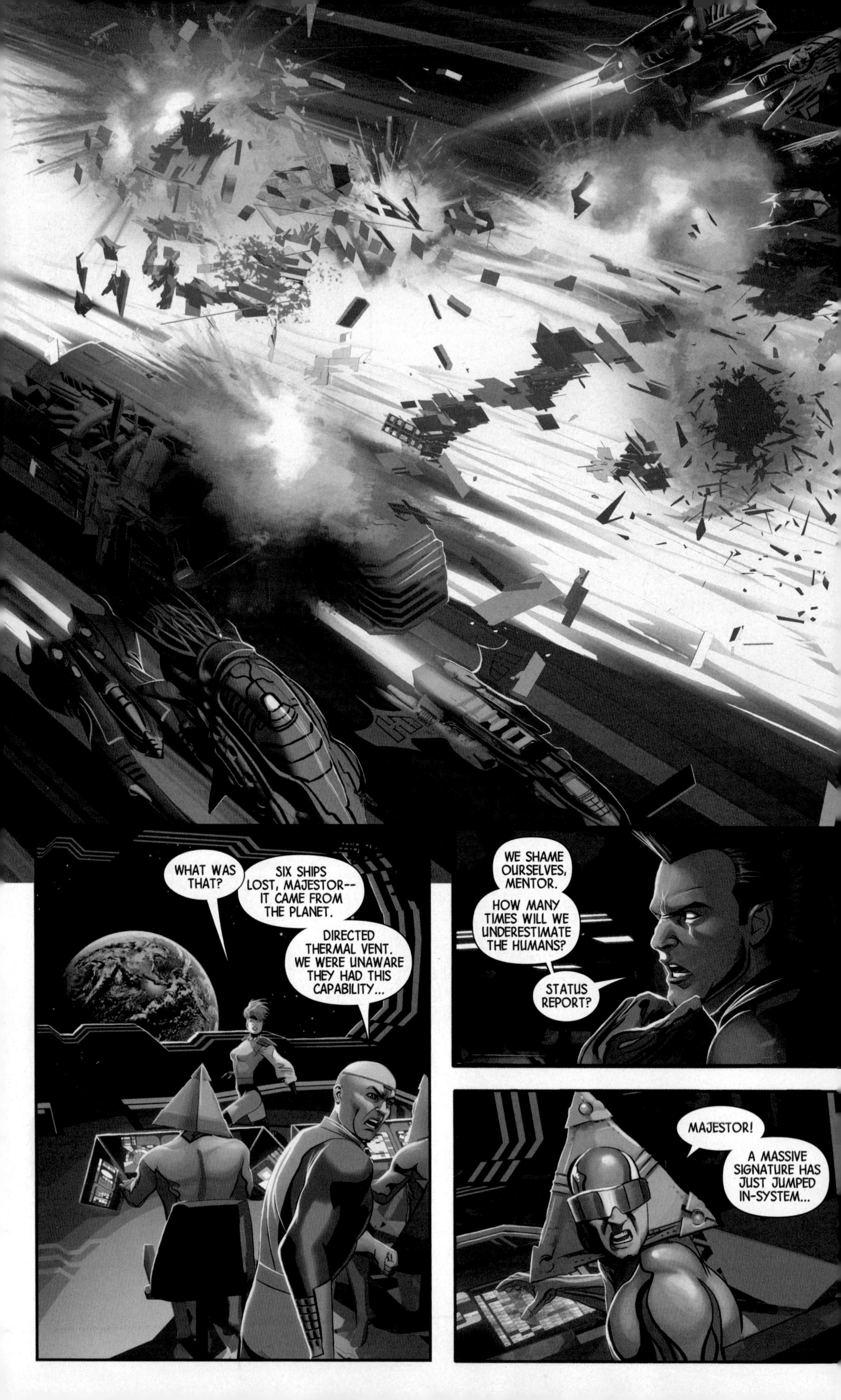
WHAT WAS THAT?
SIX SHIPS LOST, MAJESTOR-- IT CAME FROM THE PLANET.
DIRECTED THERMAL VENT. WE WERE UNAWARE THEY HAD THIS CAPABILITY...
WE SHAME OURSELVES, MENTOR.
HOW MANY TIMES WILL WE UNDERESTIMATE THE HUMANS?
STATUS REPORT?
MAJESTOR!
A MASSIVE SIGNATURE HAS JUST JUMPED IN-SYSTEM...

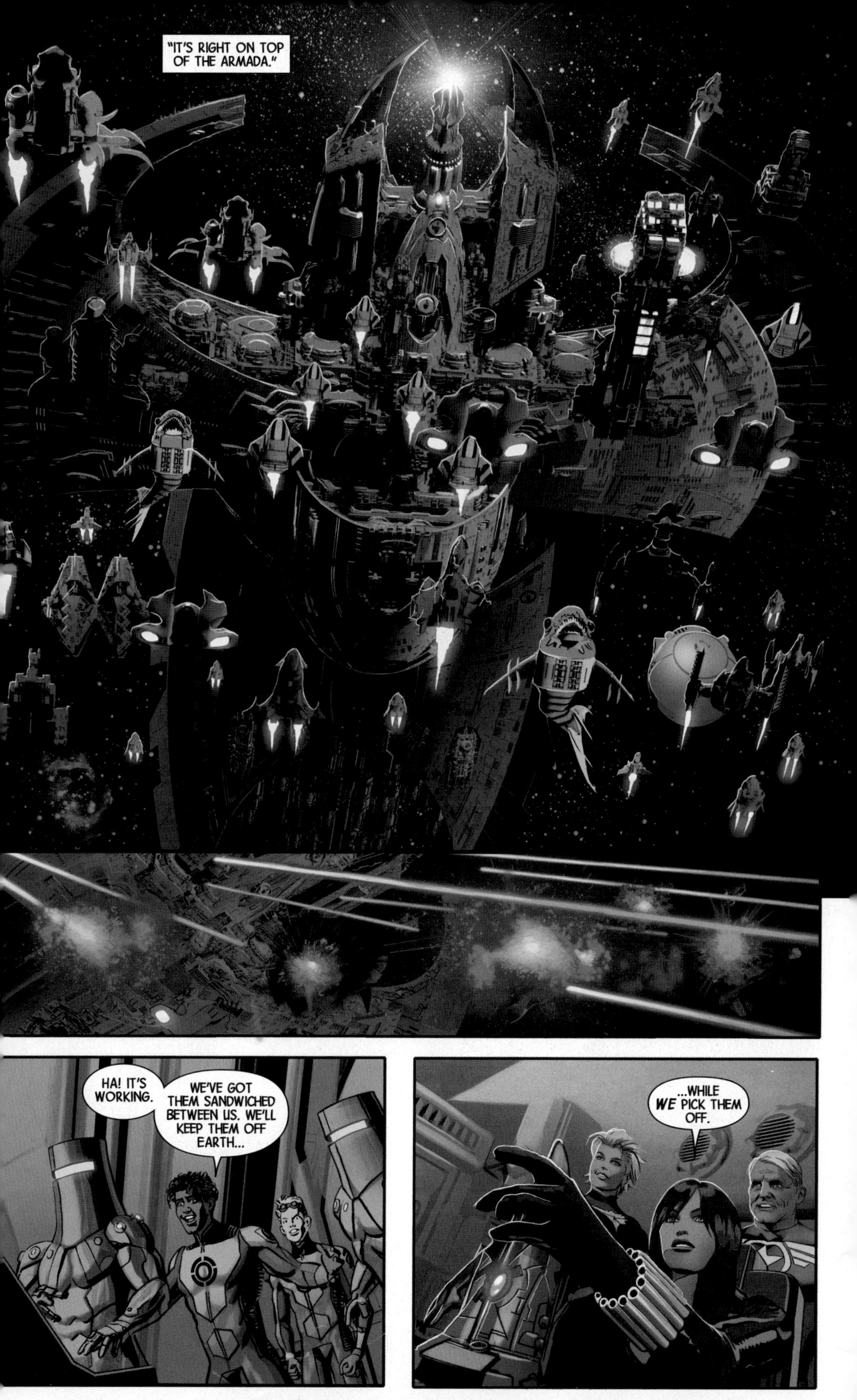
"IT'S RIGHT ON TOP OF THE ARMADA."
HA! IT'S WORKING.
WE'VE GOT THEM SANDWICHED BETWEEN US. WE'LL KEEP THEM OFF EARTH...
...WHILE WE PICK THEM OFF.

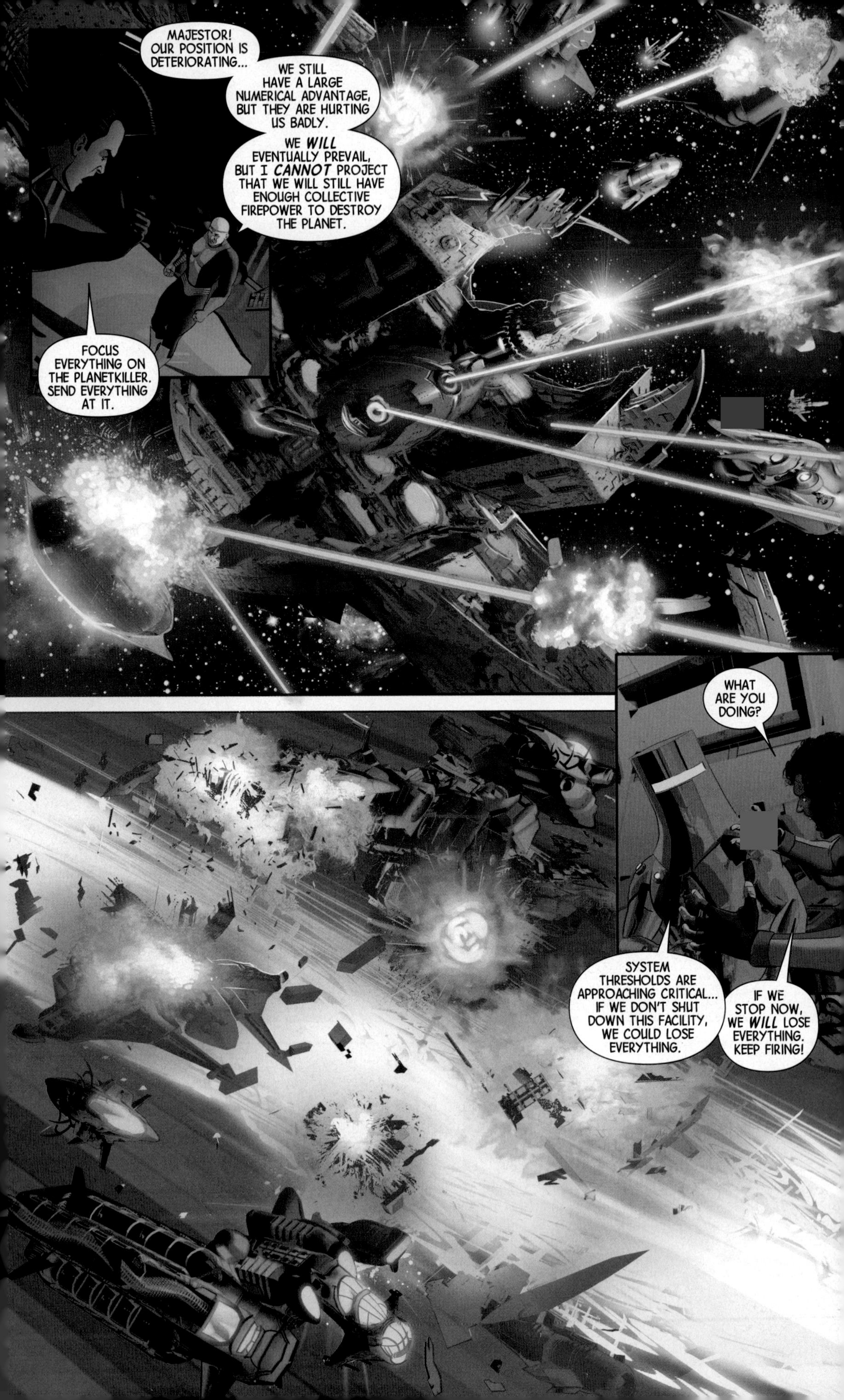

MAJESTOR! OUR POSITION IS DETERIORATING...
WE STILL HAVE A LARGE NUMERICAL ADVANTAGE, BUT THEY ARE HURTING US BADLY.
WE WILL EVENTUALLY PREVAIL, BUT I CANNOT PROJECT THAT WE WILL STILL HAVE ENOUGH COLLECTIVE FIREPOWER TO DESTROY THE PLANET.
FOCUS EVERYTHING ON THE PLANETKILLER. SEND EVERYTHING AT IT.
WHAT ARE YOU DOING?
SYSTEM THRESHOLDS ARE APPROACHING CRITICAL... IF WE DON'T SHUT DOWN THIS FACILITY, WE COULD LOSE EVERYTHING.
IF WE STOP NOW, WE WILL LOSE EVERYTHING. KEEP FIRING!

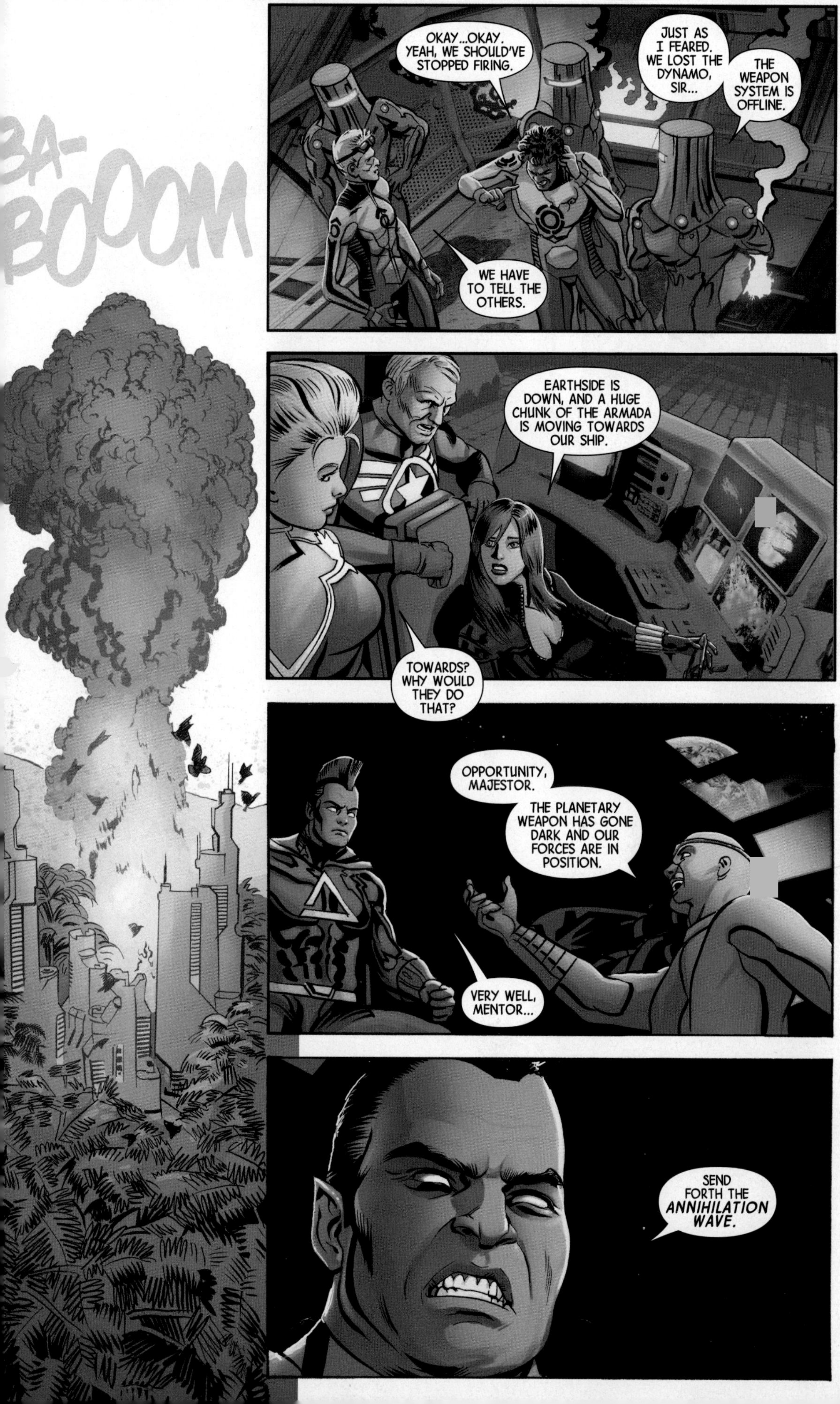
BA-BOOOM
OKAY...OKAY. YEAH, WE SHOULD'VE STOPPED FIRING.
JUST AS I FEARED. WE LOST THE DYNAMO, SIR...
THE WEAPON SYSTEM IS OFFLINE.
WE HAVE TO TELL THE OTHERS.
EARTHSIDE IS DOWN, AND A HUGE CHUNK OF THE ARMADA IS MOVING TOWARDS OUR SHIP.
TOWARDS? WHY WOULD THEY DO THAT?
OPPORTUNITY, MAJESTOR.
THE PLANETARY WEAPON HAS GONE DARK AND OUR FORCES ARE IN POSITION.
VERY WELL, MENTOR...
SEND FORTH THE *ANNIHILATION WAVE.*

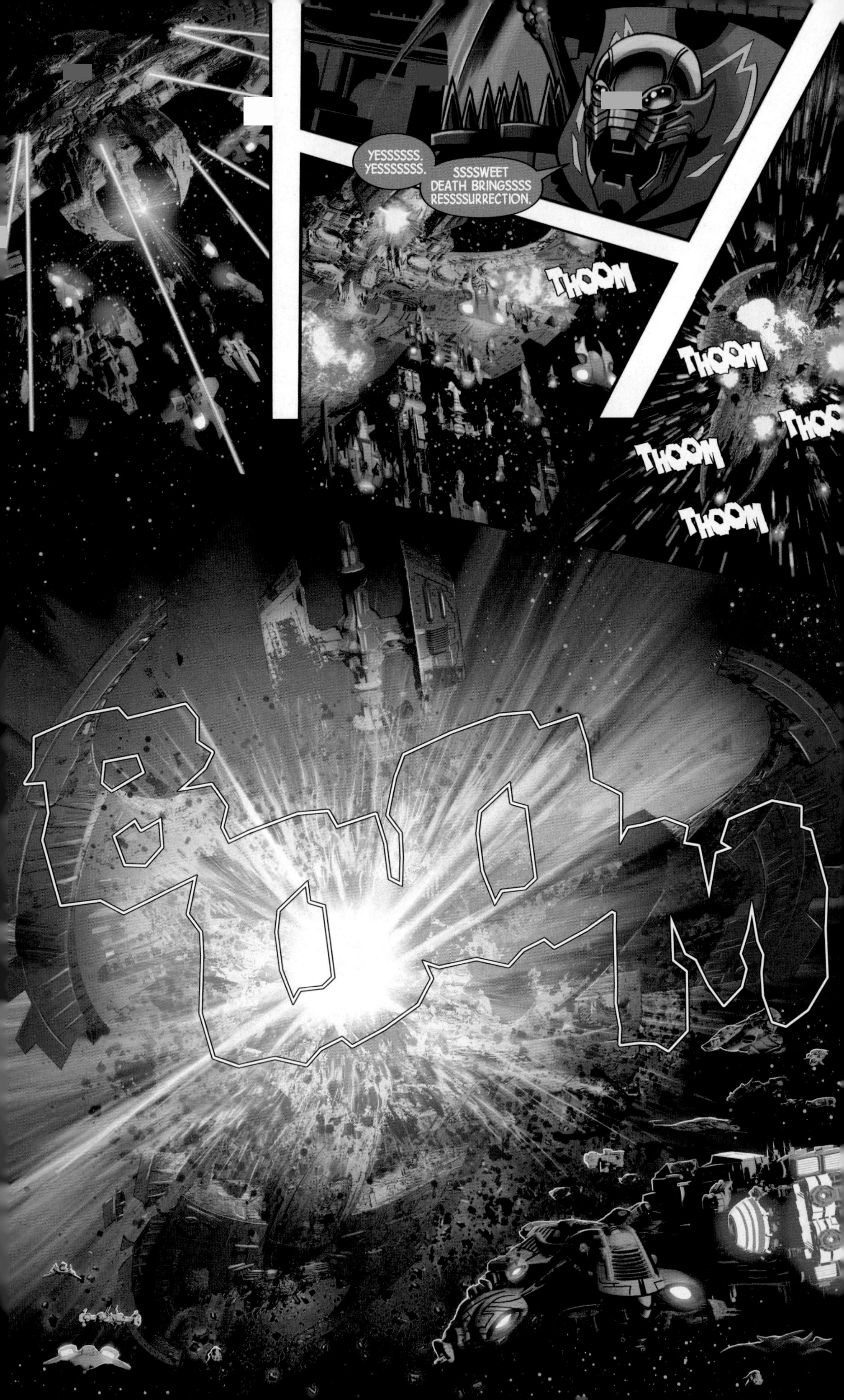
YESSSSSS. YESSSSSSS.
SSSSWEET DEATH BRINGSSSS RESSSSURRECTION.
THOOM
THOOM
THOOM
THOOM
BOOM

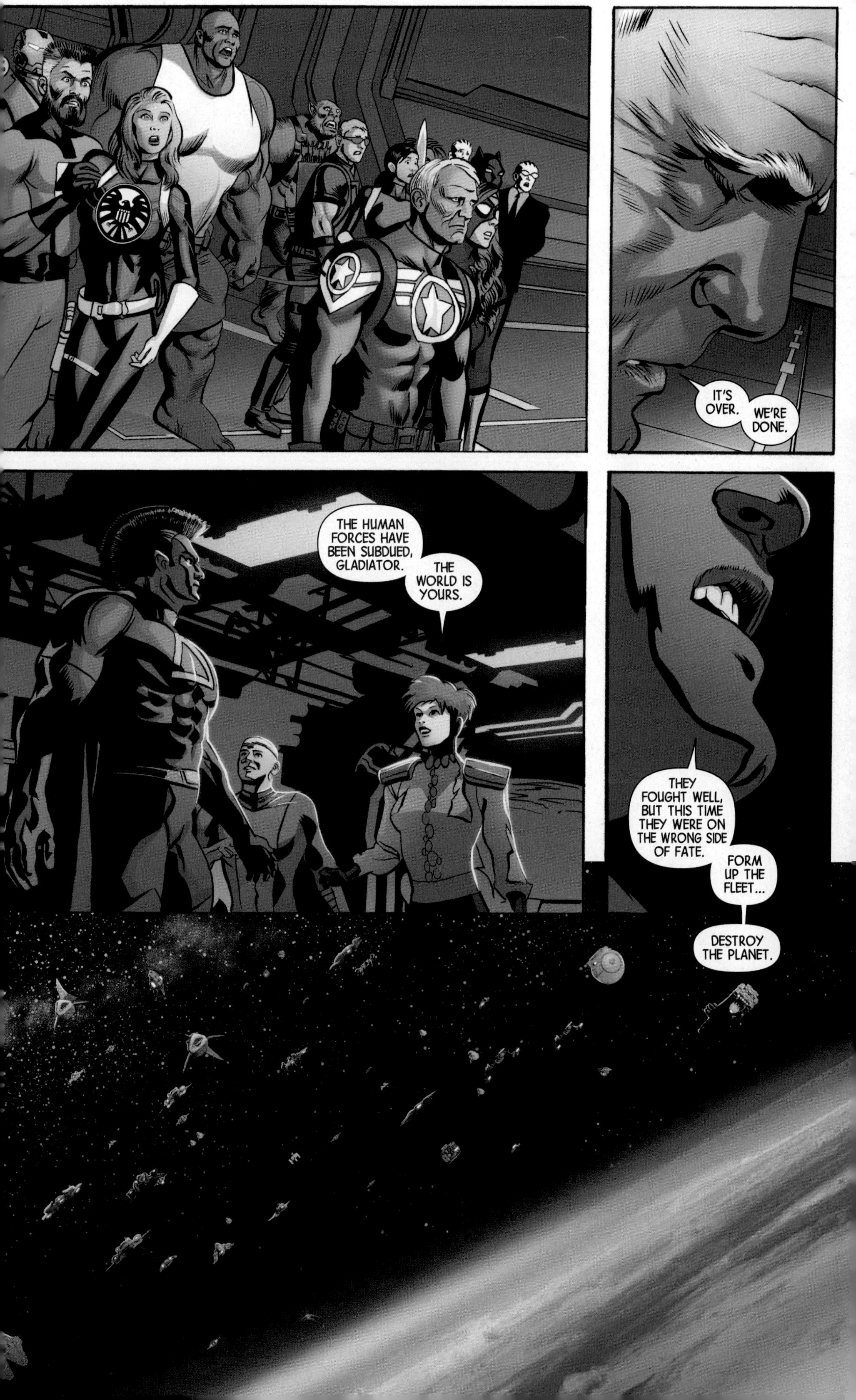
IT'S OVER.
WE'RE DONE.
THE HUMAN FORCES HAVE BEEN SUBDUED, GLADIATOR.
THE WORLD IS YOURS.
THEY FOUGHT WELL, BUT THIS TIME THEY WERE ON THE WRONG SIDE OF FATE.
FORM UP THE FLEET...
DESTROY THE PLANET.

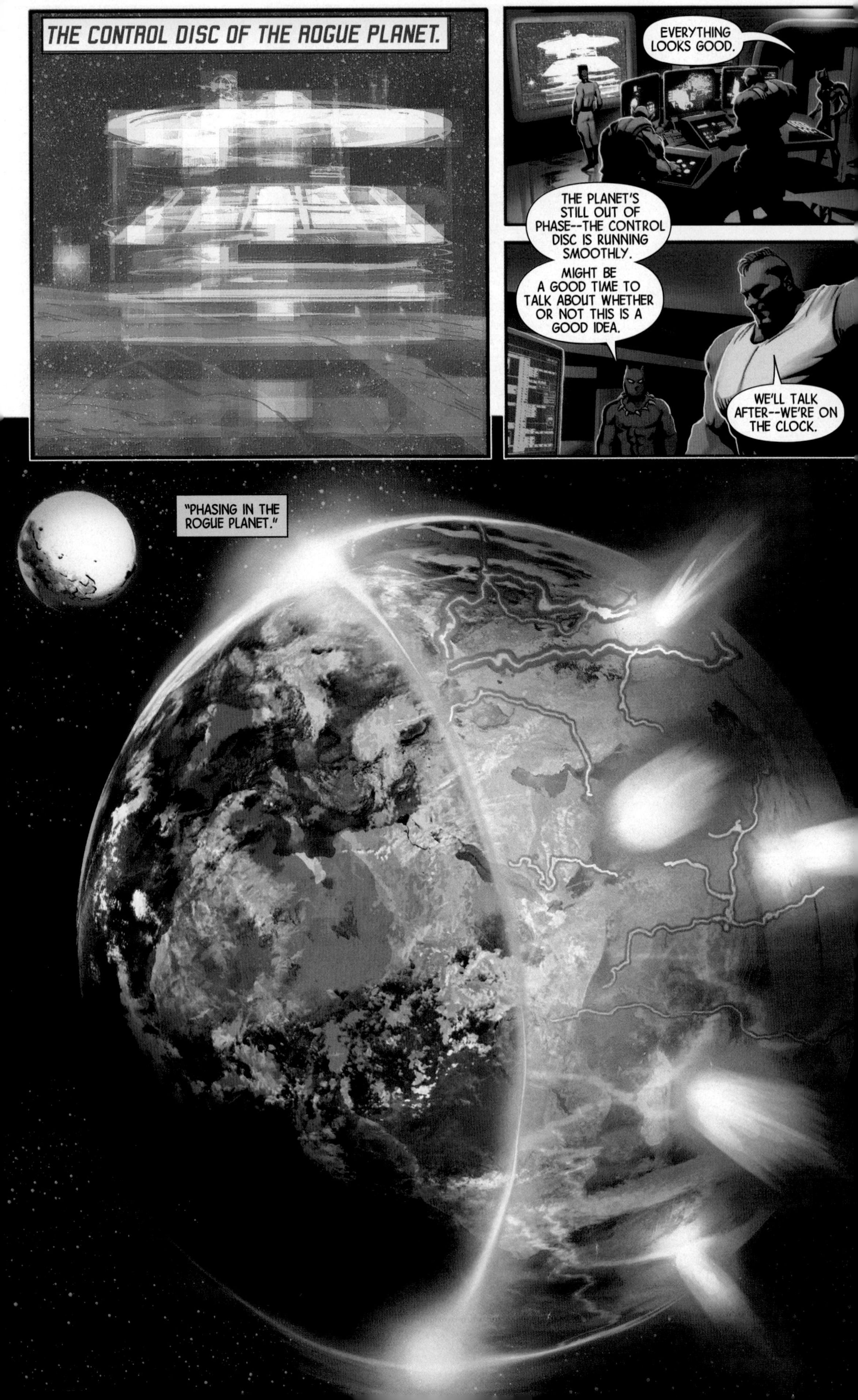
THE CONTROL DISC OF THE ROGUE PLANET.
EVERYTHING LOOKS GOOD.
THE PLANET'S STILL OUT OF PHASE--THE CONTROL DISC IS RUNNING SMOOTHLY.
MIGHT BE A GOOD TIME TO TALK ABOUT WHETHER OR NOT THIS IS A GOOD IDEA.
WE'LL TALK AFTER--WE'RE ON THE CLOCK.
"PHASING IN THE ROGUE PLANET."

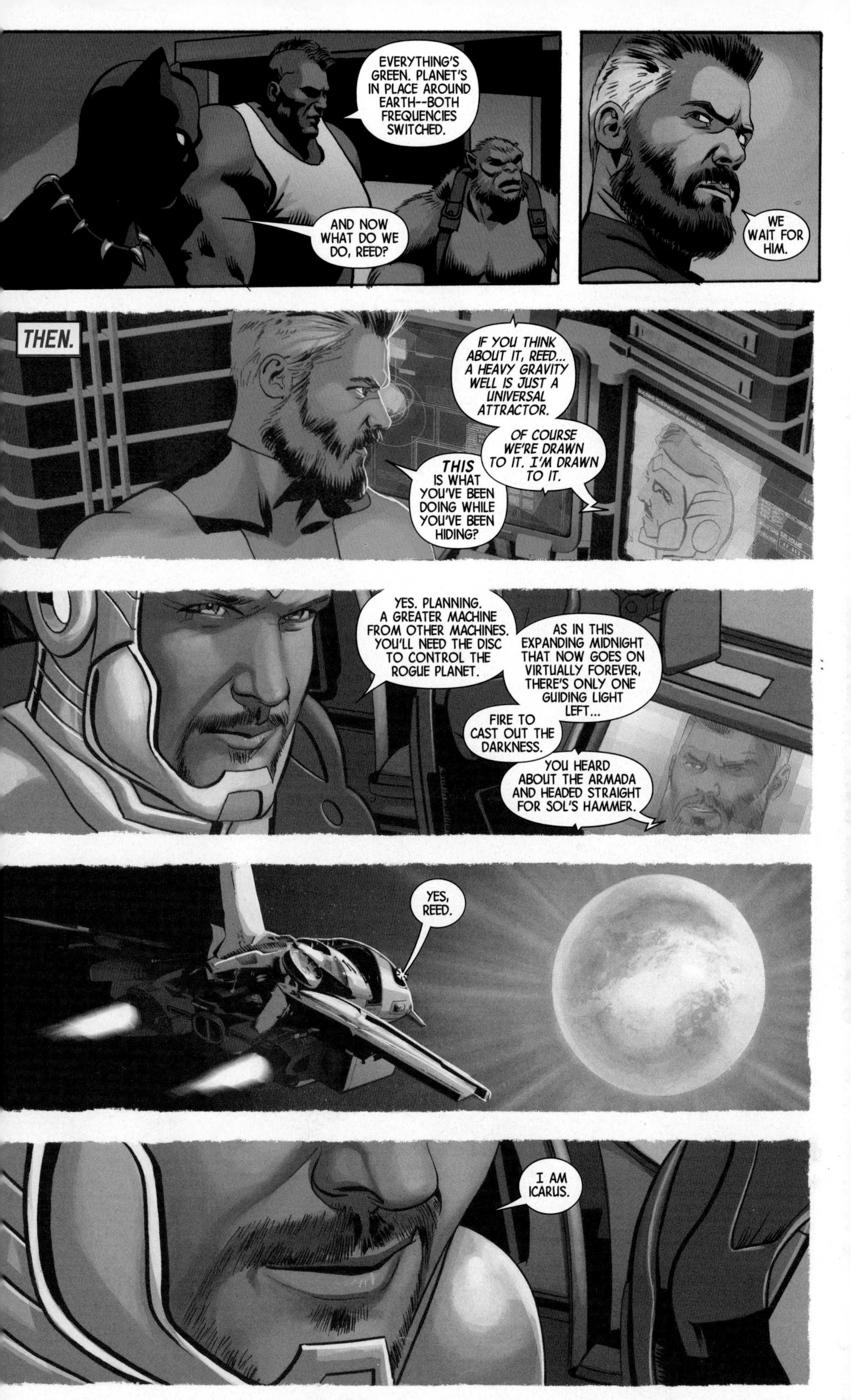

EVERYTHING'S GREEN. PLANET'S IN PLACE AROUND EARTH--BOTH FREQUENCIES SWITCHED.
AND NOW WHAT DO WE DO, REED?
WE WAIT FOR HIM.
THEN.
IF YOU THINK ABOUT IT, REED... A HEAVY GRAVITY WELL IS JUST A UNIVERSAL ATTRACTOR.
OF COURSE WE'RE DRAWN TO IT. I'M DRAWN TO IT.
THIS IS WHAT YOU'VE BEEN DOING WHILE YOU'VE BEEN HIDING?
YES. PLANNING. A GREATER MACHINE FROM OTHER MACHINES. YOU'LL NEED THE DISC TO CONTROL THE ROGUE PLANET.
AS IN THIS EXPANDING MIDNIGHT THAT NOW GOES ON VIRTUALLY FOREVER, THERE'S ONLY ONE GUIDING LIGHT LEFT...
FIRE TO CAST OUT THE DARKNESS.
YOU HEARD ABOUT THE ARMADA AND HEADED STRAIGHT FOR SOL'S HAMMER.
YES, REED.
I AM ICARUS.

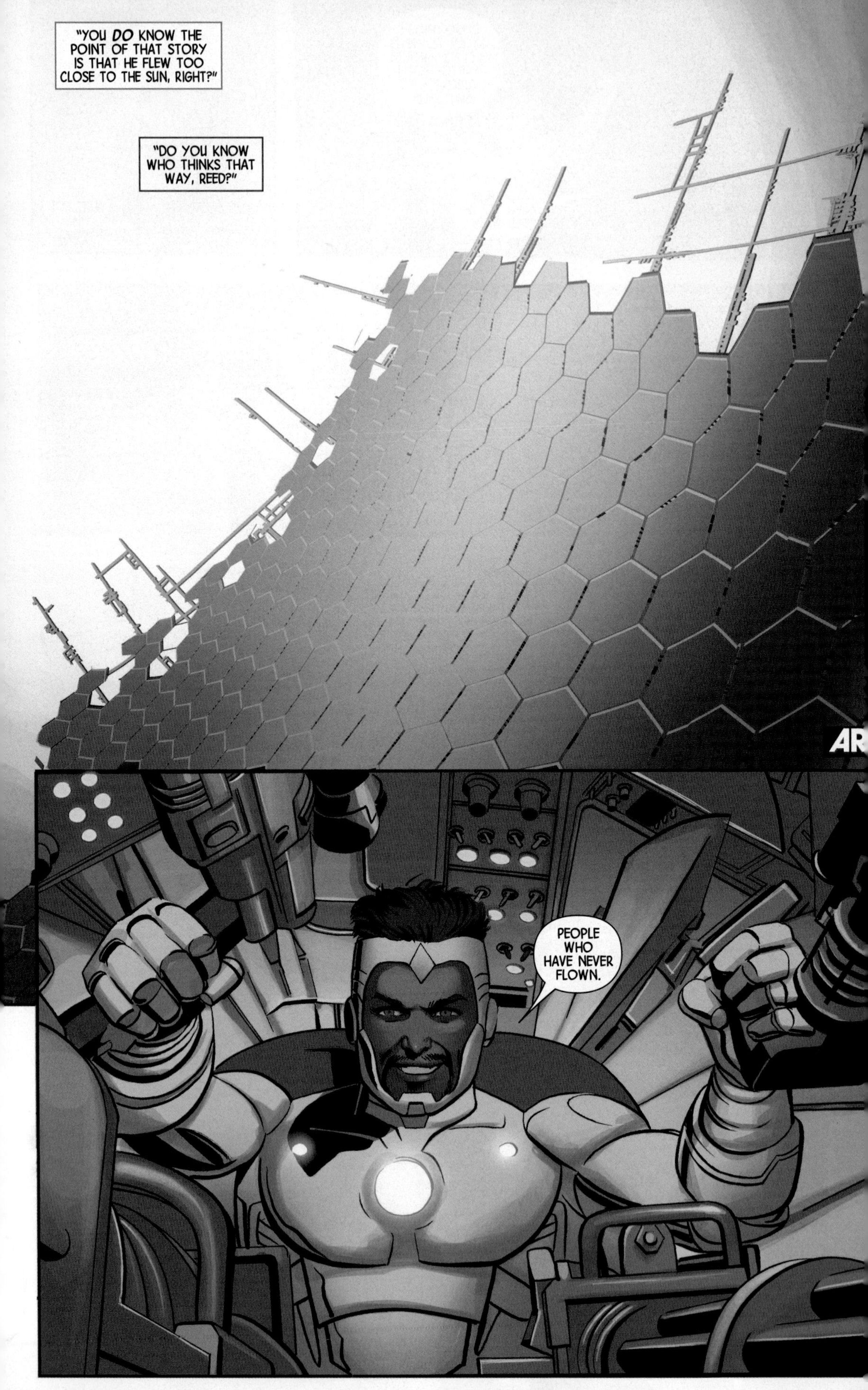
"YOU DO KNOW THE POINT OF THAT STORY IS THAT HE FLEW TOO CLOSE TO THE SUN, RIGHT?"
"DO YOU KNOW WHO THINKS THAT WAY, REED?"
PEOPLE WHO HAVE NEVER FLOWN.

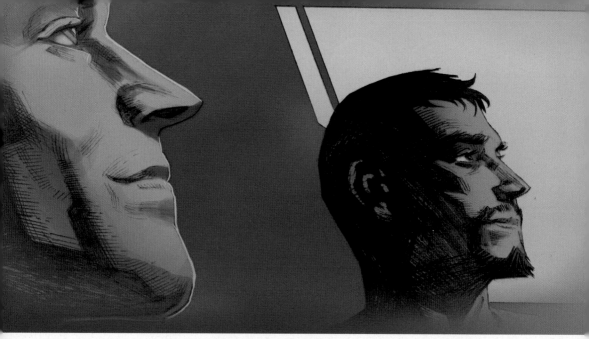

"ONE WAS LIFE. ONE WAS DEATH."

THE ILLUMINATI

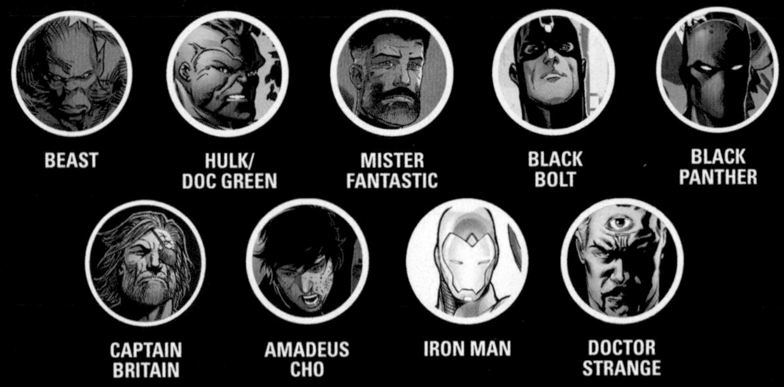
BEAST
HULK/ DOC GREEN
MISTER FANTASTIC
BLACK BOLT
BLACK PANTHER
CAPTAIN BRITAIN
AMADEUS CHO
IRON MAN
DOCTOR STRANGE

S.H.I.E.L.D. AVENGERS

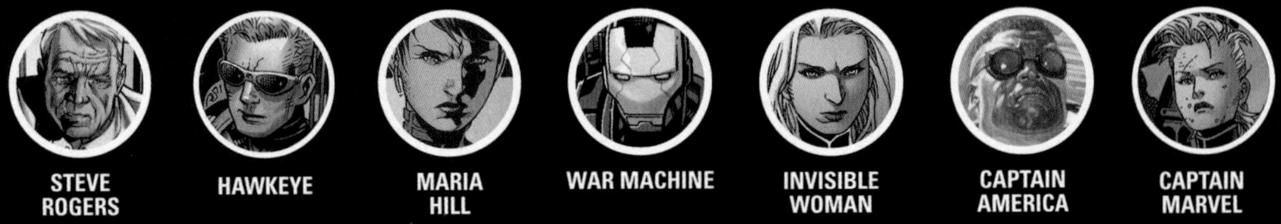
STEVE ROGERS
HAWKEYE
MARIA HILL
WAR MACHINE
INVISIBLE WOMAN
CAPTAIN AMERICA
CAPTAIN MARVEL

NEW AVENGERS

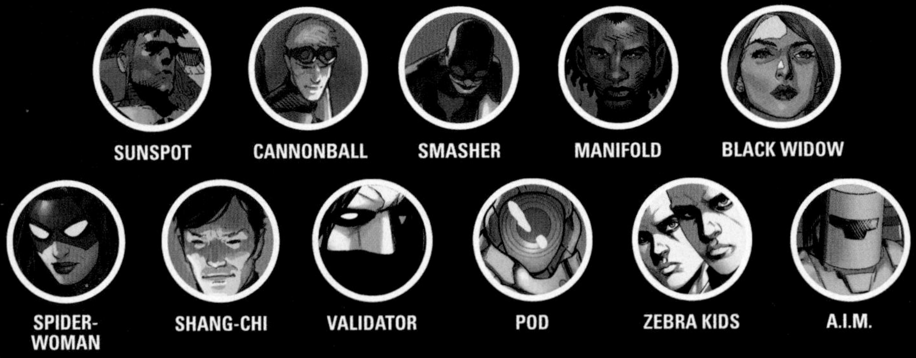
SUNSPOT
CANNONBALL
SMASHER
MANIFOLD
BLACK WIDOW
SPIDER-WOMAN
SHANG-CHI
VALIDATOR
POD
ZEBRA KIDS
A.I.M.

THE CABAL

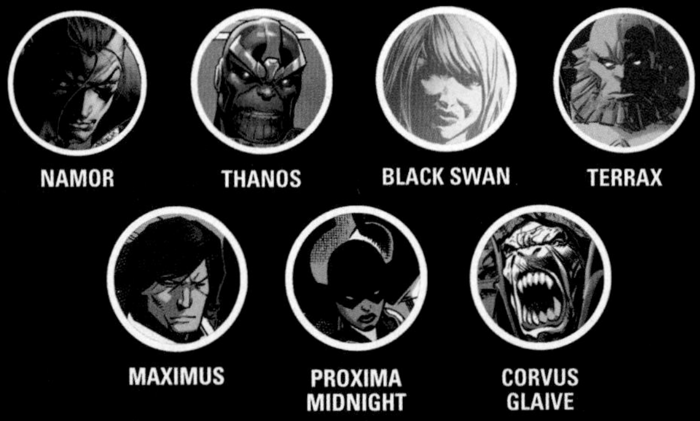
NAMOR
THANOS
BLACK SWAN
TERRAX
MAXIMUS
PROXIMA MIDNIGHT
CORVUS GLAIVE

ULTIMATE UNIVERSE

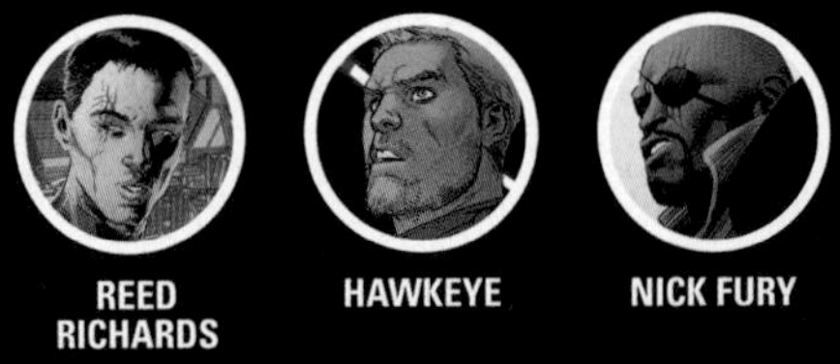
REED RICHARDS
HAWKEYE
NICK FURY

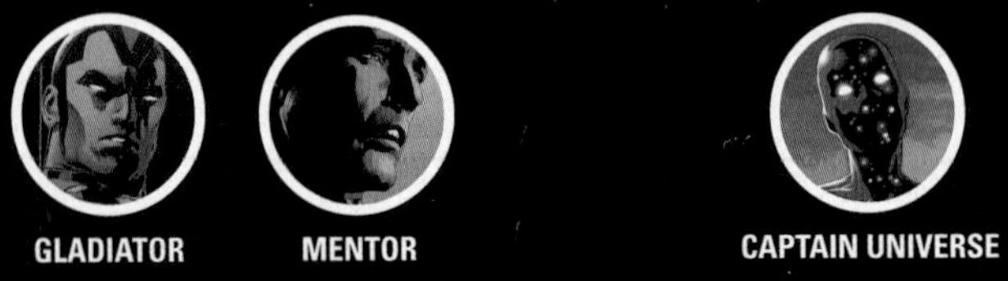
GLADIATOR
MENTOR
CAPTAIN UNIVERSE

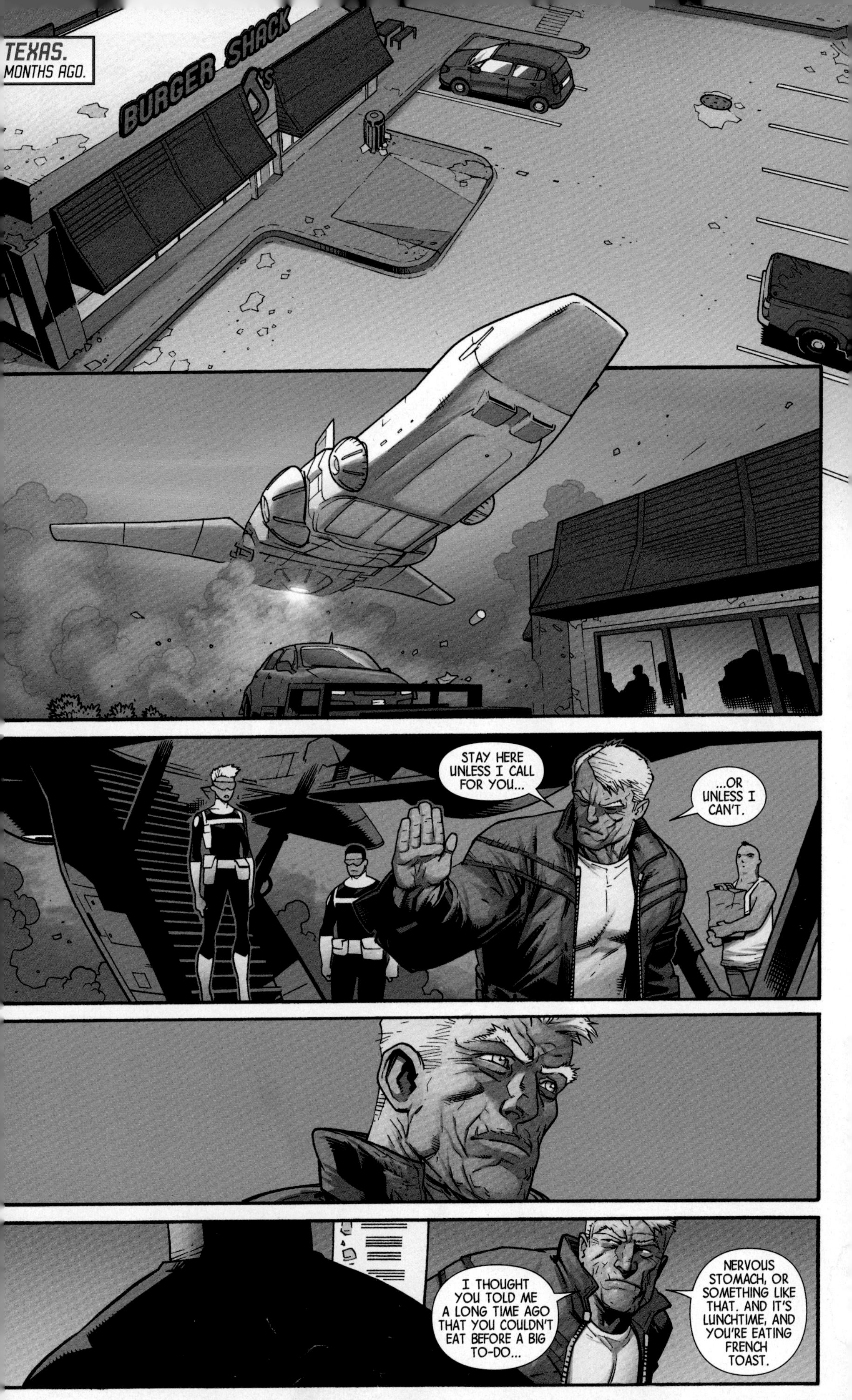
TEXAS.
MONTHS AGO.
BURGER SHACK
STAY HERE UNLESS I CALL FOR YOU...
...OR UNLESS I CAN'T.
I THOUGHT YOU TOLD ME A LONG TIME AGO THAT YOU COULDN'T EAT BEFORE A BIG TO-DO...
NERVOUS STOMACH, OR SOMETHING LIKE THAT. AND IT'S LUNCHTIME, AND YOU'RE EATING FRENCH TOAST.

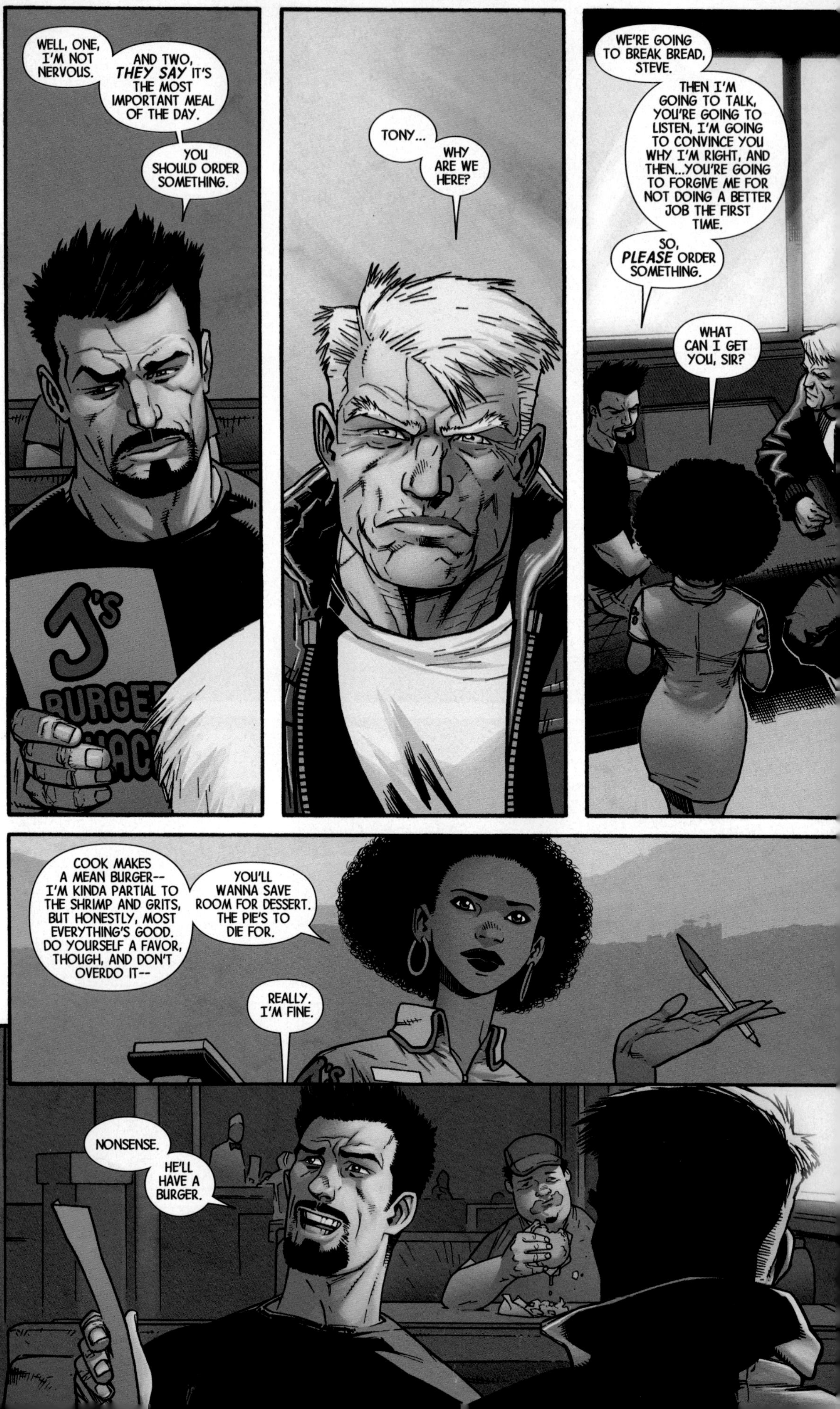
WELL, ONE, I'M NOT NERVOUS.
AND TWO, THEY SAY IT'S THE MOST IMPORTANT MEAL OF THE DAY.
YOU SHOULD ORDER SOMETHING.
J's BURGER SHACK
TONY...
WHY ARE WE HERE?
WE'RE GOING TO BREAK BREAD, STEVE.
THEN I'M GOING TO TALK, YOU'RE GOING TO LISTEN, I'M GOING TO CONVINCE YOU WHY I'M RIGHT, AND THEN...YOU'RE GOING TO FORGIVE ME FOR NOT DOING A BETTER JOB THE FIRST TIME.
SO, PLEASE ORDER SOMETHING.
WHAT CAN I GET YOU, SIR?
COOK MAKES A MEAN BURGER-- I'M KINDA PARTIAL TO THE SHRIMP AND GRITS, BUT HONESTLY, MOST EVERYTHING'S GOOD. DO YOURSELF A FAVOR, THOUGH, AND DON'T OVERDO IT--
YOU'LL WANNA SAVE ROOM FOR DESSERT. THE PIE'S TO DIE FOR.
REALLY. I'M FINE.
NONSENSE.
HE'LL HAVE A BURGER.

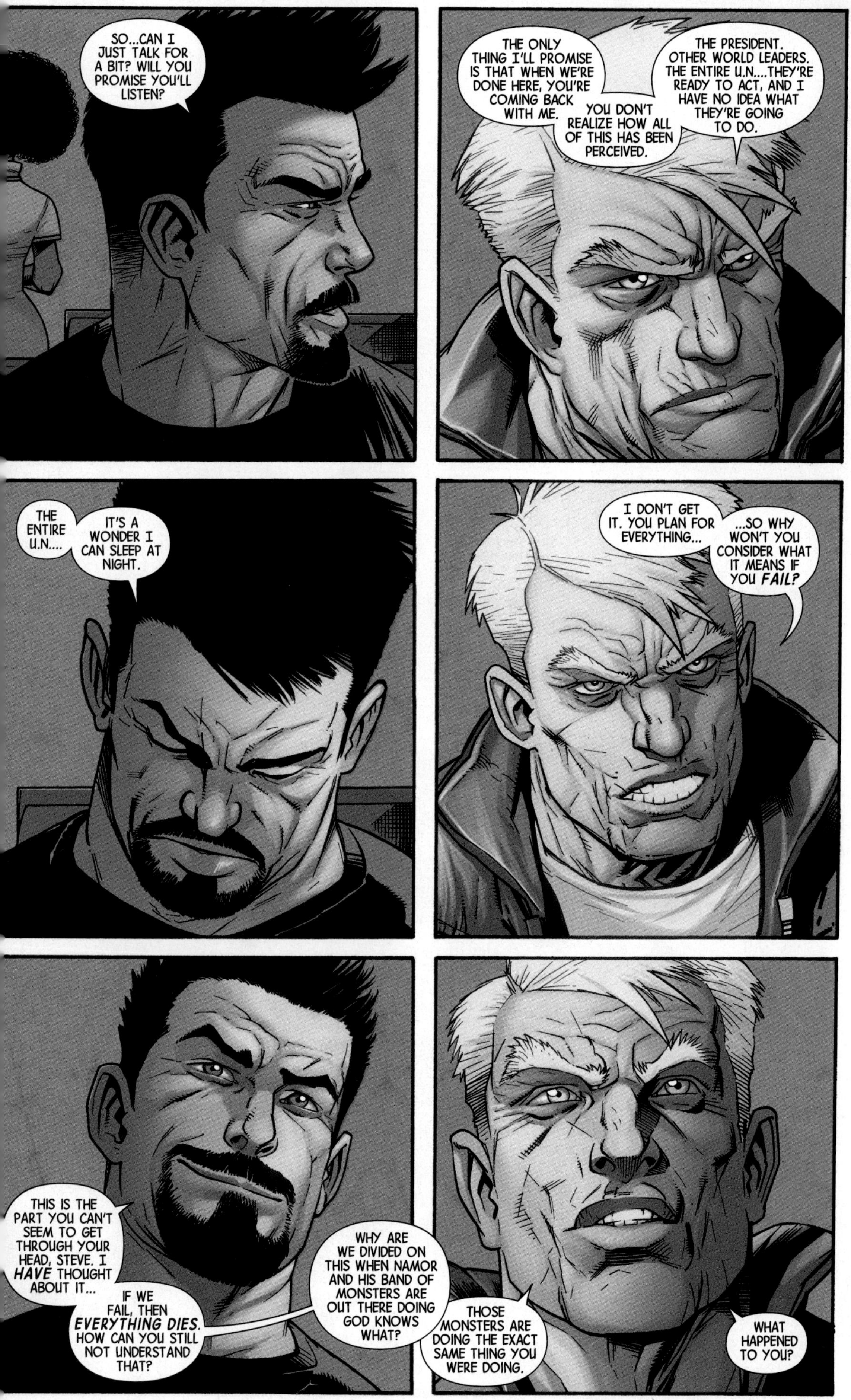

SO...CAN I JUST TALK FOR A BIT? WILL YOU PROMISE YOU'LL LISTEN?
THE ONLY THING I'LL PROMISE IS THAT WHEN WE'RE DONE HERE, YOU'RE COMING BACK WITH ME.
YOU DON'T REALIZE HOW ALL OF THIS HAS BEEN PERCEIVED.
THE PRESIDENT. OTHER WORLD LEADERS. THE ENTIRE U.N....THEY'RE READY TO ACT, AND I HAVE NO IDEA WHAT THEY'RE GOING TO DO.
THE ENTIRE U.N....
IT'S A WONDER I CAN SLEEP AT NIGHT.
I DON'T GET IT. YOU PLAN FOR EVERYTHING...
...SO WHY WON'T YOU CONSIDER WHAT IT MEANS IF YOU *FAIL?*
THIS IS THE PART YOU CAN'T SEEM TO GET THROUGH YOUR HEAD, STEVE. I *HAVE* THOUGHT ABOUT IT...
IF WE FAIL, THEN *EVERYTHING DIES.* HOW CAN YOU STILL NOT UNDERSTAND THAT?
WHY ARE WE DIVIDED ON THIS WHEN NAMOR AND HIS BAND OF MONSTERS ARE OUT THERE DOING GOD KNOWS WHAT?
THOSE MONSTERS ARE DOING THE EXACT SAME THING YOU WERE DOING.
WHAT HAPPENED TO YOU?

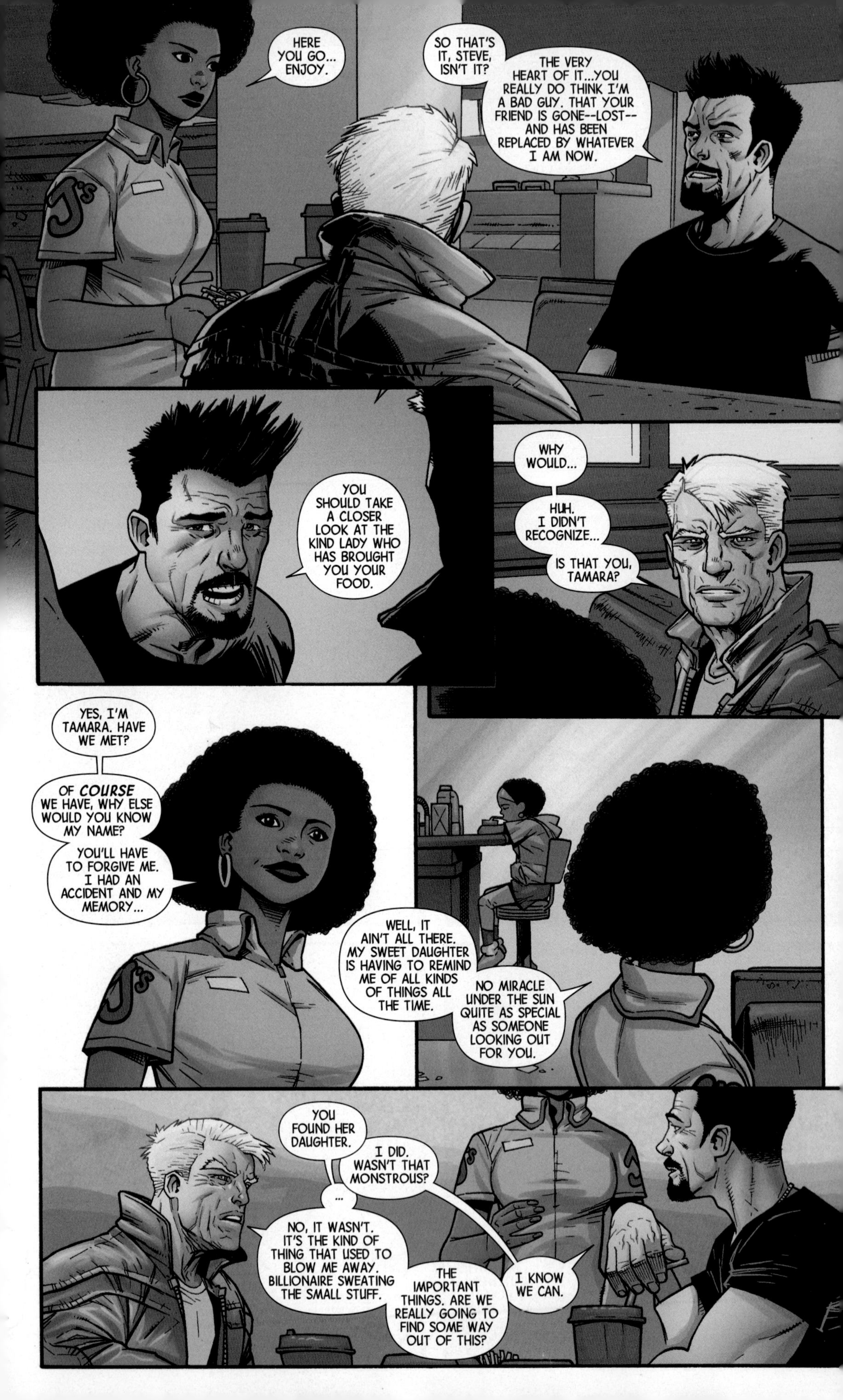
HERE YOU GO... ENJOY.
SO THAT'S IT, STEVE, ISN'T IT?
THE VERY HEART OF IT...YOU REALLY DO THINK I'M A BAD GUY. THAT YOUR FRIEND IS GONE--LOST--AND HAS BEEN REPLACED BY WHATEVER I AM NOW.
YOU SHOULD TAKE A CLOSER LOOK AT THE KIND LADY WHO HAS BROUGHT YOU YOUR FOOD.
WHY WOULD...
HUH. I DIDN'T RECOGNIZE...
IS THAT YOU, TAMARA?
YES, I'M TAMARA. HAVE WE MET?
OF COURSE WE HAVE, WHY ELSE WOULD YOU KNOW MY NAME?
YOU'LL HAVE TO FORGIVE ME. I HAD AN ACCIDENT AND MY MEMORY...
WELL, IT AIN'T ALL THERE. MY SWEET DAUGHTER IS HAVING TO REMIND ME OF ALL KINDS OF THINGS ALL THE TIME.
NO MIRACLE UNDER THE SUN QUITE AS SPECIAL AS SOMEONE LOOKING OUT FOR YOU.
YOU FOUND HER DAUGHTER.
I DID. WASN'T THAT MONSTROUS?
...
NO, IT WASN'T. IT'S THE KIND OF THING THAT USED TO BLOW ME AWAY. BILLIONAIRE SWEATING THE SMALL STUFF.
THE IMPORTANT THINGS. ARE WE REALLY GOING TO FIND SOME WAY OUT OF THIS?
I KNOW WE CAN.

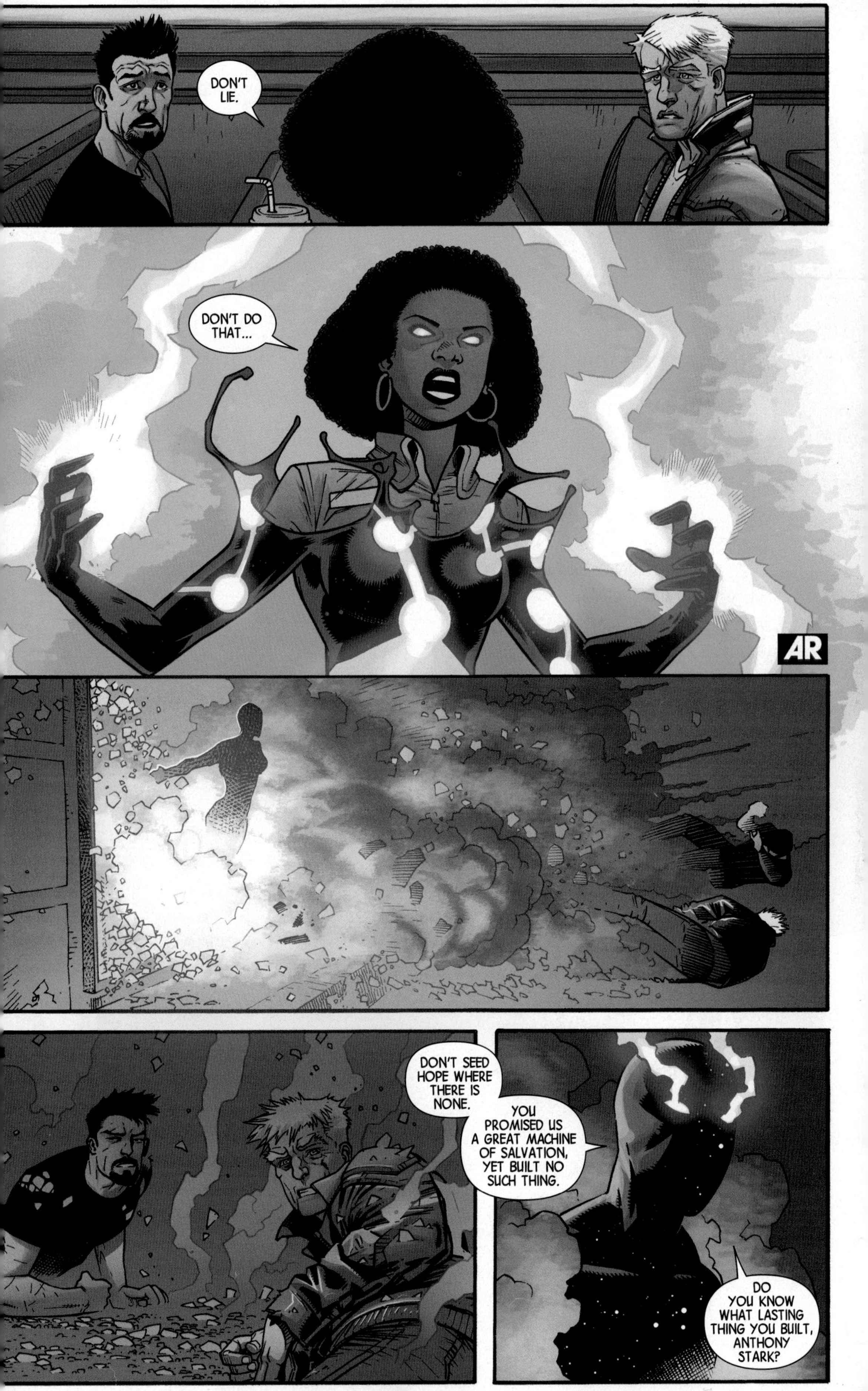
DON'T LIE.
DON'T DO THAT...
AR
DON'T SEED HOPE WHERE THERE IS NONE.
YOU PROMISED US A GREAT MACHINE OF SALVATION, YET BUILT NO SUCH THING.
DO YOU KNOW WHAT LASTING THING YOU BUILT, ANTHONY STARK?

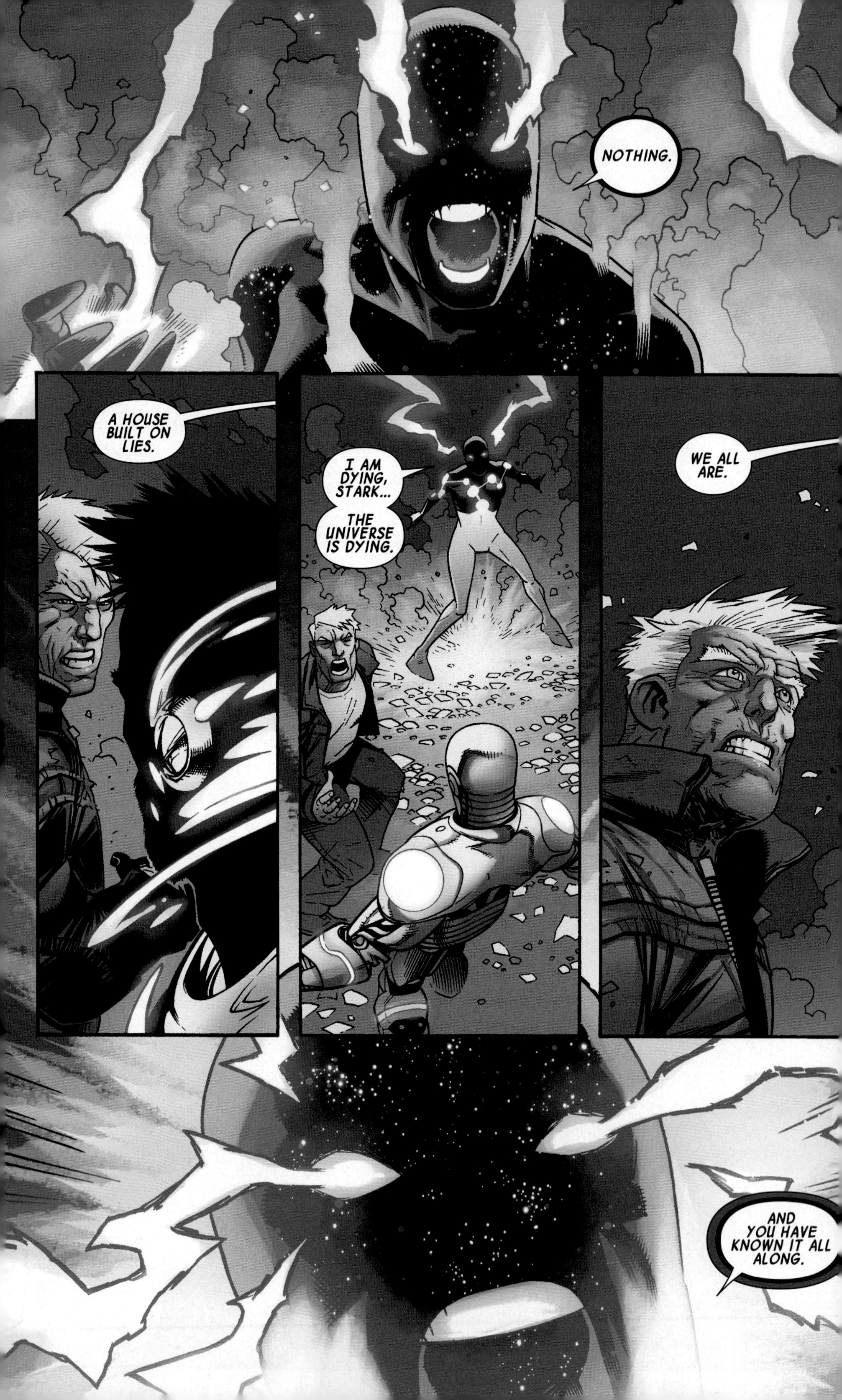
NOTHING.
A HOUSE BUILT ON LIES.
I AM DYING, STARK...
THE UNIVERSE IS DYING.
WE ALL ARE.
AND YOU HAVE KNOWN IT ALL ALONG.

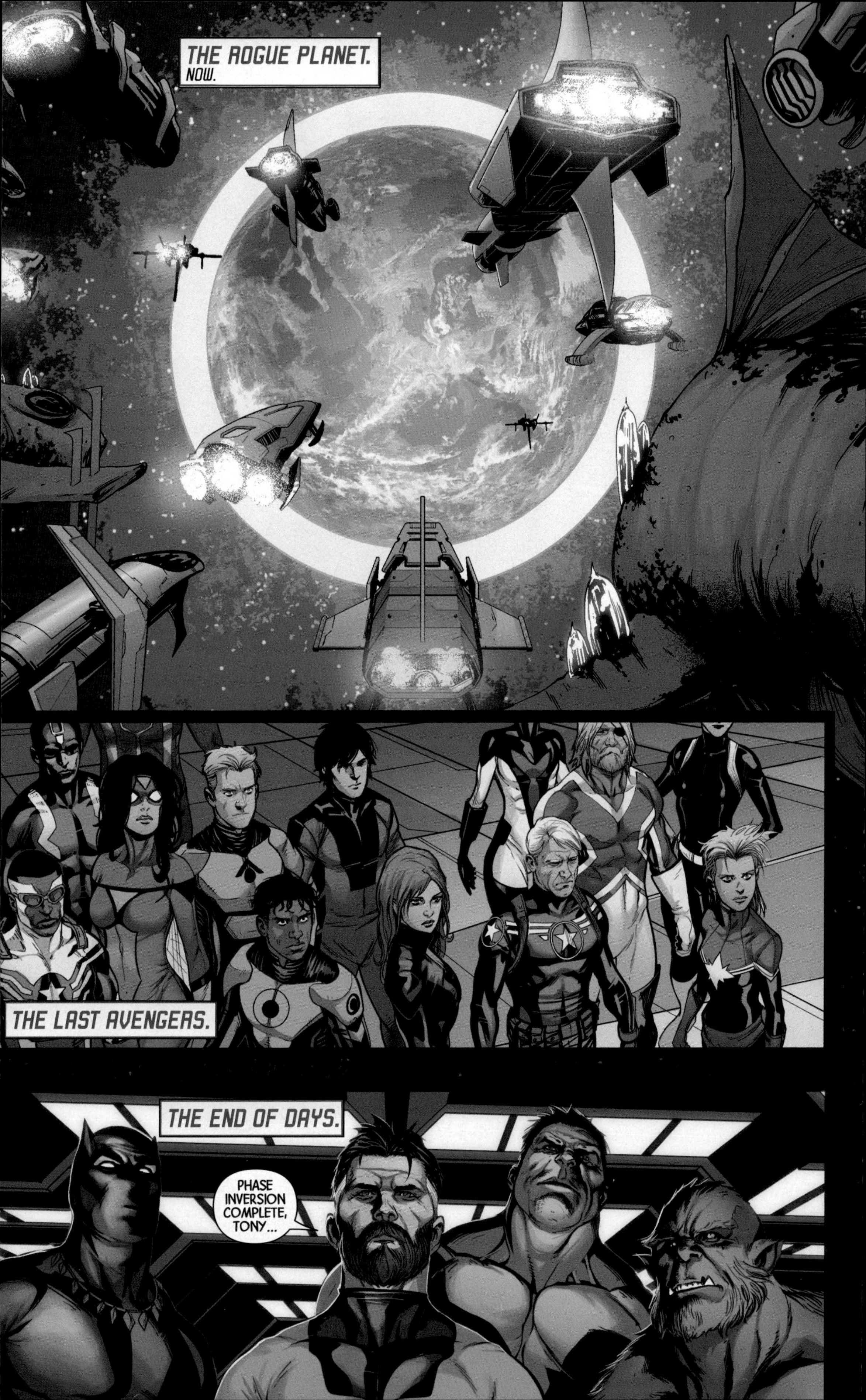
THE ROGUE PLANET.
NOW.
THE LAST AVENGERS.
THE END OF DAYS.
PHASE INVERSION COMPLETE, TONY...

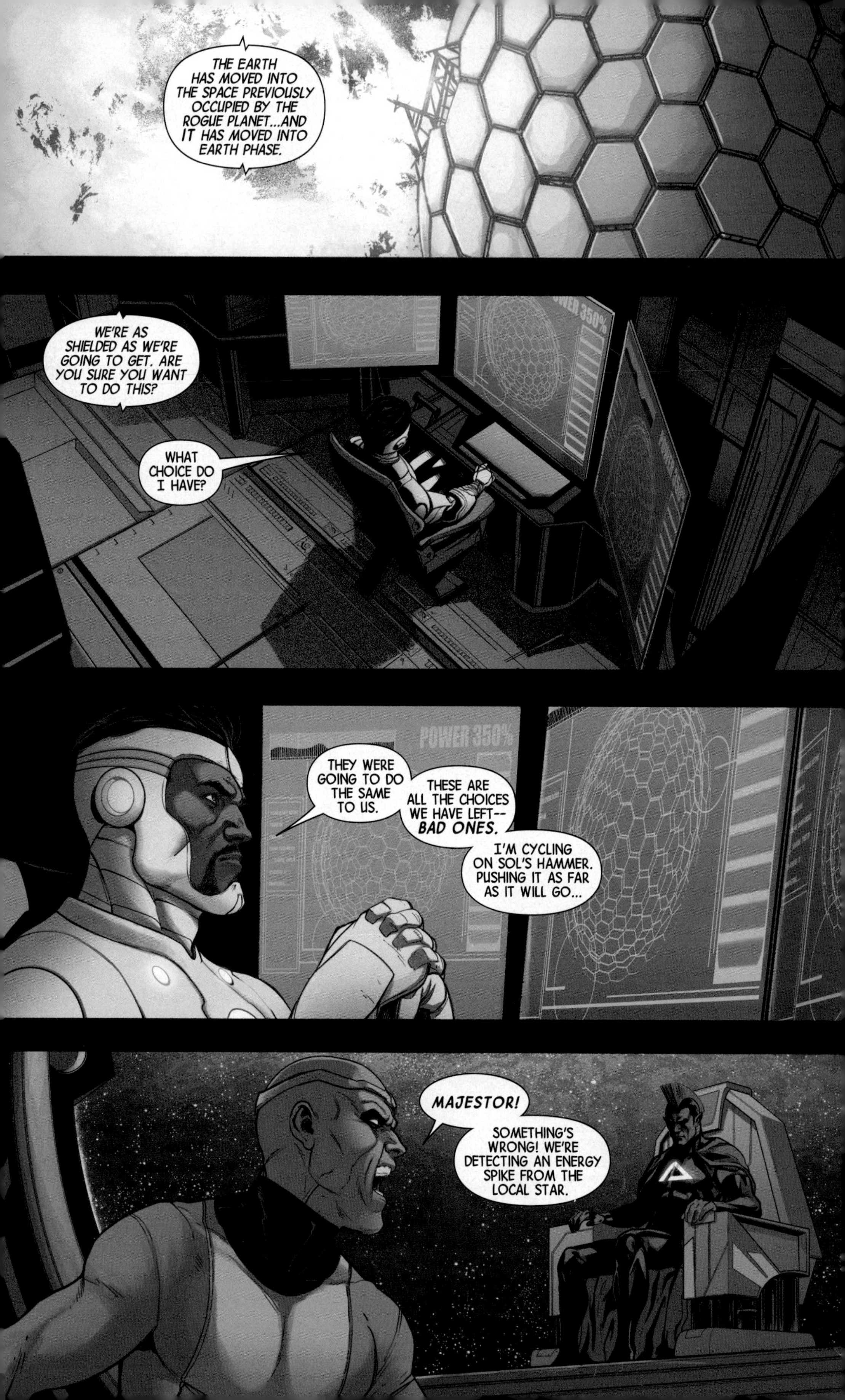
THE EARTH HAS MOVED INTO THE SPACE PREVIOUSLY OCCUPIED BY THE ROGUE PLANET...AND IT HAS MOVED INTO EARTH PHASE.
WE'RE AS SHIELDED AS WE'RE GOING TO GET. ARE YOU SURE YOU WANT TO DO THIS?
WHAT CHOICE DO I HAVE?
POWER 350%
THEY WERE GOING TO DO THE SAME TO US.
THESE ARE ALL THE CHOICES WE HAVE LEFT-- BAD ONES.
I'M CYCLING ON SOL'S HAMMER. PUSHING IT AS FAR AS IT WILL GO...
MAJESTOR!
SOMETHING'S WRONG! WE'RE DETECTING AN ENERGY SPIKE FROM THE LOCAL STAR.

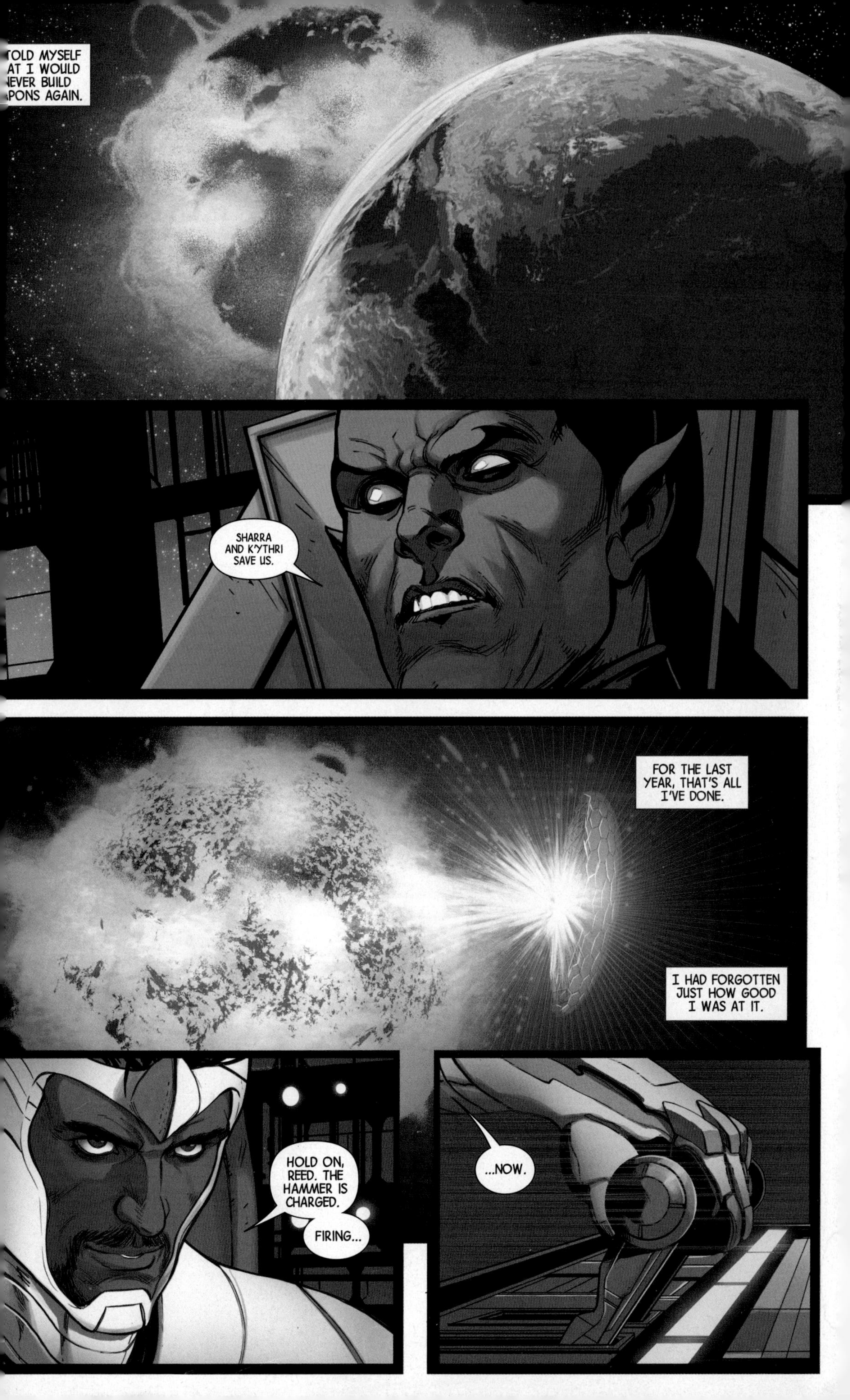
TOLD MYSELF
AT I WOULD
NEVER BUILD
APONS AGAIN.
SHARRA AND K'YTHRI SAVE US.
FOR THE LAST YEAR, THAT'S ALL I'VE DONE.
I HAD FORGOTTEN JUST HOW GOOD I WAS AT IT.
HOLD ON, REED. THE HAMMER IS CHARGED.
FIRING...
...NOW.

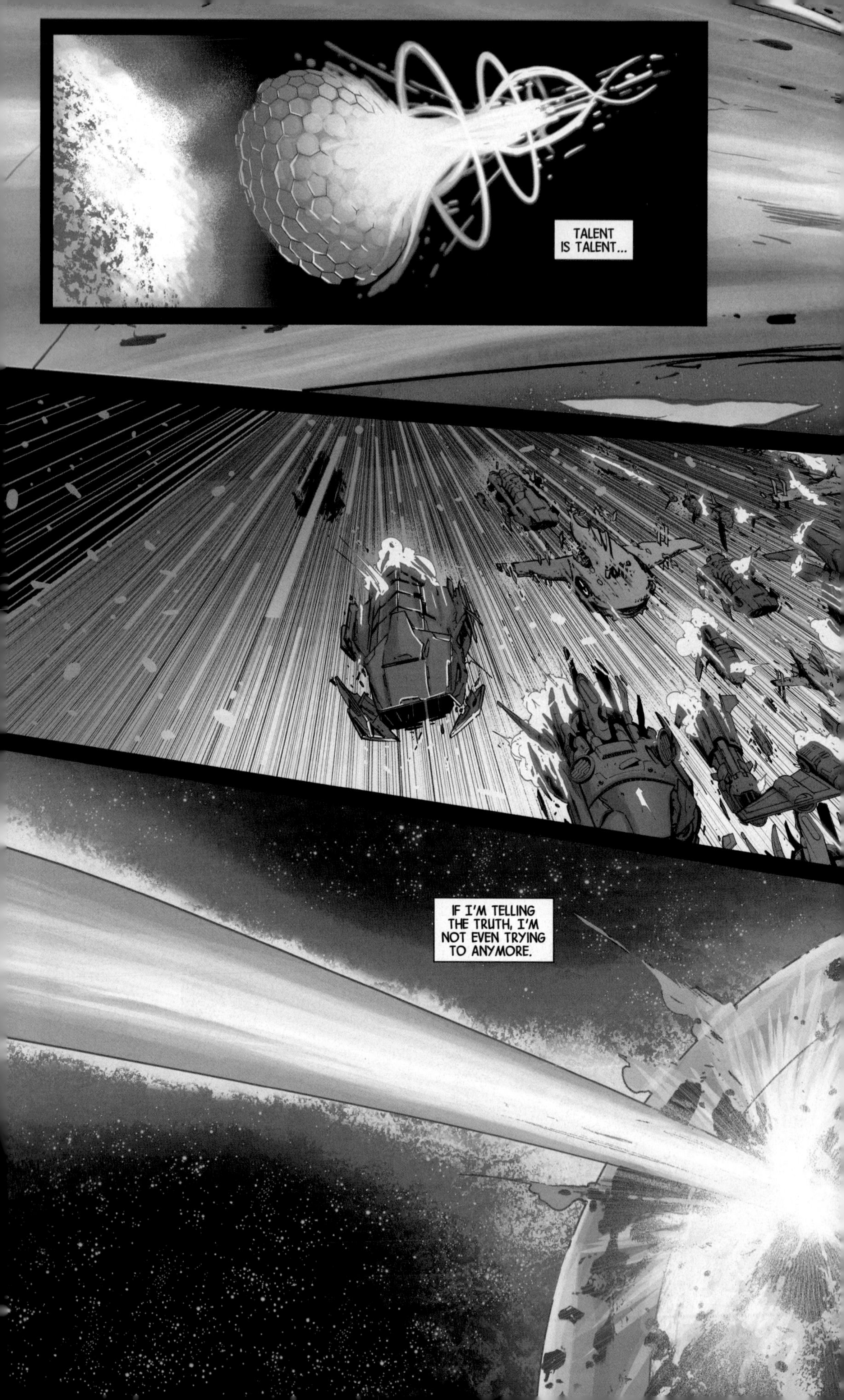
TALENT IS TALENT...
IF I'M TELLING THE TRUTH, I'M NOT EVEN TRYING TO ANYMORE.

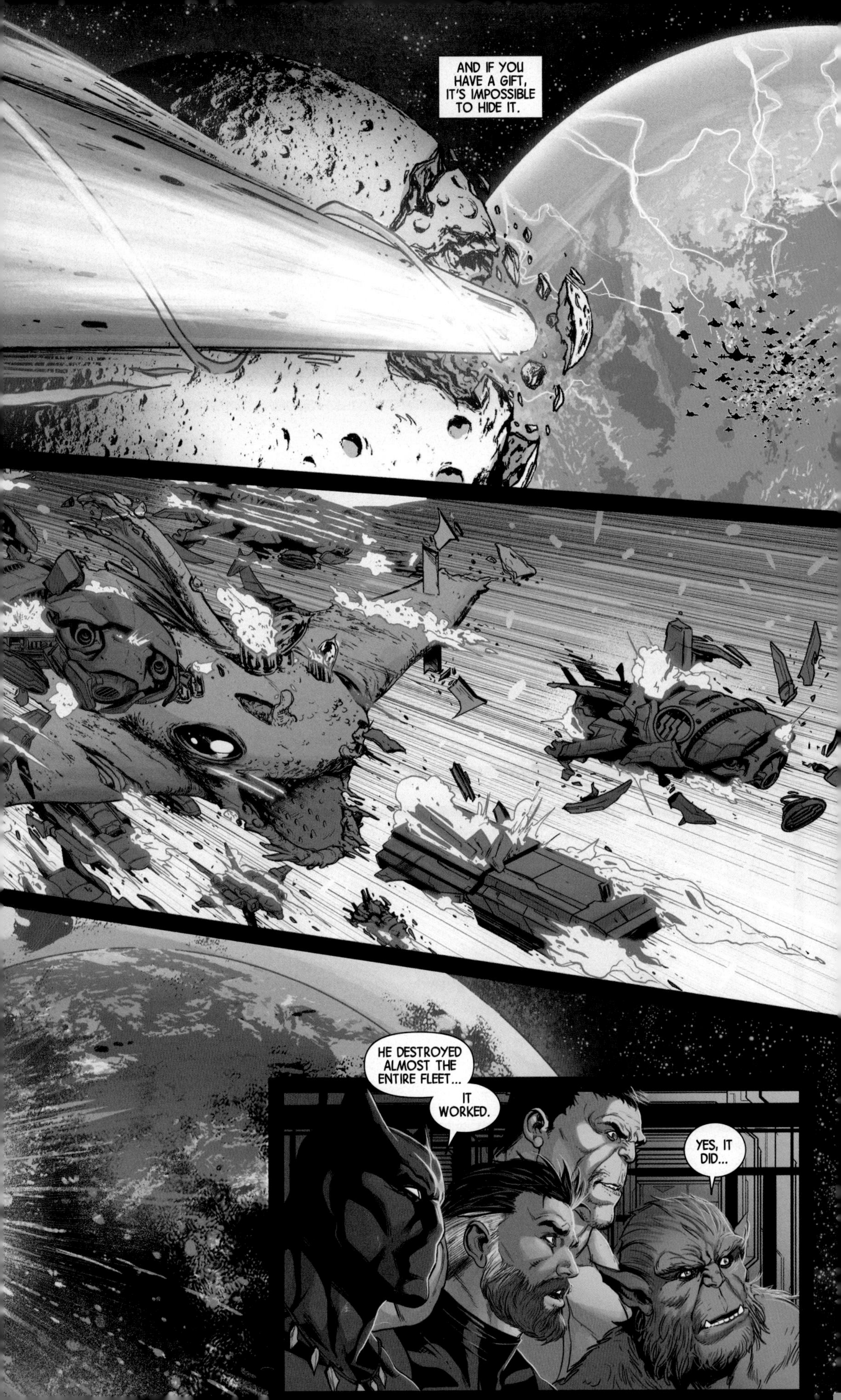
AND IF YOU HAVE A GIFT, IT'S IMPOSSIBLE TO HIDE IT.
HE DESTROYED ALMOST THE ENTIRE FLEET...
IT WORKED.
YES, IT DID...

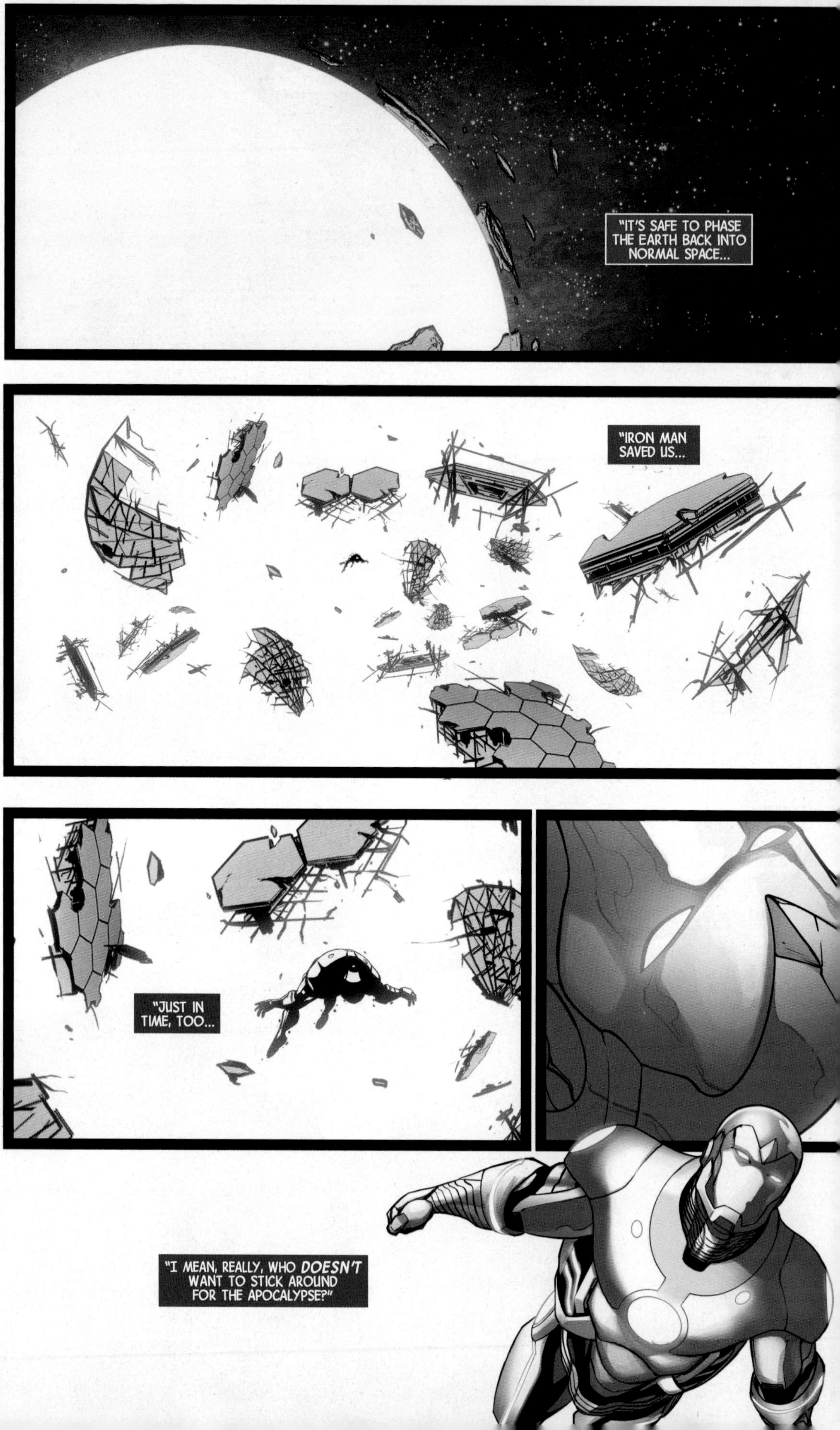
"IT'S SAFE TO PHASE THE EARTH BACK INTO NORMAL SPACE...
"IRON MAN SAVED US...
"JUST IN TIME, TOO...
"I MEAN, REALLY, WHO DOESN'T WANT TO STICK AROUND FOR THE APOCALYPSE?"

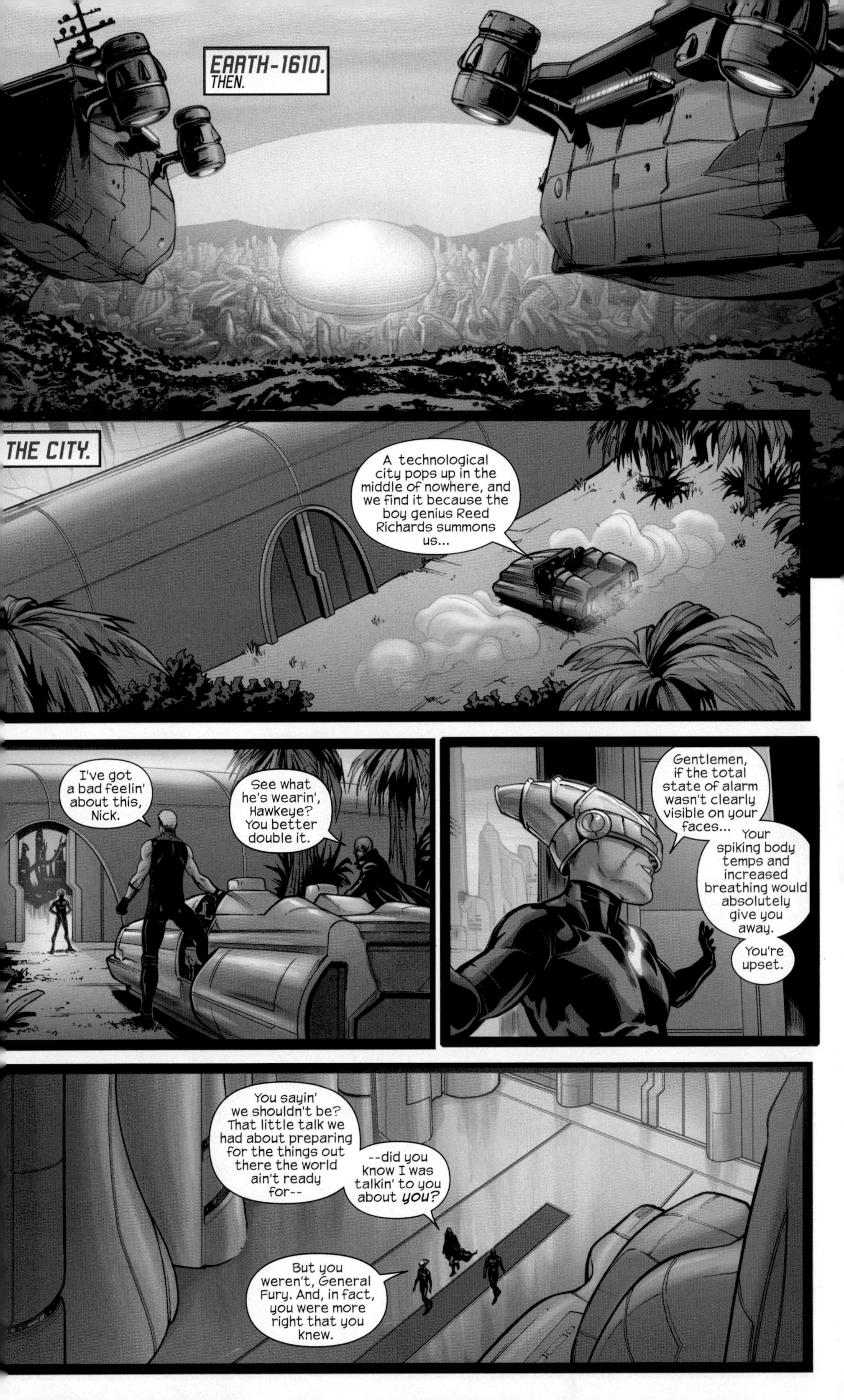
EARTH-1610.
THEN.
THE CITY.
A technological city pops up in the middle of nowhere, and we find it because the boy genius Reed Richards summons us...
I've got a bad feelin' about this, Nick.
See what he's wearin', Hawkeye? You better double it.
Gentlemen, if the total state of alarm wasn't clearly visible on your faces...
Your spiking body temps and increased breathing would absolutely give you away.
You're upset.
You sayin' we shouldn't be? That little talk we had about preparing for the things out there the world ain't ready for--
--did you know I was talkin' to you about *you*?
But you weren't, General Fury. And, in fact, you were more right that you knew.

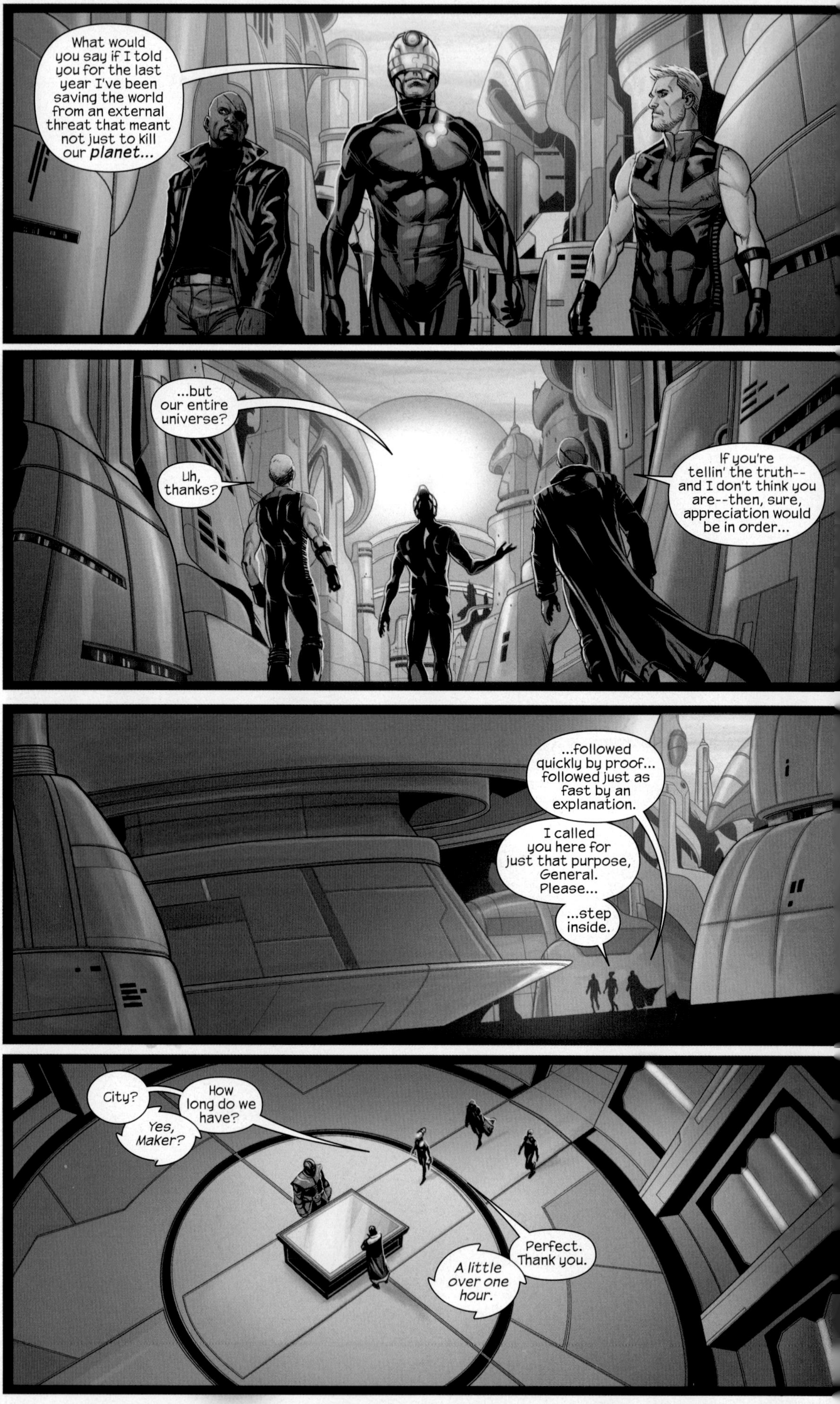
What would you say if I told you for the last year I've been saving the world from an external threat that meant not just to kill our *planet*...
...but our entire universe?
Uh, thanks?
If you're tellin' the truth-- and I don't think you are--then, sure, appreciation would be in order...
...followed quickly by proof... followed just as fast by an explanation.
I called you here for just that purpose, General. Please...
...step inside.
City?
How long do we have?
Yes, Maker?
A little over one hour.
Perfect. Thank you.

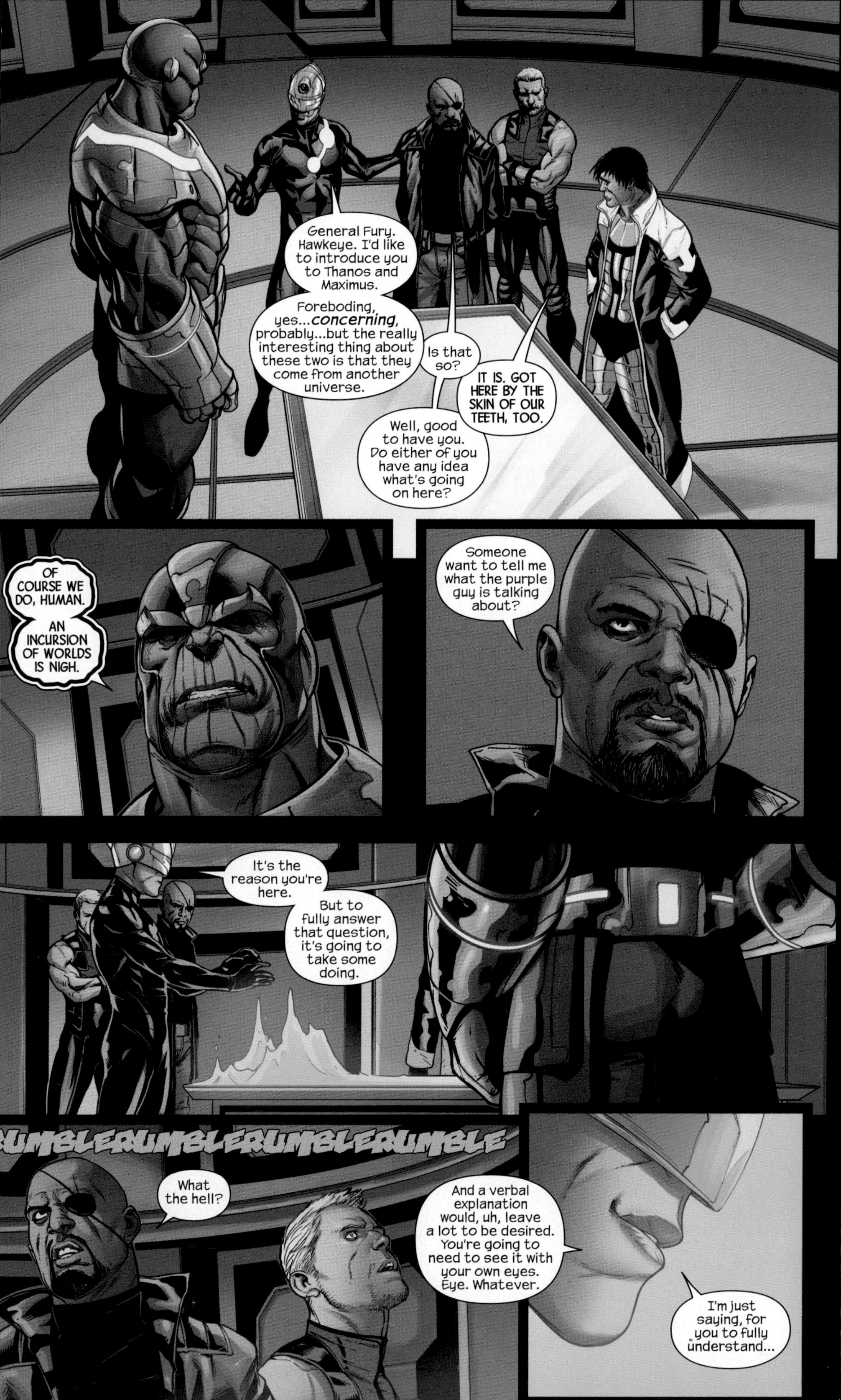

General Fury. Hawkeye. I'd like to introduce you to Thanos and Maximus.
Foreboding, yes...concerning, probably...but the really interesting thing about these two is that they come from another universe.
Is that so?
IT IS. GOT HERE BY THE SKIN OF OUR TEETH, TOO.
Well, good to have you. Do either of you have any idea what's going on here?
OF COURSE WE DO, HUMAN.
AN INCURSION OF WORLDS IS NIGH.
Someone want to tell me what the purple guy is talking about?
It's the reason you're here.
But to fully answer that question, it's going to take some doing.
RUMBLERUMBLERUMBLERUMBLE
What the hell?
And a verbal explanation would, uh, leave a lot to be desired. You're going to need to see it with your own eyes. Eye. Whatever.
I'm just saying, for you to fully understand...

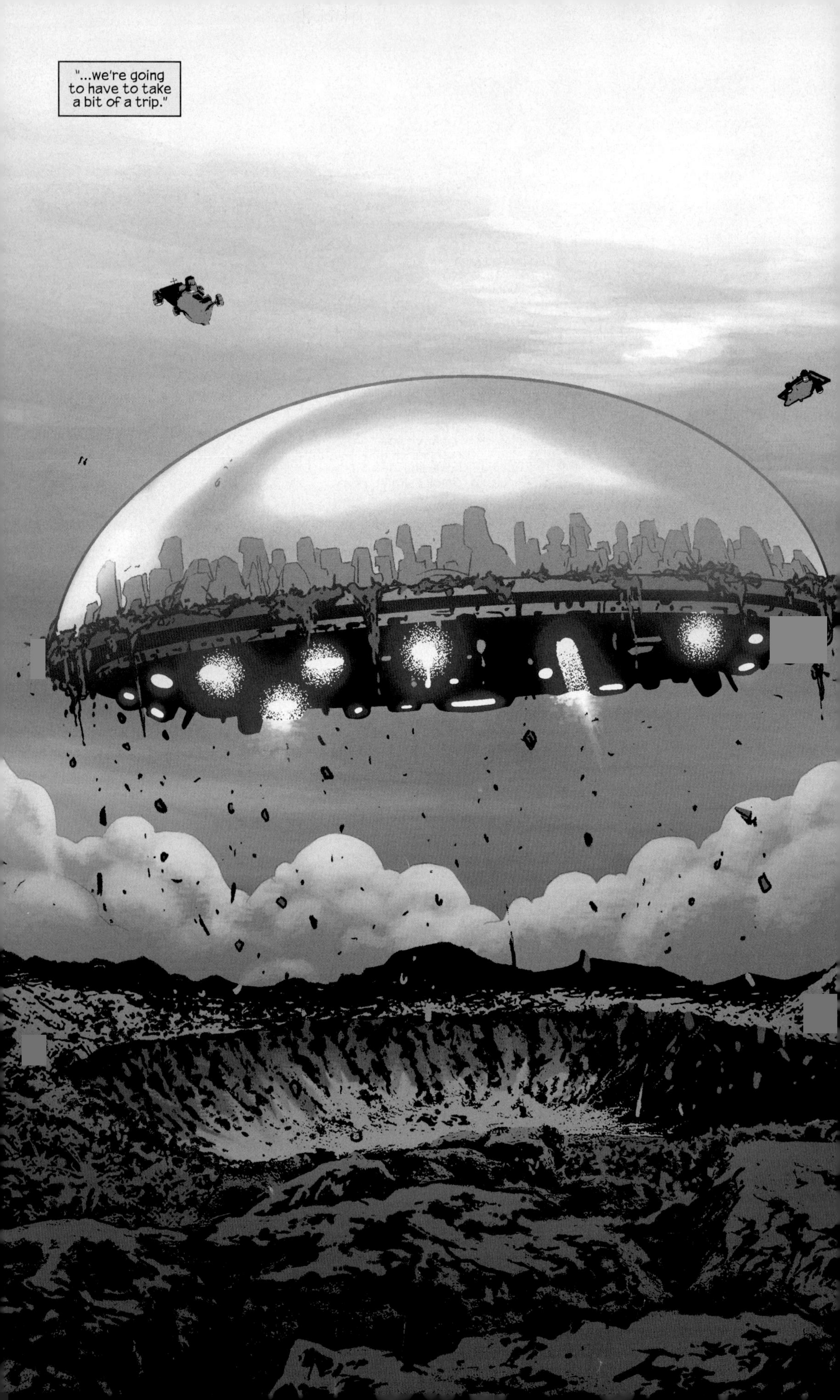
"...we're going to have to take a bit of a trip."

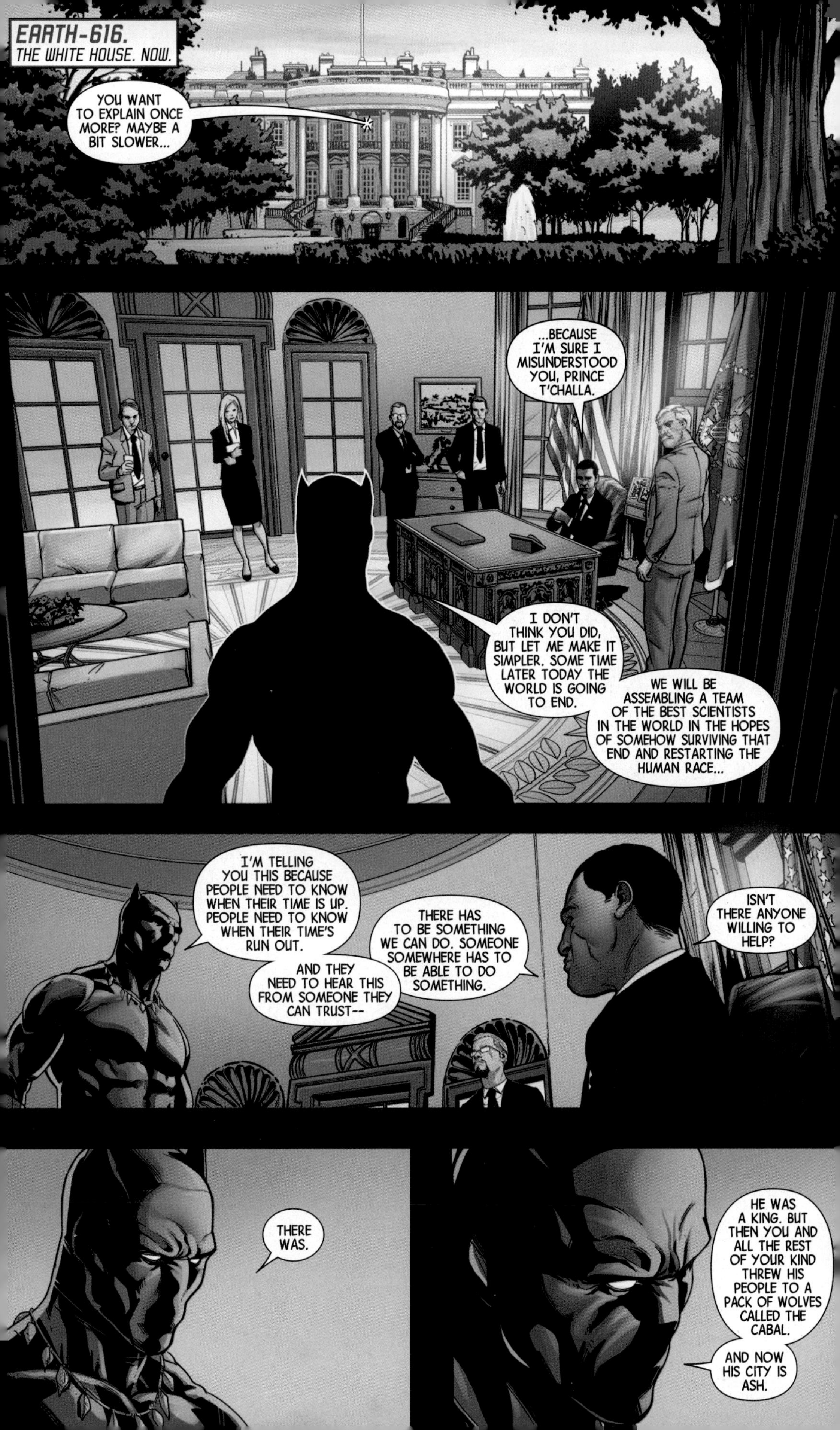
EARTH-616.
THE WHITE HOUSE. NOW.
YOU WANT TO EXPLAIN ONCE MORE? MAYBE A BIT SLOWER...
...BECAUSE I'M SURE I MISUNDERSTOOD YOU, PRINCE T'CHALLA.
I DON'T THINK YOU DID, BUT LET ME MAKE IT SIMPLER. SOME TIME LATER TODAY THE WORLD IS GOING TO END.
WE WILL BE ASSEMBLING A TEAM OF THE BEST SCIENTISTS IN THE WORLD IN THE HOPES OF SOMEHOW SURVIVING THAT END AND RESTARTING THE HUMAN RACE...
I'M TELLING YOU THIS BECAUSE PEOPLE NEED TO KNOW WHEN THEIR TIME IS UP. PEOPLE NEED TO KNOW WHEN THEIR TIME'S RUN OUT.
AND THEY NEED TO HEAR THIS FROM SOMEONE THEY CAN TRUST--
THERE HAS TO BE SOMETHING WE CAN DO. SOMEONE SOMEWHERE HAS TO BE ABLE TO DO SOMETHING.
ISN'T THERE ANYONE WILLING TO HELP?
THERE WAS.
HE WAS A KING. BUT THEN YOU AND ALL THE REST OF YOUR KIND THREW HIS PEOPLE TO A PACK OF WOLVES CALLED THE CABAL.
AND NOW HIS CITY IS ASH.

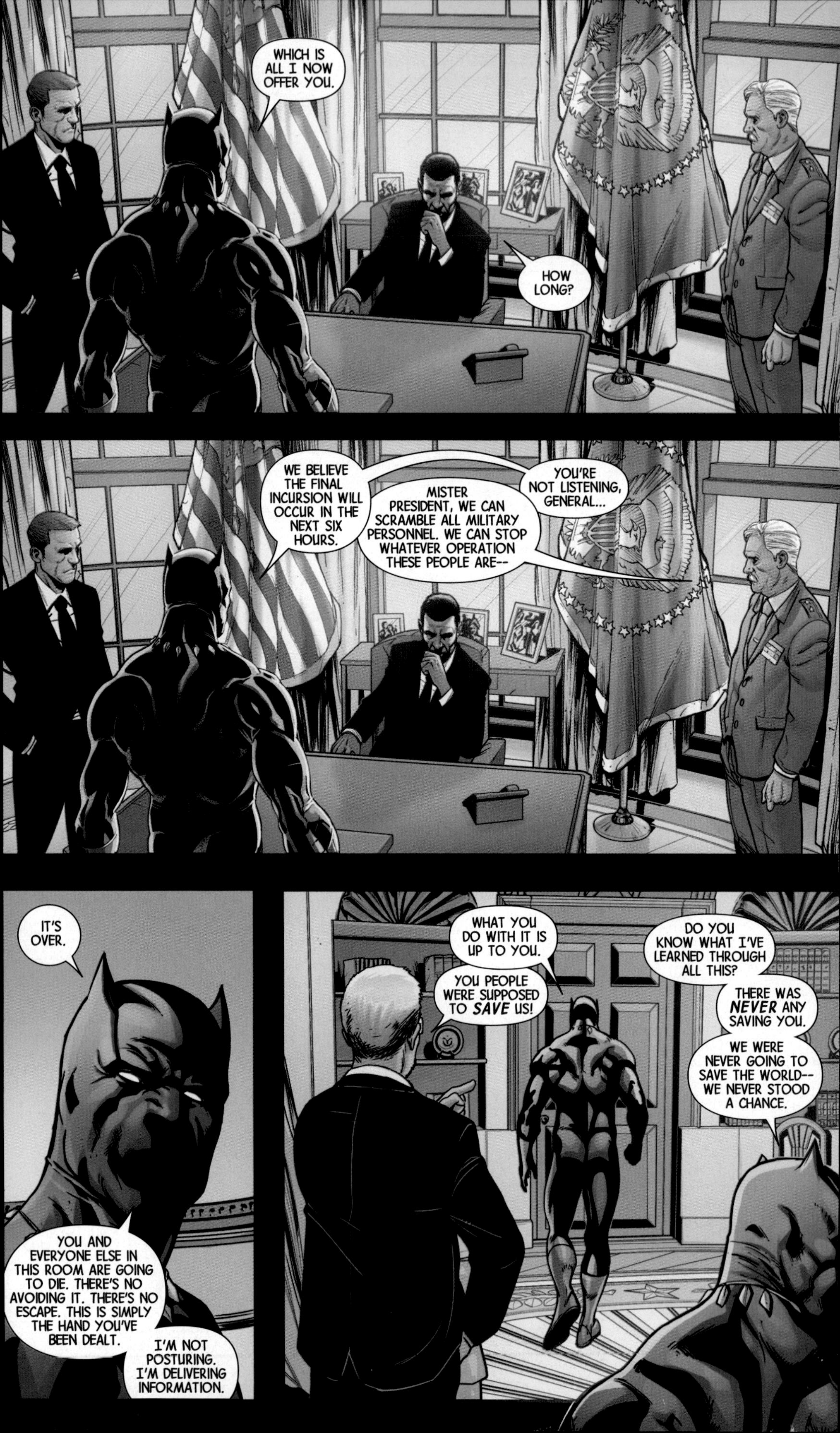
WHICH IS ALL I NOW OFFER YOU.
HOW LONG?
WE BELIEVE THE FINAL INCURSION WILL OCCUR IN THE NEXT SIX HOURS.
MISTER PRESIDENT, WE CAN SCRAMBLE ALL MILITARY PERSONNEL. WE CAN STOP WHATEVER OPERATION THESE PEOPLE ARE--
YOU'RE NOT LISTENING, GENERAL...
IT'S OVER.
YOU AND EVERYONE ELSE IN THIS ROOM ARE GOING TO DIE. THERE'S NO AVOIDING IT. THERE'S NO ESCAPE. THIS IS SIMPLY THE HAND YOU'VE BEEN DEALT.
I'M NOT POSTURING. I'M DELIVERING INFORMATION.
WHAT YOU DO WITH IT IS UP TO YOU.
YOU PEOPLE WERE SUPPOSED TO *SAVE* US!
DO YOU KNOW WHAT I'VE LEARNED THROUGH ALL THIS?
THERE WAS *NEVER* ANY SAVING YOU.
WE WERE NEVER GOING TO SAVE THE WORLD-- WE NEVER STOOD A CHANCE.

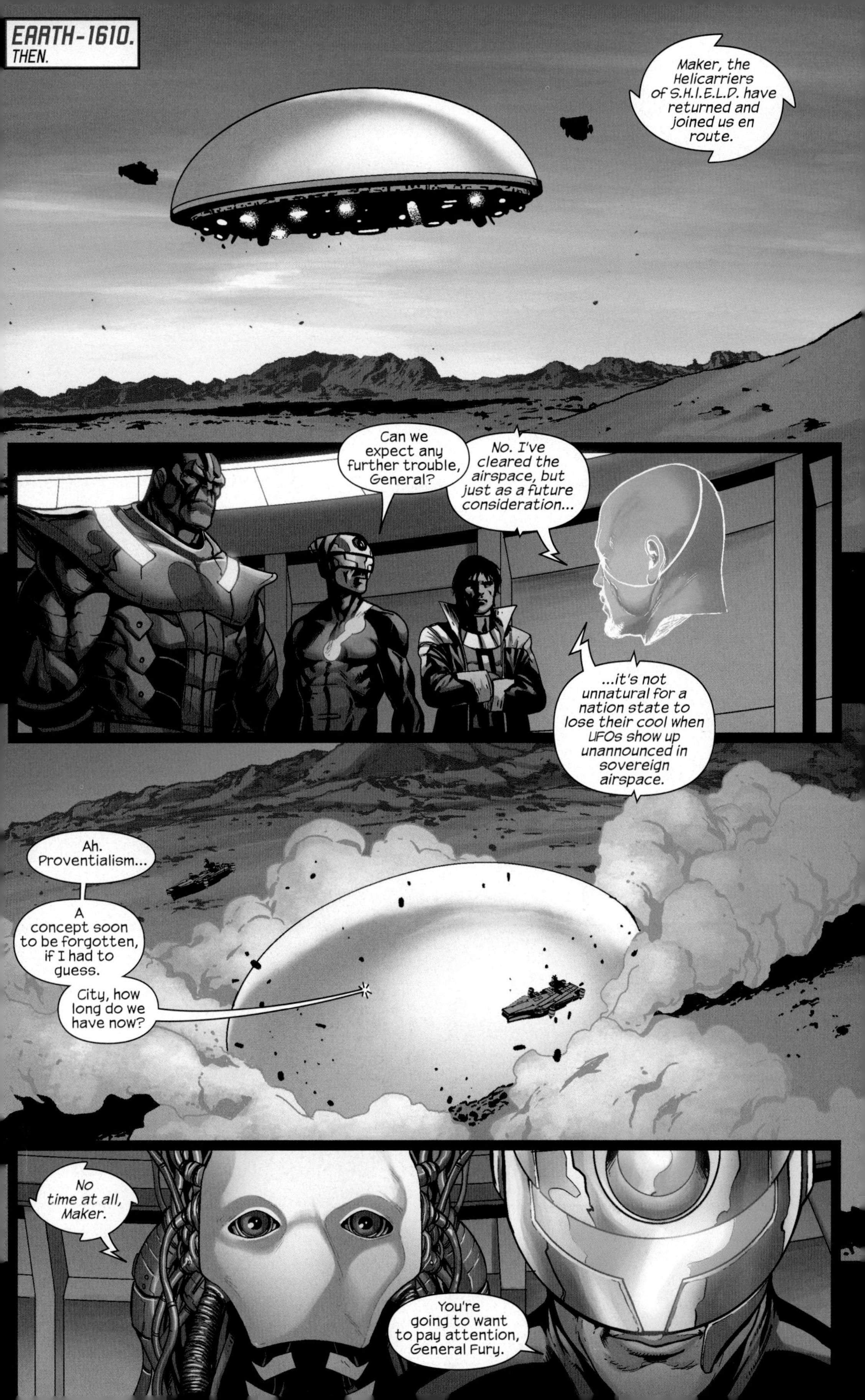
EARTH-1610.
THEN.
Maker, the Helicarriers of S.H.I.E.L.D. have returned and joined us en route.
Can we expect any further trouble, General?
No. I've cleared the airspace, but just as a future consideration...
...it's not unnatural for a nation state to lose their cool when UFOs show up unannounced in sovereign airspace.
Ah. Proventialism...
A concept soon to be forgotten, if I had to guess.
City, how long do we have now?
No time at all, Maker.
You're going to want to pay attention, General Fury.

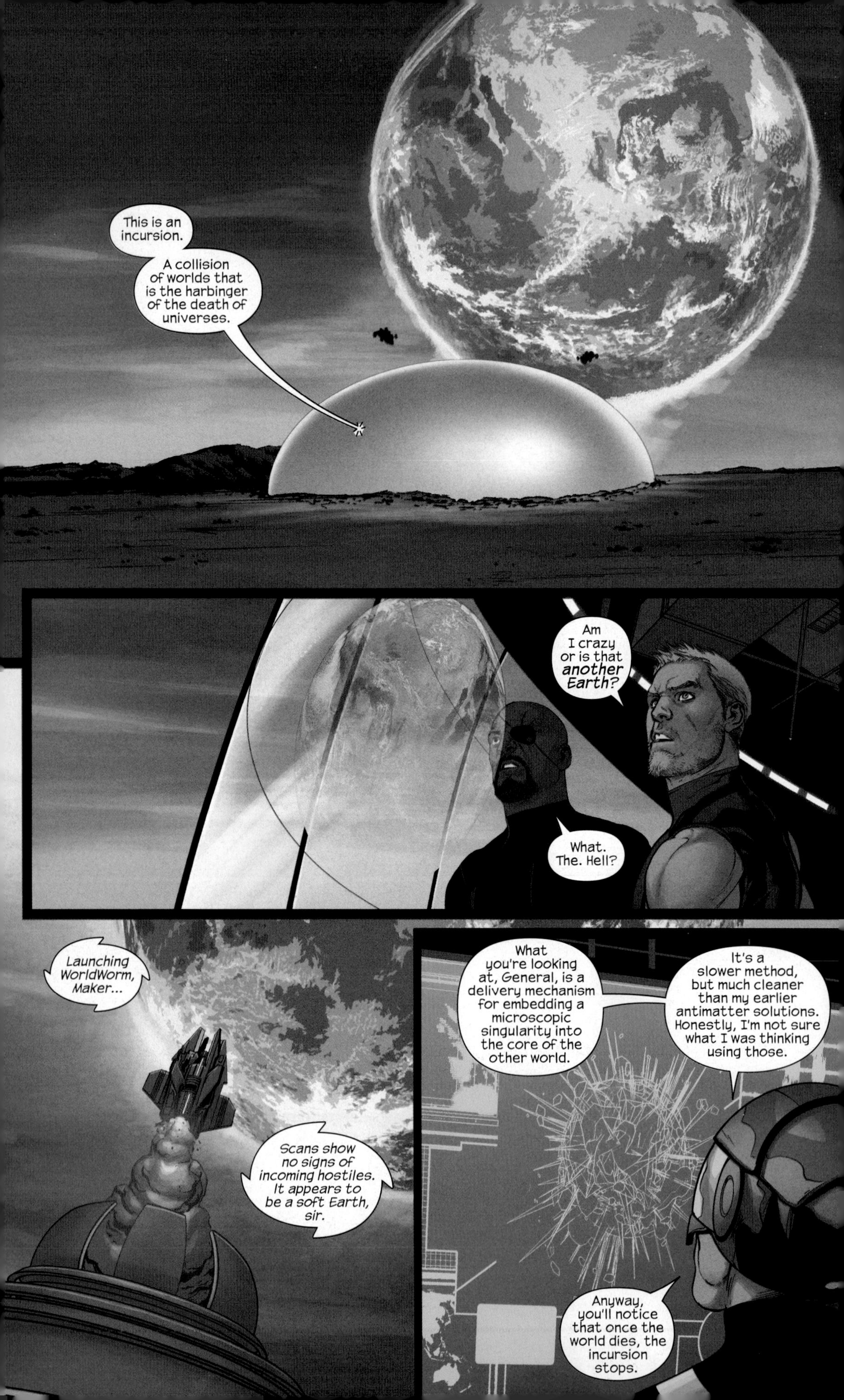
This is an incursion.
A collision of worlds that is the harbinger of the death of universes.
Am I crazy or is that *another Earth*?
What. The. Hell?
Launching WorldWorm, Maker...
Scans show no signs of incoming hostiles. It appears to be a soft Earth, sir.
What you're looking at, General, is a delivery mechanism for embedding a microscopic singularity into the core of the other world.
It's a slower method, but much cleaner than my earlier antimatter solutions. Honestly, I'm not sure what I was thinking using those.
Anyway, you'll notice that once the world dies, the incursion stops.

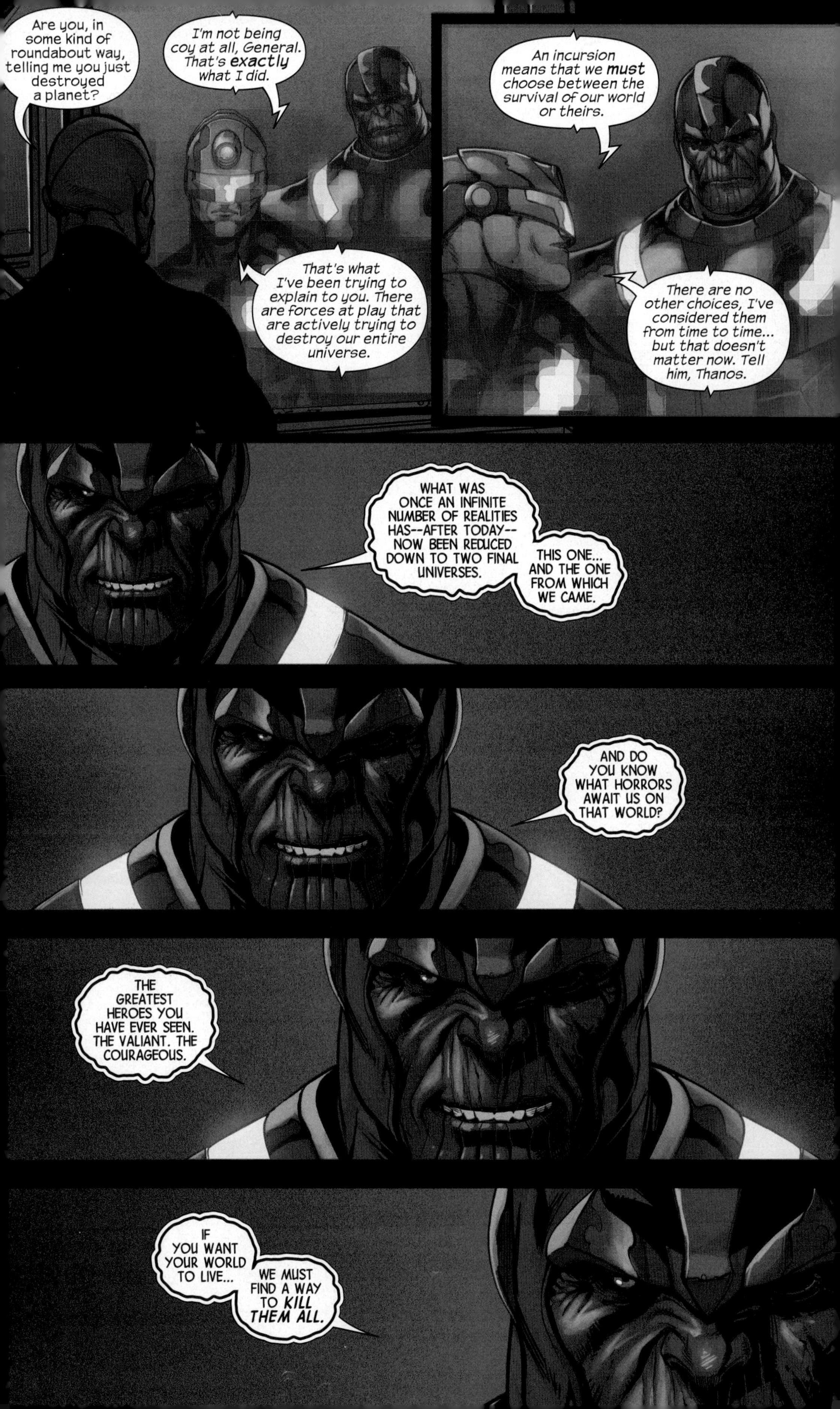

Are you, in some kind of roundabout way, telling me you just destroyed a planet?
I'm not being coy at all, General. That's **exactly** what I did.
That's what I've been trying to explain to you. There are forces at play that are actively trying to destroy our entire universe.
An incursion means that we **must** choose between the survival of our world or theirs.
There are no other choices, I've considered them from time to time... but that doesn't matter now. Tell him, Thanos.
WHAT WAS ONCE AN INFINITE NUMBER OF REALITIES HAS--AFTER TODAY--NOW BEEN REDUCED DOWN TO TWO FINAL UNIVERSES.
THIS ONE... AND THE ONE FROM WHICH WE CAME.
AND DO YOU KNOW WHAT HORRORS AWAIT US ON THAT WORLD?
THE GREATEST HEROES YOU HAVE EVER SEEN. THE VALIANT. THE COURAGEOUS.
IF YOU WANT YOUR WORLD TO LIVE...
WE MUST FIND A WAY TO ***KILL THEM ALL.***

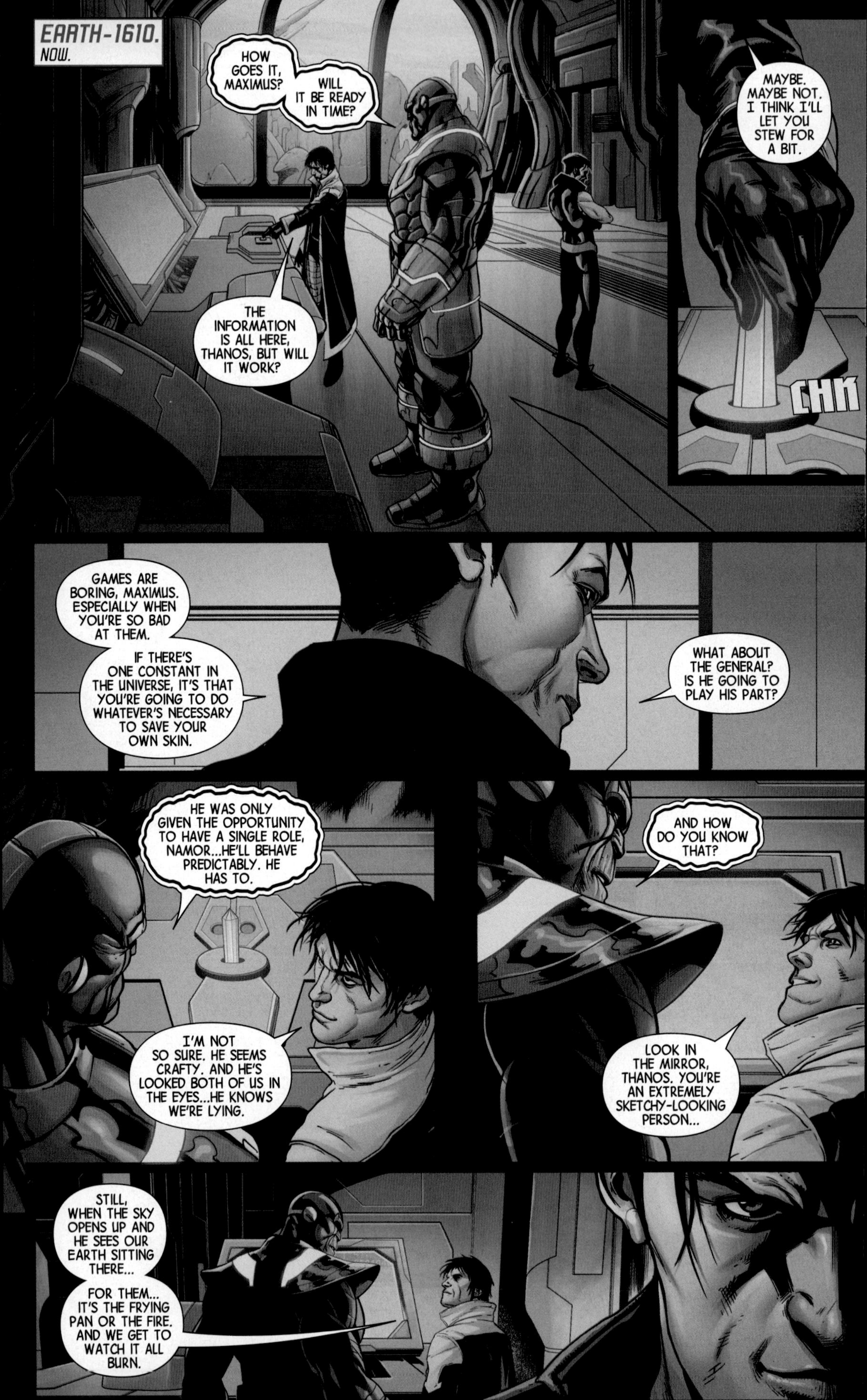
EARTH-1610. NOW.
HOW GOES IT, MAXIMUS?
WILL IT BE READY IN TIME?
MAYBE. MAYBE NOT. I THINK I'LL LET YOU STEW FOR A BIT.
CHK
THE INFORMATION IS ALL HERE, THANOS, BUT WILL IT WORK?
GAMES ARE BORING, MAXIMUS. ESPECIALLY WHEN YOU'RE SO BAD AT THEM.
IF THERE'S ONE CONSTANT IN THE UNIVERSE, IT'S THAT YOU'RE GOING TO DO WHATEVER'S NECESSARY TO SAVE YOUR OWN SKIN.
WHAT ABOUT THE GENERAL? IS HE GOING TO PLAY HIS PART?
HE WAS ONLY GIVEN THE OPPORTUNITY TO HAVE A SINGLE ROLE, NAMOR...HE'LL BEHAVE PREDICTABLY. HE HAS TO.
I'M NOT SO SURE. HE SEEMS CRAFTY. AND HE'S LOOKED BOTH OF US IN THE EYES...HE KNOWS WE'RE LYING.
AND HOW DO YOU KNOW THAT?
LOOK IN THE MIRROR, THANOS. YOU'RE AN EXTREMELY SKETCHY-LOOKING PERSON...
STILL, WHEN THE SKY OPENS UP AND HE SEES OUR EARTH SITTING THERE...
FOR THEM... IT'S THE FRYING PAN OR THE FIRE. AND WE GET TO WATCH IT ALL BURN.

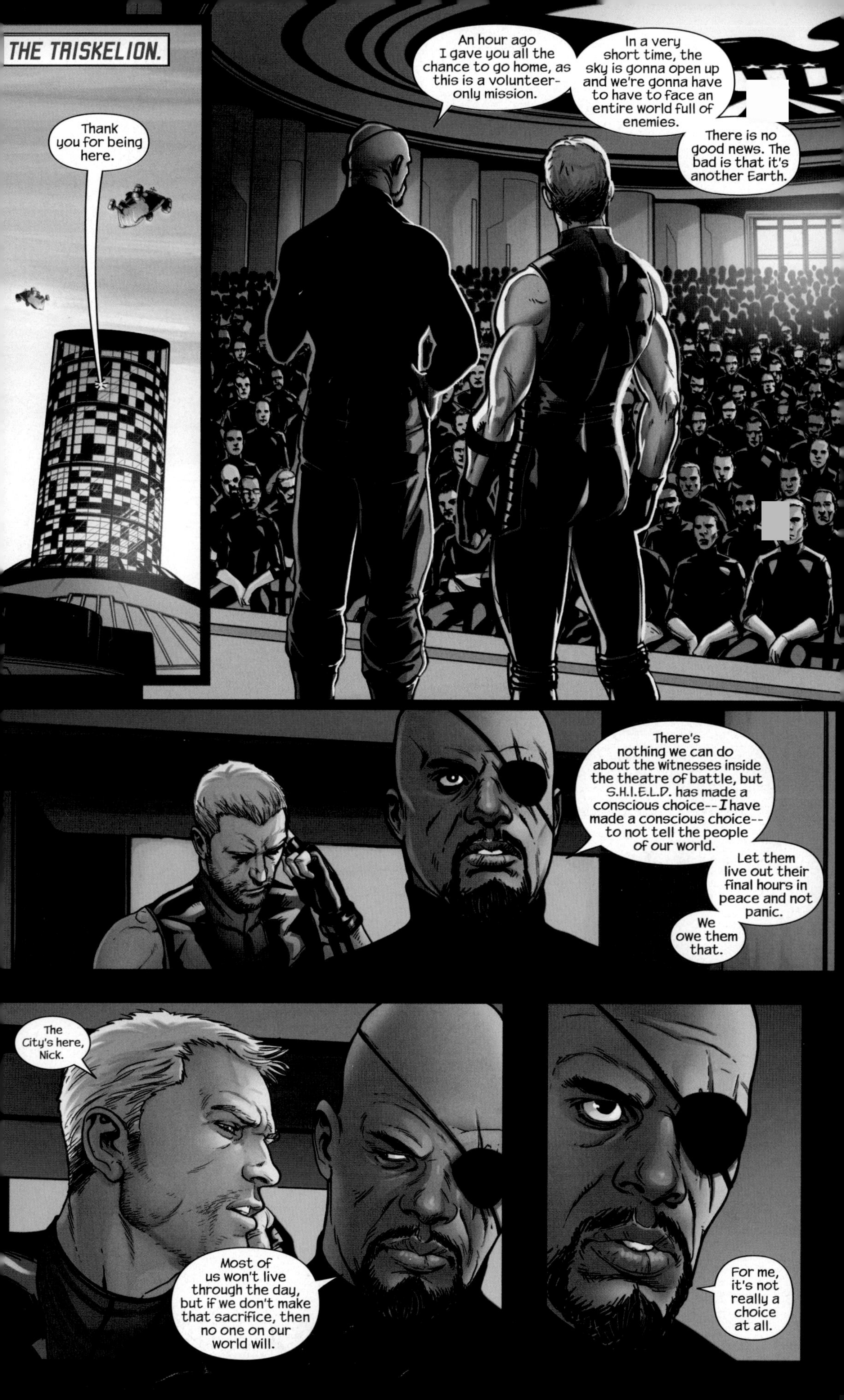
THE TRISKELION.
Thank you for being here.
An hour ago I gave you all the chance to go home, as this is a volunteer-only mission.
In a very short time, the sky is gonna open up and we're gonna have to have to face an entire world full of enemies.
There is no good news. The bad is that it's another Earth.
There's nothing we can do about the witnesses inside the theatre of battle, but S.H.I.E.L.D. has made a conscious choice-- I have made a conscious choice-- to not tell the people of our world.
Let them live out their final hours in peace and not panic.
We owe them that.
The City's here, Nick.
Most of us won't live through the day, but if we don't make that sacrifice, then no one on our world will.
For me, it's not really a choice at all.

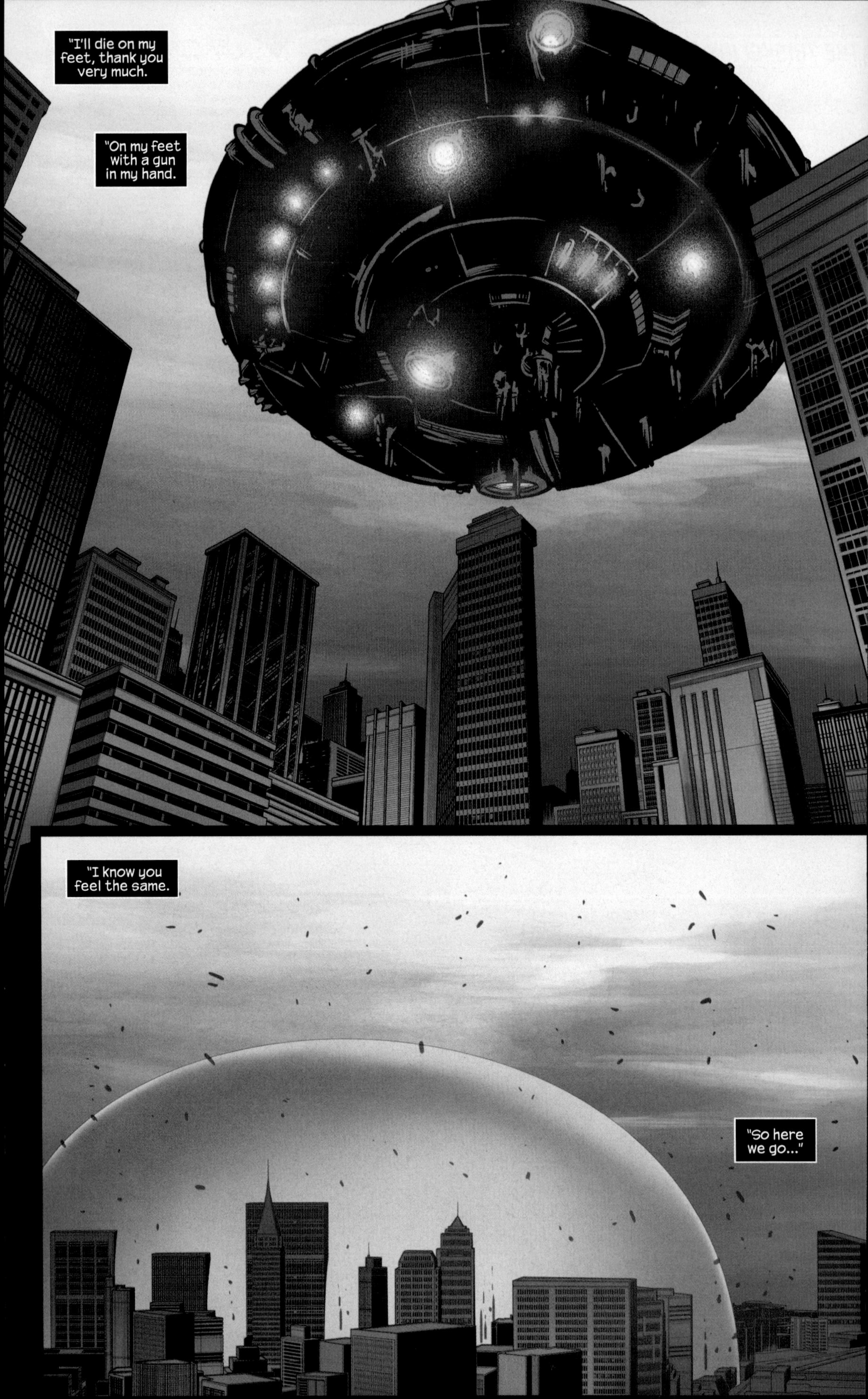
"I'll die on my feet, thank you very much.
"On my feet with a gun in my hand.
"I know you feel the same.
"So here we go..."

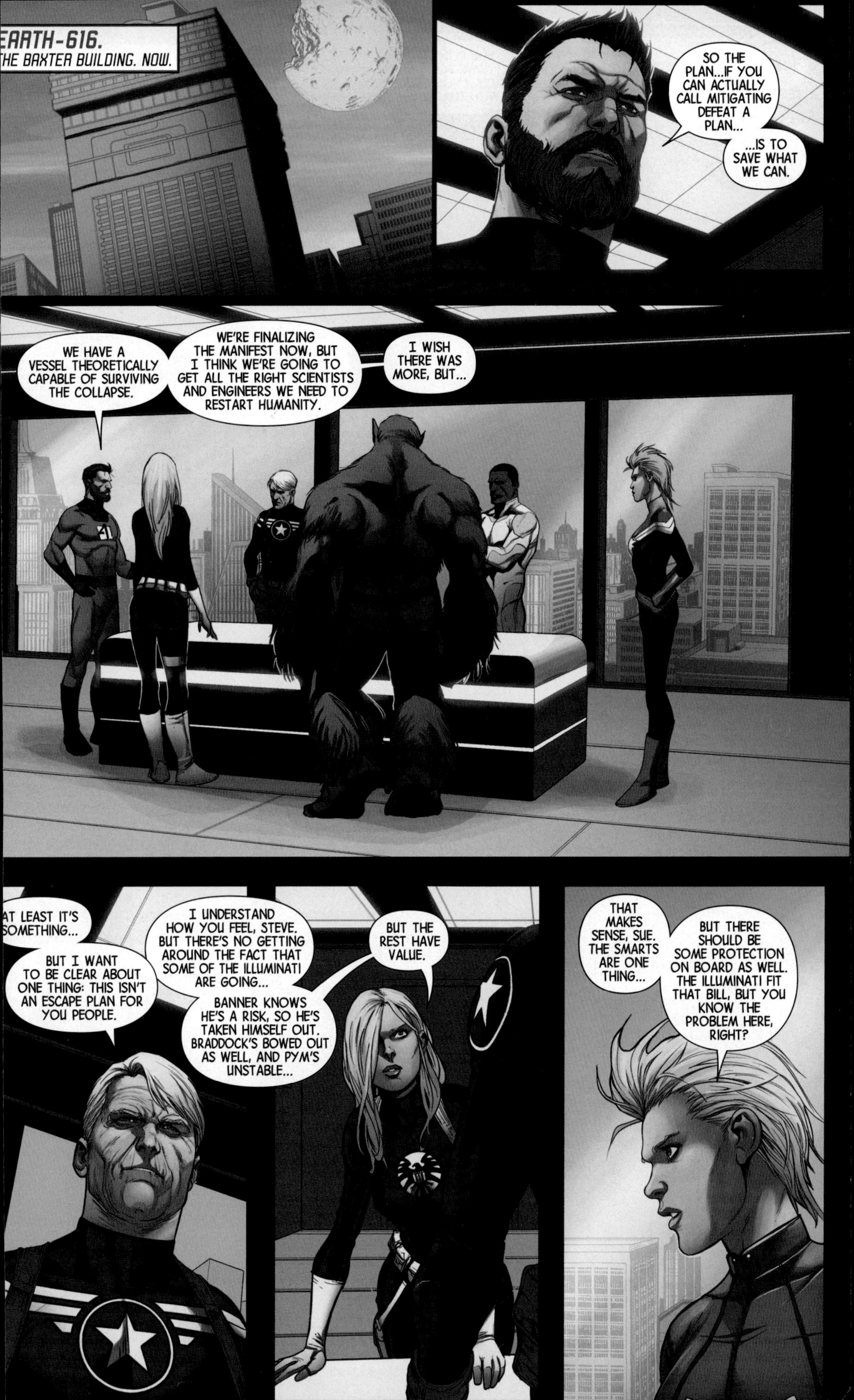
EARTH-616.
THE BAXTER BUILDING. NOW.
SO THE PLAN...IF YOU CAN ACTUALLY CALL MITIGATING DEFEAT A PLAN...
...IS TO SAVE WHAT WE CAN.
WE HAVE A VESSEL THEORETICALLY CAPABLE OF SURVIVING THE COLLAPSE.
WE'RE FINALIZING THE MANIFEST NOW, BUT I THINK WE'RE GOING TO GET ALL THE RIGHT SCIENTISTS AND ENGINEERS WE NEED TO RESTART HUMANITY.
I WISH THERE WAS MORE, BUT...
AT LEAST IT'S SOMETHING...
BUT I WANT TO BE CLEAR ABOUT ONE THING: THIS ISN'T AN ESCAPE PLAN FOR YOU PEOPLE.
I UNDERSTAND HOW YOU FEEL, STEVE. BUT THERE'S NO GETTING AROUND THE FACT THAT SOME OF THE ILLUMINATI ARE GOING...
BANNER KNOWS HE'S A RISK, SO HE'S TAKEN HIMSELF OUT. BRADDOCK'S BOWED OUT AS WELL, AND PYM'S UNSTABLE...
BUT THE REST HAVE VALUE.
THAT MAKES SENSE, SUE. THE SMARTS ARE ONE THING...
BUT THERE SHOULD BE SOME PROTECTION ON BOARD AS WELL. THE ILLUMINATI FIT THAT BILL, BUT YOU KNOW THE PROBLEM HERE, RIGHT?

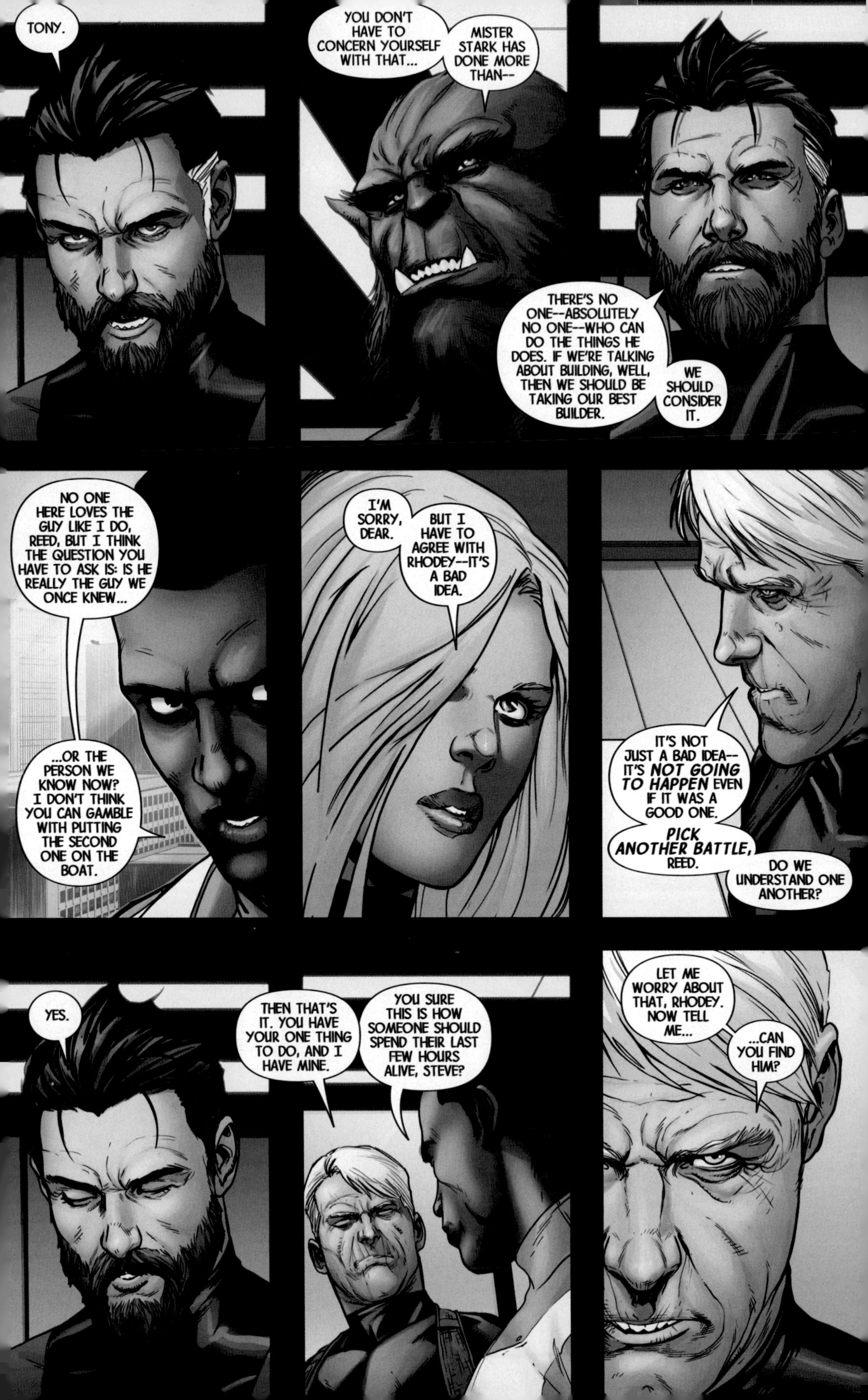
TONY.
YOU DON'T HAVE TO CONCERN YOURSELF WITH THAT...
MISTER STARK HAS DONE MORE THAN--
THERE'S NO ONE--ABSOLUTELY NO ONE--WHO CAN DO THE THINGS HE DOES. IF WE'RE TALKING ABOUT BUILDING, WELL, THEN WE SHOULD BE TAKING OUR BEST BUILDER.
WE SHOULD CONSIDER IT.
NO ONE HERE LOVES THE GUY LIKE I DO, REED, BUT I THINK THE QUESTION YOU HAVE TO ASK IS: IS HE REALLY THE GUY WE ONCE KNEW...
...OR THE PERSON WE KNOW NOW? I DON'T THINK YOU CAN GAMBLE WITH PUTTING THE SECOND ONE ON THE BOAT.
I'M SORRY, DEAR.
BUT I HAVE TO AGREE WITH RHODEY--IT'S A BAD IDEA.
IT'S NOT JUST A BAD IDEA--IT'S NOT GOING TO HAPPEN EVEN IF IT WAS A GOOD ONE.
PICK ANOTHER BATTLE, REED.
DO WE UNDERSTAND ONE ANOTHER?
YES.
THEN THAT'S IT. YOU HAVE YOUR ONE THING TO DO, AND I HAVE MINE.
YOU SURE THIS IS HOW SOMEONE SHOULD SPEND THEIR LAST FEW HOURS ALIVE, STEVE?
LET ME WORRY ABOUT THAT, RHODEY. NOW TELL ME...
...CAN YOU FIND HIM?

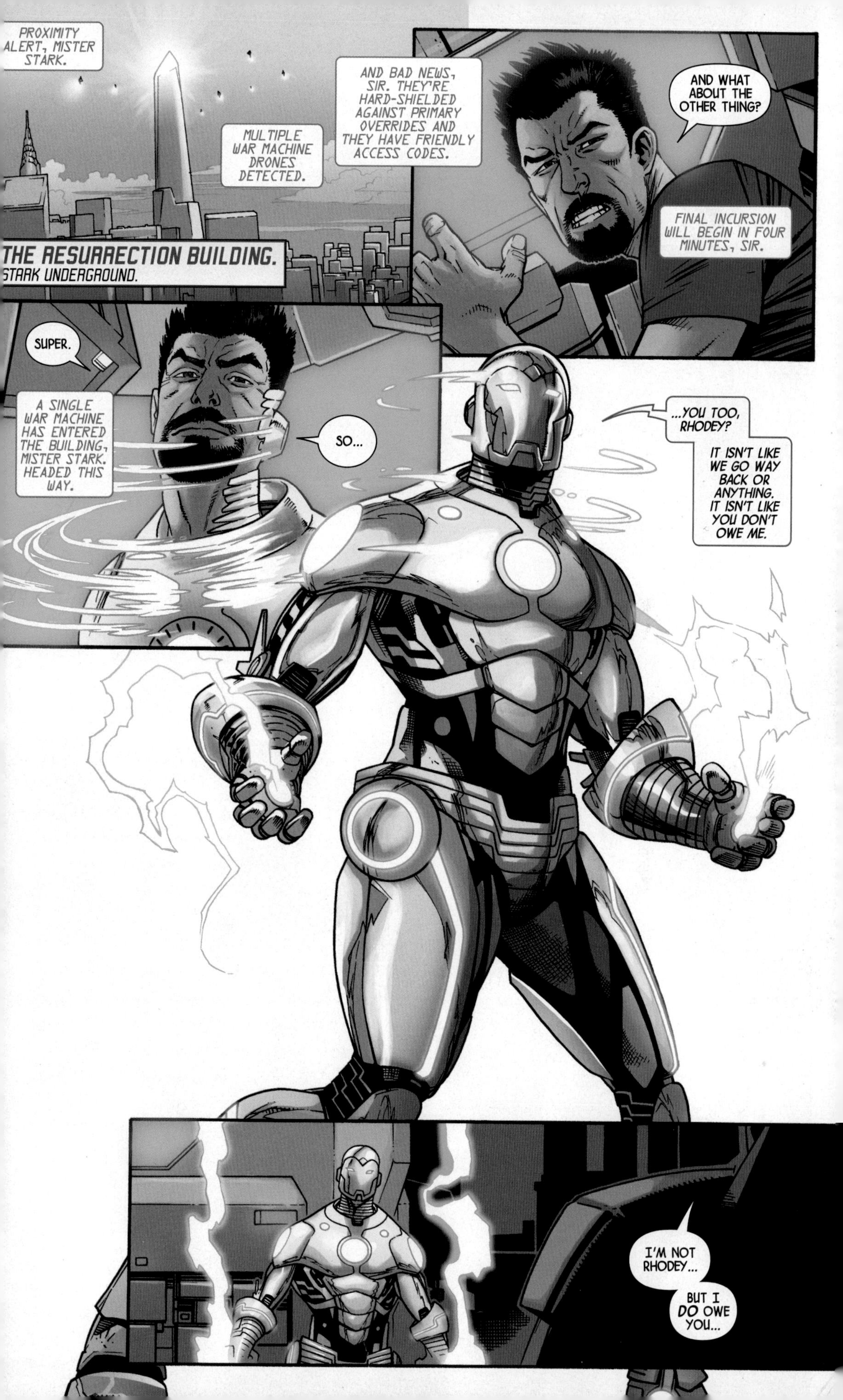
PROXIMITY ALERT, MISTER STARK.
MULTIPLE WAR MACHINE DRONES DETECTED.
THE RESURRECTION BUILDING.
STARK UNDERGROUND.
AND BAD NEWS, SIR. THEY'RE HARD-SHIELDED AGAINST PRIMARY OVERRIDES AND THEY HAVE FRIENDLY ACCESS CODES.
AND WHAT ABOUT THE OTHER THING?
FINAL INCURSION WILL BEGIN IN FOUR MINUTES, SIR.
SUPER.
A SINGLE WAR MACHINE HAS ENTERED THE BUILDING, MISTER STARK. HEADED THIS WAY.
SO...
...YOU TOO, RHODEY?
IT ISN'T LIKE WE GO WAY BACK OR ANYTHING. IT ISN'T LIKE YOU DON'T OWE ME.
I'M NOT RHODEY...
BUT I DO OWE YOU...

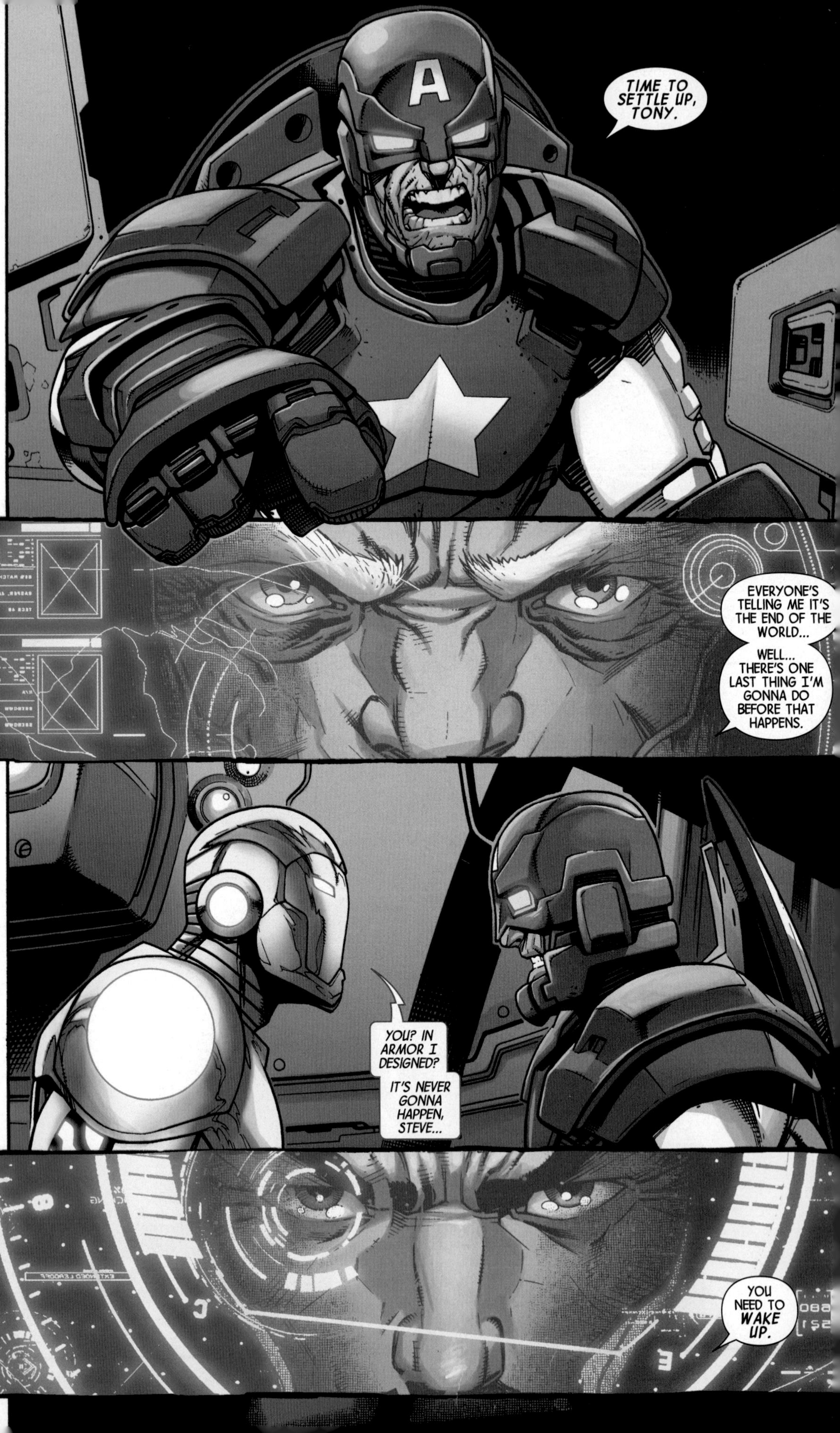
TIME TO SETTLE UP, TONY.
EVERYONE'S TELLING ME IT'S THE END OF THE WORLD...
WELL... THERE'S ONE LAST THING I'M GONNA DO BEFORE THAT HAPPENS.
YOU? IN ARMOR I DESIGNED?
IT'S NEVER GONNA HAPPEN, STEVE...
YOU NEED TO WAKE UP.

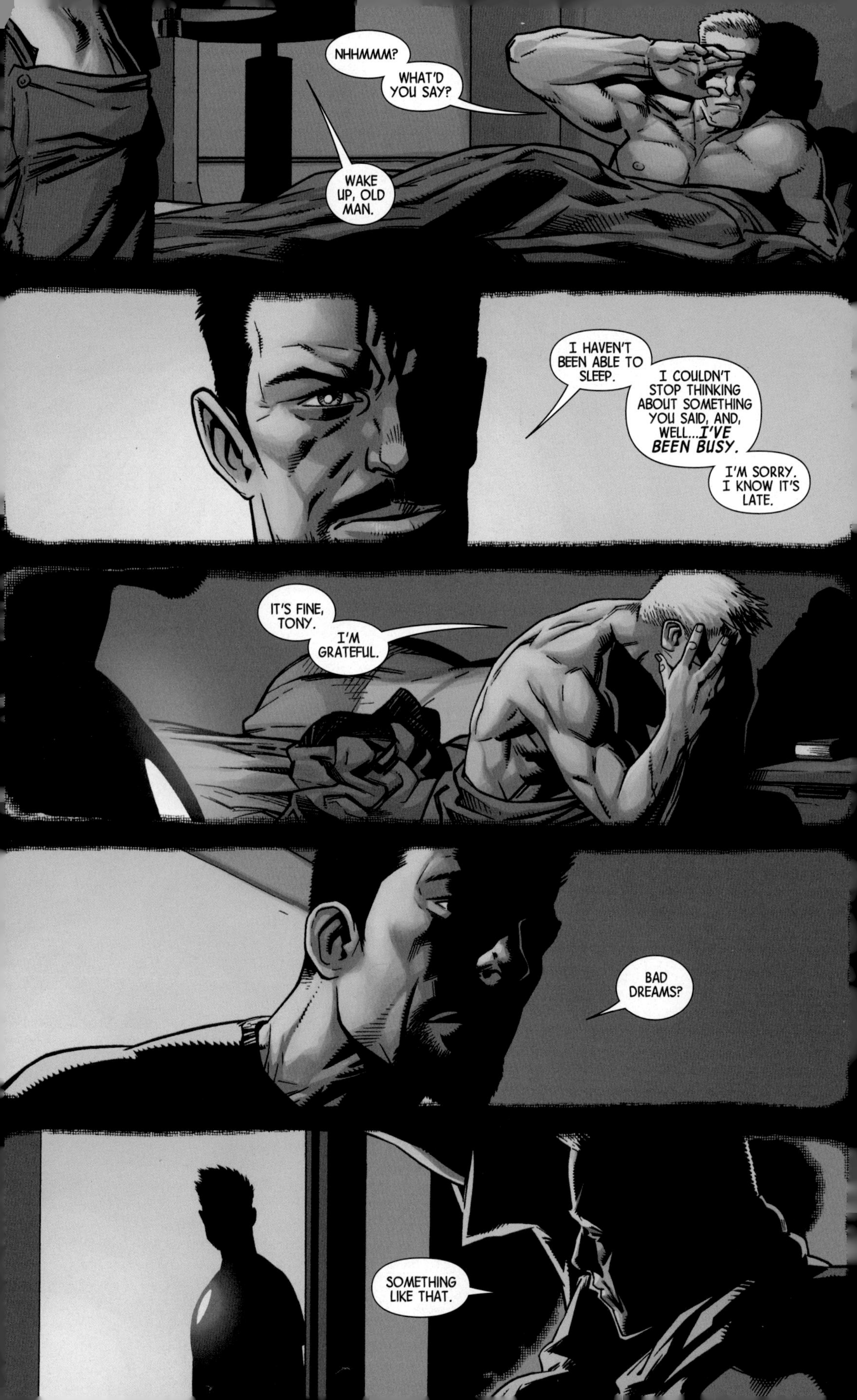
NHHMMM?
WHAT'D YOU SAY?
WAKE UP, OLD MAN.
I HAVEN'T BEEN ABLE TO SLEEP.
I COULDN'T STOP THINKING ABOUT SOMETHING YOU SAID, AND, WELL... *I'VE BEEN BUSY.*
I'M SORRY. I KNOW IT'S LATE.
IT'S FINE, TONY.
I'M GRATEFUL.
BAD DREAMS?
SOMETHING LIKE THAT.

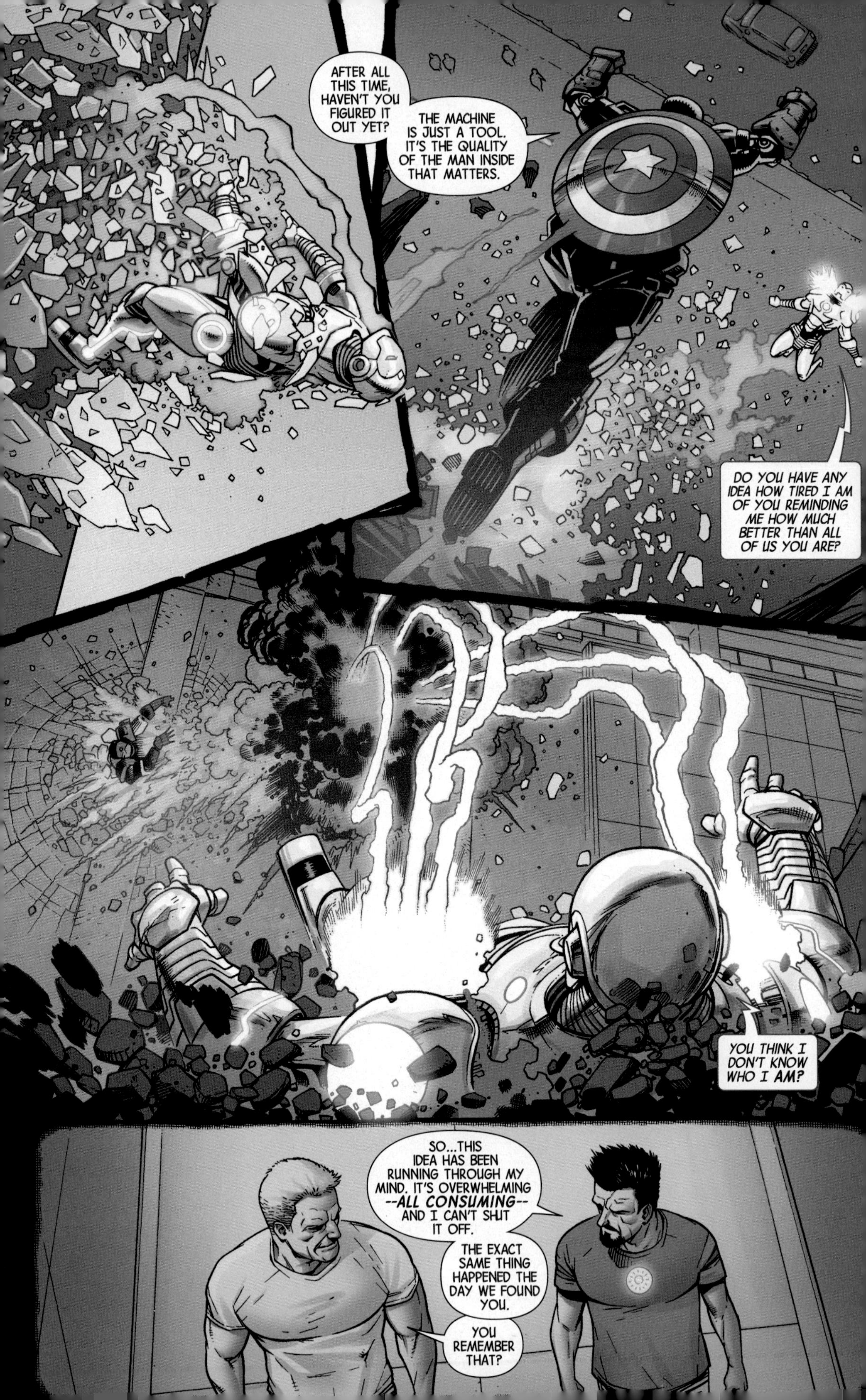

AFTER ALL THIS TIME, HAVEN'T YOU FIGURED IT OUT YET?
THE MACHINE IS JUST A TOOL. IT'S THE QUALITY OF THE MAN INSIDE THAT MATTERS.
DO YOU HAVE ANY IDEA HOW TIRED I AM OF YOU REMINDING ME HOW MUCH BETTER THAN ALL OF US YOU ARE?
YOU THINK I DON'T KNOW WHO I *AM?*
SO...THIS IDEA HAS BEEN RUNNING THROUGH MY MIND. IT'S OVERWHELMING --*ALL CONSUMING*-- AND I CAN'T SHUT IT OFF.
THE EXACT SAME THING HAPPENED THE DAY WE FOUND YOU.
YOU REMEMBER THAT?

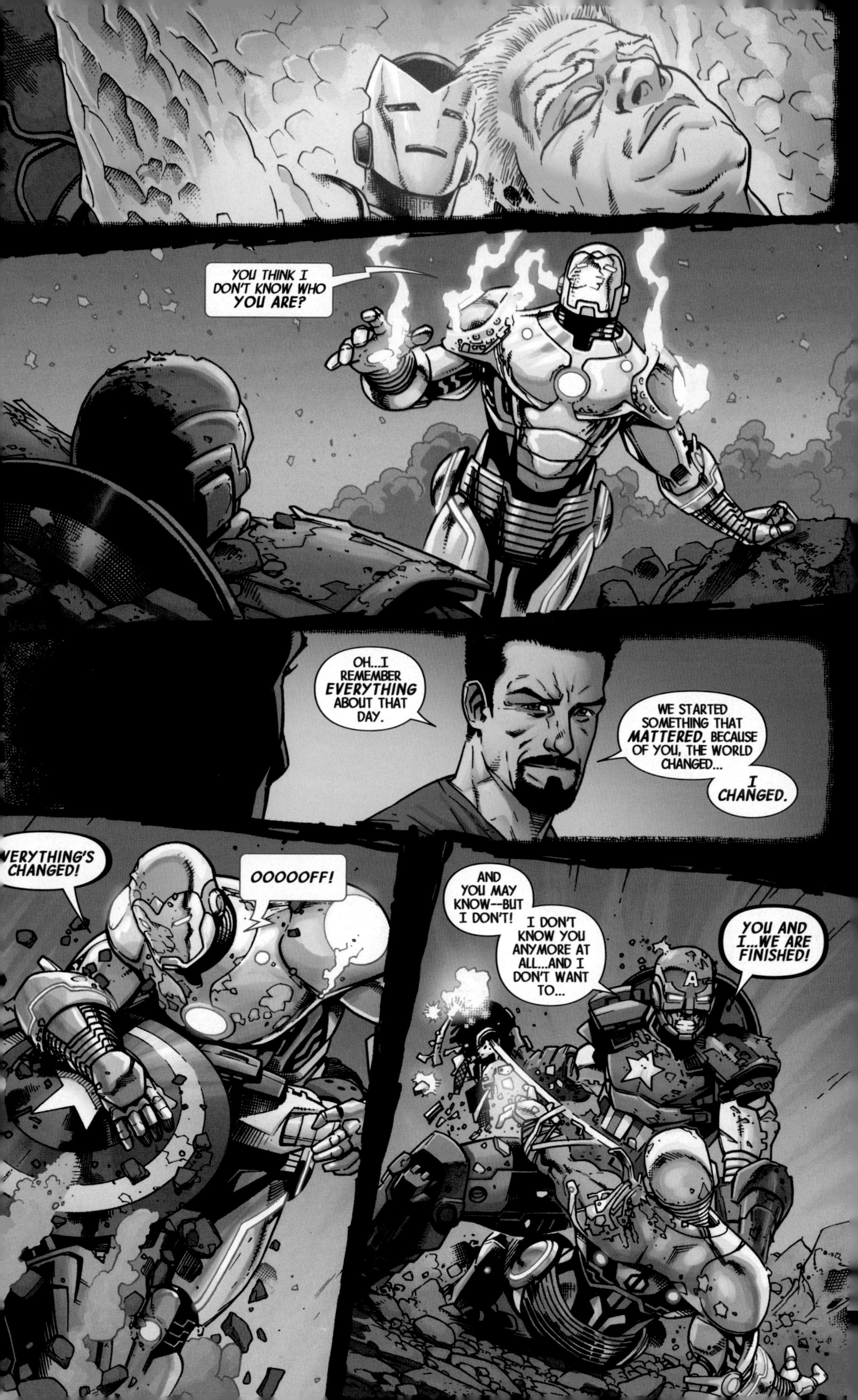

YOU THINK I DON'T KNOW WHO YOU ARE?
OH...I REMEMBER EVERYTHING ABOUT THAT DAY.
WE STARTED SOMETHING THAT MATTERED. BECAUSE OF YOU, THE WORLD CHANGED...
I CHANGED.
VERYTHING'S CHANGED!
OOOOOFF!
AND YOU MAY KNOW--BUT I DON'T!
I DON'T KNOW YOU ANYMORE AT ALL...AND I DON'T WANT TO...
YOU AND I...WE ARE FINISHED!

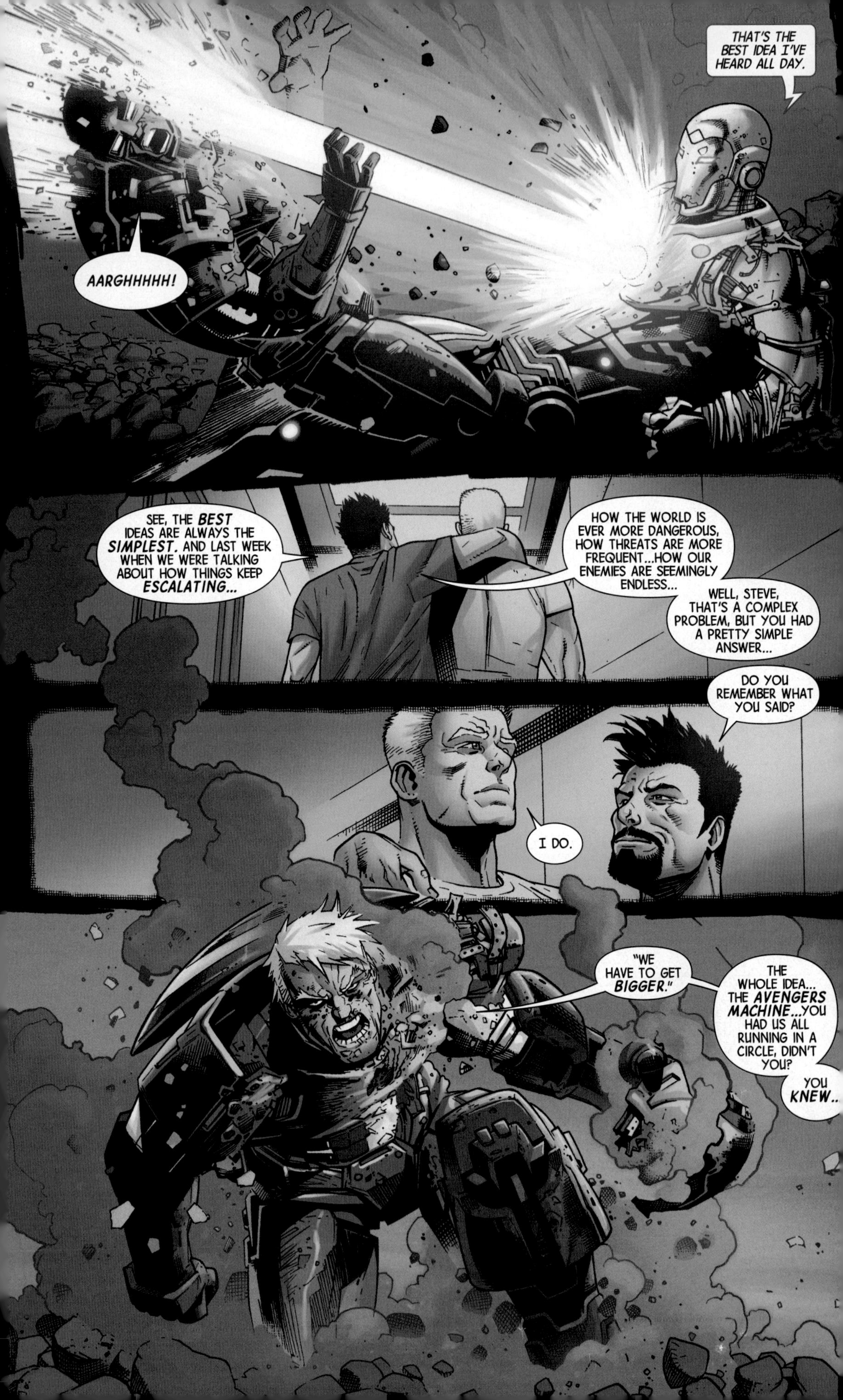
THAT'S THE BEST IDEA I'VE HEARD ALL DAY.
AARGHHHHH!
SEE, THE BEST IDEAS ARE ALWAYS THE SIMPLEST. AND LAST WEEK WHEN WE WERE TALKING ABOUT HOW THINGS KEEP ESCALATING...
HOW THE WORLD IS EVER MORE DANGEROUS, HOW THREATS ARE MORE FREQUENT...HOW OUR ENEMIES ARE SEEMINGLY ENDLESS...
WELL, STEVE, THAT'S A COMPLEX PROBLEM, BUT YOU HAD A PRETTY SIMPLE ANSWER...
DO YOU REMEMBER WHAT YOU SAID?
I DO.
"WE HAVE TO GET BIGGER."
THE WHOLE IDEA... THE AVENGERS MACHINE...YOU HAD US ALL RUNNING IN A CIRCLE, DIDN'T YOU?
YOU KNEW..

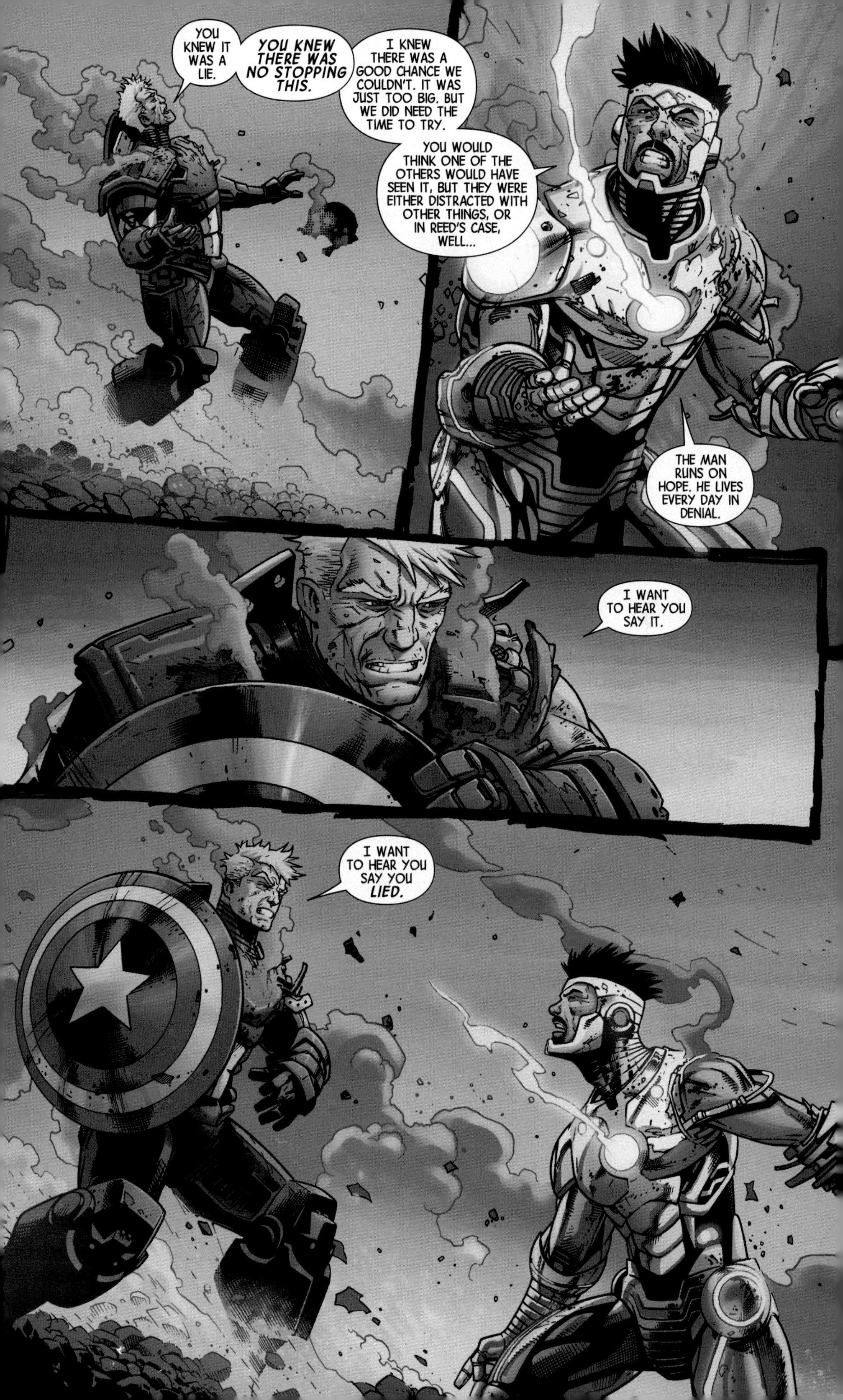
YOU KNEW IT WAS A LIE.
YOU KNEW THERE WAS NO STOPPING THIS.
I KNEW THERE WAS A GOOD CHANCE WE COULDN'T. IT WAS JUST TOO BIG. BUT WE DID NEED THE TIME TO TRY.
YOU WOULD THINK ONE OF THE OTHERS WOULD HAVE SEEN IT, BUT THEY WERE EITHER DISTRACTED WITH OTHER THINGS, OR IN REED'S CASE, WELL...
THE MAN RUNS ON HOPE. HE LIVES EVERY DAY IN DENIAL.
I WANT TO HEAR YOU SAY IT.
I WANT TO HEAR YOU SAY YOU LIED.

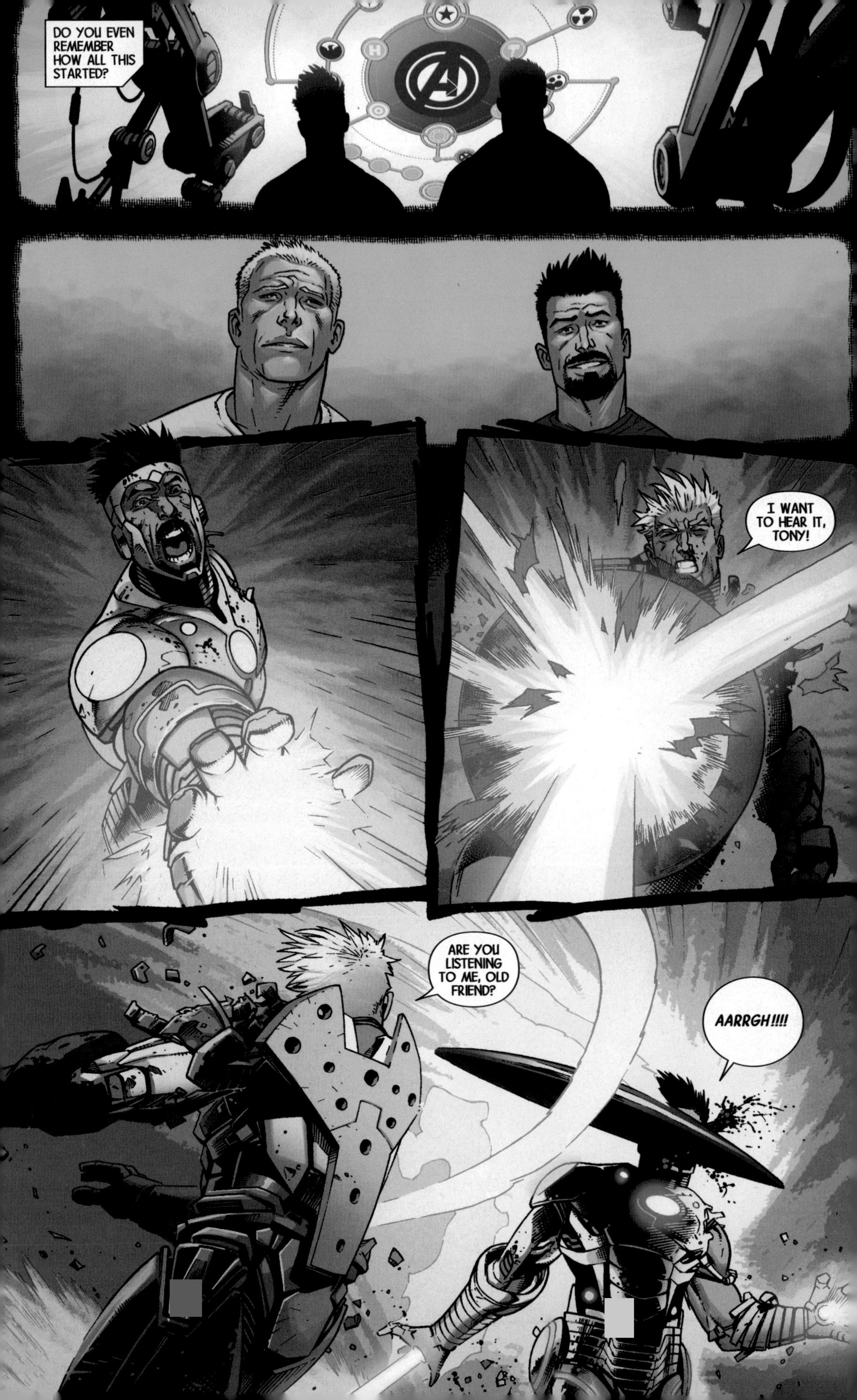
DO YOU EVEN REMEMBER HOW ALL THIS STARTED?
I WANT TO HEAR IT, TONY!
ARE YOU LISTENING TO ME, OLD FRIEND?
AARRGH!!!!

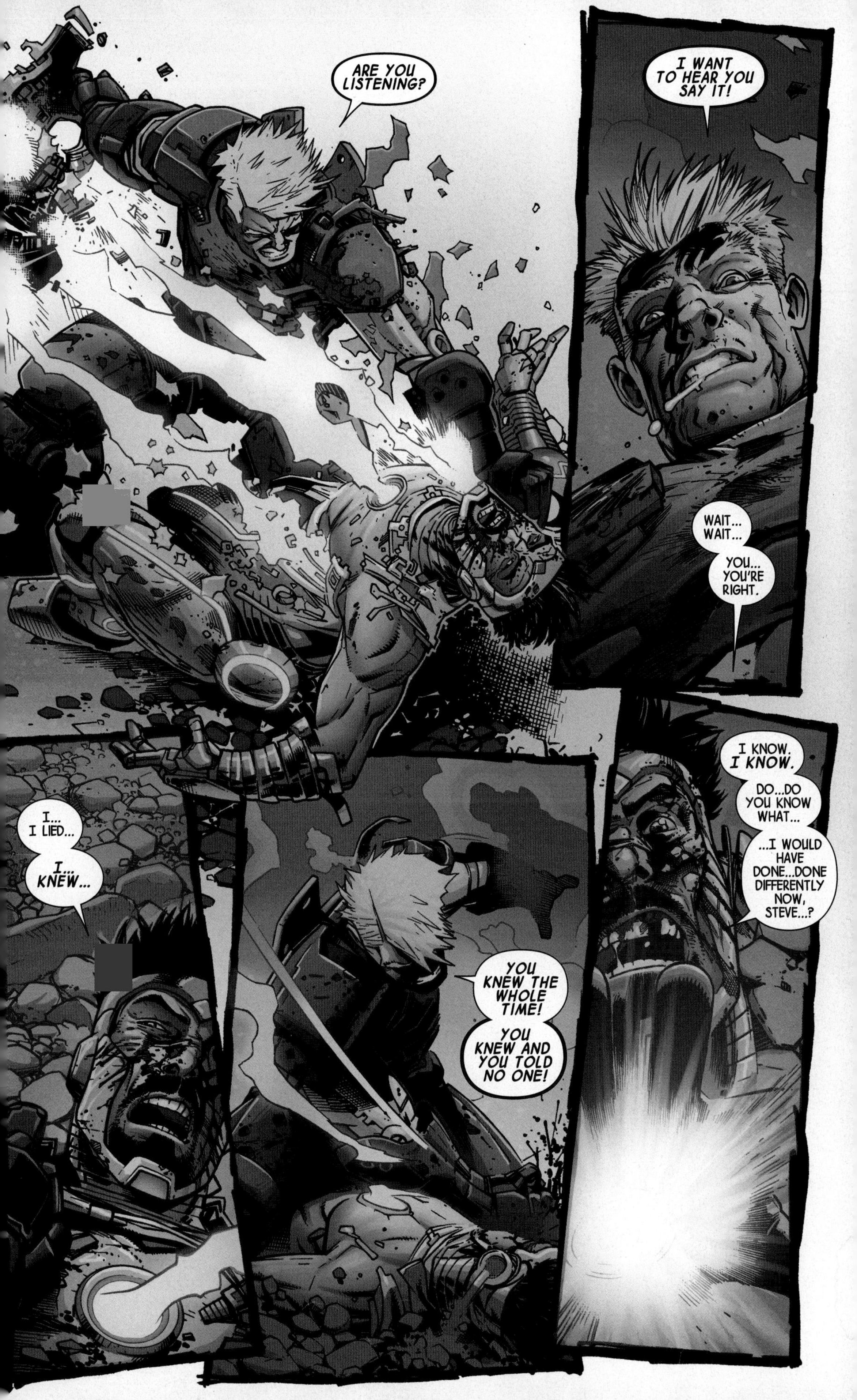
ARE YOU LISTENING?
I WANT TO HEAR YOU SAY IT!
WAIT... WAIT...
YOU... YOU'RE RIGHT.
I... I LIED...
I... KNEW...
YOU KNEW THE WHOLE TIME!
YOU KNEW AND YOU TOLD NO ONE!
I KNOW. I KNOW.
DO...DO YOU KNOW WHAT...
...I WOULD HAVE DONE...DONE DIFFERENTLY NOW, STEVE...?

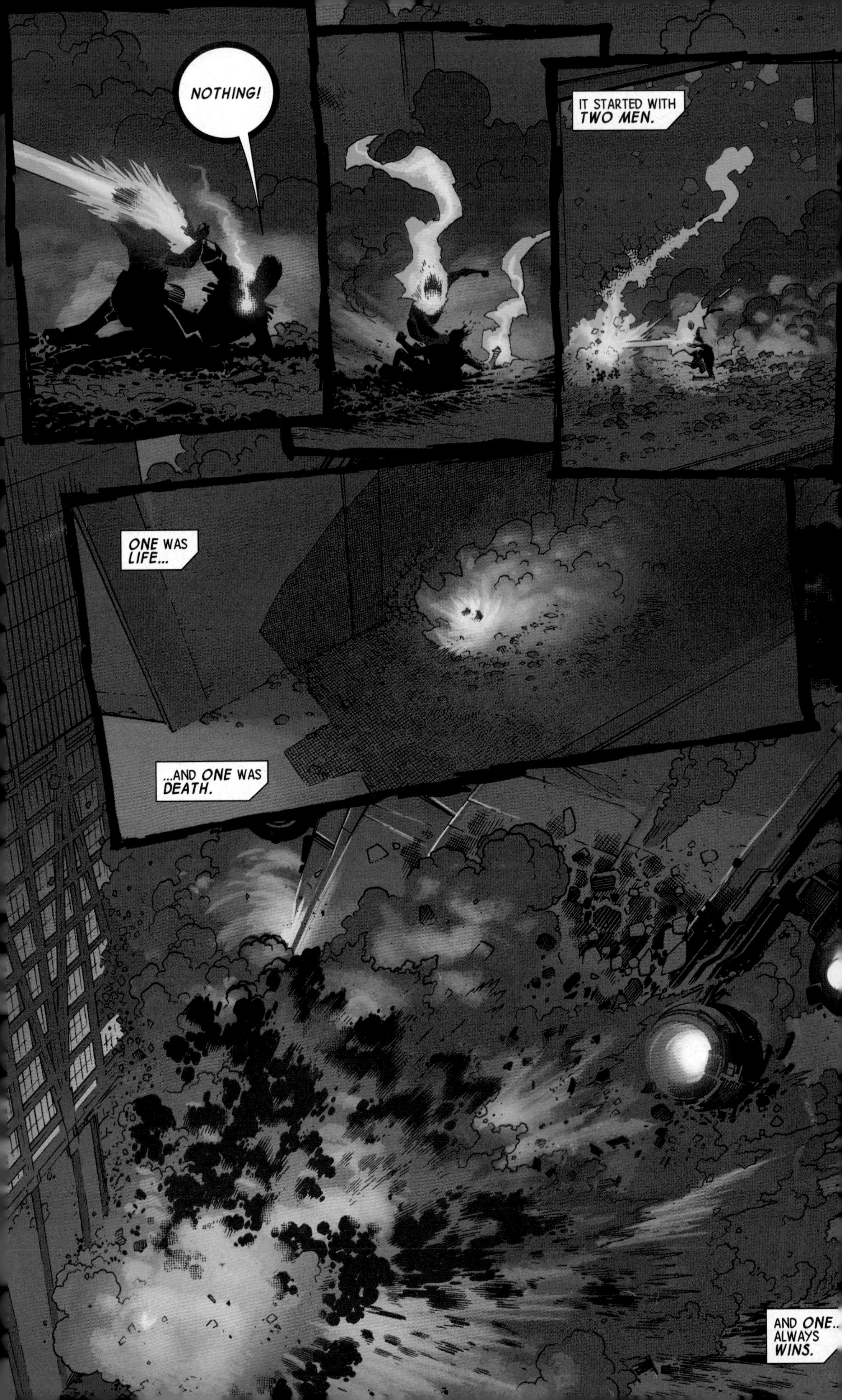
NOTHING!
IT STARTED WITH TWO MEN.
ONE WAS LIFE...
...AND ONE WAS DEATH.
AND ONE... ALWAYS WINS.

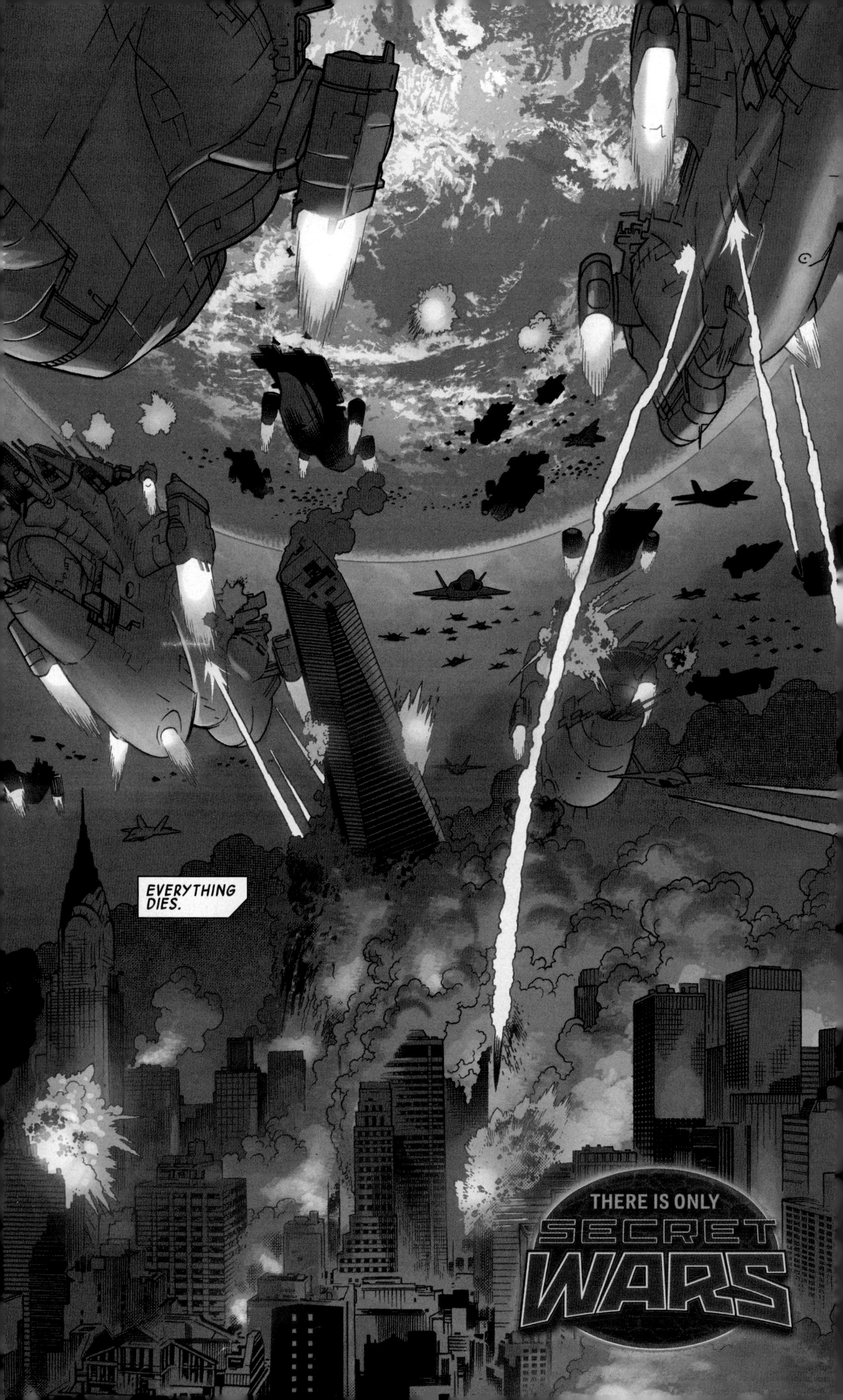

EVERYTHING DIES.
THERE IS ONLY
SECRET
WARS

NEW AVENGERS #31

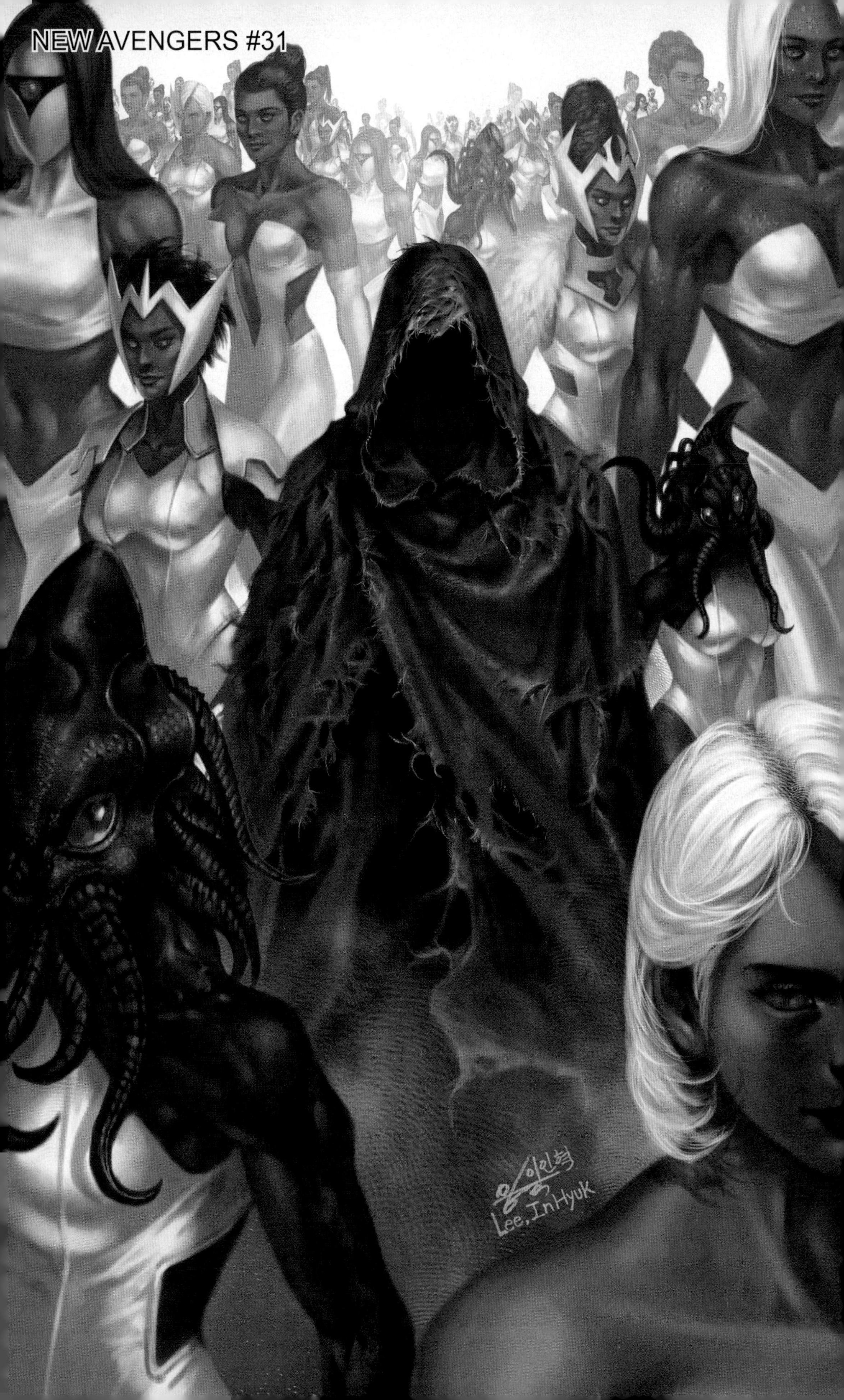
이인혁
Lee, InHyuk

NEW AVENGERS #32

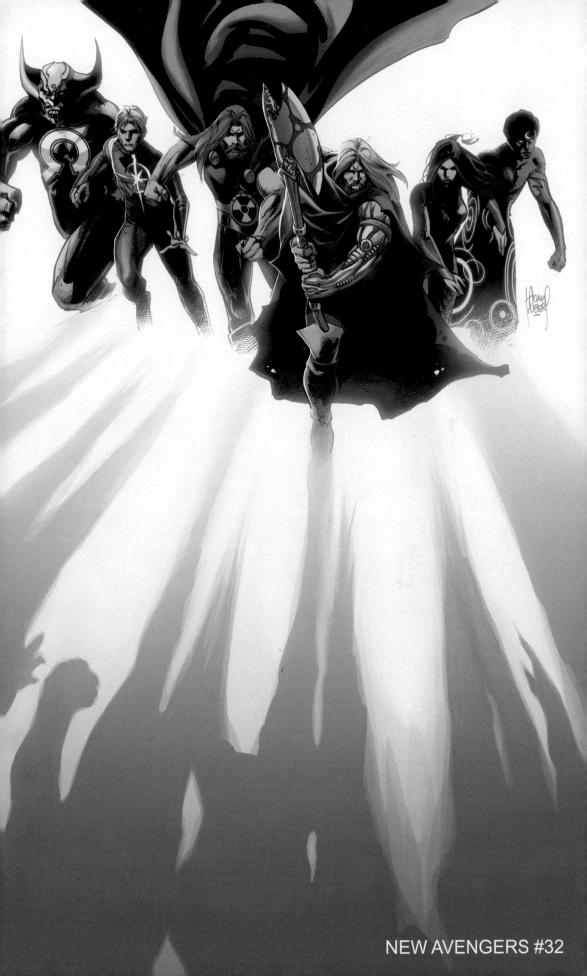

NEW AVENGERS #33

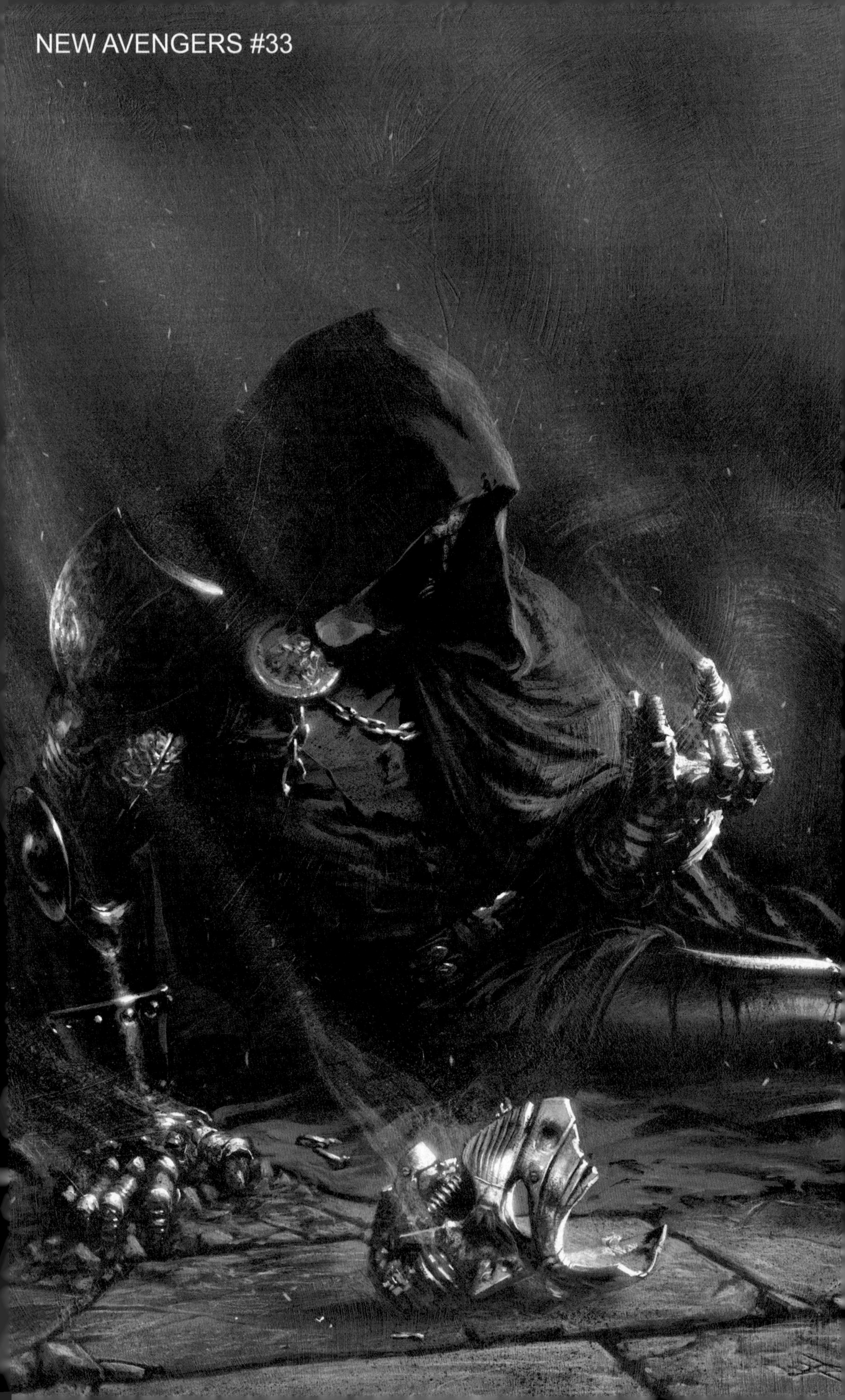

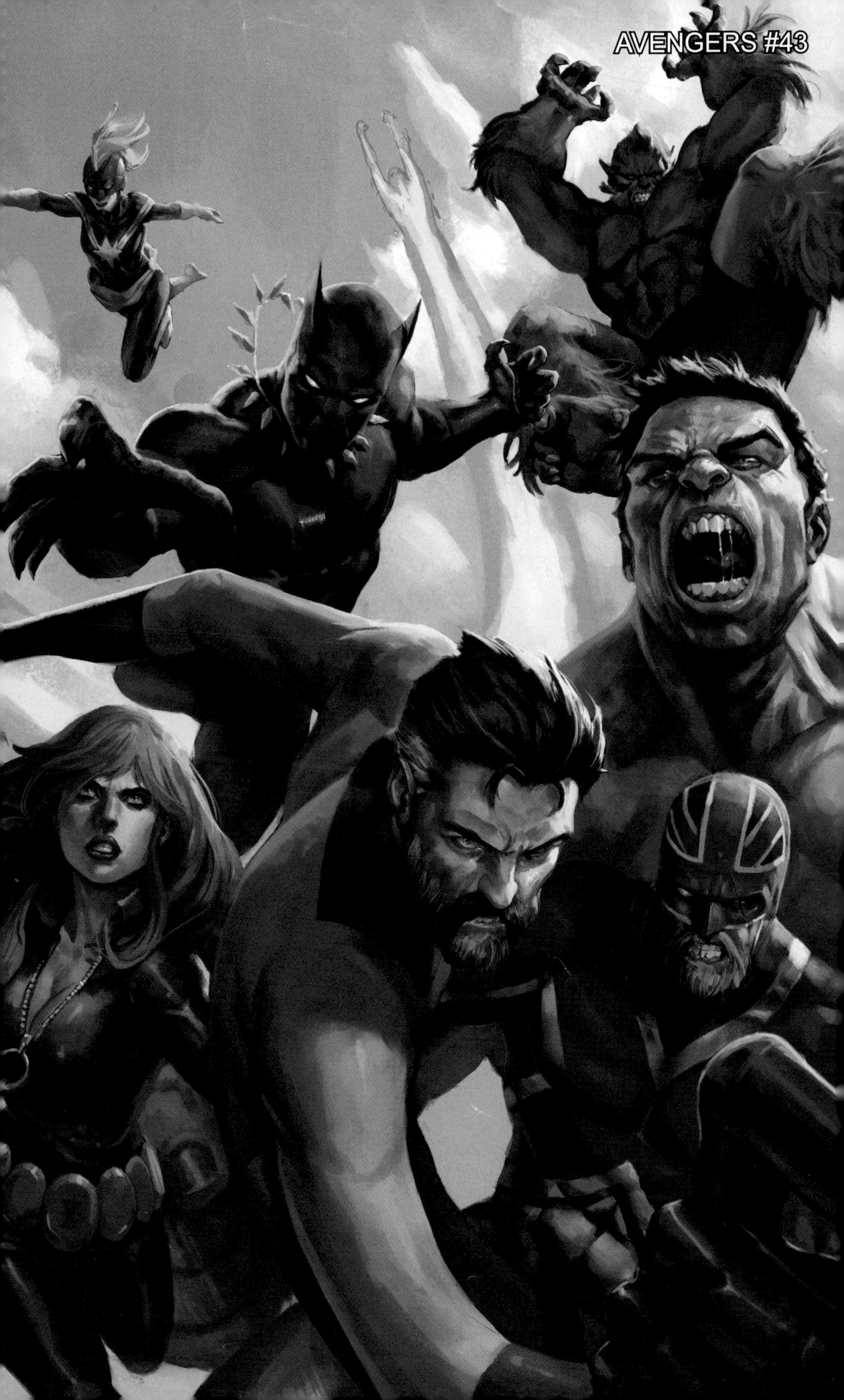
AVENGERS #43

AVENGERS #44

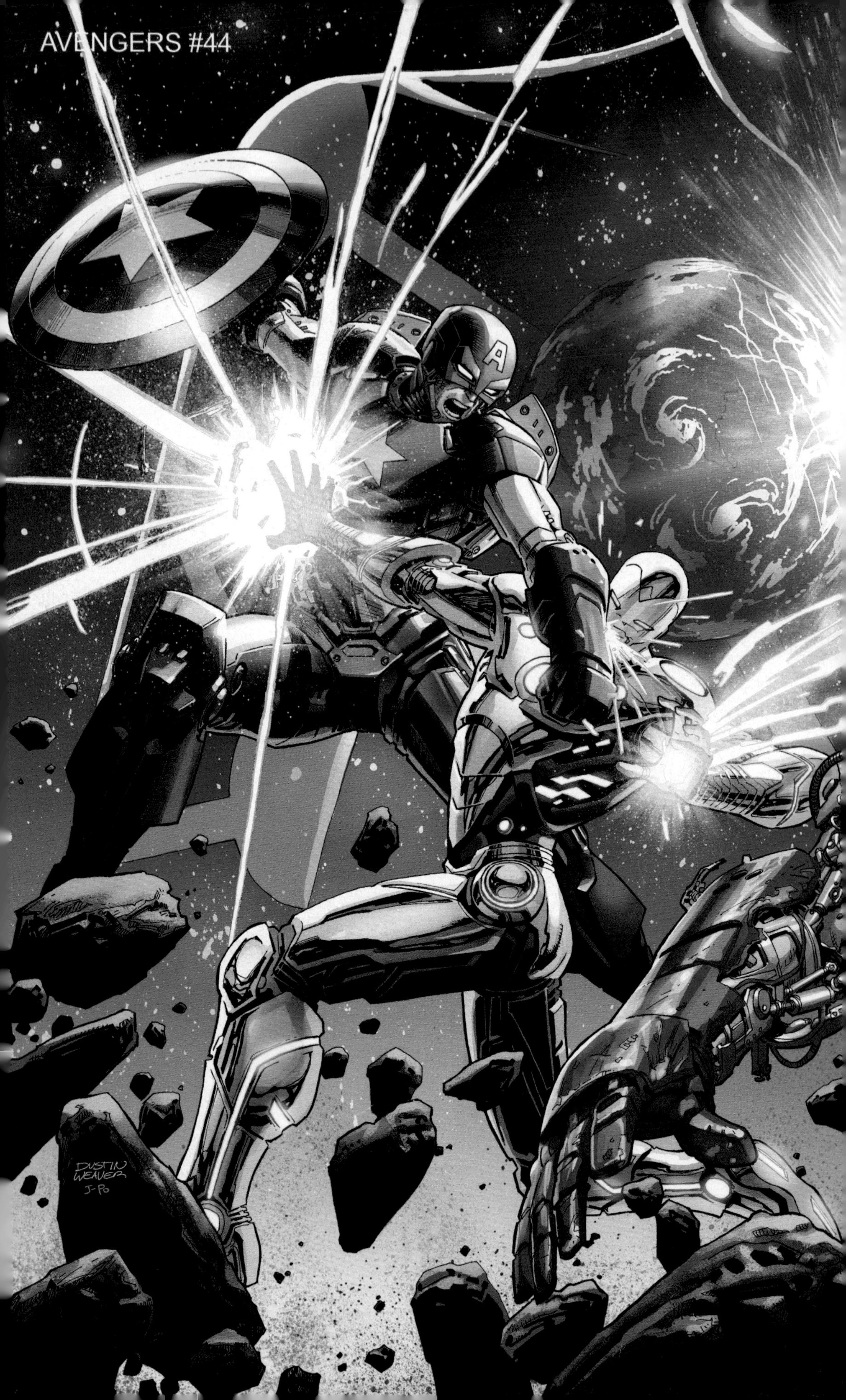
DUSTIN
WEAVER
J-Po

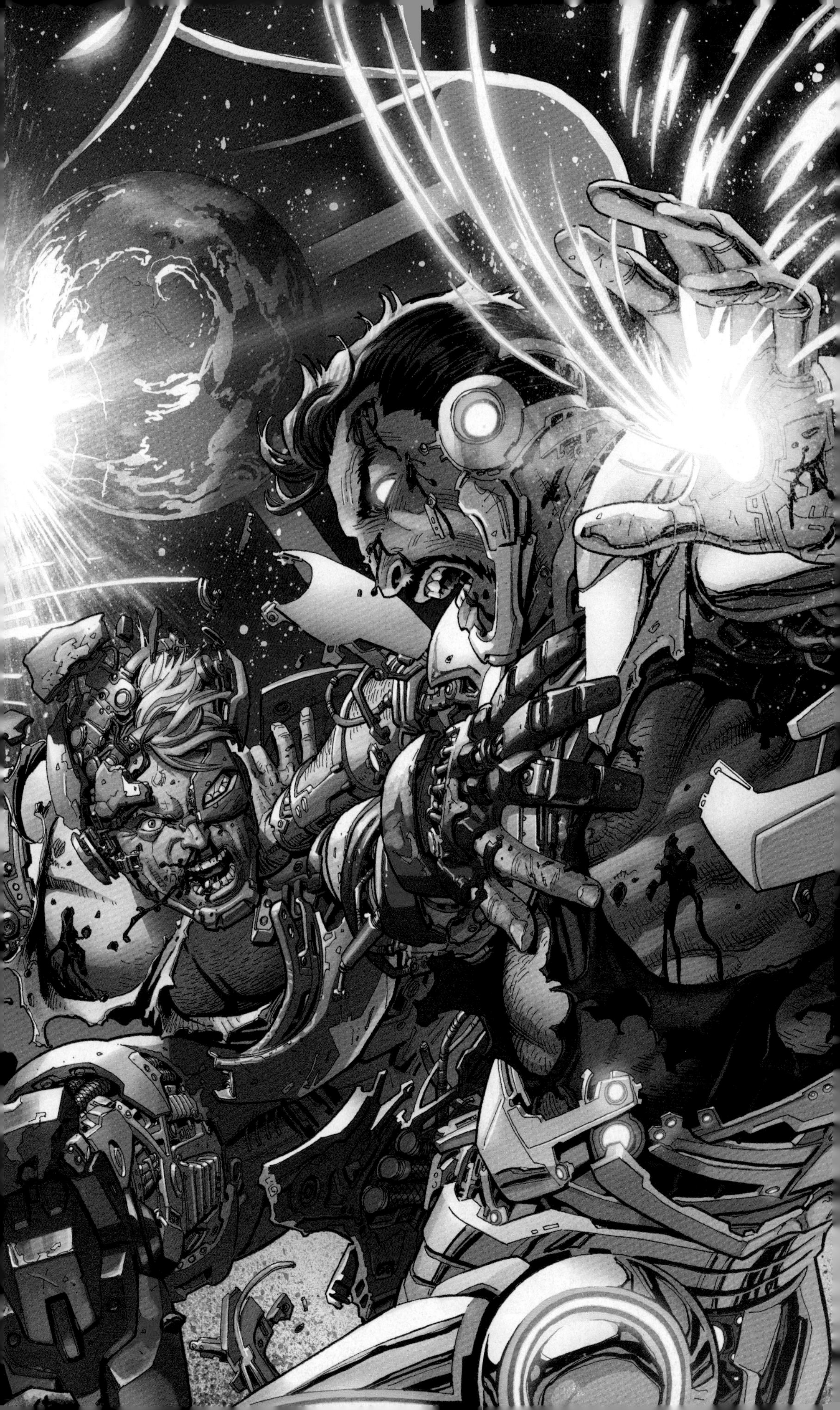

MARVEL AUGMENTED REALITY (AR) ENHANCES AND CHANGES THE WAY YOU EXPERIENCE COMICS!

AUGMENTED REALITY

TO ACCESS THE FREE MARVEL AR CONTENT IN THIS BOOK*:

1. Locate the **AR** logo within the comic.
2. Go to Marvel.com/AR in your web browser.
3. Search by series title to find the corresponding AR.
4. Enjoy Marvel AR!

*All AR content that appears in this book has been archived and will be available only at Marvel.com/AR – no longer in the Marvel AR App. Content subject to change and availability.

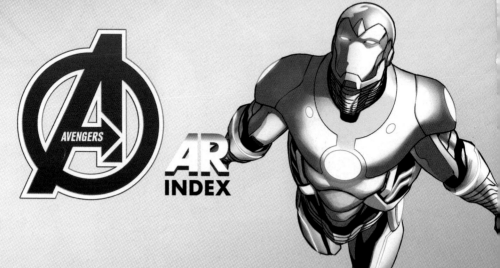

AVENGERS

AR INDEX

TO REDEEM YOUR CODE FOR A FREE DIGITAL COPY:

1. GO TO MARVEL.COM/REDEEM.
   OFFER EXPIRES ON 6/17/17.
2. FOLLOW THE ON-SCREEN INSTRUCTIONS TO REDEEM YOUR DIGITAL COPY.
3. LAUNCH THE MARVEL COMICS APP TO READ YOUR COMIC NOW!
4. YOUR DIGITAL COPY WILL BE FOUND UNDER THE *MY COMICS* TAB.
5. READ & ENJOY!

YOUR FREE DIGITAL COPY WILL BE AVAILABLE

MARVEL COMICS APP
FOR APPLE® iOS DEVICES

MARVEL COMICS APP
FOR ANDROID™ DEVICES